THE TIME OF THE CANNIBALS

THINKING FROM ELSEWHERE

Series editors:

Clara Han, Johns Hopkins University
Bhrigupati Singh, Ashoka University and Brown University
Andrew Brandel, Harvard University

International Advisory Board:

Roma Chatterji, University of Delhi
Veena Das, Johns Hopkins University
Robert Desjarlais, Sarah Lawrence College
Harri Englund, Cambridge University
Didier Fassin, Institute for Advanced Study, Princeton
Angela Garcia, Stanford University
Junko Kitanaka, Keio University
Eduardo Kohn, McGill University
Heonik Kwon, Cambridge University
Michael Lambek, University of Toronto
Deepak Mehta, Ashoka University, Sonepat
Amira Mittermaier, University of Toronto
Sameena Mulla, Emory University
Marjorie Murray, Pontificia Universidad Católica de Chile
Young-Gyung Paik, Jeju National University
Sarah Pinto, Tufts University
Michael Puett, Harvard University
Fiona Ross, University of Cape Town
Lisa Stevenson, McGill University

THE TIME OF THE CANNIBALS

On Conspiracy Theory and Context

ELIZABETH ANNE DAVIS

FORDHAM UNIVERSITY PRESS   NEW YORK   2025

Fordham University Press gratefully acknowledges financial assistance and support provided for the publication of this book by Princeton University.

Copyright © 2025 Fordham University Press

All rights reserved. No part of this publication may be reproduced, stored in a retrieval system, or transmitted in any form or by any means—electronic, mechanical, photocopy, recording, or any other—except for brief quotations in printed reviews, without the prior permission of the publisher.

Fordham University Press has no responsibility for the persistence or accuracy of URLs for external or third-party Internet websites referred to in this publication and does not guarantee that any content on such websites is, or will remain, accurate or appropriate.

Fordham University Press also publishes its books in a variety of electronic formats. Some content that appears in print may not be available in electronic books.

Visit us online at www.fordhampress.com.

Library of Congress Cataloging-in-Publication Data available online at https://catalog.loc.gov.

Printed in the United States of America

27 26 25   5 4 3 2 1

First edition

CONTENTS

Introduction: The Time of the Cannibals . . . 1

Part 1 On Conspiracy Theory and Context 27

    1. The Symptomatic Approach, 28
    2. The Epistemological Approach, 47
    3. The Particularist Approach, 54
    4. The Psychoanalytic Approach, 63
    5. The Political Approach, 76
    6. Toward Conspiracy Attunement, 87

Interlude: The Body Itself 110

Part 2 On Conspiracy Attunement: A Case Study . . 153

    1. Discourse on Division, 155
    2. The President's Body, 168
    3. Recursion and the Curse of Cyprus, 193

Inconclusion (Recontextualization) 217

    Acknowledgments 227
    Notes 231
    Bibliography 253
    On the Frontispiece 273
    Index 275
    Insert follows page 150

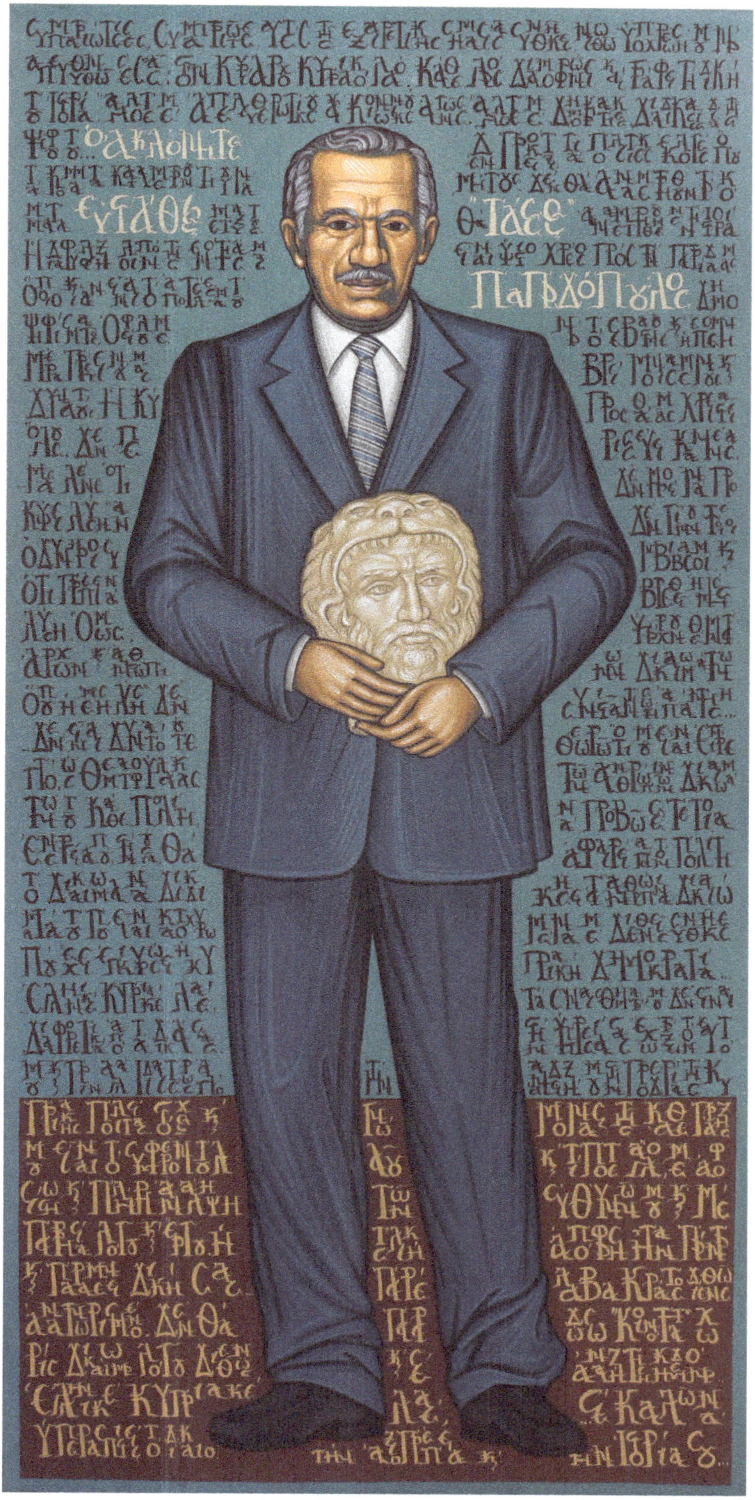

INTRODUCTION:
THE TIME OF THE CANNIBALS

> Consulting many people at this time, one signal came in most clearly. Don't go against Tassos Papadopoulos or he will eat you for breakfast. For the first time I felt fear. The people telling me this were from the sixties generation, the time of the cannibals, and they knew a few things. I had nightmares in which I was being turned over a fire like a piglet on a spit. Gathered around were Tassos and his ministers discussing my progress and deciding what to spread over my half-burnt skin. In the end, this is the problem in Cyprus. Everyone is frightened of being barbecued. (Angastiniotis 2005, 44)

I quote this passage from a short book by Tony Angastiniotis, a Cypriot photojournalist and activist who is probably best known for his documentary films, *Voice of Blood* (2004) and *Voice of Blood 2: Searching for Selden* (2005). These films expose the massacres of Turkish-Cypriot villagers at Murataǧa, Atlılar, and Sandallar committed by Greek-Cypriot irregulars and National Guardsmen in the summer of 1974.[1] That July, an attempted coup by right-wing extremist Greek Cypriots, backed by the junta in Greece, provoked the invasion of the island by Turkish military forces. The war that ensued caused mass casualties and massive displacement, as Greek Cypriots evacuated to the south of the island and Turkish Cypriots to the north.[2] This de facto division between north and south—enforced until 2003 by an impassable border, and since 2003 by the discretion of checkpoint police and soldiers—put a provisional end to two decades of civil, paramilitary, and state violence, but also led to the indefinite occupation of the north by the Turkish military: an enduring state of affairs known colloquially as "the Cyprus Problem."

The *Voice of Blood* films made by Tony Angastiniotis have been widely seen in the north of Cyprus, but in the south, they have never been broadcast or publicly screened,[3] and Angastiniotis himself—who identifies as Greek Cypriot (among other things)[4] and is taken as a traitor by Greek ethnonationalists in the south—has been the target of press attacks and personal death threats. His films are available on YouTube, where they appear to have found a large audience in the Cypriot diaspora in the United Kingdom and the United States. I came across this passage when I was reading his book, *Trapped in the Green Line: The Story behind the Documentary, "Voice of Blood"* (2005), which he wrote as a companion to the films once they had started to gain notice internationally. I was reading the book for other reasons, but when I came across the name of Tassos Papadopoulos, it affirmed my sense of his heavy presence everywhere in the modern history of Cyprus. Papadopoulos was president of Cyprus when Angastiniotis was making his films and feeling that mortal fear. His nightmares resound in what happened to Papadopoulos's own body.

On July 15, 2010, midway through the first sweltering summer I spent in Cyprus, when I was living in the southern coastal city of Limassol and making a habit of watching the evening news on several Greek-language TV channels (as broadcasts in Turkish from the north were inaccessible without a satellite dish), I caught a short segment on the public news channel covering the opening day of the trial of three men for the theft of Papadopoulos's body. Although I mentioned it in my field notes later that night, the segment passed through my attention as quickly as the other headlines of the day: commemorations of the attempted coup in 1974, a Turkish infraction of Cypriot airspace, the decision on a Cypriot property case made by the European Court of Human Rights. A few weeks later, however, I was enlightened by a British expatriate—a financial adviser who had been working at an offshore bank and living in Cyprus for many years—at a dinner party hosted by a Cypriot language teacher we both knew. The banker was commenting on all the "embarrassing events," as he called them, that had occurred in Cyprus in just the past few weeks, including the theft of 175 kilos of ammunition from a National Guard camp, which, he said, must have been facilitated by an "inside man"; the discovery of a living, prematurely born baby in the laundry at Nicosia General Hospital; and the disappearance of Christopher Metsos, alleged paymaster of a Russian spy ring traveling under a fake Canadian passport, who had been arrested on an FBI warrant in Larnaca airport and released on bail only a few weeks earlier. Metsos's escape from Cyprus, the banker insisted, could only be explained by pressure exerted on then-president of Cyprus, Demetris Christofias—head of the Communist Party who had been educated in the USSR—by then-president of Russia, Dmitry Medvedev, just as Gazprombank, the financial services wing of the Russian energy company, Gazprom, was establishing offices in Limassol and bringing to Cyprus a massively lucrative contract for natural gas exploration.

And then, the banker continued, there was the saga of the underworld crime figure Antonis Prokopiou Kitas. Known as the "Al Capone" of Cyprus, Kitas had been in prison since 1994 for the rape and murder of two immigrant women. In 2008, he had escaped from custody during a three-month stay at a hospital in Nicosia, the capital city, where he had seen associates and family members every day, liberally used his cell phone and laptop, and impregnated his second wife during a conjugal visit. Although he had been apprehended a few weeks later and sent back to prison, he was in the news again now, in July 2010, because, along with his younger brother and an employee of their family, he was on trial for the theft of the body of former president Tassos Papadopoulos. The employee had apparently attempted to extort a ransom for the body from the Papadopoulos family and had instead gotten himself and his co-conspirators caught. According to the news broadcast I saw, the arrest of the culprits had put an end to months of high-pitched speculation about the identity and possible motives of the thieves. *What is this?* the banker exclaimed, snorting into his gin and tonic. *This is what we're dealing with in Cyprus!*

"This" was my introduction to the foreigner's mythology of Cyprus as an exotic land of geopolitical intrigue, mix-ups, cover-ups, and organized crime—crime in which not only the British banker himself may have been implicated, as an employee of one of the best-known local money-laundering firms, but multiple presidents of Cyprus as well. In the time that followed, as I spent months turning to years in Cyprus, I learned to know better—to see past the folly and intrigue and to find the wit and the story of power behind them. Yes, I got very accustomed to looking behind visible surfaces in Cyprus to see what they were obscuring from view. And that is part of the problem I face in interpreting this mythology, filtered (still) through a foreigner's lens: the challenge that secrecy poses to knowledge in the "drama of revelation," as Michael Taussig frames the exposure of public secrecy, in which nothing is revealed but the play of surface and depth that gives the seductive impression of a truth behind appearances (Taussig 1999, 58, 51).

In any case, the story of the president's body stuck with me over the years, and it sticks with me still. In part, this is because it perfectly epitomizes the conspiracism in which Cypriots are so often accused of indulging—most often, by Cypriots themselves. One such accuser is Yiannis Ioannou, a Cypriot professor of comparative literature at the University of Cyprus and author of *Conspiracy Theory and the Culture of Partition: Essay on the Political Culture of Cyprus*. This book was published in 2009, on the eve of the sixty-year anniversary of Cyprus's independence from Great Britain; it takes as its point of departure the period from 1950 to 1974, when histories of modern Cyprus often begin. This period is what Tony Angastiniotis called *the time of the cannibals*: the time of anticolonial struggle and then decolonization after the founding of the Republic in 1960, when Cypriot sovereignty was inaugurated within the intimate divisions of Greek and Turkish ethnonationalism strategically nurtured by British colonial rule. In the 1950s, EOKA, a Greek-Cypriot armed resistance group, waged a successful guerilla campaign against the British with the ultimate aim of uniting Cyprus with Greece—also targeting Turkish-Cypriot civilians as well as members of TMT, a Turkish-Cypriot organization of armed irregulars then forming in response to EOKA's actions.[5] Instead of union with Greece, the 1960 Constitution established the independent sovereignty of Cyprus and a power-sharing framework for Greek-Cypriot and Turkish-Cypriot communities contested almost from its inception by Greek-Cypriot authorities— including the Republic's first president, Archbishop Makarios—who were still intent on union with Greece. The irredentist movement initiated by EOKA in the 1950s was revived between 1971 and 1974 by its successor group, EOKA-B, an overtly ethnonationalist parastate terrorist organization that targeted not only Turkish Cypriots but also Greek-Cypriot leftists and even moderate supporters of President Makarios, who by then had distanced himself from the project of union with Greece. The alignment of EOKA-B with Greek military officers and Greek political operatives representing the interests of the Greek junta (1967–1974) in finally "restoring" Cyprus to its Greek "homeland" led directly to the attempted coup, the invasion of Cyprus by the Turkish military, the war in the summer of 1974, the de facto division of the island, and the occupation of the north by Turkish forces ever since.

This postcolonial history of war has thus established "Greek" and "Turkish" as the given coordinates of social and political division that work to stabilize power in ethnonational terms. In the postcolonial geography of Cyprus, "Greek" maps onto the Republic of Cyprus, the regime in the south that enjoys international recognition and membership in the European Union, while "Turkish" maps onto the regime in the north, which unilaterally declared its sovereignty as the Turkish Republic of Northern Cyprus (TRNC) in 1983 but is recognized as such only by Turkey, the occupying power.[6] In this book, I use the term "Republic" to refer to the region and the state apparatus in the south, in its exclusion of the TRNC—an exclusion that figures prominently in the story of Papadopoulos's body.

The so-called Green Line dividing the northern and southern regions of Cyprus endures at the time of this writing; it survived an island-wide referendum on the only reunification plan ever proposed to Cypriot publics, in April 2004. Known as the Annan Plan, after UN secretary-general Kofi Annan, it was supported by most Turkish Cypriots but rejected by most Greek Cypriots, discouraged by an unlikely coalition of political leaders, including then-president Tassos Papadopoulos and then-president of the House of Representatives, Demetris Christofias, who defeated Papadopoulos in the next presidential election and was in power when he died. UN-mediated negotiations between Greek-Cypriot and Turkish-Cypriot authorities in 2008–2010, 2010–2012, 2014, 2015–2017, and 2021 opened and closed without a settlement.

In his book about conspiracy theory in Cyprus, Yiannis Ioannou uses concepts such as "political culture," "culture of division," and "culture of paranoia" to theorize the growth of Hellenic and Christian conservatism in the south, in the form not of right-wing factionalism on the margins of political life but rather of mainstream Greek ethnonationalism. He associates this transformation in Cypriot political culture in the south with widespread "belief" in what he calls "satanic conspiracies" behind the division of the island from 1974 through to the present—a time when many Greek Cypriots were displaced from their ancestral lands, radically isolated from

Turkish Cypriots, and entrained in long-term processes of urbanization and middle-class formation. In the afterlives of British colonialism, these processes have taken public discursive form as development, modernization, and prosperity.

Ioannou's diagnosis is despondent and bitter as he considers what Greek Cypriots have allowed themselves to become in the absence of "proper reason" [ορθός λόγος]. The conspiracy theories of the division that he dubs "satanic" variously depict the control of Cyprus by outside forces, or forms of secret governance within Cyprus, that have remained invisible and unaccountable to democratic processes since Cyprus's independence. They refer to secret deals between foreign powers and Cypriot authorities; interventions by the CIA, KGB, and MI6; and covert orchestration by the deep state in Turkey and the parastate in Greece under the junta of irregular insurgency and counterinsurgency groups that perpetrated much of the violence during periods of what is often called "intercommunal" conflict in 1963–1964, 1967, and 1974.

These conspiracy theories trade in and comment on Cold War geopolitics, characterizing the roles played in Cyprus by the United States, the United Kingdom, Greece, and Turkey by way of their socialist or anticommunist ideological alignments and economic arrangements. (That Cyprus was part of the Non-Aligned Movement after its independence in 1960 helps to explain its vulnerability to the play of these "great powers" and "parent states."[7]) The "paranoia" these theories express, for Ioannou, can thus be seen as a Cold War haunting, or what Joseph Masco (2014) calls a "national security affect"—an affective "infrastructure" connecting the Cold War to the present.[8] Conspiracy theories about the division of Cyprus take the Cold War as a causal force in Cypriot history that continues to shape foreign interests today—on the part of the United Kingdom, the United States, Russia, Israel, the Gulf states, China—in the exploitation of Cypriot lands and off-shore zones for natural resource extraction, tax havening, money laundering, and investment prospecting facilitated by the purchase of property and citizenship.[9] Thus, for Ioannou, while conspiracy theories about the division of Cyprus have specific historical referents in the period 1950–1974, they continue to animate contemporary political life in Cyprus as a filter for the interpretation of everything that has happened since—not least the chronic failure of peace talks[10]—as a repetition or exacerbation of the division:

It is clear how the culture of conspiracy [in Cyprus] is fortified and strengthened, and how it counteracts any lucid, rational comprehension and analysis of phenomena. It favors a comforting interpretation of developments that renders all Cypriot heroes innocent, and attributes tribulations, failures, and catastrophes to factors outside Cyprus. A persecution complex and xenophobia replace substantive political analysis. The terrorization of the people activates their survival instinct, prodding them to rally around their leaders and return them to office time after time. (Ioannou 2009, 119–20)

In this depiction, conspiracy theories about the division of Cyprus frame the division as both the beginning and the end of history: a wound inflicted by the Great Powers that will never heal, collapsing past and present in an enduring "culture of conspiracy."

In this book, I want to problematize this notion of a Cypriot "culture of conspiracy" by treating the *time* of Cypriot conspiracy theory as a question rather than a foregone conclusion. This ambition was inspired in part by my reading of a vast and growing academic literature on conspiracy theory—mostly anglophone, some of it Cypriot, much of it American, for reasons I address below. This literature—which I call *conspiratology*, meaning theory about conspiracy theory[11]—is characterized by a great deal of intertextuality, cross-referencing, and self-conscious intervention into ongoing debates, features that facilitate my treating it as a corpus or genre. Another of its characteristic features is the insistence by authors on the specificity and urgency of conspiracy theory in the moment when they are writing. Many of the works I consulted when I initiated my research in Cyprus nearly fifteen years ago were written between the mid-1990s and the early 2000s, a time that authors explicitly framed as millennial: marked by the rise of finance capitalism, the internet, and the so-called New World Order forming in the wake of Soviet collapse, leaving popular culture haunted by a muddle of Cold War ghosts.[12] Peter Knight, for example, cleanly opens the first chapter of his book, *Conspiracy Culture: From Kennedy to the X-Files*, with the line, "At the turn of the millennium in America, it seems that conspiracy theories are everywhere" (Knight 2000, 1). Jodi Dean, writing about alien abduction and "American paranoia" in *Aliens in America: Conspiracy Cultures from Outerspace to Cyberspace*, writes, "It's a symptomatic or extreme form of what is widespread in everyday life at the millennium"

(Dean 1998, 5). Jack Bratich, in *Conspiracy Panics: Political Rationality and Popular Culture*, goes so far as to describe the 1990s as the "conspiracy decade" and diagnoses the profusion of conspiratology scholarship at the time as a "conspiracy panic" (Bratich 2008, 63). James Faubion's pensive philosophical ethnography of the Branch Davidians, *The Shadows and Lights of Waco* (2001), is subtitled *Millennialism Today*, which really says it all.

Although each of these theorists (and many others besides) approached the fringe cultures that interested them quite differently and with disparate objectives, millennial parameters were crucial to all of their framing of conspiracy theory as an object for analysis at that time, and to the epistemological disorientation that pervaded—again, explicitly and self-consciously—their own analytic maneuvers. Thus, in his preface to perhaps the most widely cited work in this literature, *Paranoia within Reason: A Casebook on Conspiracy as Explanation*, published in 1999 as part of a series entitled Cultural Studies for the End of the Century, George Marcus explains,

> The short-term time-space of this series is signaled by the loaded label, fin de siècle, in which it periodizes and limits itself, and cultivates a certain detachment, while understanding that this is not the old claim to value neutrality enabling the truth. Detachment arises from and is a way to cope with bewilderments and cynicisms that seem so much part of the age. (Marcus 1999, xi)

Even Susan Lepselter's much more recent book, *The Resonance of Unseen Things*, a study of "a vernacular American poetics" on themes of captivity and independence, drawing largely from UFO stories of alien abductions, takes the 1990s as its explicit "time frame," despite a lapse of some twenty years between the experiences she writes about and the writing itself (Lepselter 2016, 1, 3). "When I think of that period now," Lepselter says, "it is like an eye in a hurricane." The storm was 9/11 and the many wars that ensued, along with the proliferation of "antigovernment conspiracy theories." Lepselter does not argue that anyone had seen it coming during the previous decade. "Yet," she explains,

> in many ways, libertarian discourses and movements based in a conspiratorial sensibility that achieved political ascendancy in the early twenty-first century were already latent, not just in the common populist strand long-standing in America, not in some quintessential "paranoid" quality

of American character, but specifically in the uncanny talk that mushroomed in the 1990s. (2–3)

Lepselter hears that "uncanny talk" in improvised, fleeting spaces of sociality that nurtured its expression and collective articulation: support groups for UFO believers; UFOlogy conferences; homes, bars, cars, and workplaces in a pseudonymized "midsize southern city" (3) and in the well-known town of Rachel, Nevada, bordering Area 51. Her text traces and evokes the "sense of resonance" animating her interlocutors' stories about their "weird experiences," insinuating the connections they perceived among those experiences and pressing their attention toward a hidden structure, a "structural something," the "powers that be," behind it all (5; 27, 11; 34; 55). Though Lepselter evokes the "senses of place" felt "deeply, ambivalently" by her interlocutors in the spaces where they talked, and though one chapter of the book is in part a rumination on a particular place that is both lived in and mythologized in American popular culture, she does not frame any of those spaces or places as the sites of a "unified, emplaced American subculture" (17). She is more interested, she explains, in the "metacultur[a]l" "real" of captivity, whose meaning as a narrative trope has formed cumulatively through the "continuous, overlapping elements" of UFO stories and a trove of other lore, especially stories about Native American abductions of white settlers in the seventeenth to nineteenth centuries.[13] Lepselter thus appreciates the complex temporality of the poetic materials she assembles in her book, but the time of the "uncanny talk" indexing the collective experience she evokes ethnographically is specific: the millennial turn. The 1990s were strange times, it seems—at least in America.

My own interest in the conspiratology emerging from those times was not, at least initially, linked to any distinctive features of millennial American culture. I had synched up with the recursive temporality of Cypriot conspiracy theory, which oriented my own analytic gaze toward the 1970s and opened indefinitely onto the horizon of the future. But here we are again. The 2010s–2020s are strange times, it seems—at least in America. Conspiracy theory is once again a matter of popular and academic concern: for many, a sign of the Trumptimes, marked by resurgent authoritarianism, the fragmentation of publics and communities, the twinning of denialism with racism and nativism, and other profoundly disturbing and surreal swerves toward the far right, epitomized by QAnon. In this connection I note that, in the first season of the popular Slate podcast *Slow Burn*, released in 2017–2018, host Leon Neyfakh argued that it was the Watergate scandal that first led to the mainstreaming of conspiracy theory in American culture; in its structure and content, the podcast drew a straight line of continuity from that time to the profusion of conspiracy theories in millennial America and again in the Trumptimes.[14] In other words, the podcast implicitly argued not only that today's strange times are a distinctive period of conspiracy theorizing in the same way that the 1970s and 1990s were but also that they are strange in that way *because* the 1970s and 1990s were.

This hypothesis of continuity leads me to ask: What do we learn about conspiracy theory by historicizing it, and specifically, by periodizing its flourishing in epochs, eras, and moments? How do we use periodization to divide up complex worlds of interconnected concepts, affects, institutions, aspirations, policies, fates, and figures associated with conspiracy? On what grounds can we disaggregate what is enduring, stable, and systemic in those worlds from what is emergent, inchoate, and fluid? What kinds of contexts do we create and destroy when we organize time in this way? These are questions about what it means to do research in complex time, apprehending distinct scales and modalities of experience and change in structural and epistemic conditions, while the concepts and theories we exercise in assessing those conditions are also shifting, transforming, fading and returning, seeming new again, in ways that are out of synch with the historical time frames that our knowledge practices render expedient.

These questions themselves are not new, and yet they may be timely. In her Frazer Lecture delivered in 1986, Marilyn Strathern gave them an intriguing inflection by thematizing the timeliness itself of concepts and theories. "Ideas seem to have the capacity to appear at all sorts of times and places," she said,

> to such a degree that we can consider them as being before their time or out of date. . . . The presence or absence of particular ideas does not seem enough to account for such movement. They collapse a sense of history into a sense of *déjà vu*. . . . For a non-historian, the problem is this: If one looks hard enough, one can find ideas anticipated long before their time, or one can trace their similarity through time. Yet, when one looks again, and considers other ideas, the sense of similarity vanishes. (Strathern 1987, 251, 253)

The concept of ethnocentrism is the "idea" Strathern probes in her Frazer Lecture—an idea around which the field of anthropology has organized itself since at least the modernist break with the work of early figures such as Sir James Frazer himself, according to the disciplinary history Strathern offers, leaning—with some irony—on I. C. Jarvie. Ethnocentrism on her account is an inclination (implicitly) or an argument (explicitly) to privilege the values and concepts belonging to one's own culture in a world *given* as plural—a set of habits, reflexes, and preferences, then, that have been tested in a special way by anthropologists (or so we make the claim) in one after another encounter with difference of one kind or another, at one level or another, on one scale or another. Cultural relativism would appear to be anthropology's corrective answer to ethnocentrism, and it is an answer associated with Bronislaw Malinowski, an heir of Frazer's and, in Jarvie's view (if not Strathern's, exactly), his assassin. In her lecture, Strathern re-envisions Malinowksi's modernist break with Frazer, author of *The Golden Bough* (1890–1915) and other exceedingly popular works in early anthropology, an "armchair anthropologist" and ethnocentrist extraordinaire, according to "received wisdom"—which wisdom, Strathern points out, reaches us by way of a retroactive recontextualization of Frazer's work in light of the modernist "revolution" brought against his ideas by Malinowski only a few years after the publication of Frazer's influential *Folklore in the Old Testament*, which Strathern takes as a paradigm of his work (254, citing Jarvie 1964, 173, 258). In putting the matter this way, Strathern is "receiving" the "wisdom" of critics of "modern social anthropology" such as Jarvie, who, she points out, positions Frazer as the "victim" of that revolution rather than as "unreadable" and "obsolete," as modernist anthropologists would have it (Strathern 254, 256, citing Boon 1982, 13, 18).

In her own "play" with context (more on this, below), Strathern juxtaposes Frazer's "historicist" approach to cross-cultural comparison—in which "diverse customs" observed piecemeal at any time, "anywhere in the world," were examined in order to "throw light" on one particular civilization and thus confirm the general laws of cultural evolution—with Malinowski's fieldwork-based approach. In the latter, she writes, the "practices and beliefs ... ideas and customs" of a people were understood in "immediate social context," and entire societies or "social systems" compared in order to hone a functionalist theory of cultural holism (254). From the vantage of functionalist theory, ethnocentrism à la Frazer appears as a problem to be redressed by placing things "in context," as Malinowski strove to do; but, as Strathern shows, it is a very particular notion of context that permits this redress. Cross-cultural comparison in the style of Malinowski, she argues, works through a more or less implicit contrast or "separation" between the culture being studied by the anthropologist and the anthropologist's own culture, into whose concepts the "other" culture can be translated and made to seem coherent in its *own* context (261). In its own context, all the ideas and practices of a people can be understood as gathering their meaning and efficacy from their interrelatedness in the "organic wholes" they compose (254). In foregrounding the "other" culture as a context in this way, Strathern observes, the anthropologist also creates a context for his own ideas to take hold through the contrast he draws between the cultural material that he discovers and the translation of it that he effects (259). In other words, both contexts are made in the process of ethnographic writing. What is compared cross-culturally, then, is those contexts, along with the concepts that "make sense" of them—concepts for which, Strathern suggests, the anthropologist's culture would have "had no ready space" before the attempt was made (269).

Strathern suggests that the dichotomy of "observer/observed," whatever else it might have meant in ethical or political terms in modernist anthropology, was, on the level of ideas, primarily a textual device used in ethnographic writing to "create a sense of alienness" and thence to "overcome" it through translation and contextualization (260). That is to say: the "separation" between the cultural context under study and the cultural context of the anthropologist's ideas was, at the very least, contrived for literary purposes. Though in a very different way from Frazer's historicism, this modernist literary contrivance, too, is ethnocentric, and its ethnocentrism would have seemed obvious to the point of being taken for granted (which is to say, decontextualized) by Strathern's audience in the 1980s. The postmodern departures from this modernist ethnocentrism that she gathered for comment in her 1986 lecture included textual techniques of juxtaposing multiple incompatible accounts of events, decentering scholarly texts as sources of authority and tools of authentication, formally incorporating multiple authorial voices to move beyond dialogue toward heteroglossia, and collapsing linear histories to "obscur[e] the line between past and present" (267). In Strathern's view, these techniques, invested as they were in unmaking the power asymmetries inherent in the observer/observed dichotomy effectuated in modernist ethnographic texts, sought to "play with context" by blurring the boundaries thus contrived and collapsing the dichotomies they supported (265).

While the ostensible object of Strathern's deliberations here is the concept of ethnocentrism, it interests me just as much that her inquiry systematically raises context itself as *the* critical issue in anthropological theory. This issue is apparent in the way she frames her venture from the outset, taking ethnocentrism as a central preoccupation of anthropology in her own time— that is, the time of her writing (if not of her training), which she describes as "postmodern" in a studiously nominalist manner: "Whether we are or are not entering a postmodern phase in social anthropology, enough people seem to be speaking as though we were for the idea to be of interest" (263). She thus nods to the so-called crisis of representation in anthropology then dominating discourse in the field and foregrounding reflexivity as an epistemological and ethical innovation. At the same time, she textually excavates ethnocentrism as a central preoccupation of the modernist "revolution" in anthropology many generations earlier. Strathern thus draws our attention to the timeliness of ideas as theoretically and, more to the point, *textually* embedded—timeliness being the foundational assumption authorizing the introduction of context into ethnographic texts: the assumption, that is, that "what people think is a 'reflection' of their times" (251).

This assumption that ideas reflect "their times" raises the question as to how it may be determined *when* "their times" are, or were. In the introduction to his book on conspiracy theory, Ioannou addresses this question in a diagnostic register:

> The meanings and values that composed the rhetoric and political discourse of the decade of the '50s—such as "our nation is the mother country"—are the ones that have shaped the political behavior [of Greek Cypriots today]. Biologically, they live in the time of today, but, having eliminated the intervening sixty years, they have stopped connecting the facts of their own time dialectically with the consequences of the sixty-year historical process they have eliminated, or bringing their political analysis to bear on those consequences. They adopt a metaphysical approach and thereby transfer the culture of that period (1950–74) to today's time—confounding and clashing with the objective historico-political facts of the last sixty years. (Ioannou 2009, 19)

In this passage, Ioannou articulates a common conception of Cyprus as "frozen" or "stuck" in time, which I have linked to paranoid epistemology in other writing about Cypriot knowledge projects concerning the past (Davis 2023). This time is captured in pervasive representations—photographs and films, poems and memoirs, documentaries and news reports—featuring people and places stranded, as if in suspended animation, in 1964 or 1974, when people abandoned their homes and villages during riots and bombings, leaving them to rot ever after, untouched. The "elimination" of all the time that has passed since then from the historical process of culture in Cyprus is "metaphysical," Ioannou writes, insisting that conspiracy theories of the division in Cyprus belong "culturally" to the past, even if they belong "biologically" to the present. This wormhole through space-time that he sees being opened by conspiracy theory in Cyprus suggests that what people think is *not* a reflection of their times, as against the assumption of timeliness that Strathern discerns and disputes in modernist ethnography and cultural theory. That Ioannou makes this observation in the form of a diagnosis—pronouncing a pathology in Cypriot political culture—suggests that he might wish for more conventional timeliness in the relation between ideas and culture in Cyprus.

Ioannou surely enjoys greater intimacy with (or at least proximity to) that culture than the modernist ethnographers whose texts Strathern examines did in relation to the cultures they studied. Ioannou's text maintains a dichotomy between observer and observed—a separation that motivates and authorizes his diagnosis of Cypriot conspiracy culture—but that dichotomy does not map onto cultural difference as foreign/native, in the style of modernist ethnography. It maps onto cultural difference in a different style—a postcolonial style, say, that maintains the modernist concept of culture as local and bounded, but operates that concept within ethnonational borders rather than across them. In this bounded culture, Ioannou locates himself in the *margins*, a position that exposes him to the destructive untimeliness of conspiracy theories.

In the previous paragraph, trying to work out Ioannou's position in relation to conspiracy theory, I have already framed and reframed the inside/outside of culture several times, and with it, the interpretive perspectives that might be associated with his position. Thus, Ioannou is like modernist ethnographers in his presumption of cultural difference between himself and those he writes about (he is "outside" mainstream culture and therefore qualifies his critical judgment of the culture by way of his experience with it rather than his alignment with it); he is unlike modernist ethnographers in his belonging to the culture that he is studying (he is "inside" the culture and therefore does not need to translate and contextualize it for his audience); he is like modernist ethnographers in his assertion of the superiority of his knowledge over that of his interlocutors (he is "outside" the culture and therefore can see what cultural insiders cannot); he is unlike modernist ethnographers in sharing the cultural identity of his interlocutors and thus knowing his lot to be thrown in with theirs (his critique is reformist, addressed to the culture from "inside"); he is like modernist ethnographers in belonging to a cultural elite positioned to make cultural diagnoses (he is "outside" the culture); he is unlike modernist ethnographers in being a colonized subject (he is "inside" the culture); and so forth. Many more framings—limitless—are possible. It would be especially easy to proliferate them if we were to take into account other axes of difference beyond ethnonational identity—such as class, gender, generation—and if we conceived of interpretive perspective as a function of historical as well as cultural position: time as well as place. Wormholes abound.

Strathern develops her line of thinking about timeliness in order to probe the "mood" of postmodern anthropology—playful, ironic—and to pinpoint its difference from modernist ethnography in its textual styles rather than its ideas; the occasion of a lecture named after Sir James Frazer and given in 1986 makes sense of that aim, perhaps. But in the spirit of her deeper and subtler provocation, and in the light of Ioannou's critical diagnosis of conspiracy culture in Cyprus, I wish to experiment with a substitution: to consider conspiracy theory, like ethnocentrism, as an idea whose self-evident timeliness demands explicit reflection and qualification. This experiment is not only a formal maneuver—substituting one idea for another to see whether the argument holds—but also a way of extending Strathern's examination of ethnocentrism. I argue in what follows that epoch and locale—time and place—are implicit, largely unexamined premises in most conspiratology, a literature that sustains many of the textual traits of modernist ethnography that Strathern, in 1986, saw starting to be dismantled by postmodern critiques. (She was not in a position, then, to see how minimal and marginal those interventions would turn out to be.) Among those traits are the observer/observed dichotomy, rigid yet implicit boundaries between the cultural context studied by anthropologists and the cultural context of their ideas, and the "sense of alienness" contrived by ethnographers in regard to the cultural materials they study in order to overcome that sense by translating and contextualizing them. These modernist textual conventions are alive and well in conspiratology, as I read it, and this literature thus models the subtle and not-so-subtle ways in which modernist ethnocentrism survives in cultural theory in the guise of *contextualization*. This is not the ethnocentrism of Frazerian anthropology and its framework of historicist comparison that took western civilization as a starting and ending point of cultural evolution. It is rather an implicit ethnocentrism enacted by taking as given a civilizational asymmetry—with cultural, political, and economic implications—between locales of theorizing and locales of ethnographic data collection. I develop this point more substantially in Part 1.6; here, I recall Ioannou's movement in and out of a modernist perspective in his writing on Cypriot conspiracy theory. The framing and reframing of his position along insider/outsider axes of differentiation that I performed above show how a postcolonial stance of antinationalism can both advance a critique of ethnocentrism and undermine it by stabilizing context in ethnonational terms. This is the central point that I take from Strathern's critique of modernist ethnocentrism as I explore the workings of context in conspiratology.

I initiate this exploration in Part 1, where I question at length both the *timeliness* and the *alienness* of conspiracy theory as it is represented in conspiratology. I recontextualize these features of conspiracy theory as entailments of ethnocentrism in cultural theory—an inheritance or, better, a hangover from the anthropological enterprise of cross-cultural comparison that so few anthropologists today pursue, at least explicitly. Strathern addresses that hangover as a disciplinary type in *Partial Connections* ([1991] 2004), a somewhat later work that reads to me as a continuation of her 1986 Frazer Lecture. Here, she identifies a characteristic "excess" or "remainder" in the movement of anthropological thought over time (Strathern [1991] 2004), xxii, passim), for which she takes cross-cultural comparison as the "exemplar for all descriptive activity" (xvi). In order to answer a particular question about how one culture is like or unlike another, she explains— her key example is whether a particular Papua New Guinean society "has" or does not "have" initiation rites—one would need to know more than the question knows: that is, more than the knowledge contained by the question.

That "excess" can be approached by asking additional questions: What counts as an initiation rite and what doesn't? Is a rite actually a subset or a type of another kind of thing? And so on. Such new questions are what Strathern calls "remainders": "material that is left over, for it goes beyond the original answer to the question to encapsulate or subdivide that position (the question-and-answer set) by further questions requiring further answers" (xxii). For Strathern, the remainder is not only what is presumed or left over by the asking of a particular question, but also the impetus to keep going: the possibility inherent in any question that the operation of asking the question can be repeated on different scales and yield additional answers that "encapsulate" previous answers and, in doing so, reframe them, establishing a new context for their elaboration. The remainder, then, is a source of creativity; it is the way "an answer is another question, a connection a gap, a similarity a difference, and vice-versa" (xiv).

I take Strathern's vocabulary of remainder and excess as a way to talk about recursion in knowledge-making practices. On her account, we develop new knowledge by doing the same thing with the knowledge that was produced by the previous doing of that thing, whether that thing is asking a question, reversing figure and ground, zooming in or panning out, changing the scale, specifying the context. As I demonstrated in working out the observer/observed distinction in Ioannou's positionality, there is always another distinction to be made, leading to a recontextualization of his position in relation to Cypriot conspiracy theory. There is no end to the contexts that can be set for social analysis. The process is theoretically endless, yet there is no radical novelty, since every bit of knowledge that is produced contains all that has come before. New knowledge entails the past and also changes it. By the same token, new knowledge does not reduce complexity but rather maintains it, no matter on what scale one seeks to approach it.

What remains cloudy for me in Strathern's otherwise dazzlingly lucid perspective on recursive knowledge-making is the starting point of the research process. If this process is recursive, then what is contained in an initial question largely reflects what the asker already knows; the question itself is some kind of outcome of the prior asking of other questions. Strathern frames this knowledge that exceeds the question being asked as an "excess," which she treats as a *consequence* of asking the question, even though, in her depiction, that excess logically precedes the asking. In other words, the initial question reflects the partialities and limitations of the asker as well as her prior knowledge. What is not contained in that initial question is not only logically prior knowledge but also the arena of the asker's ignorance, and that is what—ideally, I think, for Strathern—the asker might ultimately approach for the first time through the process of pursuing remainders, assuming a research process ambitious enough not to rest on swift conclusions. The risk of any research process, then, lies with the misrecognition of the starting point as a question that is valid in its own terms, without regard to the context in which it became the answer to a prior question—a context in which some knowledge was surely foreclosed. Strathern's depiction of knowledge-making as the management of excess in the pursuit of remainders does not address how research questions are thus determined—or *overdetermined*—by contextual foreclosures in the first place. This "first place" is not an anyplace in abstract logical space, as subject to the recursivity of knowledge production as any other. It is the special and unique place where the ethical freight of knowledge production rests—where the "value" of truths sought in social science is presupposed by the subjective categories of thought that give empirical knowledge its "objectivity," as Weber observed a century ago (Weber [1904] 1949, 110). It is what motivates research in the form of a desire to know more on the part of the researcher.

The overdetermination of the division of Cyprus as the starting point of my own research process, and my own desire to know more, is what remains to be accounted for here. If this were a problem *only* for me, I could work to resolve it by engaging in a rigorous practice of reflexivity to account for my shifting positionality along the insider/outsider axes of differentiation—some of whose possibilities I traced for Ioannou, above—over the course of my research and writing. I do strive after this practice in this book. But reflexivity alone cannot disentangle my thinking from the problem of division. As I have written elsewhere, I have found as a researcher that the division of Cyprus has colonized knowledge production about Cyprus to such an extent that other struggles and divisions inevitably appear in relation to it: as dimensions and effects of it, or, on the other hand, as social and political problems in their own right that the division mystifies and obscures (Davis 2023, 11–15, 41–43, 161ff.). Cypriot anthropologist Olga Demetriou captures this problem beautifully in framing as "minor losses" all the rethinking context and cross-contextual comparison. This evidence includes the writings of Cypriot and foreign journalists, scholars, and lay researchers who have turned to state archives in Cyprus, the United States, and the United Kingdom in order to substantiate or refute conspiracy theories about the events leading up to the division of Cyprus. I have spoken with several of these researchers, though my emphasis here is on their print discourse, especially works circulating in the capacious world of self-published books in Cyprus. Most of the evidence, however, comes in the form of diverse contributions to the Cypriot press coverage of the theft of the president's body in December 2009: news stories, op-eds, and letters to the editor published in an array of newspapers in the south and the north, in Greek and Turkish (and in a few instances, English). I read this press coverage as public discourse about conspiracy theory that presumes and anticipates conspiracy theory as a condition of public discourse in Cyprus, in a historically deep and recursive way. I construe this metadiscourse on conspiracy theory as evidence of a Cypriot context of conspiracy attunement that could be compared, as such, to other contexts with different historical-temporal and geographical-cultural boundaries.

Between Part 1 and Part 2 is an Interlude in which I explore political theologies and theories of sovereignty in relation to the dead bodies of political leaders. Since many such bodies have taken momentous and often scandalous itineraries, provoking public talk in many times and places, this topic is well suited to my project of rethinking context for comparative purposes. Leading up to the case study on Tassos Papadopoulos's remains in Part 2, then, I explore in the Interlude several other cases in which the dead bodies of political leaders have been exhumed, handled, studied, debated, moved, and most directly to the point, desecrated and re-sacralized. Comparing the profusion of conspiracy theories about the meaning of Papadopoulos's body with the apparent unspeakability of his missing remains, I argue that conspiracy theories about the theft cannot be analyzed without recourse to the body itself, and I venture some thoughts about what the body itself might be.

At the time of this writing, the division of Cyprus in its broadest contours has endured for sixty years, and those who lived through the violence of the 1960s and 1970s are now very much in the minority on both sides of the divide. It is therefore crucial to understand how the politics of division are reproduced in younger generations of Cypriots, for whom division cannot be accounted to the direct experience of perpetrators and survivors. Younger Cypriots, having adjusted to the division as a "new normal"—though in ways quite different for those living in the south and those living in the north—may not be as compelled politically by settlement talks and public debates on the Cyprus Problem as they are by international solidarity movements or transnational fascist mobilizations.[16] The division is surely not in the foreground of everyday life for many Cypriots in any case. Yet conspiracy theories continue to carry the division into the emergence of the everyday. This was how the story of the president's body first came to my own attention—that is, as a news item on a Greek-language TV channel, wrapped up along with other items into a package of the day's import, each one refracting the division in some way: commemorations of the attempted coup in 1974, foregrounding the invasion by Turkish military forces that it provoked; a Turkish infraction of Cypriot airspace, counted as an infraction only in the south, given the long-standing occupation of the north by Turkish military forces; and a decision by the European Court of Human Rights on a lawsuit brought by a Greek-Cypriot refugee against the Republic of Turkey, seeking compensation for property in the north to which they had had no meaningful access since 1974. The trial of the men charged with stealing the remains of Papadopoulos—presented by the reporter as the *true culprits*—appeared in the broadcast as the truth-seeking process that would finally put to rest rampant conspiracy theories attributing the crime to Turkish nationals, Turkish Cypriots, Greek-Cypriot leftists, and even Greek-Cypriot supporters of Papadopoulos. It was one among many events that day that reintroduced the division as a condition of everyday life.[17]

And what was the story of the president's body told in that trial? Almost three months after the theft, in March 2010, Papadopoulos's remains were found by the Greek-Cypriot police, acting on an anonymous tip, and conclusively identified by DNA analysis. They had been placed inside a tomb belonging to someone other than Papadopoulos, in a different cemetery located in the southern Nicosia neighborhood of Strovolos. One of the alleged thieves, Sarbjit Singh, an undocumented Indian national, identified eventually as the source of the anonymous tip, confessed his involvement and named his employers as the key players in the plot. These employers were two brothers, Antonis and Mamas Prokopiou Kitas, who reputedly ran a criminal organization based in Nicosia. The defendants all pled not guilty;

PART 1
On Conspiracy Theory and Context

As I noted in the Introduction, much of the scholarly writing on conspiracy theory to date is intertextual, cross-referential, and interventionist. These features facilitate—even insist on—my treating this writing as a distinctive body of literature: conspiratology. My own commentary in the pages that follow is intended as a contribution to the debates recurrently addressed in this literature, rather than as an exhaustive overview of the literature itself, which would be impossible as well as uninteresting, I think, given how summary and repetitive much of the literature is. The texts I have chosen to read closely here are exemplary of particular interpretive and argumentative strategies that are robustly represented and widely cited in the conspiratology literature. My overarching concerns in Part 1 are to characterize this literature rigorously, to locate points of agreement and articulate my disagreements with other conspiratologists, and to establish a way to move beyond the well-rehearsed approaches that dominate this literature. My engagement, then, is with conspiratology and not with conspiracy theory itself, since, as I argue throughout Part 1, conspiracy theory *itself* is an impossible object of analysis.

The approaches to conspiracy theory that I examine here are not mutually exclusive; they are tendencies or habits of thought that may overlap and synergize (as in the symptomatic and political approaches) and may even entail one another (as the symptomatic entails the particularist approach, and the psychoanalytic entails the political approach). From a sociology of knowledge perspective, it is noteworthy that conspiratologists tend to take approaches that align with their disciplinary heritage: philosophers seem more wedded to the epistemological approach, for example, and anthropologists more to the particularist approach, even if they have epistemological or at least definitional moments in their thinking that align them with philosophers. But the symptomatic approach is broadly shared by conspiratologists across the board, at least as a background condition of their argumentation. My aim in distinguishing these approaches, then, is to specify the tools conspiratologists use to analyze conspiracy theory, and to confront directly the stakes and implications of using those tools. As I demonstrate through the sections of Part 1, all these approaches treat conspiracy theory as a viable object of analysis. I pursue a contrary approach, shifting focus from conspiracy theory as an object toward *conspiracy attunement* as a context, a shift that I sketch out in Part 1.6 and then demonstrate in Part 2.

1. THE SYMPTOMATIC APPROACH

As many conspiratologists have observed, the term "conspiracy theory" is not a neutral, merely descriptive term. Its normative usage is to dismiss the referential truth of the theory in question, often without any evaluation of evidence. Cultural studies scholar Jack Bratich contends,

> Conspiracy theories ... in a neutral marketplace of ideas ... *could be* one kind of descriptive narrative among many. But this is not the case. Conspiracy theories exist as a category not just of description but of disqualification. (Bratich 2008, 3)

Bratich is drawing directly here from Foucault's work on subjugated knowledges, a small piece of his wide-ranging studies on methodology in the social and human sciences. In a lecture given in 1976, Foucault presented the concept of subjugated knowledge as a kind of defense against what he described as the "inhibiting effect of global, *totalitarian theories*" such as Marxism and psychoanalysis (Foucault 1980, 80–81 [emphasis original]). All too briefly, he identified two kinds of subjugated knowledges that, combined together, had animated the critiques of institutions founded on scientific knowledge that he and colleagues had been developing for some time, by then, under the rubric of "genealogy." He described one kind of subjugated knowledge as "buried knowledges of erudition"—that is, "blocs of historical knowledge" that had been "disguised" within modern scientific discourse (82). The other kind, which Bratich and other conspiratologists have associated with conspiracy theory, was a more expansive category comprising "inadequate ...

naïve knowledges, located low down on the hierarchy, beneath the required level of cognition or scientificity . . . low-ranking . . . unqualified, even directly disqualified knowledges . . . a popular knowledge . . ." (82). The issue of disqualification is crucial here, as it expresses Foucault's fundamental wariness about the will to power animating claims to official knowledge—for which he offers the general term "science," along the lines spoken in this lecture:

> What kinds of knowledge do you want to disqualify in the very instant of your demand: "is it a science"? Which speaking, discoursing subjects—which subjects of experience and knowledge—do you then want to "diminish" when you say: "I who conduct this discourse am conducting a scientific discourse, and I am a scientist"? Which theoretical-political *avant garde* do you want to enthrone in order to isolate it from all the discontinuous forms of knowledge that circulate about it? (85)

We do not have to see conspiracy theory as an altogether subjugated knowledge to grant that the label itself has often, if not mostly, been used to disqualify claims to knowledge and those making the claims. (In his more recent work, Bratich explores how the political terrain during Trumptimes has undermined the effectiveness of the label to, in fact, disqualify—a point to which I return in Part 1.5.) In recognition of this condition of conspiracy talk, in prior writing on this topic, I have placed scare quotes around the term "conspiracy theory" with every usage as a tactic to forestall the naturalizing common sense that so easily forms around conspiracy theory (Davis 2024). I saw this is as a practice of documenting the attributions others make of conspiracy theory without qualifying or disqualifying the referential truth of any theory in particular, and in doing so, I aimed to draw attention to unexamined premises in conspiratology as well as presumptions of mutual understanding—as in, "We know it when we see it," a form of inductive reasoning that, as Bratich notes, aspires but fails to position us to draw definitive distinctions between conspiracy theory and other kinds of theory (Bratich 2008, 2). However, I have come to think that, while this practice may effectively distance me from other conspiratologists, it might also distance me from conspiracy theory in an ironic mode, and actualize a kind of nominalism in relation to conspiracy theory that I explicitly reject (see Part 1.2). I argue throughout Part 1 that conspiracy theory is an impossible object of analysis because it is a radically unstable object; attempting to stabilize my own analytic position in relation to conspiracy theory as a metacommentator on a social phenomenon would mean standing outside the phenomenon rather than acknowledging the way my own thinking is "contaminated" by it, as Kathleen Stewart writes about cultural critique that "can grasp its object only by following along in its wake, tracing its interpretive moves and their actual effect" (Stewart 1991, 395). In the end, in this book, I decided not to use scare quotes from here on out, in the hopes that readers might more easily track their own impulses to stabilize conspiracy theory as an object and thus to qualify or disqualify it; the success or failure of those impulses will surely be instructive.

One of the procedures commonly used by conspiratologists to disqualify specific conspiracy theories in the way Bratich indicates is to diagnose those theories, or their proponents, as paranoid. Robert Robins and Jerrold Post (1997) are exemplary in this regard, defining conspiracy thinking as a form of "political paranoia," as Jodi Dean reads them: "a distortion, caricature, or parody of the useful, prudent, and sound practices of normal political behavior" (Dean 2002, 50). With a very different political objective, Mark Fenster characterizes conspiracy theory as "hyperactive semiosis," explicitly aligning himself with Richard Hofstadter's perspective in his famous and much-cited essay, "The Paranoid Style in American Politics," published in *Harper's* in 1964 (Fenster 1999, 78). To be sure, most scholars of conspiracy theory are careful to specify that they do not deploy the diagnostic term "paranoia" clinically. Hofstadter himself explains,

> In using the expression "paranoid style" I am not speaking in a clinical sense, but borrowing a clinical term for other purposes. I have neither the competence nor the desire to classify any figures of the past or present as certifiable lunatics. In fact, the idea of the paranoid style as a force in politics would have little contemporary relevance or historical value if it were applied only to men with profoundly disturbed minds. It is the use of paranoid modes of expression by more or less normal people that makes the phenomenon significant. (Hofstadter 1964, 77)

Hofstadter possibly introduced and certainly popularized what has become since then the dominant approach to conspiracy theory: namely, *symptomatic reading*. Best and Marcus describe symptomatic reading as the prevailing mode of literary analysis from the 1970s onward that "took meaning to be hidden, repressed, deep, and in need of detection and disclosure by an interpreter" (Best and Marcus 2009, 1). While they have a broad-ranging interpretive strategy in mind that could be applied to any text, when it comes specifically to conspiracy theory, paranoia is always in play as the hidden meaning to be detected and disclosed as the author's overt truth claims are rejected. The generalization of paranoia beyond mental pathology is the key to the liberality with which symptomatic readers accept and explain the meaningfulness of particular conspiracy theories while denying their plausibility.

The appealing notion of "paranoia within reason"—which resonates nicely with Hofstadter's phrase "more or less normal"—was popularized if not coined by George Marcus in his introduction to his "casebook" by that title. Marcus is interested here in paranoid tendencies of thought that remain within the orbit of plausibility; he operates a distinction between "exotic and excessive" forms of paranoia and those that are merely "distorted, even playful," and indeed, he observes, "commonsensical in certain contexts" (Marcus 1999, 5, 2). The primary such context he identifies is the post–Cold War era globally and, more specifically, scenarios of regime change in postsocialist and other postconflict states, as Cold War legacies of "paranoid social thought and action" and "paranoid policies of statecraft and governing" reverberated in the growth of "wild capitalism" and organized crime (2, 3).

The other main context Marcus identifies is social theory itself—that is, academic theories of society and power—indexed to the same Cold War legacy of paranoia that he finds in social and political life. Dominant forms of cynical rationality such as game theory, he writes, interacted with the "crisis of representation" in the social sciences and humanities from the 1980s onward to produce a situation of radical epistemological uncertainty with a paranoid tinge.[1] Marcus notes that accounts of these developments at the turn of the millennium (the moment of his writing, too) reflected the emergence of global relations of power and knowledge on such a massive scale, and of such intricate complexity, that social theorists could only grasp at fragments they found impossible to reconcile coherently within now-dismantled and discredited "metanarratives and conceptual frames" (Marcus 1999, 4). Among these, perhaps—Marcus does not name them explicitly—are liberalism, nationalism, historicism, cultural relativism, and realism. (Many contributors to the *Casebook* still felt comfortable with Marxism at the turn of the millennium.) Paranoid conspiracy theories—whether about transnational capital, the New World Order, or the end of days—arose to account for the "social and ethnographic facts of the world" that demanded but defied those conventional forms of explanation (4).

Marcus's *Casebook* is by no means the only influential work to frame conspiracy theory as a symptom of failures in social theory to address the scale, intricacy, and complexity of post–Cold War relations of power and knowledge.[2] Many scholars have taken this symptomatic approach, citing remarks by Fredric Jameson—identified by Best and Marcus as the preeminent "symptomatic reader" (2009, 3, 5, passim)—in *Postmodernism* and an earlier essay:

> Conspiracy theory (and its garish narrative manifestations) must be seen as a degraded attempt—through the figuration of advanced technology—to think the impossible totality of the contemporary world system. (Jameson 1992, 38)[3]
>
> Conspiracy, one is tempted to say, is the poor person's cognitive mapping in the postmodern age; it is the degraded figure of the total logic of late capital, a desperate attempt to represent the latter's system, whose failure is marked by its slippage into sheer theme and content. (Jameson 1988, 356)

Jean and John Comaroff take an equally symptomatic view in their conclusion to Harry West and Todd Sanders's 2003 volume, *Transparency and Conspiracy*, where they develop a line of argument they had initiated in an earlier paper (Comaroff and Comaroff 1999):

> Conspiracy, in short, has come to fill the explanatory void, the epistemic black hole, that is increasingly said to have been left behind by the unsettling of moral communities, by the so-called crisis of representation, by the erosion of received modernist connections between means and ends, subjects and objects, ways and means. (Comaroff and Comaroff 2003, 287–88)

The gesture to the meta-discursivity of conspiratology made by the Comaroffs here in their phrasing—"the explanatory void . . . that is *increasingly said* to have been left behind" and the "*so-called* crisis of representation"—both presumes and affirms the distinction between social theory and conspiracy theory that conspiratologists wield to assess the legitimacy of theory and attribute it to some (social theories) and not others (conspiracy theories). From this perspective, social theories are deployed not only as explanations of society and power to which conspiracy theories offer alternative accounts, but also as explanations of conspiracy theories themselves. The failure of social theories to explain what they purport to explain is identified by Jameson, Marcus, and others as a causal factor in the rise of conspiracy theory as a sociopolitical phenomenon.

Quite a few ethnographers have made a point of muddying the distinction between social theory and conspiracy theory advanced by these scholars while nevertheless performing a symptomatic reading. One such piece is Susan Harding and Kathleen Stewart's "Anxieties of Influence: Conspiracy Theory and Therapeutic Culture in Millennial America," also published in West and Sanders's 2003 volume. Moving swiftly from neurasthenia at the turn of the twentieth century to conspiracy theory at the turn of the twenty-first, Harding and Stewart take these affective-mental disorders in the United States both as vocabularies or "idioms" of social malaise and as symptoms of it (Harding and Stewart 2003, 259). Proliferating predicates as they go along, they characterize conspiracy theory as a "structure of feeling" (260, 282), as a "fiel[d] of feeling" (263), as "some sort of therapy" (263), and as an "embodied anxiety" (264), which, entangled with contemporary "therapeutic culture," communicate experiences of uncertainty and contradiction in American "postwar paranoid culture" (264) as well as "cures" and other forms of "redemption" (259) for those experiences. Their brief case studies take them to two marginal communities in California that formed in the 1970s but came conspicuously into public view in the 1990s: Calvary Chapel, a fundamentalist evangelical megachurch in Orange County, and the Heaven's Gate group in San Diego, which combined Christian eschatology with UFO/alien cosmology. The forms of "paranoia" Harding and Stewart find in these groups—which, in radically discrepant ways, concerned salvation at the end of days as an escape from powerful groups seeking their corruption and exploitation—are quite remote from the sort of "paranoia within reason" marked out for study by Marcus; presumably this is among the reasons Harding and Stewart turned their attention to them, designating Heaven's Gate in particular as "ultrafringe" due to the mass suicide of all thirty-nine members in 1997 after the passage of the Hale-Bopp comet. Given the marginality of these groups, the authors find it easy to dismiss their practices, but their decisive analytic maneuver is to diagnose those practices in a symptomatic register by connecting them to features of less marginal "hippie/drug culture," pop culture representations of space travel, and evangelical Christianity, among other sources (280). In multiplying these connections, Harding and Stewart obscure the division they themselves have drawn between the fringe groups they study and the extremely broadly construed "therapeutic culture" of millennial America that they take as a context for understanding those groups. It is that division that authorizes their own diagnostic judgment, implicitly locating them in the reasonable center of American culture even if they are also subject in some ways to its characteristic anxieties.

A more straightforward piece of symptomatic reading is Didier Fassin's 2011 essay "The Politics of Conspiracy Theories: On AIDS in South Africa and a Few Other Global Plots." Here, Fassin examines a scandal that arose in South Africa in 2000, when Manto Tshabalala-Msimang, then minister of health, expressed her "affinities not only for heterodox science"— specifically, the theory, supported by then-president of South Africa, Thabo Mbeki, that AIDS was not caused by a virus—"but also for conspiracy theories" (40) about Freemasons, the Illuminati, and the assassination of JFK, among other things. As against unnamed "commentators" who "underscore the irrationality of such beliefs without examining their meaning" (41), Fassin offers a classic symptomatic reading, looking behind the overt content of Mbeki's heterodox theory of AIDS to find its real and collective meaning in "the political history of AIDS" (41) in South Africa. He shows that this theory—widely held among Black South Africans but widely ridiculed by the "white liberal elite," he observes (40)—was entangled with the long history of viciously racist policies pursued by the white South African government throughout the twentieth century, especially tactics of forcibly segregating and displacing Black South Africans to "native locations" on the pretext of protecting public health during epidemics of plague and tuberculosis. Fassin notes the popularity of "heterodox AIDS theories" (42) in other contexts, as well—notably, the United States, where, he writes, 15 percent of African Americans polled in 2005 "viewed AIDS as a form of genocide against black people" (45)—in order to argue for a "political reading" of such beliefs among "historically dominated or discriminated groups" (46). In this political reading, Fassin shares with Marcus his distinction between the "exotic form" of conspiracy theory and its "ordinary expression" (40), using the term "counter-narratives" (40, 41) to recontextualize conspiracy theories as ordinary, even banal "beliefs" (41, 42, 45, *pas-*

sim) that dismantle the "cognitive consensus" about reality held in "normal times," and that thereby "reveal deep divisions in society" (40), *pace* Victor Turner.[4] That these divisions were obvious all along to some members of society while they remained invisible to others—in other words, that there never were "normal times," nor a "cognitive consensus"—is surely a crucial part of the political history Fassin begins to narrate here.

In his more recent writing on conspiracy theory, Fassin revisits the AIDS epidemic in South Africa, in part to redress what he perceives as "presentism" and "ethnocentrism" in contemporary media discourse on conspiracy theory (Fassin 2021, 128, 130). On his account, this discourse—his references are to US and European, especially French, media—is sloppy, alarmist, and denunciatory, characterized by "often biased, judgmental and in the end impoverished debate"; and though it newly features anxieties about "fake news," it does not otherwise, Fassin suggests, distinguish today from any other "conspiratorial moment" (128, 129). He perceives a widespread failure here to distinguish conspiracy theory from both skepticism and critique, and a certain bad-faith handwringing among media commentators about the "conspiratorial climate" to which they are in the process of contributing (129). The presentism Fassin targets for his own critique pertains to the pervasiveness of specific theories circulating "these days" (with references to COVID-19 and QAnon); he infers ethnocentrism from the absence of talk about theories arising from and addressing the world outside the United States and Europe ("in the Muslim world, in Asia, and in Africa," 128). The redress he offers comes in the form not of provincializing the Euro-American media discourse on conspiracy theories, or specifying its conditions of possibility,[5] but rather of looking again to South Africa and to the past in order to analyze conspiracy theories that emerged there during the AIDS epidemic—to "take these theories seriously," he writes, by "trying to understand what they mean," along the lines established in his earlier article (135).

Fassin takes a rather nominalist tack in this paper, asserting the social facticity of conspiracy theories and finding heuristic value in "examining these phenomena for what they can tell us about the social worlds in which they are embedded" (130, 134)—specifically, the "felicity conditions" that dispose people to be "pervious" or "permeable" to conspiracy theories (132, 133)—without "ridiculing" or "condemning" them (130). He reserves his ridicule and condemnation for American and European media commentators on conspiracy theories that originate and circulate in their own milieu, while rendering a respectful symptomatic reading of the "conspiratorial web that surrounded AIDS in South Africa" as a "window to the embodied memory of a painful past, the present political climate of mistrust, and the persisting racial and social tensions that goodwill had not sufficed to erase" (136). Fassin thus reproduces an asymmetry—characteristic of symptomatic readings, as I show in Part 1.3—between locales in which conspiracy theories are understood as such (e.g., France and the United States) and locales in which conspiracy theories should be understood heuristically (e.g., South Africa, and "the Muslim world . . . Asia, and . . . Africa" more generally), because it is in these latter locales—and presumably not in the former—that "the boundary between conspiracy and conspiracy theories may be blurred" (134).

In his 2004 paper on a cholera epidemic in the Orinoco Delta of Venezuela, Charles Briggs takes a more generative but nevertheless symptomatic approach, contextualizing the meanings of conspiracy theories of the epidemic and showing how those meanings functioned to normalize long-standing, multidimensional rifts between *criollo* and Indigenous Venezuelans. Studying the circulation of all accounts of the epidemic—from theories expressed by public health officials about contaminated shellfish to those expressed by Indigenous Delta residents about their deliberate poisoning by government officials and agents of oil companies—Briggs traces the specific processes by which the latter came to be labeled and dismissed as conspiracy theories. Focusing on the structural conditions of racism in which state power is embedded in Venezuela and globally, he identifies with the radical doubt cast on official theories of the epidemic by Indigenous residents and interprets their conspiracy theories as artifacts of the "unequal distribution of symbolic capital" by which Indigenous Delta residents are deprived of access to legitimate public speech (Briggs 2004, 178). These theories are not *only* artifacts, however; Briggs is ultimately interested in mobilizing his analysis of conspiracy theories to develop a critique of the structural inequalities across which symbolic capital is (thus) unequally distributed. For my purposes here, it is most important to note the diagnostic tenor of this critique, which positions conspiracy theories as symptoms whose meaning refers to social, economic, and political inequity and injustice rather than to the actors and events invoked by their overt semantic content.

Briggs's line of argument ultimately runs up against the approach developed by anthropologist Mathijs Pelkmans and political theorist Rhys Machold in their 2011 paper, "Conspiracy Theories and Their Truth Trajectories," although they share with Briggs a preoccupation with structural asymmetries in the social field. In what I am referring to as symptomatic readings of conspiracy theory, Pelkmans and Machold find a "lingering functionalism" that "fails to interrogate systematically the links between power and truth" (Pelkmans and Machold 2011, 68). This lingering functionalism is especially evident to them in works that characterize conspiracy theories as "subaltern strategies" to "make sense of impersonal and opaque forces" and other disempowering conditions of social and political life (68)—a functionalist perspective, as I understand their argument, because it explains conspiracy theories in terms of how they function to reproduce the social-political order: that is, the work they do to render people's worlds coherent, and thus to maintain the very conditions whose inequities and contradictions give rise to these theories in the first place.

Whether conspiracy theories actually do this work for people must, I think, be an open ethnographic question rather than a categorical assertion. Do people indeed make sense of their world by connecting the dots via untrue theories—thinking their way toward a coherence, however groundless in reality, that eludes them in daily life? It is surely a possibility that, on the contrary, people may be making *nonsense* of their world—not producing coherence in their social and emotional lives, but rather doing something much more destructive: tearing through the fragile social relations and political foundations that might offer them a sense of sense of connection and stability if they had not already been rejected as false and harmful.

To evade the trap of functionalism, Pelkmans and Machold turn their attention instead to conspiracy theories that have what they call a "use value" other than "sense-making" (68). They offer a counterexample: the theory that Saddam Hussein was amassing weapons of mass destruction and "conspiring with Al Quaeda" to attack the United States in the early 2000s (67)—which theory, they point out, was universally discredited but never socially labeled a conspiracy theory, though it clearly entailed a conspiracy to misinform the public on the part of Bush II administration operatives. Pelkmans and Machold identify the use value of this theory as "serv[ing] the political status quo" (68). Their approach, shifting from conspiracy theories to *theories of conspiracy* as their object of analysis, has the benefit of bracketing the truth claims of conspiracy theories rather than leaving truth implicit (because already known), as symptomatic readers do. Instead, they propose quite radically suspending the evaluation of truth in order to show how all theories move through "asymmetric fields of power" and come either, on one hand, to be accepted as true or false representations of reality, or, on the other hand, to be labeled as conspiracy theories.[6] Their approach thus illuminates another discursive space, outside the regime of truth, in Foucault's term—a space where conspiracy theories are "not even wrong,"[7] as Bratich notes, which is to say: disqualified in advance as candidates for truth.

Symptomatic readers miss this other space. Their critique operates "within the true," as Foucault named the parameters of truth regimes (Foucault 1971, 24),[8] and it is from these parameters—however rigorously and subtly contextualized—that they derive their certainty that *something is wrong*. They do not argue that people who are "paranoid within reason" are right to think what they think; the concept of reasonable paranoia enables symptomatic readers instead to acknowledge that a conspiracy theory makes sense "in context"—that it is plausible, meaningful, and even productive somehow for people who inhabit that context—*even though it is wrong*. The key is what the readers know to be true, as opposed to what the others believe.

When we presume that a conspiracy theory is false in this way, we are obliged to ask why others believe it if we want to make sense of it; as Fassin notes, "Making sense of what seems irrational and rendering the intelligibility of what appears to be incomprehensible represent a crucial contribution of the social sciences to our understanding of contemporary societies" (Fassin 2011, 42). Symptomatic reading in this sense bears the mark of the "empiricist paradigm" in anthropology that Byron Good explored in his 1990 Lewis Henry Morgan Lectures. In the published text (Good 1994), Good notes a strong resonance between this empiricist paradigm and the salvation ideology enacted by colonial missionaries; since the earliest days of the discipline, on his account, anthropologists have shared with "religious fundamentalists" a deep and abiding concern with the false beliefs of others (7–8). It is perhaps no accident, then, that anthropologists have most often focused their attention on belief when studying religions and "folk sciences" (20), conventionally glossed as *belief systems*. Conspiracy theory fits easily into or alongside these other systems, as attested by a wealth of ethnographic studies comparing conspiracy theory to magic, witchcraft, and fringe religions such as paganism.[9]

Good shows that anthropologists on both sides of the rationality debate of the early twentieth century—that is, the debate as to whether "primitives" could be understood as rational[10]—implicitly construed beliefs as propositions about the world: true or false statements that could be tested against reality. He ties this understanding of belief to "a particular folk psychology" that he associates with Euro-American rationalism in anthropology: "[a] view of culture as propositional, mentalistic, voluntaristic, and individualistic" (23). Anthropologists working in this rationalist tradition have taken for granted that culture can be studied as it manifests itself in the verbal statements people make about what they think and feel; and in turn, that their minds, to which anthropologists have no direct access, have contents that are reflected accurately in those statements. Rationalist anthropologists, Good observes, therefore face the special challenge of explaining how people whom they take to be rational nevertheless persist in holding "apparently irrational beliefs":[11]

> [They] have often argued either that seemingly irrational statements must be understood symbolically rather than literally or that they represent a kind of proto-science, an effort to explain events in the world in an orderly fashion that is the functional equivalent of modern science. (11–12)

Good finds the distinction between *our knowledge* and *their belief* to be pervasive in the empiricist-rationalist canon of anthropology, from Evans-Pritchard's defense of "primitive rationality" in *Witchcraft, Oracles, and Magic among the Azande* (1937) to much of the medical anthropology literature of the mid-twentieth century that construed the confrontation between biomedicine and Indigenous diagnostic and healing practices as a central problem in the development of what was then called "the third world" or, by some, the postcolonial world. Sabina Magliocco's (2012) work on magic and vernacular healing practices in Italy deftly shows how Good's colonial framing of the knowledge/belief dichotomy may be remapped onto the internal geography of Europe, in line with Michael Herzfeld's (1987) theorization of the locales of ethnography and anthropological theory in which Greece has played such a central role (see Part 1.6). In this remapping, Magliocco finds that southern Europe is often understood as the last bastion of a "pre-Enlightenment worldview" (Magliocco 2012, 7), hospitable to superstition and magical thinking, as against the self-conceptions of northern and western Europeans (and Euro-Americans) as rigorous rationalists. This framing of southern Europe, as I show in Part 1.6, has a great deal to do with the Cypriot context of conspiracy attunement.

Addressing the apparent confrontation between biomedicine and "native belief systems" that Good sketches out, Stacy Leigh Pigg (1996) relates how she was drawn into complex talk about Nepalis' belief in shamans during her fieldwork in Nepal in the mid-1980s. Such talk was complex due to the range of professions her Nepali interlocutors made about their own beliefs and doubts, which she contextualizes in part by the influence of development discourse and especially the discourse of "modern medicine" (162, passim), which positioned shamans as the personification of ignorance, superstition, and corruption that development must overcome. Compared with the intricacy, subtlety, and situatedness of different Nepalis' different kinds of talk about their belief in shamans, Pigg finds development discourse remarkably flat-footed and naïve in its depiction of unyielding, unquestioning, undifferentiated belief in shamans among Nepali villagers. The "distinction between knowledge and belief" (176) that Good associates with the empiricist-rationalist paradigm in anthropology is very much in play in the "cross-talk" that Pigg observes (and engages in) among Nepali villagers and development workers.

In response, Pigg develops what she calls a "structuralist reading" of modernization discourse (I would call it an analogy between structuralism and modernization discourse), noting that this discourse introduces the very dichotomies—modern and traditional, knowledge and belief—in terms of which it analyzes cultural material and attributes value and meaning. This circularity works both to confirm the central premise of modernization (viz., that villagers are indeed superstitious believers) and to exclude Nepali points of view entirely—most important, their skepticism about shamans: "In order for the position of 'people who understand' to exist," Pigg notes, "there must be a credulous 'other'" (177). Even so, she writes, "the modern dichotomies seem to wobble even as they are asserted" (177). Thus, in her presence, development and health-care workers sometimes "played" at shamanism, engaging in a mimetic performance in order to persuade villagers that medicine *works*, and then finding (and showing) that, thus "enmeshed in the very superstitions it opposes" (177), it does indeed. Pigg takes such performances of shamanism, in which it was not clear to anyone "who fooled whom," as emblematic of the "displacements" of people and culture effected by globalization, which is also to say the displacement of concepts and categories of difference (193, 195n8). Her own interactions with Nepali villagers and Nepali development workers were situated, dynamic, and, she insists, "dialogical"—meaning that in talking with her and one another, Nepalis were "oriented toward listeners" whom they did not presume to share their views, and from whom they "anticipate[d] responses that might come from various perspectives" (171). Thus, Pigg concludes, "Assertions of belief stake out speaking positions in a dialogical context" (190); the way one talks about belief establishes who one is, what one knows, and what one can make happen in that context.

Like Pigg, Good explores the positionality embedded in the distinction between *our* knowledge and *their* belief, situating it within two historical shifts in the meaning and use of the word "belief" in the anglophone Christian world, as outlined by the historian of religion Wilfred Cantwell Smith. First is a shift from performative use (an oath or pledge to God or a feudal lord) to propositional use (a judgment about the truth or falsity of a statement); second, and related, is a shift from first person ("I believe") to third person ("they believe"). Inspired by Smith's sensitivity to the pragmatic dimensions of language use, Good, like Pigg (1996, 194),[12] follows anthropologist Jeanne Favret-Saada away from the semantics of belief and toward its performativity—toward an analysis that does not take professed beliefs as propositional statements about reality, nor as representations of the mental states of speakers, but rather as tools for establishing one's position in a field of power.[13] This field might be a witchcraft scenario, as in Favret-Saada's ethnography *Deadly Words*, where witchcraft talk in rural France appears as a "battle of powerful wills, a fight to the death" (Good 1994, 13).

Favret-Saada's crucial ethnographic observation—mind-bending for those of a rationalist-empiricist bent—is that no one in the dialogical context of witchcraft occupies the position of witch; no one admits or aspires to being a witch, and indeed Favret-Saada asserts that there is no such person. Witch is an imaginary position that cannot be occupied, but accusations that specific persons are witches carry enormous power: the power to cause social death and even biological death. In this situation, there is no position a speaking subject can take except that of bewitched (sufferer) or unwitcher (healer). A sure way for an anthropologist to remain outside this field of power, Favret-Saada shows, is to speak with interlocutors *about* witchcraft, announcing one's utter irrelevance to their concerns by blathering on about their beliefs.

One does not have to be in a witchcraft situation to privilege the pragmatic over the semantic dimensions of talk about belief; Good extends the dialogical context in ethnographic research to any scenario in which an anthropologist might be addressed by interlocutors as a conduit of power or value. This kind of analysis opens a way around "the usual arguments about the nature of rationality" (19), as he puts it, that have cropped up time and again in anthropological debates about the status of belief. I come back to this "way around" later, in Part 1.6, where I frame my interest in conspiracy attunement—as against conspiracy theory—as an interest in reflexivity and styles of talk in the longue durée as contexts for social analysis. Like Pigg and Good, I take my lead from Favret-Saada's study of witchcraft; her theorization of witchcraft talk as a battle of wills entails an exploration of the unconscious defenses and desires (especially the violent drives) that motivate that talk. This theorization marks a deliberate and knowing departure from the learned habit she observed among French urban elites of describing the rural peasants who supposedly believe in witchcraft as gullible, backward, irrational, and semantically in earnest when they speak. On Favret-Saada's description, these elites come off as the pitiably credulous ones, earnestly believing in the beliefs of others, thereby missing the point entirely and backing themselves into a scientific dead end. Sabina Magliocco makes this point elegantly, recounting her fieldwork with vernacular healers in Italy: "I was always careful not to ask about belief, conscious that, as Dégh writes, 'The question itself provokes distortion'" (Magliocco 2012, 6, citing Dégh 1996, 39).

I do not want to overstate the resemblance between witchcraft and conspiracy theory scenarios as dialogical contexts. But among other parallels, one is especially clear: there is no subject position for the conspiracy theorist. This label exists as an attribution but not an identity. That is not to suggest that people may not speak the words "I am a conspiracy theorist"; they surely may. But if they do, it is by way of reappropriating a label of disqualification in a playful or oppositional mode. Even if the label does not in fact effectively disqualify, as Bratich argues in his recent work (2017), it is nevertheless an attribution whose purpose is to disqualify, marginalize, ostracize, and exclude: to place the person thus-called outside the sphere of social and political legitimacy. It names a position that cannot be occupied by a person engaged in a dialogical situation with others. To say "I am a conspiracy theorist" in a non-ironic way is to say, "You cannot trust me. Do not believe a word I say." Meaningful communication is nullified. If we wish to talk about people who believe in conspiracy theories, then, we commit ourselves to concluding not only that they hold false beliefs—which an atheist might easily say about a Christian—but also that they cannot *profess* their beliefs.

In their ethnographic work on conspiracy theorists in the Netherlands, Jaron Harambam and Stef Aupers (2017) show that people *they* have identified as conspiracy theorists due to their activity in "'places' generally given the label 'conspiracy theory'" (117)—websites, film screenings, performances of well-known conspiracy figures such as David Icke—do not identify *themselves* as conspiracy theorists, and in fact use that term to "distance themselves" (118) from others in the milieu whom they find irrational or too radical. These people instead see themselves as skeptics, activists, dreamers, or "critical free thinkers" (118, 119, 122, 126), whereas they might identify a conspiracy theorist as a "fear monger," a "loon," or a "demagogue" (121). Harambam and Aupers present the "Dutch conspiracy milieu" as a subcultural and "interactional context" (114, 115) in which self-alignment and self-differentiation in relation to others are the key modes of identity formation. In this context, the label "conspiracy theorist" continues to carry the pejorative charge of disqualification derived from the dominant culture—a meaning that is only confirmed by their interlocutors, whose use of the label, they observe, "ultimately discredits the whole group" (126). Within this milieu, they argue, "The adage, 'I am not a conspiracy theorist' functions . . . as a trope to reclaim rationality in a cultural climate where 'official' truth claims are increasingly contested" (126).

In direct response to this argument, in his most recent article on conspiracy theory (2022), Theodoros Rakopoulos observes a great deal more "ambivalence" (51) on the part of people labeled as conspiracy theorists in relation to the "dynamic" "ascription" of that label (48). His interlocutors in Thessaloniki are authors of conspiracy theory literature that "they (and their readership) call 'conspiratorial,' 'alternative,' 'marginal,' 'unconventional,' 'revelatory,' 'anti-establishment' and 'truth-seeking'" (47). Given their long-term experience going back to the 1990s, and their long-standing preeminence in the milieu, they are able to position themselves as "gatekeepers," "experts" and "'arbiters' in the field of conspiracy theory in Greece" (46, 49). Rakopoulos seeks to "demystify and de-essential[ize]" (55) this context by paying attention to the conflicts, contradictions, diversity, dynamism, and "internal differentiat[ion]" (57) within it:

> The milieu is . . . characterised by different worldviews and internal strife but does not confirm the adage "I am not a conspiracy theorist" identified among lay conspiracists (Harambam and Aupers 2017) . . . Though the actors in this field are ambivalent about their identity as conspiracy theorists, they embrace their branding as such by the "powers that be." They would primarily identify their craft as an unconventional and radical way to talk about "the political." . . . I must underline that many, indeed most, of my interlocutors, even when sometimes denying the term "conspiracy theory," did promote the notions of "conspiracy" and "conspiracism" to discuss their ideas about the world. (2022, 49, 51)

It seems that, while Rakopoulos's interlocutors did not always distance themselves from the label "conspiracy theorist" (they did not always say "I am *not* a conspiracy theorist"), they often did so; and when they instead embraced it, this was done in the mode of reappropriating a disqualifying label from the "powers that be" in order to qualify themselves as legitimate critics of those powers. Rakopoulos reads their rejection or embrace of the label as situated choices that depended on whom they were addressing and to what ends they were speaking. Likewise, he notes that practitioners deployed terms like "paranoid" or "fascist" to denigrate or debunk the claims made by other practitioners with whom they disagreed (55). All these terms were available to people in this milieu—producers and consumers of conspiracy theories alike—to position themselves in relation to others in the milieu, but none of them was claimed as an earnest, stable self-description or identity.

Turning back to symptomatic readings of conspiracy theory, we can see that the concept of reasonable paranoia operated by many symptomatic readers shares in the structuralist dichotomies of modernization discourse on belief, *pace* Pigg. The notion of context implicit in the concept of reasonable paranoia is a classically ethnocentric one; it effects precisely the "separations" that characterize modernist ethnography on Strathern's account, even if the contextual boundaries that do the separating are not always thematized as cultural (though they often are). It explicitly disavows the clinical and pathological connotations of "paranoia," while implicitly mobilizing those connotations to dismiss the referential truth of the theories in question. The concept of reasonable paranoia makes no sense at all unless we redefine paranoia as a normal and healthy response "in context"; but if we make that contextualizing move, relativizing the meaning of the paranoid theories in question, then we lose the analytic edge that paranoia offers us to distinguish irreality from reality, and delirium from truth, on a universal scale. This is too costly a sacrifice for many social theorists, and perhaps that is why so many have taken up "paranoia within reason" as a sort of half-measure: one that allows relativism and universalism to coexist—relativism when it comes to meaning, universalism when it comes to truth—but on different registers, thus obscuring the contradiction between them. When symptomatic readers interpret the meaning of conspiracy theories that others appear to believe in *their* contexts, they implicitly treat the truth-making procedures they follow in their own analysis as *contextless*—which is to say, producing truth regardless of context.

As I noted earlier, the focus Pelkmans and Machold train on the fields of power in which "truth and untruth are created" puts them at quite a distance from symptomatic reading (Pelkmans and Machold 2011, 66); in declining to evaluate the truth claims of the theories they study, they also decline to pathologize or disqualify the proponents of those theories. In this, they approach the tack that Jack Bratich takes in his 2008 book, *Conspiracy Panics*. In this work, Bratich does not attempt to find the deep meaning of conspiracy theory, but rather presents it as a "metaconcept signifying the struggles over the meaning of the concept" (Bratich 2008, 6). From this meta-perspective, he examines the process by which theories are disqualified as conspiracy theories in favor of hegemonic knowledge claims, and how those processes of disqualification produce meaning and reproduce power. He therefore shifts his analytic sights from conspiracy theories to conspiracy *panics*—that is, to fretful and despairing discourses about conspiracy theory that have surfaced at particular historical moments.

In examining conspiracy panics rather than conspiracy theories, Bratich embraces what he calls the "symptomatological" approach, according to which, "conspiracy theories are taken as a sign of something else" (14)—some kind of collective dis-ease, malaise, anxiety, anomie.[14] On his own account, what sets Bratich's "symptomatology" apart from what I have been describing in this section as symptomatic reading is that he takes conspiracy panics rather than conspiracy theories as his object, and thus renders an "immanent diagnosis," an "analysis from within," probing the "'unstated presuppositions and problematics'" of conspiracy panic rationalities (Bratich 2008, 15, 16, quoting Read 2003, 12). His immanent diagnosis stands in contrast to the more familiar transcendent diagnosis of conspiracy theory performed by symptomatic readers, in which a special position of authority, outside and above conspiracy talk, is reserved for those who know the truth of the matter. Indeed, the truth of the matter, and whether people believe the truth, are not Bratich's concerns. He instead examines how truth claims operate in conspiracy panics to "define the normal modes of dissent" by relegating conspiracy theories to the irrational fringes of society and framing them as "a symptom of a culture or a climate of paranoia" (11). In substituting the "diffuse threat" of conspiracy theory for any clearly defined object of fear, he argues, conspiracy panics mobilize generalized anxiety that reveals "presuppositions" about rationality and morality that are not "articulated" explicitly within conspiracy panic discourse (11, 16). While Bratich is, thus, very interested in collective dis-ease, he sees it as an effect of conspiracy panics rather than a cause of conspiracy theories.

In *Conspiracy Panics*, Bratich argues that the relevant context for understanding conspiracy theories is the context of their disqualification: the discourses, events, and processes through which conspiracy theories come into being *as* disqualified (*as such*, he often writes), and "visible and intelligible" (6) in their disqualification. It is in this sense that, for him, context is "constitutive" of conspiracy theories rather than a separate matrix, such as local culture or political economy, to which we might turn to understand them (19); conspiracy panics, he explains, are "part of a conceptual context" (13). When he describes his diagnosis of conspiracy panics as "immanent" rather than "transcendent," then, it is to this constitution of conspiracy theories by context that he is referring, acknowledging the absence of any external criteria or scale by which to determine their meaning. His tactic of immanent diagnosis entails delving deeper into the panicked public discourse on conspiracy theory, as represented in US media, in order to determine the implicit conceptual preconditions of this discourse.

But what kind of context is media discourse? Though searingly incisive, Bratich's immanent diagnosis of conspiracy panics does not offer access to the performative dimension of public talk about conspiracy theory. Ethnographers need other tools if they wish to analyze media discourse *in* a context (as I do in Part 2.2) rather than *as* a context in itself—in other words, to examine conspiracy theory in a context where the discursive meets the dialogical. In Part 1.6, I develop the concept of conspiracy attunement as just such a tool. Conspiracy attunement is a "dialogical context," in Pigg's term, in which public discourse about conspiracy theory becomes a performative meta-discourse. In this context, self-representations and representations of others as theorists of one kind or another work as tactics in a field of power in which conspiratologists are also active and implicated.

2. THE EPISTEMOLOGICAL APPROACH

As I showed in the previous section, the symptomatic approach frames conspiracy theories as expressions of paranoia that is collective—social—in nature. This approach entails an epistemological premise that is worth interrogating in its own right: namely, that conspiracy theory can be categorically distinguished from other kinds of theory on the basis of distinctive features that occur in all conspiracy theories but do not occur in other kinds of theories. This epistemological premise of the symptomatic approach has, itself, been treated to substantial attention by conspiratologists in their attempts to define and stabilize conspiracy theory as an object of analysis.

What I am calling the *epistemological approach*, here, is the attempt to define and classify conspiracy theory by its distinctive theoretical features, which I elaborate in this section. Epistemology itself has a much broader ambit, touching any problem of knowledge: what it is, where it comes from, what forms it takes, what it asks of us, what it inspires us to do. A much narrower set of questions is posed by the epistemological approach to conspiracy theory: how do we know it when we see it, and how does it fail as a way of knowing? In my reading of the conspiratology literature, it is most often philosophers, psychologists, and political scientists who take this approach to conspiracy theory; anthropologists, sociologists, and cultural studies scholars appear less keen on this endeavor, perhaps due to the awareness of difference within and across conspiracy theory contexts that their research necessitates. Nonetheless, many of the latter group of conspiratologists, including most of the symptomatic readers I discussed in the previous section, proceed inductively, assuming a commonsense consensus among writers and readers as to what we all mean by conspiracy theory. Others take an implicitly nominalist stance, identifying conspiracy theory as nothing more or less than what their interlocutors in the social field say it is. This nominalist approach is closer to Bratich's, in the sense that conspiracy panics, for Bratich, are discourses *about* conspiracy theory; we do not need to agree on a definition of conspiracy theory to analyze discourses about it. But Bratich does not pursue comparative analysis across contexts (except historical ones, a point to which I return in Part 1.3); if we extend his concept of conspiracy panics beyond the context he examines—say, to US media culture—it quickly reveals itself to be just as unstable a ground for analysis as conspiracy theory: just as much in need of definition and just as unable to provide one.

As for implicit nominalism, which follows the meanings and usages of the term conspiracy theory across different contexts: this path seems to me to lead inexorably to analytic incoherence. In asserting the same concept—conspiracy theory—to describe a variety of cultural and political practices that are called "conspiracy theory" in their own contexts, we must either flatten the differences among those practices in order to contain them within the concept—thus making them unrecognizable as conspiracy theory within their own contexts—or we must go without knowing why such different practices go by the same name in all those contexts. In other words, if conspiracy theory is just what people say it is, then we cannot compare conspiracy theory across contexts in which different people say it is different things. Conversely, if we work inductively, and assume that everyone agrees on a general definition of conspiracy theory independent of context, then many practices that go by the name "conspiracy theory" will be excluded from that definition. A general theory of conspiracy theory is impossible to develop from either starting point.

In light of this problem, a number of conspiratologists have offered loose or preliminary definitions of conspiracy theory without asserting their universal applicability. Jodi Dean, for instance, sensibly dismisses several narrative and authorial features by which other academics have identified (and derided) conspiracy theory as such: for example, "style," "plot," and "pathological motivations" (2002, 49). She lands instead on a particular kind of literalism as the distinctive feature of conspiracy theory: that is, "the way conspiracy theory *takes the system at its word*" (2002, 53, emphasis original). Theodoros Rakopoulos, who seeks to "update our anthropological knowledge of conspiracy theory" by reading it through capitalism (2018, 378), gives a gloss on contemporary European conspiratology in the figure of Pierre-André Taguieff, who apparently follows the symptomatic approach rather closely: "Conspiracy theory's chief feature," Rakopoulos says of Taguieff's work, "is seen to be its capacity to provide intellectual convenience in an increasingly complex world" (377). Clare Birchall gamely offers a "working definition": "In its simplest terms, conspiracy theory refers to a narrative that has been constructed in an attempt to explain an event or a series of events to be the result of a group of people working in secret to a nefarious end" (Birchall 2004, n.p.; Birchall 2006, 34). Yet Birchall quickly complicates this definition, styling conspiracy theory as "hyperreal knowledge" (2006, 73ff.) and pinpointing its many affinities with other kinds of theory.

Philosopher Brian Keeley, in a widely cited piece, attempts to work out a more global definition on epistemological grounds. "A conspiracy theory," he writes, is "a proposed explanation of some historical event (or events) in terms of the significant causal agency of a relatively small group of persons—the conspirators—acting in secret" (Keeley 1999, 116). He presents this as a "bare bones" and neutral definition that may apply to theories of conspiracy in which we ought to believe as well as those we ought not (116). He helpfully assumes that we are and may always be in a position of limited knowledge of the truth; the question as to how we might distinguish between conspiracy theories and legitimate theories, then, is a question of what it is reasonable to believe under these conditions of limited knowledge.

The distinction Keeley pursues between warranted and unwarranted conspiracy theories maps cleanly on to the distinction George Marcus and others maintain between reasonable and unreasonable paranoia. Rather than relating conspiracy theories to their context in order to arrive at a judgment of reasonableness, however, as Marcus and others do, Keeley proceeds to discount unwarranted conspiracy theories by identifying and discrediting their characteristic epistemological features, which appear (on his account) to inhere in conspiracy theories regardless of the context in which they appear. These features include their contestation of a "received" or "official" account, their stipulation of secrecy and "nefarious" intentions, their connection of "seemingly unrelated events," and their reliance on "errant data" (117). Keeley moves beyond these distinguishing features of unwarranted conspiracy theories—which are not, for him, reason enough to reject them in advance—in order to consider the "outdated" picture they hypostatize of an ordered world in which everything fits. He implies that belief in these theories constitutes a moral choice to inhabit that sort of ordered world instead of "an irrational and essentially meaningless" one in which causes and effects have no proportionate relation—the latter being an "absurdist" position, in his term (125).[15] The distinction he asserts between warranted and unwarranted conspiracy theories thus ends up resting, he writes, on how much "skepticism . . . we can stomach" (126).

Keeley is admirably clear by the end of his paper about the moral nature of the distinction he has developed between warranted and unwarranted conspiracy theories. His relativism is grounded in his assumption of our limited access to truth; judgment of a theory's legitimacy therefore takes the form: *this theory is more plausible than that one*. Keeley's relativism is epistemological rather than contextual, and thus does not entail any assessment of the effect that the context in which one is exercising judgment may have on one's judgment about the plausibility of a particular theory. Pelkmans and Machold point to this problem in their careful reading of Keeley:

> One peculiarity of the attempt to pinpoint the epistemological characteristics of conspiracy theorizing [as Keeley does] is that these presumed epistemological characteristics turn out to be sociological ones when scrutinized. The issue of the fundamental attribution error is ultimately about the relation between theory and theorizer—about how data are interpreted and given weight by social actors. (Pelkmans and Machold 2011, 69–70)

I follow Pelkmans and Machold in this line of argument, which, by insisting on contextualization, takes us to the limit of the epistemological approach to conspiracy theory. My own view is that conspiracy theory cannot, on epistemological grounds, be categorically distinguished from social theory or any other kind. This is because, first, the questions about expertise and legitimate authority that are often raised by critics of conspiracy theory are also, equally, raised by social and critical theory. Clare Birchall neatly demonstrates this intimacy, drawing close parallels between conspiracy theory and cultural studies as an academic field in terms of both their interpretive procedures and their "undecidability around the issue of legitimacy" (Birchall 2006, 85). Robyn Marasco (2016) likewise finds deep similarities between psychoanalytic procedures and paranoid thought, which I discuss in Part 1.4. Such resonance between conspiracy theory and social and critical theory is a point to which many social and critical theorists seem comfortable acceding when engaging in cultural critique—their legitimation of "subjugated" and "populist" knowledges attests to this comfort, as I show in Part 1.5—but often less so when they are rejecting conspiracy theory.

Second, as conspiratologists readily acknowledge, there are actual conspiracies in the world, and a conspiratorial form of causal agency—a multiple, collusive, secretive agency, as Keeley has it (Keeley 1999, 116)[16]—is indisputably at work sometimes in the social, economic, political, and cultural phenomena studied by social and critical theorists. These conclusions are shared by many conspiracy theorists and social and critical theorists; Durkheim's theory of social cohesion around ritual elites, Marx's theory of primitive accumulation, Althusser's theory of ideology, even John L. Jackson's (2017) theory of race-thinking as a conspiracy (among anthropologists, among others), stand as obvious, if contestable, examples. The very prospect of contesting the classification of these theories as conspiracy theories—as in Karl Popper's defense of Marx as "one of the first *critics* of the conspiracy theory [of society]," for instance (Popper [1963] 2002, 167n3)—is what lures some conspiratologists into drawing categorical distinctions between conspiracy theory and social and critical theory that are not warranted on epistemological grounds.

Mark Fenster observes popular leftist critics of conspiracy theory, such as Noam Chomsky and Michael Albert, engaging in precisely this kind of line-drawing, worried that leftists have been or will be seduced by conspiracy theory's focus on the individual agency of purported conspirators, and thus be "distracted" from real critique and reform oriented toward systemic or structural problems (2008, 43, 45–47).[17] Structural agency may seem to such critics a better, less conspiracist place to land in the social analysis of power. But while the explanatory appeal of structural agency may be obvious to the point of self-evident for many social theorists, it is not a causal concept of agency unless it is linked with a theory of false consciousness (a Marxian approach) or with the actions of individuals taken in the aggregate (a sociological approach). Pierre Bourdieu's dialectical theorization of *habitus* (Bourdieu [1980] 1990), for example, straddles these two approaches in its explanation of *practice*. We may pinpoint the effects of structural agency—rather, we may hypostatize it as a cause of effects we can pinpoint—but the concept in itself does not offer an alternative causal explanation to that of individual agency. When pressed to show how structural agency is causal, scholars often end up recurring to individual agency, re-describing individuals as class members or subject positions in a discourse—that is, as representatives of collective nodes in structural matrices that are occupied (though not authored) by individuals.[18] This issue is one of long-standing and intricate debate among social scientists and social theorists; for my limited purposes here, the important point is that notions of structural agency do not answer the question as to how to distinguish conspiracy theory from social theory on epistemological grounds. Theories of structural agency just kick the epistemological black box of agency down the road.

American literature scholar Timothy Melley (2000) is especially astute and persuasive on this point.[19] He notes that "concepts of structural agency have long been a staple feature not only of economic and social theories but also of aesthetic approaches such as literary naturalism, the late-nineteenth-century movement coupled to the development of sociology, machine culture, and deterministic theories of human behavior" (2000, 5). The "agency panic" he diagnoses in American conspiracy narratives at the turn of the millennium bears, he writes, "an important likeness" to "sociological thinking" in "illuminating the obscure sources of social regulation" (15). Thus, he finds "a problem inherent in the definition of paranoia": namely, that "despite the seemingly obvious marks of extreme (or pathological) cases of paranoia, it is remarkably difficult to separate paranoid interpretation from 'normal' interpretive practices" (17). Eve Kosovsky Sedgwick's now-classic essay on paranoid reading and reparative reading hews to this line of thinking; she examines paranoia as a dominant practice of interpretation and critique that mirrors precisely the overdetermination and inevitability of "systemic oppressions" postulated by critical theorists (Sedgwick 2003, 124). Her essay catalogues the "suspicious" techniques of demystification, revelaion, exposure, and decipherment of hidden violence and false consciousness rough which such theorists establish their own distance from power and w their sharp political teeth. Sedgwick offers this depiction of paranoid 'ing as a sort of self-portrait in which her own readers—addressed as \gues—might see themselves.

epistemological approach to conspiracy theory has taken an inter-urn during the Trumptimes, which many critics regard as especially \le to conspiracism. In their recent book, *A Lot of People Are Say-* *Jew Conspiracism and the Assault on Democracy* (2019), for exam-:al scientists Russell Muirhead and Nancy Rosenblum explore erm "the new conspiracism" (Preface, 5, 8, passim), or "conspiracy without the theory" (x, 2), which they associate with the Trump presidency. To establish the novelty of the new conspiracism, the authors develop an epistemological account of "classic conspiracism" (10, 19, passim), or "classic conspiracy theory" (20, 23, passim), in contrast to which they define the new conspiracism privatively. Indeed, on their account, the new conspiracism is not an epistemology at all. Its defining features are its "shedding" of explanation, theory, argument, and evidence (24, 28, 31); its "typical form," Muirhead and Rosenblum write, is "bare assertion" (25), or "innuendo" (27), or "free-floating allegation disconnected from anything observable in the world" (26). What seems to most trouble them about the new conspiracism is its lack of theory—its disconnection from any political ideology, values and principles, worldview, program of reform, "theory of justice" (35), or "sense of history" (28). They view it as "sheer negativity" (33, 39), whose product and sole purpose is "delegitimation" (33ff.): specifically, the delegitimation of democratic institutions and processes.

By contrast—and this is the interesting turn—Muirhead and Rosenblum present "classic conspiracy theory" as a long-standing feature of political life in democratic societies, presented here as a prelapsarian Beforetimes. They go to some trouble to show that it was a crucial factor in the founding of the United States, as the Revolutionary War that established its independence from Great Britain and thereby its sovereignty was motivated by a "conspiracy theory about Britain's secret intention to extinguish liberty in North America" (21). They are not interested in distinguishing conspiracy theory from legitimate theory; on the contrary, they borrow Keeley's distinction between warranted and unwarranted conspiracy theories, noting "there are no bright lines" between them, and that "there is nothing that makes conspiracy theories as such irrational or erroneous" (10). Classic conspiracy theory, on their account, like all political theory, "tries to make sense of the political world" (20) by "connecting the dots and identifying patterns" (26–27), and shares with other epistemologies the basic practice of marshaling evidence to support arguments and offer explanations. It is, then, precisely by rejecting any distinction between conspiracy theory and legitimate theory on epistemological grounds that Muirhead and Rosenblum are able to define the new conspiracism as a political tactic without an epistemology.

I suggest that theorists who attempt to establish a distinction between (illegitimate) conspiracy theory and (legitimate) social and critical theory on epistemological grounds—such as a priori definitions of agency as multiple, collusive, and secretive, or "leap[s] in imagination" linking together pieces of evidence[20]—are engaged in a process of begging the question.[21] What they offer as the conclusion of their argument—namely, that a particular theory is in fact a conspiracy theory—is actually its premise. Conspiracy theory cannot be distinguished on epistemological grounds from other kinds of theory. Nor, for the same reasons, can it be defined as a category or genre of knowledge in relation to other low-status knowledges with which it is often compared or equated: fake news, propaganda, rumor, gossip. There is no such thing as conspiracy theory per se; there is only theory: good and bad, well-evidenced and not, persuasive and not, enlightening and not, desirable and not. Denouncing or dismissing a particular theory by reclassifying it as a kind of theory (i.e., conspiracy theory) obscures other, more compelling grounds for critique: its falseness, its destructiveness, its use in bad faith. From this perspective, to the extent that the conspiracy theory label is used by critics to distinguish it from legitimate theory, the term can only be a red herring and a muddying of the waters—a futile attempt to stabilize a position from which truth will appear self-evident.

3. THE PARTICULARIST APPROACH

In the Introduction, I suggested that many approaches to analyzing conspiracy theory operate and in fact depend on a fundamentally ethnocentric use of context. In what I will call the *particularist approach*,[22] locale and epoch operate as unexamined, mutually entailing premises, forming an implicitly distinctive context that conspiratologists understand as "making sense" of theories that would not make sense elsewhere and elsewhen. From these unexamined premises follow the critical distinction between reasonable and unreasonable paranoia that makes symptomatic reading possible.

Rather than start from locale and epoch as contextual premises, in this section I start instead from the question: *What is a context?* Roy Dilley, in his reflections on "the problem of context" in anthropology, remarks on the flexibility of context as a framework for conceptualizing culture—so flexible, in fact, as to lack a distinctive shape or scale:

> The concept of culture became the defining feature of social anthropology after Malinowski, and it came to represent that which is local, particular and distinctive, compared to the global, general and common. The

word context became part of a stock anthropological vocabulary used to denote a bewildering variety of characteristics, domains and environments. Contexts could be cultural, social, political, ritual and religious, economic or ecological; they could be interactional, systemic or historical. The term, it seems, is sufficiently elastic to be stretched in numerous directions for diverse purposes. (Dilley 1999, 26)

One way to examine the "purposes" for which context has been "stretched" in conspiratology is to observe a commonplace division of analytic labor between the various locales and epochs of conspiracy theory. Part I of George Marcus's *Casebook* (1999), for example, entitled "Paranoia within Reason," comprises chapters on theories and knowledges developed by reasoning experts of various kinds—philosophers, quantum physicists, attorneys, psychotherapists, climate scientists—based in European or North American locales that are not thematized as contexts for the theories and knowledges being examined. Part II of the book, "Paranoid Histories," shifts toward what are styled as Cold War "legacies" playing out during the 1990s: fascism in Italy, dictatorship in Brazil, Stalinism in Russia, and Yugoslav socialism in Slovenia—a series of locales that are overtly thematized as contexts. The papers in Part III of the book, "Paranoid Presents," engage the same "present" as those in Part II—that is, the 1990s—but, in Marcus's framing, rather than the past, they address "what may be emerging" in the form of "visceral and immediate responses to contemporary events and experiences" (Marcus 1999, 8), such as a mafia trial in Italy, a neofascist movement in London, Gulf War illness and evangelical millennialism in the United States. This split in the present moment between historical legacy and present emergence is a function of the specific locales in which the conspiracy theories in each chapter are examined. What is most striking to me about the arrangement of material in the *Casebook*, however, is not this division in the work of historical time between the places represented in Parts II and III, but rather the division between Part I and the rest of the book—between, that is, theories and knowledges whose locale is not thematized or addressed explicitly at all, and "histories" and "presents" whose locale forms the central explanatory context.

Another widely cited collection, *Transparency and Conspiracy: Ethnographies of Suspicion in the New World Order*, edited by Harry West and Todd Sanders (2003), advances a more purposively cross-cultural understanding of locale, featuring case studies in South Korea, Nigeria, Mozambique, Indonesia, Tanzania, and China as well as post-Soviet Russia and the United States. In the introduction, reflecting explicitly on the problem of locale, West and Sanders warn readers not to reproduce the dichotomies we have inherited between "the west and the rest" and all those connected with it: between "the global and the local, modernity and tradition, rationality and conviction" (2003, 6). They find these dichotomies undergirding a more specific split in conspiratology between conspiracy theory and occult cosmology. Their own distinction between these two categories is grounded in the scope and scale of the beliefs in question; occult cosmologies, in their view, regard the entire world and its operations, whereas conspiracy theories may concern themselves only with specific domains or fragments. While this distinction may not be tenable, as I discuss shortly, it stands as a useful reminder that "local" and "global" are heuristic rather than descriptive concepts that always raise "a problem of scale," as Jean and John Comaroff pointed out in their now-classic paper on occult economies (Comaroff and Comaroff 1999, 294). This is the point to which Strathern returns time and again in *Partial Connections*; it is the fundamental problem raised by a historical shift she was observing in anthropology at the time of her writing: the shift from a "perspectival" to a "postplural" vision of the world (Strathern [1991] 2004, xvi). On her account, anthropologists—those in the untimely postmodern vanguard, at least—were moving from a *relativism* necessitated by the fact of multiple perspectives (I see the world from my perspective, you from yours) toward a *partiality* necessitated by the fact of fractal perspectives (I see infinitely multipliable and recombinant facets of worlds, rather than a whole world—and you do, too). This "postplural" epistemology, for Strathern, does not speak to or about wholes; it connects facets across scales, and thereby reconfigures relations. In her terms, then, West and Sanders are still working with a perspectival, relativist vision of the world, mapping wholes onto locales and then accumulating locales in order to prove the existence of multiple perspectives.

The "problem of scale," as the Comaroffs put it, has attracted much attention in the conspiratology literature. Yet the thematization of scale as an analytic problem does not seem to have emboldened many anthropologists to radicalize their own orientation as observers or interpreters toward what they take to be "local" or "particular" epistemologies—which is to say, epistemologies they do not share. Many remain modernist ethnographers, in Strathern's terms, relativizing the practices and values of others to the contexts in which those others are located, without subjecting their own context to scrutiny; the observed/observer distinction is reinforced by the description of context for the observed and the disappearance of context from the observer. These ethnographers already know that the conspiracy theories they examine are false, but they seek to understand why and how people are nevertheless compelled by those theories by placing them (only) in *local context*.

This strategy of placing others' beliefs in local context is what I am calling the *particularist approach*, taken by nearly all the symptomatic readers I discussed in Part 1.1. In the chapter by Harding and Stewart, for example, scale and context are essential to their analysis but taken for granted rather than worked out conceptually; Calvary Church and Heaven's Gate remain small, local groups whose practices and apparent beliefs can be contextualized in terms of American therapeutic culture but not shared by anyone outside their communal boundaries. Even Pelkmans and Machold ultimately take a somewhat particularist approach, characterizing "organizational features of societies"—such as hierarchy and secrecy—or collective situations of "conflict or political transformation" that make it reasonable for ordinary people to be paranoid, skeptical, or cynical (Pelkmans and Machold 2011, 71). While they are agnostic with respect to potentially distinctive epistemological or rhetorical features of conspiracy theory, then, they assent to sociocultural criteria for distinguishing "realistic" theories from "fantastical" ones (72), maintaining the implicit premise of sociocultural boundaries that create local contexts in which the distinction between reasonable and unreasonable conspiracy theories could usefully if not durably pertain.

On this point, to imagine appropriate contexts for examining conspiracy theory beyond local culture, West and Sanders engage insightfully with Arjun Appadurai's conceptualization of "ideoscapes," which they gloss as "chains of ideas, terms, and images that can be condensed into key words (e.g. freedom, welfare, rights, sovereignty, representation, democracy) and exported to new contexts" (West and Sanders 2003, 10, citing Appadurai 1996, 36–37). But even this attempt to comprehend the nonlocalized fluidity of modes of thinking and feeling entails the fixity of the "geographical landscapes" "over" which "cultural flows" like ideoscapes "move," and "on" which they "superimpose themselves," as well as a linear chronology in their movement from one landscape to another (10). West and Sanders thus depend on a categorical distinction between the contexts in which modes of thinking and feeling originate and those in which they arrive and insinuate themselves.

This perplexity around local context finds a fascinating and instructive expression in David Sutton's article "Poked by the 'Foreign Finger' in Greece: Conspiracy Theory or the Hermeneutics of Suspicion?" (2003). Here, Sutton takes up the prevalent stereotype of Greeks as conspiracy theorists in relation to the 1999 NATO bombing of Yugoslavia during the Kosovo War, then being interpreted by Greek protestors—as the earlier wars in Yugoslavia had been—as an attempt to advance the material and political interests of the "Great Powers" rather than as a humanitarian intervention, as it was branded by the United Nations. Sutton uses rich ethnographic evidence from his discussions with residents of the Greek island of Kalymnos to demonstrate the cultural embeddedness of a "traditional Greek hermeneutics" (Sutton 2003, 205) that he reads as a "hermeneutics of everyday suspicion" (203). This cultural way of knowing, on his reading, has served to align ever-unfolding events of political importance with the historical pattern of Greece's domination by the Great Powers (202), which are understood to be hiding the truth of their material interests behind the appearance of civilization, development, and humanitarianism.

Sutton's avowed interest here is to rebut two key works of conspiratology that he takes to be nonsensical and inflammatory: namely, *The Hidden Hand* (1996) and *Conspiracy* (1997), written by American neoconservative historian and political commentator Daniel Pipes, who argues that "conspiracy theories flourish among the world's losers" (193), according to Sutton. On one hand, Sutton distinguishes Greek hermeneutics of suspicion from conspiracy theory by characterizing this way of knowing as a "sensemaking practic[e]" articulated in a "Greek cultural idio[m]" (2003, 200), along the lines that earlier anthropologists had taken in interpreting witchcraft in other locales. On the other hand, Sutton seems to suggest that these Greek "narratives," as he calls them (200), are not essentially different from conspiracy theories that Pipes himself argues were "'imported' from the west" to other locales (Sutton, 2003, 202), where they took hold and then traveled back to the west—though only, in Pipes's view, to fringe communities there. For his part, Sutton makes no claim that these narratives or theories are Greek (or local) in origin, nor *essentially* Greek (or local) in any sense. He ends by observing the "convergence" between Greek hermeneutics of suspicion and "Western conspiracy thinking" (205) around a general theory of patronage in social relations, which anthropologists in other contexts would, I think, not hesitate to consider legitimate social theory. In his final lines, Sutton even jokes that, given this convergence, Greek hermeneutics of suspicion would appear to be ahead of American conspiracy theory in elaborating this theory of social power (205). The indeterminacy of locale here—the undecidability between "the global and the local, modernity and tradition, rationality and conviction," in West and Sanders's terms—engenders an instability in the contexts that would otherwise ground the cross-cultural comparison Sutton seems to be after.

Among other perplexities of the particularist approach, many of the conspiracy theories that scholars have examined in locales ranging from the United States to Russia, Greece, India, and Brazil are understood by those scholars to be *the same* theories everywhere they are found: for example, those involving the New World Order, the Great Powers, the Masons, UFOs, etc.[23] That these are identifiably the same theories, and thus can be understood as having traveled widely—perhaps as ideoscapes, in Appadurai's term—means that how any particular locale is explanatory is a question for comparative analysis: a question of how one locale in comparison to others may explain the emergence, meaningfulness, and efficacy of these theories. What kinds of differences among local contexts would we need to grasp and elaborate in order to show how *the same* theories arise and work *differently* in those contexts? Instead of asking this question, many conspiratologists take local context to be inherently explanatory, and work to pinpoint the meaning of the theory in question in local terms as if the theory distinguished that context from all the others in which it had also appeared. To suggest, as many conspiratologists do, that such conspiracy theories are how locals make sense of their world—the "lingering functionalism" to which Pelkmans and Machold object—is not a way of specifying local context. It is rather the opposite: a judgment, however implicit, that local difference is really not so different after all. This strain of erratic and opportunistic particularism, in which context remains entirely untheorized if routinely invoked, thus ends in the same impasse as the implicitly nominalist stance I described at the beginning of Part 1.2; it undermines the potential of ethnographic research to help us understand both the particularity *and* the generality of conspiracy theory.

As for locale, I would argue, so for epoch. The apparently special moments in historical time when conspiracy theories have flourished, according to many symptomatic readers, is better described, I think, as conspiracy *panics*, in Bratich's term: as "historical conjunctures" in which conspiracy theory has been overtly problematized, as he puts it (Bratich 2008, 8). Conspiracy theory, the ostensible object of these panics, does not share those historical-conjunctural parameters, in his view. But Bratich's rubric of conspiracy panics is not as comprehensive or generalizable as we might wish it to be when specifying a relevant context for analyzing particular conspiracy theories. Panics, as he describes them, seem to entail a periodic or resurgent crisis temporality that breaks into "normal times," as Fassin reads Turner (Fassin 2011, 40), dismantling the reigning social consensus and inaugurating a new epoch.

The temporal logic underlying such notions of crisis and panic is a chronological linearity that is "conventionally recognized by the term 'historicism,'" as Charles Stewart writes (2017, 130). Exploring alternative historical temporalities, Stewart pinpoints "post-Ottoman topological historicizing," where "the past is not in its expected place" (130). He dubs this temporality "topological" because, as in the geometric concept, a form endures even as parts of it twist, bend, and stretch through analogies and affects, producing changes *and* continuities without rupturing the form itself. When it comes to temporality, Stewart suggests, the post-Ottoman world—as distinct (though not entirely or categorically) from "Western societies" in European and North American locales where linear chronology is dominant (130)—is itself such a topological form, made up of so many lifeworlds where "the past, present, and future may be bent around one another rather than ordered linearly" (abstract, 129). The post-Ottoman world may, he observes, be so rich in topological historicizing due to the deterritorialization and fragmentation of "local histories" ensuing from the collapse of the Ottoman Empire, itself constructed over six centuries. Its breakdown instigated violence and social rupture—many and widespread wars—over the course of the twentieth century that yielded "pulsating communal complaints" and durable irredentist "fantasies of restitution" in light of the "sheer impossibility of recovering the past" (130–31)—a past when people belonged in the places where they lived, or so it appears in such imaginings. Stewart characterizes the topological histories produced in such places as "uncanny"; they "surprise and shock" and ultimately "violate" the "genre of historicism" (129, 139) that has become an "intuitive temporal ontology" in academic history developing from "Enlightenment reason" (139, 130), and in "Western time" (129) more broadly, even if it is complicated and enriched by other temporalities in people's phenomenal experience of history in western locales.

In the light of such alternative historical temporalities and their multiplicity, especially in a post-Ottoman locale like Cyprus, it seems to me that it would be a sort of naïve historicism to contextualize conspiracy theory in terms of symptomatic eruptions caused by social-economic-political conditions particular to a historical moment. As Stewart has observed, historicism in this naïve sense is a mode not of historical contextualization but rather of decontextualization: of separating a particular historical moment from *its* connections and continuities with other moments.[24] A deeper historical contextualization, on the contrary, would trace how conspiracy theories emerge and change, fragmenting and morphing, overlapping with other theories and changing again, sustained and animated by people's talk about them. This is the sort of metadiscursive historical contextualization I have in mind with the concept of recursion, which, as I argued in the Introduction, is a more appropriate concept for analyzing discourse about conspiracy theories in historical time—the concept that best describes the ordering process by which people apprehend apparently new theories and thereby reframe apparently old ones. Instead of seeing particular conspiracy theories as symptoms of historically novel social, economic, and political conditions, then, I aim to examine the recombination, repurposing, and recontextualization of vocabularies and narrative details that have been there all along, shifting status from ground to figure, from micro to macro, from local to global, and vice versa. These are all recursive processes that cannot be accessed via naïve historicism.

I come back to this point about historicism in Part 1.6. Here, I wish to foreground the recursive nature of context itself, again leaning on Roy Dilley's expansive overview of the concept in anthropology. "'Meaning is context-bound, but context is boundless,'" Dilley asserts, echoing literary theorist Jonathan Culler:

> First, there is no limit to its contents, it is unsaturable and is always open to further description; second, any definition of context can itself be contextualized by means of a new context, and the process is open to infinite regression. (Dilley 1999, 22, 36, citing Culler 1983, 123)

What we take context to be, in other words, is one of those "remainders" that Strathern theorizes in *Partial Connections*. Dilley, avowedly influenced by Strathern here, notes that context can expand or contract, incorporate or exclude, shift or regress, depending on the delimiting choices made by analysts. He characterizes context as a conceptual device that defines the interdependence of relativism and universalism in cross-cultural comparison, whether it is implicit or explicit:

> One of the purposes of anthropological contextualism—the invoking of local cultural contexts—has been to produce a counter to universalist, context-free knowledge. Both approaches to knowledge—via contextualism or "context-freeism"—are mutually implicated and necessary, for one makes little sense without the other. (Dilley 1999, 36)

Strathern likewise argues there is no way to stabilize the process of cross-cultural comparison with reference to "external criteria," scales, or contexts. Since cultural features do not exist in the abstract, any cultural feature that might be compared cross-culturally must be developed from "local meanings," and thus cannot "escape contamination" by those meanings. "Scales," she concludes, "have to be created by the anthropologist" (Strathern [1991] 2004, 75). By the same token, moving from one scale to another entails "information loss" that cannot be recuperated on the new scale (xix). And thus we circle back to the problem of scale that is broached by the particularist approach. If meaning is *only* conceived as local, and if, moreover, what counts as local is conceived in bounded culturalist terms, then the local contextualization of meaning is tantamount to ethnocentrism—a point with which I imagine Strathern would surely agree. The particularist approach to conspiracy theory, which relativizes the meaning of conspiracy theory to local context, is thus intrinsically connected to the symptomatic approach, which interprets the meaning of conspiracy theory as a reflection of deeper social disorder or malaise within that context. The very premise of the symptomatic approach is a local culture whose particularity—whose irrational beliefs, to put a finer point on it—can only be explained in local terms, constituting one of many perspectives in a world given as plural.

Distinctions between reasonable and unreasonable paranoia, as between social theory and "conspiracy theory," are thus tethered to boundaries between here and there, now and then, that are neither warranted nor desirable so long as they demarcate such discrete and stable contexts. Boundaries rest on and also generate distinctions; they are not to be avoided for that reason, of course. The task at hand—the task I take up in this book—is rather to ascertain what kind of distinctions are entailed by the boundaries we observe, and vice versa, when we are defining a context for analysis. Ultimately, I argue that it is futile to try and pin conspiracy theory to any particular context. My approach is rather to show how choosing a different object for analysis—conspiracy attunement rather than conspiracy theory—allows us to understand context itself differently, and thus to think not cross-culturally but rather cross-contextually.

4. THE PSYCHOANALYTIC APPROACH

I should note at the outset of this section why I have framed the approach I address here as *psychoanalytic* and not *psychological*. This decision reflects a stark divide in expertise and explanatory ambition among the contributors to scholarship on conspiracy theory referring in some way to the psyche. Those taking what I would call a psychological approach—which I do not entertain in this section—are clinical and social psychologists; their contributions are styled as hypothesis-driven research deliverables that measure the extent of belief or tendencies toward belief in conspiracy theory within specific populations, or that categorize personality traits and social-psychological factors that might predict individuals' receptivity or vulnerability to such belief.[25] As these contributions beg the question at every step—taking for granted precisely what they propose to explain about belief and personality, not to mention conspiracy theory—they are open to the same criticisms around nominalism and inductive reasoning that I leveled at the epistemological approach in Part 1.2. Too, as these contributions are behaviorist, broadly speaking, they do not entail a theorization of the psyche that would add a distinctive kind of explanation to the symptomatic, particularist, and political approaches I examine elsewhere in Part 1.

That distinctive kind of explanation is, however, offered by the psychoanalytic approach that I explore in this section. Those who take the psychoanalytic approach are literature scholars, cultural studies scholars, critical theorists, political theorists, even a few anthropologists; they are connected not by disciplinary formation but rather by a shared interest in the explanatory power of psychoanalytic theory in accounting for the sociopolitical histories and dynamics that shape and animate fantasy. The psychoanalytic approach affirms the power of the social within the symbolic processes of the individual psyche; conspiracy theories are understood from this perspective as fantasies stemming from psychic conflicts that are widely shared in society because they are caused by society. A psychoanalytic account of why and how people come to be attracted to conspiracy theory necessarily recurs to the society whose arrangements of power—whose forms of stratification and solidarity—furnish the content of their fantasies. Contributors to the psychoanalytic literature on conspiracy theory thus hypostatize the psyche as a symbolic system that offers analytic access to individual motivation in the form of desire, which in turn sheds light on the individual's saturation with the social.

Given its critical orientation toward the social, I understand the psychoanalytic approach as an articulation—a subset—of the symptomatic approach. My reservations about symptomatic readings, developed in Part 1.1, therefore extend to psychoanalytic readings, even if the latter offer more precise and comprehensive explanation. For reasons different from mine, Nebojša Blanuša and Todor Hristov (2020), on whose overview of psychoanalysis and conspiracy theory I lean heavily in this section, find symptomatic readings of conspiracy theory insufficient; in focusing on the "social function" of conspiracy theories, they argue, symptomatic readings do not explain "the particular objects the conspiracist desire latches onto" (73). The psychoanalytic approach offers such an explanation; indeed, it is the most powerfully explanatory of all the approaches to conspiracy theory that I examine in Part 1, and that—as I discuss below—is one of its pitfalls.

Many psychoanalytic accounts of conspiracy theory take as a point of departure Sigmund Freud's theorization of paranoia in his case study (first published in [1911] 1963) of German Senate president Daniel Paul Schreber, based on Schreber's own memoir of his "nervous illness" published in 1903.[26] In the study, Freud argues that paranoia can be traced to the subject's fixation at an early stage in libidinal development: the (normal) stage of homosexual desire, which is (normally) repressed under the force of social and familial prohibition. In paranoia, however, the libido, barred from an external same-sex object of desire, attaches instead to the subject's own ego, generating a narcissistic structure that may develop into megalomania.[27] For Freud, then, paranoia is typified by the subject's withdrawal of attachments from the outside world. Delusions of persecution represent the subject's attempt to recover an attachment to others, often through a regressive libidinal surge toward a new object ([1911] 1963, 138). But this new object that "instigates" the attachment—a substitute for a parent or sibling—becomes, instead, a persecutor and an enemy. The subject's love, experienced first internally, is repressed and then projected onto the substitute and inverted: one's love for the other becomes the other's hatred for oneself, which then justifies one's fear of the other. Because the subject's repression of forbidden love is unconscious, the subject experiences that love-turned-hate as extrinsic. Persecutory fears and resentments that arise from this repression are, for Freud, attempts by the subject to form relations with others and attachments to the world, but since those fears are delusional, they cannot actually furnish the materials for such repair.

Taking distance from Freud's case study method, Blanuša and Hristov (2020) are keen to frame paranoia not as a clinical pathology but rather as the general structure of desire that accounts for the appeal of conspiracy theory in the imaginary space of fantasy. They go to some trouble to elaborate Jacques Lacan's theory of desire, starting from the observation that "desire is originally a form of jealousy" (73). At an early stage of psychological development, they explain, desire is driven by need—for food, comfort, protection—but need can only be communicated to others as a "demand" in terms those others will recognize: that is, in terms of shared language, which, at this stage, is a proxy for the symbolic order that will later be fleshed out in the social arrangements of power (family structure, gender norms, morality, law) as a person matures and assumes a social role. As Blanuša and Hristov read Lacan, one must learn to desire in recognizable terms if one's desire is to be recognized by others, and so one desires first by identifying with others and learning to desire what they desire. Since one can never really be another, however, one can only imagine what the other desires. Desire thus inaugurates an imaginary process, operating on the level of fantasy, in the form of a question about what the other wants (so that one can know what to want). But this question is never answered by the symbolic order (75); one must try to answer it oneself. Is it a lover? a partner? a house? a child? a high-status job? an expensive education? something else, something more? In this way, desire is displaced from object to object, each failing to satisfy one's desire, each failure requiring a new object to sustain one's desire. Fantasy thereby works to cover over the void that is opened by desire, but it never works completely or permanently. Fantasies driven by desire move through one's identifications with others who one suspects might experience more enjoyment than oneself, since what one is experiencing is not really enjoyment but rather the perennial failure of fantasies to provide satisfaction: *someone else is having a better time at my expense.* It is in this sense that, for Lacan, the structure of desire is paranoid.

Blanuša and Hristov present this Lacanian theory of desire as the framework for understanding paranoia as a general psychosocial condition, rather than as a clinical pathology: "Lacan normalizes paranoia as a phenomenon and makes it a part of everyday psychosocial functioning" (76). It is with this normalization in mind that they apply Lacan's theory of paranoid desire to conspiracy theory. They present the figure of the conspiracist as one who relentlessly seeks more and more evidence of hidden truths that will never fully reveal themselves. This structure of unsatisfiable desire accounts for the futility of debunking conspiracy theories, as any piece of veridical evidence that might be presented to counter a conspiracy theory can be interpreted by the conspiracist as evidence of a further conspiracy: a cover-up. In this light, debunking might be experienced unconsciously by conspiracy theorists as an attempt to ruin their pleasure; as a threat in this sense, debunking might provoke anger, fear, and aggression. From a psychoanalytic perspective, then, debunking conspiracy theory misses the point entirely.

The psychoanalytic approach would have nothing more to offer than clinical analysis of paranoia if it did not account for conspiracy theory on the collective level. Blanuša and Hristov turn to Slavoj Žižek to make the leap from psyche to society—or, more precisely, to show how the dynamics of fantasy in individual psychic lives are already shaped and populated by the social. In a number of his works (1989; 1997; 2006), Žižek traces conspiracy theory to disruptions in the symbolic order caused by collective traumatic events or broader breakdowns in social and epistemic authority—Blanuša and Hristov cite "postmodernism" as one such (77)—which precipitate a breakdown in the fantasies that sustain desire in the terms of the reigning symbolic order.[28] Žižek thus associates the "proliferation" of conspiracy theories with the "depleted power of the Other," meaning the power hypostatized by the subject as subtending the symbolic order. This depletion instigates the compensatory fantasy of a yet more powerful Other—a "positing of an Other of the Other . . . imagining that behind the apparent curtain of the apparent social order exists true reality ruled by a conspiracy of malevolent and powerful actors responsible for societal troubles" (77). This fantasy posits an enemy that poses a threat to society, an enemy that is "stealing our enjoyment" (77) by disrupting the very terms of connection and recognition with which we have learned to operate.

As fantasies, Blanuša and Hristov conclude, conspiracy theories are means of repairing trauma experienced as a disruption in the symbolic order (77):

> The general function of conspiracy theories is thus identificational: Defining the enemy in order to define oneself as its mirror image and therefore to anchor the signifiers that identify one's own group, community, or society, ... [conspiracy theories] articulate deeper political cleavages running through the political field by means of interpreting previous traumatic events and processes as encounters with supposed enemies. (78)

Other scholars who take the psychoanalytic approach likewise frame conspiracy theory as repair of trauma in this sense. Robyn Marasco (2016)—reading Freud and Melanie Klein—notes that introjection and projection, the key psychical mechanisms in paranoia, are also the mechanisms by which people form relationships generally; paranoia is, then, among other things, an attempt at relationality (114).[29] The "relations" formed through paranoia, Marasco observes, "are not always genial.... But even persecutory fear and projected hatred are efforts to establish relationships, however distorted" (114).

Zahid Chaudhary (2022) places such "distorted" relationships at the center of his account of QAnon before and during the insurrection of January 6, 2021, when many thousands assembled and attempted to take over the Capitol in Washington, DC. Chaudhary pays special attention to the "gamification of paranoia" (107) in LARPing—live action role-playing—that Anons performed online leading up to the insurrection; for him, it is in the LARP that we can see how "psychodynamics ... are indissociable from their economic and political aspects" (104). Key to his argument is the way LARPing effects a blurring between fantasy and reality, a "convergence of the unreal with the real" (109) in the virtual space of QAnon sociality that flourished on 4chan and other online forums. In this space, he observes, LARPing has special meaning that it does not have in real-life role-playing, as the online personae of ordinary folks with no special status or insight may profess access to secret insider knowledge and thereby gain advantage in the online game of conspiracy theory (107). Yet this does not mean that online sociality among Anons is reducible to pure dissimulation and manipulation; on the contrary, Chaudhary explains, it is a kind of play, in which shared tropes are deployed and information titrated in the "half-light of conscious conviction"—a state resembling hypnosis, for Freud, in which emotions feel real and phony at the same time (114). Chaudhary locates LARPing on a continuum of online make-believe practices of self-presentation that all, in one way or another, connect "performance" with "community formation" (108).

This notion of community formation might seem to offer grounds for commensurating conspiracy theory with paganism, witchcraft, magic, and other mystical mindsets and practices that overcome their denigration as irrational and false with a reparative vision of the world in spiritual terms. Sabina Magliocco frames such reparative visions as "reenchantment" (Magliocco 2012, 7), which inspires participants to accept the efficacy of their beliefs insofar as they are situated in ritual practices that create the conditions of "participatory consciousness" (5, 20)[30] and a shared sense of community. Chaudhary indeed considers the January 6 insurrection as such a performative, even ritual, context for Anons, in which they enacted attempts at relationality as a "form of self-recuperation and self-cultivation" (106). However, though the community "made real" in this process may have worked a reenchantment for Anons, it was not a reparative outcome. Chaudhary recounts the horrific LARPs performed by Anons during the insurrection—"involving napalm, blackface, and 'Allah ak Bar'" as well as the "hanging noose" and reenactments of the murder of George Floyd—writing, "Such are the Schreber-like healing attempts that aim to rebuild the world" (113). And they were no more effective for Anons than Schreber's were for him:

> Destructive forms of mass projection are an elaborate LARP, investing the world with forms of the group's psychic needs and wishes, but such a solution spells disaster because it ensures that the image of the world reflected back to the paranoid subject is a repetition of itself, caught now in pathological forms of symbol formation that assure certitude but fail to relieve anxiety. (118)

In framing conspiracy theories as fantasies gone disastrously wrong under deformative social, political, and economic conditions, the psychoanalytic approach also offers a way for those who do not think of themselves as paranoid, fearful, or hateful to countenance and relate to the *pleasures* of conspiracy theory. Marasco, citing Richard Hofstadter's essay on the paranoid style, pays special attention to the "satisfactions . . . that come with being *in the know*" offered by conspiratorial reason—satisfactions not only of knowing but also of being right and righteous. But, she suggests, "the satisfactions of conspiratorial reason run much deeper" than this (236); they run to the "seductions" (237) wreaked by fantasies of power that may be especially appealing to Americans:

> Conspiracy thinking registers a certain idealization of big power. What is more, conspiratorial reason is an idealization of power itself, in which power really is what it says about itself, really is all-powerful, really does have clear and known ends, and really can meet these ends with exactness and efficiency. Like all idealizations, this view of power is comforting and consoling. It assures its adherents that power is always purposive and predictable, that it never misses its mark, that it is perfectly rational. (Marasco 2016, 238)

The centrality of power in these fantasies speaks to the political ambitions of the psychoanalytic approach. No one contributing to this literature is asking questions about the psychic life of conspiracy theory who is not asking for political reasons—that is, with the objective of accounting for connections and synergies they find disturbing among conspiracy theory, right-wing populism, and fascist ideology. Scholars taking the psychoanalytic approach work to de-pathologize paranoia in the clinical sense, as noted earlier, but they do not normalize it entirely. They acknowledge that real psychological disturbance is in play, but they locate the disturbance at the level of the collective rather than the individual. The idea that a sick society makes people sick psychologically, that paranoid critical theory is apt for analyzing political paranoia in our times, that there is something deeply wrong in the very conditions of social and political life today: these common assertions align the psychoanalytic approach with the political approach I examine in Part 1.5, and even presume it.

At the same time, and by the same token, these assertions distance the psychoanalytic approach from the "paranoia within reason" tack I discussed in Part 1.1, which—paradoxically, I suggested—normalizes paranoia by relativizing it to specific contexts (though only over there—not here). On the contrary, it is by way of political critique that the psychoanalytic approach pinpoints paranoia as a collective problem in the first place. Thus, in her reading of Freud's case study on Schreber, Marasco criticizes Freud for not attending to "how Schreber's personal, professional, social, or political life [got] expressed in his symptoms" (240). In other words, Freud's theory of paranoia is limited by his failure to see this psychological disturbance as social and political in origin and implication.

Although most contributors to the psychoanalytic literature are careful to observe that paranoia characterizes extremism of all kinds, rather than being essentially politically right- or left-wing, they are, across the board, concerned politically with right-wing paranoia. Marasco, for example, notes, "Paranoia knows no party affiliation or ideological division—it joins the extreme left and the extreme right, and those with no clear political convictions whatsoever" (237). Yet she also argues, reading Fanon, that "paranoia flourishes in the colonial context," and she is especially concerned with the "the paranoid dimensions of fascist authority" as theorized by Adorno and Horkheimer (238). She lands in agreement with this "earlier generation of critical theorists," who understood conspiracy thinking as fundamentally dangerous "for its attachment to repressive authority and its libidinal investments in power" (240).

Blanuša and Hristov offer a closer reading of Adorno, showing that he understood conspiracy theory as "a symptom of the general powerlessness" that individuals faced in "modern mass society" (72). Tracing the similarities between conspiracy theory and mass advertising—especially "how they tapped into the desire of the public" (71)—Adorno hypothesized a "psychological type vulnerable to conspiracy theories" (71), which he read as "defence mechanisms against frustration caused by the social order" (72). Blanuša and Hristov connect Adorno's analysis of conspiracy theory to that of Žižek, who frames conspiracy theory as a mystification of political interest in capitalist society: "Although many researchers in cultural studies, sociology or anthropology claim that conspiracy theories could have emancipatory potential," they write, "from the perspective of Lacanian psychoanalysis, they are the last ruse of power trying to mask its impotence by representing itself as a mask of an omnipotent clandestine Other" (78, citing Žižek 2006, 219). It is for this reason, perhaps, with this skepticism, that contributors to the psychoanalytic literature on conspiracy theory for the most part do not celebrate the subversive and oppositional politics they as-social world, which discloses the contingency of any particular social arrangements of power: things have been and could be otherwise than they are now. Breakdown in a social order yields difference in the form of a before and after the breakdown, as well as between self and other within the now-disordered social world; where there was identity, there is now multiplicity and division.

Along emerging lines of difference in such a scenario, however those lines are drawn, collectives may form, driven by shared attraction to certain fantasies of shared identity whose scale is different from before, and whose boundaries exclude some people who have been inhabiting the same social world but are now perceived as enemies who do not belong. The psychoanalytic approach presumes that social forces are in play in this kind of identity formation but offers no social theory that would explain why some individuals are attracted to a particular fantasy of identity while others in the same social world are not. Breakdown in a social world experienced psychically as the symbolic order, then, always raises a question as to whether a people who are now divided indeed ever inhabited the same social world—that is, the question of multiplicity. Can a fundamentally heterogeneous social world be countenanced, from a psychoanalytic perspective? What kind of context is a social world that can be internalized psychically by individuals? Psychoanalytic theorists cannot answer these questions as long as they pose the problem of difference and multiplicity only within social worlds rather than between them.

Within social worlds, the psychoanalytic approach to conspiracy theory displaces onto the discursive level what psychoanalytic theory explores on the dialogical level—that is, the space of the encounter, where the analyst is at stake along with the analysand in a situation of mutual implication. The analyst's management of the analysand's transference—their willingness to serve, if partially and provisionally, as a screen or object of the analysand's projections in order to facilitate the emergence of their repressed thoughts, wishes, and memories—also entails the management of their own countertransference: the fantasies elicited or animated in the analyst by the analysand. The therapeutic efficacy of psychoanalysis, in theory, depends on this radically situated context of dialogical and sensory interaction. The psychoanalytic approach to conspiracy theory, instead, conjures a sociopolitical context in which the fantasy life of the collective may be interpreted. But the intimacy between interpreter and interpreted that pertains to the psychoanalytic encounter does not pertain to the critique of this sociopolitical context, where it is instead the radical alterity of the Other that drives interpreters to render a psychoanalytic critique in the first place.

This misplacement of intimacy suggests to me that closer attention is warranted to the ways in which psychoanalytic theorists draw boundaries and deploy context in their symptomatic readings. The implicitness of context in the psychoanalytic approach is not unique to this approach; as I showed in Parts 1.1 and 1.3, this problem is common to the symptomatic and particularist approaches. What is unique—uniquely contextless—about the psychoanalytic approach is its postulation of a relationship between individual and society that subtends the general applicability of the theory across contexts in the absence of any actual encounter with cross-contextual difference. This problem of context in psychoanalytic readings is related to the definitional problem I raised in Part 1.2 about the inductive approach to conspiracy theory ("I know it when I see it"), which assumes a commonsense consensus among writers and readers as to what "we" all mean by conspiracy theory. It is also a distinct facet of the long-standing problem posed by anthropology to psychoanalysis—a problem of much longer standing and much wider scope than debates about the universality of the Oedipus complex, for example, taken up and synthesized magnificently by Gananath Obeyesekere in *The Work of Culture* (1990).[33]

The crux of the matter, here, is that the psychoanalytic approach presumes universal psychic processes that might instead distinguish rather specific coordinates of psychic life in a particular social world—those coordinates being (or including) patriarchy, capitalism, and Judeo-Christian faith traditions in Europe and Euro-America. The only way to know whether these psychical processes are indeed universal is to countenance radical difference between social worlds, but this is precisely what the psychoanalytic approach does not do. In the small sample of this literature that I discuss here, none considers conspiracy theories outside the United States and Europe; none explicitly addresses the context of their analysis in terms that would distinguish it from any other context. Blanuša, for example, does a symptomatic reading of conspiracy theories in Croatia by way of Žižek, and, with Žižek, frames conspiracy theories as, themselves, symptomatic readings par excellence (Blanuša 2009, 114n1). In this reading, the Croatian nation is taken for granted as context; Blanuša deploys a survey about "political controversial events and processes in recent Croatian history" to test the prevalence of "conspiratorial beliefs" in the "general population" of Croatia (113–114). Marasco, as noted above, leaves the United States as a political context so implicit that it is not even named except through her invocation of the title of Hofstadter's essay. Nation remains the consistent, and consistently implicit, context for these works. The contextual premise of nationhood is especially evident in Žižek's writing on "the Nation-Thing" (Žižek 1992), in which national borders operating symbolically as social boundaries inaugurate political subjectivity.

Chaudhary, on the contrary, does not take nation as the collective context for QAnon, but rather virtual spaces overlapping with algorithmic media spheres and markets. The absence of clear and stable social, cultural, and political boundaries seems to be the point for what he describes as the "community" of Anons: "QAnon is first and foremost a community, however diffusely and heterogeneously constituted" (2022, 109). For participants in this community, the social is no longer tethered to locale, if it ever was; it instead resides immanently in the blurred lines between online and "real" life whose very blurriness is exploited for lulz by community members, a means of establishing rather conventional forms of recognition and like-mindedness. Chaudhary shows that the Anons who participated in the January 6 insurrection acted as members of a community that they were "making real" through their participation in the event. He traces the contours of this community prior to the insurrection in the distinctions participants deployed to identify themselves—for example, the designation of "people outside of this community" as "normies" (109)—as well as "'inside terms,' codes for particular people or particular alliances" (109), and a shared "mood of supreme irony" reinforced by public shaming in the virtual space (109), which Chaudhary dubs "QAnon land" (110). Quoting Jim Watkins, identified here as the "owner of websites that hosted QAnon," Chaudhary writes, "This began as a LARP and 'it became real. It's American history now'" (114). In Watkins's swift, seemingly seamless movement from *becoming real* to *making American history*, the implicit national frame becomes explicit. It is that national frame that defines the insurrection at Capitol Hill as a pseudo-patriotic coup against the US government. In that sense, the United States serves as a floating context for Anons, available to them whenever the need arises to define their thought and action as oppositional, but not explanatory of their thought and action in the way the virtual spaces of QAnon activity are for Chaudhary.

Regardless of whether they take nation or a different collective formation as the grounds and parameters of the social, psychoanalytic theorists postulate a symbolic system in the psyche as a proxy for the social. The nature of social relations, and changes in the structure of society, can only be extrapolated from the analysis of psychic life, which is already understood in terms of this proxy relation. There is no place, empirically, where the theory touches down on the social. Within this theoretical framework, the existence of difference on a collective scale can only be understood dialectically, which is to say, as a hypothetical particularization of the universal whose assimilation by the universal leads to a new synthesis. Difference remains abstract insofar as it remains legible at the level of the universal. In Part 1.6, I explore further the complexities of locale that I began to address in Part 1.3, in order to argue that this play between universal and particular that constitutes dialectical thinking cannot generate criteria for comparative thinking about conspiracy theory across contexts. In the psychoanalytic approach to conspiracy theory, the implications of dialectical thinking are a bit different, if related. I indicated at the outset of this section that the psychoanalytic approach is overly explanatory, and I can now qualify this suggestion by way of acknowledging the bold ambition of psychoanalytic theory to account for the saturation of the individual by the social in a context that defies comparative thinking. The psychoanalytic approach to conspiracy theory explains how individual fantasies reflect and represent social division and conflict, but only at the cost of a social theory that would account for how different societies work in and on individuals differently.

5. THE POLITICAL APPROACH

[I]n a paper written some years into the recent era of austerity in Greece, [d]rawing from his personal and ethnographic experience of the widespread [an]d enduring protests initiated there at the start of the economic crisis in [200]8, Dimitrios Theodossopoulos (2014) argues for *resistance* as a special [and] integral topic in anthropology. He critically examines two dominant [mode]s in the analysis of power that routinely denigrate, marginalize, pa[troniz]e, idealize, or otherwise distance or discredit subaltern practices of [resista]nce: pathologization and exoticization. These modes of analysis [m]irror the two dominant approaches to conspiracy theory that I have [describe]d, respectively, as symptomatic and particularist. Theodossopoulos links them together—as I have done—showing them to be not only mutually complicit but also mutually entailed. While Theodossopoulos does not thematize directly the politics claimed by the scholars conducting such analyses, his writing hints at political positioning behind both the denigration *and* the celebration of resistance that he is ruing so persuasively and in such rich detail.

I hear a warning, from Theodossopoulos, not to reduce conspiracy theory to "politics." I want to dwell on this point for a moment, in order to insist that neither conspiracy theory nor its debunking has any inherent or obvious alignment with right or left politics, nor in fact any particular political valence. I insist on this because the right-wing sources and audiences of certain conspiracy theories have inclined some leftist scholars, especially in the United States, to dismiss them as intrinsically or effectively pathological. For others, again especially in the United States, the populist, insurgent, insurrectionist, even revolutionary potential of conspiracy theory has presented some appeal. John Fiske—an example of "bad" leftist scholarship in the judgment of several conspiratologists, including Clare Birchall and Mark Fenster—characterizes as "counter power" (278, passim) and "localizing power" (288, passim) the theories and rumors of white conspiracy perpetrated against African Americans that, he observes, have attained widespread currency in African American communities. Fiske presents one such, known as the Cress Theory, as a "Black reading" of "white supremacy" in America (Fiske [1993] 2016, 242ff. and Chapter 13)[34]—his gloss on the widely read essay by Afrocentrist psychiatrist Frances Cress Welsing, "The Cress Theory of Color-Confrontation and Racism (White Supremacy): A Psycho-Genetic Theory and World Outlook," first published in 1970. Her theory accounts for the origins of racism in a genetic mutation that produced whiteness as a deficiency of melanin, leading to the ejection of "albinos" from Africa and the development of white supremacist imperialism on the part of white people as a defensive "reaction formation" to their own inferiority, and the projection of their hostility toward Black people onto Black people themselves (reimagined thus as "hating us"), thereby creating a psychical pretext for total racial domination by whites.[35] It is, I gather, the totalization of all social relations as "color confrontation" by Cress that has led many critics to dismiss the Cress Theory as a conspiracy theory, while others, such as Fiske, view it quite straightforwardly as subjugated knowledge in the Foucauldian sense, which they should legitimate by their own scholarship. Fiske narrates his experience of learning about the Cress theory from a Black student and coming to treat it as a compelling object of research:

> One publisher's reader of this manuscript [*Power Plays Power Works*] called [the Cress Theory] racist and warned me that in not criticizing it as I summarized it I ran the risk of endorsing it. Other whites have pathologized it as paranoid or have denigrated Cress Welsing's book as poorly argued, lacking in evidence, or as just naïve. But there are other whites who have received its jolt and have allowed it to deconstruct, even if only by a little, the knowledge structure by which they know themselves as white. ([1993] 2016, 282)

Writing explicitly from his subject position as "a white professor in a major university," Fiske explains, "I do then endorse the Cress Theory and equivalent Black knowledges, not for any essential 'truth,' but for their deconstructive counter to white ways of knowing whiteness" (283).

That the broad acclamatory position Fiske takes here on "counter-knowledges" (283) is appealing to leftist academics, especially white leftist academics such as himself, depends on his distance from, or his inattention to, right-wing conspiracy theories—a point that Mark Fenster makes at length in his "Afterword" (2008, 224). Here, Fenster discusses *The Turner Diaries*, a "virulently fascist, racist, patriarchal, and anti-Semitic novel" (xxi) about a conspiracy of the federal government (dubbed "The System") to police and criminalize racism and hate, and a reactive conspiracy (dubbed "The Organization") among white separatists to exterminate all non-Aryan whites. The novel is thought to have inspired Timothy McVeigh to bomb the Alfred P. Murrah Federal Building in Oklahoma City in 1995, which killed 168 people, including 19 children, and injured many hundreds more (*Washington Post*, 2001). Fenster presents *The Turner Diaries* as a fundamental challenge to the populist politics animating some leftist academic approaches to conspiracy theory. Here, he observes, as he does throughout his book, the ineffectiveness of conspiracy theory across the political spectrum—its failure to mobilize a political agenda at the collective level, beyond acts of subversion or terrorism undertaken by one person or a small group—as one of the reasons not to overemphasize politics in the academic analysis of popular culture (more on this point below).

Clare Birchall similarly objects to the reduction of conspiracy theory to a political agenda, right or left. "As a transcendental signifier," she writes,

> "politics" organizes and limits the kinds of questions that can be asked of conspiracy theory and even of politics itself. If made to respond only to this agenda, if mobilized only within this discourse, many aspects of conspiracy theory remain unthought. (2006, 69)

A number of conspiratologists have made this point, noting that people who identify themselves as leftist *and* as right-wing have been accused of conspiracy theorizing and have also made such accusations, both today and in the past (Melley 2000, 11; Harding and Stewart 2003, 261). Timothy Melley shows, for example, how accusations of conspiracy that were at "ideological cross-purposes" in the United States in the 1950s—such as J. Edgar Hoover's writing on communism and Vance Packard's writing on capitalism—attributed "national crisis" to "a large and powerful program designed to manipulate unwitting Americans" in uncannily similar terms (Melley 2000, 2). Muirhead and Rosenblum likewise argue that "classic conspiracy theory" has no partisan affiliation, and while the new conspiracism has a definite "partisan penumbra" (5, 95ff.)—meaning that "the extremes of the Republican Party" have aligned with it while "the Left" has not (5)—they insist that it is "tribal" affiliation rather than political affiliation that accounts for its appeal to Trump supporters (49). Theodoros Rakopoulos (2022) shows how conspiracism "dovetails" with far-right fascist thinking *and* with leftist anthropological thinking insofar as all these approaches to human diversity entail a "post-racial and culture-centred belief in ontological alterity" and a proposition of "cultural incommensurability" among different communities and societies (46, 47). Rakopoulos also makes explicit what is sometimes backgrounded in the political approach to conspiracy theory: namely, the emancipatory ambitions of many conspiracy theories—freedom of thought and freedom from domination. These overtly political stakes are obscured by the label "conspiracy theory," and possibly muddled further by their swift dismissal as cynical bad-faith tropes by conspiratologists intent on assigning them a partisan valence.

Fenster, in the revised edition of *Conspiracy Theories: Secrecy and Power in American Culture* (2008), offers case studies in conspiracy theories whose promoters span the political spectrum, from the white separatist militia movement of the 1990s (chapter 2) to the 9/11 truth movement (chapter 7); the latter, he writes, "assume[d] an anti-imperialist, anticorporate cast" easily assimilated to "leftist causes" (43–44). He also examines what he calls the "left-progressive political critique" of "right-wing populist conspiracy theory" that is "frequently funded by conservative groups or circulated by conservative media outlets" (43). In terms borrowed from Michael Rogin (48–51), Fenster characterizes these leftists as "realists," who foreground the motives or interests of elites in promoting conspiracy theory and their tactics of manipulating the public into believing them. This "activist" position, for Fenster (50), forms a strong contrast with the "centrist" and even "apolitical" position taken by the "symbolists"—those who see conspiracy theories as collective expressions of political or economic crisis, and whose explanations recur to cultural or mass psychological causes. (These are symptomatic readers, in the term I have borrowed from Best and Marcus.) The symbolists, he observes, share with Richard Hofstadter his functionalist conception of political paranoia as a collective anxiety "produced by [the] political and economic situation" (48) and manipulated by demagogues to suit their purposes. In elaborating and criticizing both the realist and the symbolist position, Fenster shows that, just as conspiracy theory has no essentially left or right politics, the debunking of conspiracy theory may also advance any political position.[36]

In the course of his critique of the symbolist approach to conspiracy theory, Fenster offers a close reading of Hofstadter's famous essay on the paranoid style, and his many other works on conspiracy theory, in order to account for Hofstadter's broad and lasting influence on conspiratology and liberal political theory more generally. He presents Hofstadter as a "consensus" historian (27ff.): a guardian of pluralist democracy who, equally "suspicious" of right-wing and left-wing "extremism" and indeed of "virtually any kind of populism" (29), defended the center of American politics by promoting pragmatism and reasoned debate. What distinguishes Hofstadter from many of his "consensus" contemporaries, on Fenster's reading, is that he developed a then-unique understanding of "popular politics" as a "symbolic realm" practiced through "rituals" and "rhetorical effort" (31, 32)—and thereby a conception of conspiracy theory as a *style* rather than a political agenda or a pathology. Fenster parts company with Hofstadter when it comes to Hofstadter's deployment of "paranoia" as a descriptor of that style, which Fenster finds "confused and confusing," and even "simplistic and useless as it has been taken up by others" (36). Its uselessness is most notable, for Fenster, in the disjuncture it perennially wreaks between "individual psychology" and "social phenomenon" (42), which renders it "unclear which are the effects and which are the causes" (41–42) of the purported political paranoia being observed.

Fenster also rejects the equation Hofstadter draws between populism and conspiracy theory. Conspiracy theory is indeed populist, Fenster argues, insofar as it evokes "an unwitting and unwilling populace in thrall to the secretive machinations of power" (84), but the converse does not hold; populism does not entail conspiracy theory, and many of its historical forms have had nothing at all to do with conspiracy theory. With this focus on historical contingency, Fenster declines to define populism as any particular political rationality or agenda; arguing that it is a "process" rather than a "content" (85), he observes, with Ernesto Laclau, its "ever-present vagueness in content and its context-specific variation in history" (84). Indeed, the ways in which populism is "unstable" (86), in Fenster's view, are also the ways in which conspiracy theory is "unstable" *within* populism (89).[37]

In this, Fenster agrees with Jeff Maskovsky and Sophie Bjork-James, who introduce their 2020 collection, *Beyond Populism*, as a response to the global rise of "angry politics," from Hindutva in India to the Indignados in Spain. They do not wish to frame angry politics as populist—or not exactly—due in part to the irresolvable fluidity and volatility of populism itself. Wary of wading into long-standing academic debates over the definition of populism, and carefully cataloguing an array of radically different political movements organized around "popular disdain, disillusionment, and disenchantment" arising in the worldwide "twilight of neoliberalism" (1, 2), they observe,

> We do not find it especially useful to pin down too precisely what is meant by populism. Indeed, a survey of populist politics across the globe would not find among them a common ideology, constituency, or set of demands. Nor are today's populists unified by their political strategies or tactics or by a shared sense of who "the people" or their antagonists are. (6)

Maskovsky and Bjork-James decline to use the term "populism" to organize such disparate and dissonant political movements into one category while refusing any stable definition of that category—a tactic that I described as *implicitly nominalist* in regard to conspiracy theory at the beginning of Part 1.2 and rejected as incoherent. Instead, they offer a different term, "angry politics," as a rubric that can encompass "neoliberal disenchantment, racialized resentments, and the rage of the downtrodden and repressed" (8); in using this term, they insist on "disaggregating" all of these politics from populism (12). I understand this move in two ways: first, as a mode of what they call "conjunctural thinking" (13), which captures the novelty of the present moment without immediately assimilating it to specific and preestablished genealogies of political thought and action; and, second, as an emphasis on the affective dimension of politics—"anger"—over (and in some cases against) its explicit goals, organizational structures, or purported causes. Admittedly, the authors themselves do not make the case for the second interpretation, but a number of the papers in the volume do—especially Jennifer Riggan's (2020) contribution—and it seems to me the only way that "angry politics" can function as a stable rubric for cross-contextual analysis of the kind ventured in this volume.

William Mazzarella (2019), too, cautions against the "definitional urge" in his examination of anthropological approaches to populism, noting the notorious "slipperiness" and "promiscuity" of the concept. He turns instead to what the "affective intensification around questions of populism" may teach us about "our political investments" (47). Mazzarella is especially concerned by the "habit" among anthropologists of using liberalism as a "foil for our critiques" (47) while holding fast to the "liberal settlement" that has implicitly, and utterly erroneously, divided the world into societies that are governed by liberal norms of public life and those that are not. More to Mazzarella's point, this "habit" has sustained a tension within anthropological thinking on populism as, on one hand, the expression of a fearsome crowd sharing "collective flesh" with authoritarian leaders (49ff.), and on the other, an authentic collective agency enjoying the "culturally situated integrity" of "nonliberal" difference (48) and bearing the potential to mobilize radical political change. Moving beyond the liberal settlement, as Mazzarella suggests in his title, requires acknowledging the role that "unconscious processes" play in "political life"—especially the affective and aesthetic dimensions of political life that most interest him—and thus of the irreducible complexity of "the social," whose analysis remains both urgent and challenging: a problem not solved, he insists, by "simple empiricism" (55). Returning, thus, to the question of "our political investments" in analyzing populism, Mazzarella entreats anthropologists (presumably leftist anthropologists) feeling embattled by the apparent rise or resurgence of racism, xenophobia, misogyny, and authoritarian brutality, not to retreat back into the liberal settlement in order to assert anthropology's relevance to politics.

Muirhead and Rosenblum (2019), for their part, take a more conventional perspective on populism, noting that it is an "elusive label" but then defining it broadly as "insistence on the sole legitimate authority of the authentic, spontaneous 'voice of the people'" (62, 63) in order to show its entanglement with Trumpism as well as its irreducibility to Trumpism. Indeed, they vigorously distinguish populism from the new conspiracism they associate with Trump, noting that "nothing in populism entails an assault on argument, evidence, and common sense" (64), and that populism is essentially "reformist" while the new conspiracism is "politically sterile" (64, 31), neither expressing nor mobilizing a political agenda.

Birchall, too, who entertains the subversiveness of conspiracy theory, nevertheless observes its political inefficacy. She concedes the "risk" articulated by Douglass Kellner, among others, that the commodification and aestheticization of conspiracy theory in 1990s popular culture may also have depoliticized it, robbing it of any "radical potential": "Conspiracy theory appears (to varying degrees in different contexts) *both* politically engaged *and* deeply ineffectual in the realm of democratic politics" (2006, 41, emphasis original). From his metadiscursive perspective, Jack Bratich offers an account of this failure. He conceives of the social field as governed by hegemonic forms of rationality that "become dominant only through struggle" with dissident forms that, in this struggle, become "productive" and "useful" for "official apparatuses" (Bratich 2008, 7, 8).[38] His overarching argument in *Conspiracy Panics* is that liberalism requires skepticism; liberal citizens are supposed to trust institutions of knowledge production that keep the parameters of legitimate skepticism intact, and those institutions are threatened by populist dissent. Conspiracy panics, specifically, in problematizing conspiracy theory as a "nonspecific threat against democracy," work to legitimate those institutions while integrating or neutralizing dissent and extremism (12, 11). The instability and slipperiness of conspiracy theory, taken as an epistemology or form of rationality, is part of this strategy, on Bratich's view; the absence of specific and consistent criteria for identifying conspiracy theory is precisely what "allows a conspiracy panic to operate," by making accusations of conspiracy theory plausible in a "free-floating way" (12). Thus, he writes, "moral panics are themselves strategies in a combative context, not simply tools for the maintenance of a social order, or a stabilizing technique" (12).

This perspective, while quite appealing in its explanatory force, and despite Bratich's welcome assertion that "there is no need to totalize a panic into the social field" (12), still rings too functionalist to my ears, insofar as it comprehends hegemony as a process of quiescence in the interest of the already-powerful. In conceiving conspiracy panics as strategies of power, Bratich leans on hegemony as a conceptualization of structural agency, without specifying whose power is being produced and maintained by panic and whose anxiety mobilized. It is thus not clear whose interests, if indeed anyone's, are served by the denunciation and disqualification of conspiracy theory. Conspiracy panic discourse does not seem to have defused dissent or opened a way for the political center (wherever, whenever) to quell or assimilate extremists. Such denunciations, like the imputed theories themselves, move in too many directions and express too many incompatible interests to serve such a function.

Indeed, perhaps with such questions in mind, Bratich himself has moved beyond his millennial conceptualization of conspiracy panics in his recent work on conspiracy theory during the Trumptimes. As he explained in a 2017 lecture, the conspiracy theory label that he had previously understood as the lynchpin of conspiracy panic discourse no longer actually disqualifies, and certainly no longer marks partisan alignment, if it ever did. He offered by way of example the release in October 2017 of some but not all classified files relating to the assassination of JFK—an apparent compromise between Trump, on the one hand, and the CIA and FBI, on the other—which positioned Trump aides as the loudest voices demanding transparency and the release of all files, leaving no "public position" for those on the left to contest state secrecy. In the "era of fake news" and the mainstreaming of conspiracy theory, Bratich suggested, we are now in a situation of "mutually assured disqualification," meaning there is no position—right or left, elite or popular, conservative or progressive—from which anyone may disqualify anyone else with the label "conspiracy theorist." Unlike "mutually assured destruction" in the Cold War nuclear arms race, he explained, "Everyone [today] is using the weaponized term of 'conspiracy theories'; therefore, it is mutually assured that everyone is getting disqualified . . . so [there is] a kind of flattening of the field . . . that produces some new things" (Bratich 2017).

The crucial new thing, on Bratich's account, drawing from Foucault, is the shift from a "regime of truth" to a "regime of war" as the matrix of everyday life. He thus sees discourses about conspiracy theory as strategies in communications warfare. In his lecture, he identified many factors that have contributed to the recent "eruption" of popular concern with conspiracy theory in the United States, including the circulation of information instantaneously and in massive volume online; a loss of faith in traditional institutions of political representation, especially political parties; a digital economy based on sharing through consumer networks; the development of popular culture as conspiracy culture from the 1990s onward; and the war on terror, which has promoted "peer-to-peer skepticism" as a model of citizenship, ratcheting up suspicion to a point "out of control." While I decline the epochal terms in which Bratich framed the distinctiveness of this conspiracy panic during the Trumptimes—I would instead frame it as a recursive movement—I readily take the factors he identifies as indications of changing and perhaps increasing conspiracy attunement in American political culture.

With these changes in mind, I circle back to Fenster's observation that conspiracy theory has been singularly ineffective in mobilizing political movements, despite the alarm it has raised in certain corners at certain moments. Given the global growth of QAnon (for example) since Trump's election and its violent mobilization in the insurrection of January 6, 2021, Fenster's view—and the attribution of political sterility to the new conspiracism by Muirhead and Rosenblum—may seem naïve, denialist, or simply unprescient. By contrast, a number of recent academic works frame QAnon in particular as a political movement with a political agenda. In a recent paper on whiteness and the rise of Trumpism, for example, Jeff Maskovsky and Julian Aron Ross (2022) describe "QAnon conspiracists" as "the content creators, or, better, the creative class, of the far-right," and strenuously argue for Trumpist conspiracies to be taken seriously as "ideological and materially productive" insofar as they "generate new ways of articulating labor to concrete projects of white supremacy" (173). For the authors, it is the articulation of "content"—conspiracy theories—with labor politics and white supremacist ideology that verifies QAnon, and Trumpist conspiracism more broadly, as a "movement" (167).

Rather than try to determine whether conspiracy theories have a politics—and whether, if they do, this is a recent or long-standing feature of the political field in the United States and elsewhere—I would rather reframe the debate. I do not think there is room for doubt that conspiracy theories can (and do) provide "content" for political mobilization in the sense Maskovsky and Ross have in mind, as I read them—a shared language, perhaps,[39] or a set of libidinally cathected images. But the very question as to whether conspiracy theories themselves have a politics leads to an analytic dead end. Conspiracy theories cannot bear this freight and will not reward analysis undertaken with this question in mind. Zahid Chaudhary's writing on QAnon, discussed in Part 1.4, suggests that the form of its political mobilization was evanescent and ludic; the insurrection was a theater of play that blurred reality and irreality, online and offline. Chaudhary attributes this mobilization not to a political agenda promoted by Q and held in earnest by followers, but rather to an "as if" belief that motivated action insofar as it was pleasurable for participants: "QAnon does not require belief in the sense of an enduring conviction whose propositions can be taken at face value; instead, belief is a provisional matter, like the temporary world of the game, held in relation to the demands of the game and discarded or revised as these demands shift" (Chaudhary 2022, 110). The pleasure of participation in this "as if" mode, according to Chaudhary, was conditioned by factors other than conspiracy theories themselves: white supremacist, heteropatriarchal, and nativist birthright ideologies chief among them, nurtured in a virtual environment where interpersonal dynamics were structured by the valorization of irony and identity play. Attributing the mobilization of Anons to conspiracism, or interpreting their mobilization *as* conspiracism, would seem to miss "the political" in these crucial respects.

The political approach to conspiracy theories that I have examined in this section forces the dichotomy between right and left politics to the surface of analysis. It compels a conceptualization of conspiracy theory as advancing a political agenda commensurable with right or left politics as they are articulated more broadly in public culture. But while conspiracy theories may certainly—as Maskovsky and Ross, Chaudhary, Marasco, and many others have shown—be articulated with right or left politics, this articulation is situated, partial, unpredictable, and often temporary, rather than integral, essential, or causal. For these reasons, in this book I aim to withstand the indeed powerful temptation to reduce conspiracy theory to politics. I hope instead to establish not only the impossibility of conspiracy theory as a concept or category but also its vacuity: to diminish the "jolt" it delivers, *pace* Fiske; to refocus attention on the political threats and crises that are obfuscated by public discourse conducted in its terms; and to develop more nimble and effective tactics of response.

6. TOWARD CONSPIRACY ATTUNEMENT

In the preceding sections, I explained why I feel compelled to abandon conspiracy theory as an object by the impossibility of grasping it analytically, locating it contextually, or using it politically. Here, in this final section of Part 1, I turn my attention to the phenomenon I am calling *conspiracy attunement*, which I see as a better avenue for analysis. As I argued in Part 1.3, conspiracy theory is not a distinctive feature of any particular epoch or locale; it is not a "reflection" of a particular time or place. But that does not mean we cannot study its meaning and efficacy contextually. The problem is how to set the context appropriately. I take conspiracy attunement as a dialogical context in which talk *about* conspiracy theories has meaning and force in the form of accusations and attributions, jokes and insults, stories and legacies, habits and weapons.

In proposing conspiracy attunement as a particular context for analysis, I am also interested in theorizing context in general. In doing this, I will have to sidle up to the concept of culture delicately and strategically. While I do not gloss contexts of conspiracy attunement as cultural contexts, that is partly because the notion of cultural context is usually understood to mean local context, in all the problematic ways I discussed in Part 1.3. In its displacement from the center of anthropological theory, it seems to me, culture has come to serve anthropologists less as a tool and more as a communicative gesture—for some, no more than a habit or tic. It means everything, in the sense that it is a pervasive descriptor for any feature of human life that has a collective dimension; and yet it means nothing specifically, lacking referential content or analytic edge. It is one descriptor among many that anthropologists use to get at the coordinates and determinants of collective life, often bundled together in a conceptual tangle—social-cultural-political-economic (perhaps also historical)—in which the specific contribution made by culture is a fuzzy notion associated with language, meaning, and consciousness. In my own search for a way to understand Cypriot conspiracy attunement as a context, having observed that cultural difference seemed to operate for many conspiratologists as an unexamined (and thus untheorized) premise of their symptomatic readings, I have turned to theorists of culture whose influential works on the subject date to a different time: the newly poststructuralist 1980s and 1990s, when the concept of culture was still being actively debated in anthropology in a way that now appears to me untimely—"before [its] time or out of date," as Strathern might suggest (Strathern 1987, 251).

Among those theorists is Arjun Appadurai, who argues, in *Modernity at Large* (1996), that "the cultural" should be understood not as a substantive term entailing particular contents, but rather as a diacritic: a tool for marking difference and introducing contrast for heuristic purposes, in a way that is itself different from the difference yielded by other diacritics (like those I named above: social, political, economic, historical, etc.). To disentangle the cultural from the ethnic or ethnonational, for example, as he is committed to doing—and as I am committed to doing here, for political reasons in addition to analytic ones, given the ethnonational terms of the division in Cyprus and its disastrous effects—he proposes that we take culture "as a marked term" emphasizing the "consciousness of [certain] attributes and their naturalization as essential to group identity" (13–14). His insistence on "consciousness," "naturalization," and "group identity" as the defining features of the cultural has helped me to arrive at conspiracy attunement as the object of my own study—inflected in a peculiar way by division as a central feature of social and political life for Cypriots. I am interested, thus, in how Cypriots reach for shared facts and shared symbols to express a sense of collective solidarity in relation to their division; in whether they in fact experience that sense of a collective; and if they do, in how satisfying and how durable it is, and in what sense it is indeed collective. These questions take me far from the symptomatic approach to conspiracy theory that would (in theory) position me to assess reasonable vis-à-vis excessive paranoia among Cypriots. They are basic questions about belonging to an unstable collective and exclusion from it, and they are questions that I think many Cypriots often ask themselves. To answer them, I cannot look only at academic and public discourses on conspiracy theory in Cyprus; I must also examine how Cypriots relate—"consciously," in Appadurai's term—to their widespread characterization as conspiracy theorists, much as Stacy Leigh Pigg examined the self-awareness that Nepalis formed in relation to their reputation among development workers as credulous and superstitious villagers, as one index of their modern identity (180–81).

I have chosen the term "conspiracy attunement" over "conspiracy consciousness" as the right way to indicate this relationally inflected self-awareness because I do not want to risk implying any kinship between conspiracy consciousness and false consciousness (in the Marxian sense), nor to insinuate any theory of the unconscious (in the Freudian-Lacanian sense). I use this term instead to capture the embodied, affective, and interpersonal dimensions of Cypriots' relation to conspiracy theory—including humor and cynicism—as well as the intellectual, symbolic, and discursive dimensions, insofar as that relation is collective rather than idiosyncratic. The extent to which, and the sense(s) in which, conspiracy attunement in Cyprus is collective are what I explore in Part 2, in my case study of the president's body.

What is at stake in the concept of conspiracy attunement that I am developing here is an alternative to paranoia, which symptomatic readers take as the deep meaning of conspiracy theory. It is an alternative way of understanding the collective psychosocial, cultural, and historical dimensions of violence and secrecy without pathologizing or dismissing the referential truth of conspiracy theories. Methodologically, working with this concept of conspiracy attunement instead of paranoia means paying attention to the tropes and modes of communication and self-understanding that we observe and use; it means tracking the attributions of conspiracy theory in situated speech through which power is channeled and enacted. It means paying attention to self-consciousness and dialogic play as pragmatic determinants of interpersonal dynamics: what people say and to whom, the way they say it, what else they are saying when they say it, and what their saying does—as opposed to what we take people to *believe* when they say it.

In framing this dialogical context as conspiracy attunement, I mean deliberately to evoke a phenomenological appreciation for the affective, relational, and performative aspects of engagement with conspiracy theory. The way a person hears a claim or question about conspiracy and turns her attention to it in response might be very much like tuning in to a musical performance. Attunement in this sense implies relationality—a sense of coming into harmony with "surroundings that include the embodied presence of others," or an "intersubjective milieu," as Thomas Csordas writes (Csordas 1993, 138–39).[40] That is not to suggest that the relationality of attunement is uniform, harmonious, or consistent; people can become attuned to one another or fall out of attunement over time. Indeed, in a context of conspiracy attunement, some people might learn to hear a "dog whistle" to which others remain deaf.[41] This kind of differential attunement is one implication of social division and political polarization, and it marks the boundaries of an attunement context. This is one of the reasons I think conspiracy attunement may offer a better lens onto shared experience and shared horizons than other tools of contextualization—cultural, historical, ethnonational, and so on—that refer to an external matrix.

Perhaps it is with this sense of attunement in mind that ethnographic conspiratologists like Rakopoulos, along with Harambam and Aupers, use the phenomenological term "milieu" to characterize the context in which their interlocutors, already contending with the label "conspiracy theorist," relate to others who are active in that context as well as to the label itself. Rakopoulos in particular emphasizes the "grassroots" milieu in which his interlocutors work, self-consciously positioning themselves as experts and gatekeepers in the professional field of "'conspiracy theory publishing'" (2022, 46, 58). Approaching conspiracy theory in this milieu at the ethnographic "eye-level" (47, 48, 50, 57, passim), as Rakopoulos puts it, means situating conspiracy theory in the "lives of the minds behind it" (57), talking with the "theorists behind the theory" (52) in order to bring their published works, which circulate in and beyond the milieu, into intelligible relation with their more situated and spontaneous self-expressions (for example, in interviews with the ethnographer). Seeking out the "roots" of conspiracy theories (57) in the ideas and commitments of their authors, Rakopoulos insists that "intention matters" (58); the intention of conspiracy theorists is what allows us to distinguish between deliberate misinformation and "inspirational narratives," as one of Rakopoulos's interlocutors describes conspiracy theories (51).[42] The author's intention can only be discerned by getting to know the author.

But intention is slippery. Even if we see conspiracy theories as intentional "political projects" that take form in "social engagement" (58), as Rakopoulos suggests, these political projects cannot actualize themselves at the collective level; an author's intentions may matter very much to the author but remain illegible or irrelevant to readers. It is surely also the case that authors' intentions may not be fully legible even to themselves, and that their intentions may shift with shifts in the milieu (for example, what seems to be at stake collectively in the Epsilon theory about a secret society of ancient Hellenes from another planet has shifted since the turn of the millennium, while the theory itself remains relevant). In Rakopoulos's paper, as in Harambam and Aupers's, the milieu seems to me the central explanatory concept, which is nevertheless not theorized directly; rather, it dissipates behind the self-understanding of individual conspiracy theorists—or those who do not wish to identify as such—even though it is only in relation to others in the milieu that their self-understanding takes shape. *How* the milieu is a collective or shared environment cannot be substantiated only by elucidating the individual perspectives of participants.

My own approach to the shared environment of conspiracy attunement is closer to Giovanna Parmigiani's (2021) analysis of position and context in her recent writing on the "apparent 'belief' in conspiracy theories" among contemporary pagans in southern Italy (Parmigiani 2021, 508). Their "apparent 'belief'" is concerning to her insofar as these theories—especially those relating to COVID and QAnon—seem to belie her interlocutors' intelligence and education (that is, she thinks they ought to be able to weigh evidence and reason properly, but they do not do so[43]), and to contradict their own espoused values of social justice and care and respect for other living beings and the environment. As an opening gambit, then, Parmigiani expresses an offended liberal sensibility as she sketches the contours of her interlocutors' collective illiberality; yet she refrains from examining their beliefs as symptomatic reflections of a fringe worldview or state of mind. She describes her interlocutors instead as a "community of sense" enacting a counterhegemonic sensory and affective politics, or *dissensus*, in Jacques Rancière's term. Distinguishing their "conspiracy-believing" from "believing in conspiracies" (509, 511, 520–21), Parmigiani aims to move away from the "psychological, cognitive, and social dynamics of *beliefs*" toward the "sensory, aesthetic, and performative dimension of *conspiracy-believing*" (515). Conspiracy-believing by pagans is, on her reading, an "explicit, populist form of *dissensus* aimed at challenging the common ways to sense and make sense of the world" (518) on the part of a community that "wants to be fully acknowledged, recognized, legitimized in their 'participatory' way to inhabit the world" (524).

Drawing on Sabina Magliocco's work on magic, Parmigiani argues that conspiracy-believing, like believing in magic, "can only be grasped contextually, and possibly, positionally—that is, in reference to the micro and macro contexts in which they are embedded and to the position of the individuals and groups vis-à-vis other individuals and society at large"

(Parmigiani 2021, 515 [cf. 521]).⁴⁴ Magliocco frames belief—in magic, the evil eye, chain letters, and so on—as a "contextual expression," a "response" to both micro- and macro-contextual "forces," and thus, as "integral to the success of certain procedures and performances" as well as a "product" of them (Magliocco 2012, 7). The question for ethnographers, then, is how to determine which contexts are relevant for the analysis of belief in this sense. The conspiracy theories that Parmigiani's pagan interlocutors discuss are sometimes localized ("based in Italy") and sometimes not ("broadly international") (508). Her interlocutors themselves are highly localized in the Apulia region of southeastern Italy, but Parmigiani seems most concerned by their receptiveness to conspiracy theories "coming from overseas" (508), especially the United States. She suggests that online forums and social media—while certainly facilitating their sense of themselves as a "community of sense"—are not the main context in which the sensory and aesthetic politics of that community have formed (517n16). Instead, she argues that their "esotericism" in regard to magic effectively conditions and possibly explains their adoption of "conspiracy culture" (518); both, she writes, entail "participatory way[s] of knowing" the world (519) that have the performative effect of affirming and enhancing practitioners' participation in "networks of belonging" (507, 509, 524). Parmigiani thus leaves open the determination of the relevant context for analysis, allowing it to shift with her interlocutors' self-positioning as they feel resonance between conspiracy narratives and their own "deep knowledge" (519–20).

Nevertheless, Parmigiani's analysis of her interlocutors as a community of sense entails Italy as an implicit frame—the body politic or "society at large" (515) with which her interlocutors are in counterhegemonic dissensus, and which thus renders coherence from their dissensus. It matters a great deal that her interlocutors are tied to a small, specific geographic locale in Italy, not because that locale explains their conspiracy-believing but rather because it constitutes a *peripheral* location for their dissensus on a national scale. This region, she indicates, is demarcated by its ancient association with Magna Graecia rather than Rome; Greek is spoken there by a long-standing ethnic minority along with Greek expatriates who have settled there recently. Parmigiani thus localizes her interlocutors on the "fringe" of national space (507), not only geographically, but also historically and culturally. I do not mean to suggest that she asserts the national scale as a delimiting context for their conspiracy-believing; indeed, she shows that her interlocutors often shift contexts or frames of reference in the process of their sense-making. Rather, I am suggesting that the analytic of dissensus takes that national scale as an implicit context. Nation—Italy—floats as a context that may be stabilized and invoked by her interlocutors at certain moments in their performative dialogue with others who, themselves, may or may not be located in or identified with Italy.

In this book, I see nation similarly as a floating context, but on a different scale. I do not follow a fringe community of conspiracy theorists within Cyprus; rather, it is the "whole" of Cyprus, or, rather, the impossibility of a "whole" Cyprus, that forms the context of conspiracy attunement for a discursive public riven by radical social and political division. Substantiating this context as a dialogical one requires careful delineation and discernment of relevant talk, be it written or spoken. In the Interlude and Part 2, where I explore the body of Tassos Papadopoulos as a discursive site, the evidence I present is largely textual: publications on the political history of Cyprus and press coverage of the theft of the president's body. This textual emphasis may have the effect of skewing my analysis, making talk about conspiracy theory appear wholly discursive when so much of it is affective, relational, and performative. As Rakopoulos observes, working with gatekeepers of "conspiracy theory" discourse whose experience, expertise, and prioritization of "printed material" mark the "generational distance they felt from a younger and more volatile scene" online, "Doing ethnography with conspiracy theorist authors implies a discursive fieldwork, in a logo-centric research environment operating on interviews and the printed textuality of conspiracy" (Rakopoulos 2022, 49, 51). He warns against the "reduction" of conspiracy theory to "the epistemic" that results from its framing as an "alternative" science or epistemology in this environment (55). The concept of conspiracy attunement helps me avoid this reduction, by connecting the discursive dimensions of conspiracy theory talk to its performative dimensions. It also provides me a path around the problem of evaluating conspiracy theories as truth claims, or crediting people's professions of belief in conspiracy theories. Picking up on people's attunement to conspiracy does not entail any particular view on their knowledge or beliefs about conspiracy.

The self-conscious humor that I have heard Cypriots express in conversations about conspiracy theory—which strike me as evidence of conspiracy attunement—leads me to Michael Herzfeld's concept of "cultural intimacy." In his 1997 book by that title, Herzfeld defines cultural intimacy as "the recognition of those aspects of a cultural identity that are considered a source of external embarrassment but that nevertheless provide insiders with their assurance of common sociality" ([1997] 2005, 3). As support for the concept, Herzfeld observes social actors in Greece oscillating between contradictory positions on cultural norms depending on audience and context—by turns valorizing and stigmatizing behaviors such as animal theft, for example—which reflect and effect power hierarchies among those actors. On his account, these contradictions do not disrupt social cohesion in Greece; on the contrary, they are mediated and resolved by the encompassing symbolic frame of the nation-state and thus, in a sense, serve to reinforce it.

It is in this telos of resolution and encompassment of contradiction that I see the limits of this concept for analyzing the Cypriot context of conspiracy attunement. In revealing multidimensional boundaries between insiders and outsiders that describe the flexible political tactics of inclusion and exclusion in a society, cultural intimacy might well explain, for example, the arguments and jokes I have observed so many times among Cypriots that thematize the possibly (though not necessarily) embarrassing stereotype of Cypriots as conspiracy theorists. But the enduring division of Cyprus—not only between regimes in the north and the south, but also between the political left and right—has fragmented the social field in a radical way, and rendered untenable any notion of the nation-state as a symbolic frame. The nation-state, such as it is, does not "work" in Cyprus to mediate contradictions in the social field, nor to stabilize or metaphorize boundaries between inside and outside. The segmentary logic of cultural intimacy presumes a homogeneity of identification at the symbolic level of ethnos or nation that does not exist, at least in this case. Rather than trying to get a fix on how conspiracy theory expresses antagonisms and their resolution in ethnonational culture, then, I am more interested in exploring how Cypriots relate to their characterization as conspiracy theorists—an attribution made as often by Cypriots as by "outsiders" of any description.[45]

This approach raises the methodological problem of how to recognize attributions of conspiracy theory when studying conspiracy attunement. How do people in a particular context know conspiracy theory when they see it, in order to take an attitude or action in relation to it? And how does anyone else (an anthropologist, for example) know that they know it? If conspiracy attunement has to do with attributions of conspiracy theory—and affects and attitudes toward conspiracy theory, and jokes and other kinds of commentary about conspiracy theory—how can conspiracy attunement itself be identified for analysis without defining conspiracy theory as the particular kind of thing that it is about? And, along these lines, how is conspiracy theory different from religion, kinship, or any other social relation that depends on context for its definition?

I venture that one difference between conspiracy theory and other relational concepts is the specificity of the very term "conspiracy theory" and its many translations; identifying its attribution in situated speech is not difficult, while identifying religion or kinship that way might be, given the broader ambit and unspecialized usage of these concepts. In addition, among other possible diacritics of conspiracy attunement that might be used for the purposes of cross-contextual comparison, I propose the social problem created by attributions of conspiracy theory. If conspiracy theory is not always and in every context taken to be toxic and harmful, it is at least understood to be untrue by definition; there is, as I argued in Part 1.1, no way to occupy the position of conspiracy theorist in meaningful communication. It is therefore divisive in its attribution—which is to say, the attribution creates a division on the matter of truth between the person making the attribution and the person thus attributed. It is the very model of a "dividing practice," in Foucault's term (Foucault 1982, 208), just as Magliocco argues about the concept of belief (2012, 9); it separates the rational from the irrational, the modern from the non- or premodern, the expert from the amateur or grassroots, and so on. But this dividing does not happen only on the level of discourse; the attribution of conspiracy theory also effects a polarization between people participating in a conversation or argument. *Dialogical polarization* may therefore serve as a useful diacritic of conspiracy theory.[46] Polarization is not a definitional feature of conspiracy theory but rather operates in the metadiscursive register of conspiracy attunement where attributions of conspiracy theory work as performative utterances.[47]

One example of this kind of attribution: On January 1, 2011, the left-leaning Greek-language Cypriot newspaper *Politis* gave its "anti-award" for "best conspiracy theory of 2010" to Giorgos Perdikis, head of the Green Party in Cyprus, for promoting the theory that the British Royal Air Force had been "spraying the clouds" over Cyprus in order to steal the rain ("The Bug" 2011, 21). I have heard about cloud spraying so many times in my everyday conversations with so many people in Cyprus that I can attest personally to the wide circulation of this theory. Other versions suggest that the Royal Air Force sprays the clouds to prevent rain and ruin agriculture on the island, thereby increasing Cyprus's dependence on foreign imports; or, alternatively, to enhance signals coming to and from the massive radar facility in the Troodos Mountains near the British Sovereign Base Area on the southern coast.[48] Several years after this item appeared in *Politis*, in February 2016, Nicos Kouyialis, the minister of agriculture in the Republic, ordered an official investigation into these allegations of "geoengineering," in order to assess the chemical composition of the cloud cover over Cyprus and to request information about Royal Air Force activities from the British Foreign Ministry. An earlier report issued in 2010 had been dismissed by Perdikis and others as a "whitewash" (Hazou 2016).

The author of the 2011 article in *Politis*, writing under the nom de plume "The Bug" [ο κοριός], praised the same Mr. Perdikis as well for his "strong stance" on the "new spying venture" undertaken by the Turks, who claimed to be constructing cell towers in the region of Achna—an abandoned village in the north, near Famagusta—but who Perdikis said were actually installing surveillance technology in collaboration with Echelon (an Anglo-American surveillance program originating in the Cold War, thought by many to have an installation at the Sovereign Base Area at Akrotiri, near Limassol) along with the "treacherous" English. And the "runner-up" for best conspiracy theory of 2010, awarded by "The Bug": "The average Cypriot, who eats whatever he's fed."[49]

My point in offering this example is not that the cloud-spraying theory (or the Turkish spying theory, for that matter) is widespread and silly, but rather that the author of this item in 2011 found it both funny and sad, and knew that his readers would appreciate the award because they were already well aware of the theory in relation to many other conspiracy theories of which they were also aware. In other words, this *Politis* piece expresses not "conspiracy culture," as Peter Knight and Jack Bratich have it (Knight 2000; Bratich 2008, 66), but rather conspiracy attunement. On this point, I have learned much from Jodi Dean's analysis of American UFOlogy in the 1990s. Considering an array of TV shows, online discussion groups, and other pop culture forms, Dean notes, "Their insight into the themes and anxieties just below the surface of American society in fact presupposes a general cultural awareness of this discourse. 'Getting it' requires prior knowledge of UFOs and alien abduction" (1998, 29). It is not the "anxieties below the surface" that I think are explanatory—these can only be hypothesized via symptomatic readings of cultural forms, and I have already rejected that approach—but rather the cultural processes Dean indicates, by which such "prior knowledge" may be developed and recursively applied in new cultural productions. It is the acute awareness among Cypriots of the prevalence of conspiracy theory in Cypriot public culture, and the need perceived by many to position themselves in relation to conspiracy theories in order to speak publicly on matters of political significance, that I think distinguishes the Cypriot context of conspiracy attunement from others. Studying particular conspiracy theories in Cyprus—such as those surrounding the theft of the president's body—requires deep knowledge of the recursive process by which conspiracy theory has been and continues to be transmitted in Cyprus as a legacy—or, as the Cypriot journalist Makarios Drousiotis has put it, a "curse" (Drousiotis 2005a).[50]

It is the cursedness of Cyprus, conceived this way, that distinguishes Cypriot conspiracy attunement from other contexts. The cloud-spraying theory in Cyprus, for example, resembles, in many of its features, certain conspiracy theories about chemtrails—vapor trails in the atmosphere created by toxic aerial spraying—that have found traction in other contexts. Alexandra Bakalaki examines one such theory that, on her account, entered public discourse in Greece in the early 2000s and had achieved widespread legibility by the time of her research in 2013. Bakalaki traces the theory to "North America in the 1990s" and asserts that it "spread around the world" via the internet after that (2016, 12). Her aim is to explain why it raised as much "popular concern" among Greeks as it did (14), focusing largely on the financial crisis starting in 2008 and its aftermath of austerity as anxiety-provoking conditions of everyday life that propelled a new kind of local sense-making. In this regard, her paper is a contribution to the corpus of symptomatic readings of conspiracy theory that presume both a collective malaise and a mode of sense-making that are local, but that presume as well the recognizability to readers of conspiracy theory as such without reference to that local context.

Yet Bakalaki complicates these presumptions about locality, too, noting that supporters of the chemtrail theory in Greece employ *both* a "localist rhetoric" of fear about the "threat to the homeland" posed by chemtrails *and* an "internationalist, cosmopolitan rhetoric" that acknowledges the global environmental effects of aerial spraying (16). Greece as a locale for this conspiracy theory is thus both local and global; Bakalaki configures a specific—Greek—relation of scale between local and global by contextualizing the chemtrail theory in light of the both local and global financial crisis and the both local and global environmental crisis. This oscillation between local and global contexts might be familiar from globalization discourse, broadly; the categories in themselves are empty and undefined, and it is the shift in perspective from one to the other, rather than the specific content of either, that helps us grasp the meaning of the chemtrail theory and the way it compels people.

The cloud-spraying theory in Cyprus, on the other hand, finds its meaning in relation to conspiracy theories of the division in Cyprus. It implicates the Royal Air Force and the military-surveillance installations at the Sovereign Base Areas belonging to the United Kingdom (and used by the United States), which are well-understood by Cypriots already to be implicated in conspiracy theories of the division. The cloud-spraying theory does not make sense in light of an external matrix, the way the chemtrail theory in Greece does in the matrix of financial crisis and climate change, on Bakalaki's account. Rather, the relationship between the conspiracy theory of cloud spraying and conspiracy theories of the division in Cyprus is recursive; the latter give rise to and make sense of the former, which, in turn, recontextualizes them.

Makarios Drousiotis deems this recursion a curse, and he is entitled to bemoan and denounce it. I do not presume to do the same; my aim is rather to examine the way recursion has given a durable social form to Cypriot conspiracy attunement. The long duration and open-endedness of this context precludes any periodization of conspiracy theory as an expression of the Cold War, post–Cold War, millennial, or any other epoch. There is no threshold or discontinuity I can pinpoint that would divide the context of conspiracy attunement between the time of the cannibals—when Papadopoulos and so many others were organizing violence and division—and the time when Papadopoulos's body was stolen, or for that matter, the time when Papadopoulos was president and Tony Angastiniotis was having nightmares about being cannibalized by him. Conspiracy theories about the division of Cyprus contextualize conspiracy theories about the president's body, which, in turn, recontextualize conspiracy theories of the division as part of their own story.

The recursivity of these conspiracy theories works against the epochal tendency of so much conspiratology, especially the literature of the millennium that I discussed in Part 1.1. Such epochal tendencies derive, I think, from the narrow focus in cultural studies (and some anthropology) on popular culture in the United States, a locale that is not marked as one cultural context among others—as a context, that is, that might be compared cross-culturally with others. The unmarkedness of the US context makes it fertile terrain for the production of general theory about conspiracy theory: argumentative claims that it is a *kind* of theory with generic traits, which works in particular ways for particular reasons in particular contexts. To be clear, what I mean by *general theory* is theory that tracks its object across contexts through a play between general and particular. In general theory, the existence of difference can only be understood dialectically, as a particularization of something general that is, itself, an ongoing synthesis of all particularizations. Comparison is a way of connecting particular versions of this general thing, which is to say, versions that are already understood to be comparable insofar as they differently instantiate the general. As I argue below and in the Interlude, the great risk of general theory in this sense is that what is taken to be general may turn out to be a particular version that is dominant, hegemonic, imperial. General theory in this sense cannot accommodate difference that is not legible as an instantiation of the particular version that is dominant.

Unmarking locale as context is one of the key mechanisms of such general theory. This is one of Susan Lepselter's (2016) most consistent interpretive moves in her remarkable book about American UFO believers, which I discussed in the Introduction. Lepselter is exceedingly careful to avoid the culturalist trap of setting or presuming essentializing boundaries around the conversations and other talk-saturated experiences she shared with her interlocutors—who were, in her rendering, peripatetic and searching, often scrambling at the edges of settled middle-class life, from which they had fallen or perceived themselves excluded. They were also, she notes as an aside, almost exclusively white, and often libertarian, loosely speaking: unaligned with dominant right-wing or left-wing politics but deeply invested in the American birthright mythology of personal freedom. Despite these demographic and situational coordinates—which help explain how her interlocutors related to what she calls "public stories" of alien abduction (111), as to the Native American captivity narratives she finds haunting and resonating within them—Lepselter explicitly refuses to "define or analyze the social categories of the people [she] describe[s] here, because there isn't one" (156). She refuses, too, to take the specific sites of her ethnographic research as places whose particularity might account for the kind of talk she heard and engaged in there. Culture, on her telling, is diffuse and roaming, and only very loosely articulated with conspiracy theory about the New World Order, which, despite its prominence in the discourse of her interlocutors, is treated as only one among many forms of their "uncanny talk."

What Lepselter gives us, then, is indeed a symptomatic reading, but without a transcendent cultural diagnosis; if she shows that talk about UFOs and alien abductions is an expression of collective malaise, it is because her interlocutors diagnose their own situation that way, telling her repeatedly that "something isn't right" (76). In this sense, her book successfully accomplishes what she, after Kathleen Stewart, calls "contaminated critique" (Lepselter 2016, 17), which "mixes with its object and includes itself as an object of its own analysis" (Stewart 1991, 395). Lepselter's theory of conspiracy theory is *their* theory, interrupted by her real-time commentary and her post-hoc textual asides. Her way of writing their theory is to follow their turns of thought and phrase, to mimic their interpretive mode of "connecting the dots" (2016, 25) and to evoke the "rushes of feeling" (156) they associate with the coherence they derive thereby.

An exceptionally compelling and persuasive text has resulted from this process; I have no interest in taking issue with *The Resonance of Unseen Things*. What I want to emphasize in Lepselter's "contaminated" conspiratology is the unmarkedness of the locale in which she conducted her research. That locale is crucial to the meaning of the stories she is telling and retelling, but it is backgrounded in her text as a setting and a poetic repertoire, rather than foregrounded as an explanation; or, to use Strathern's terms, it is a "ground" that never becomes "figure." What is foregrounded analytically as a context in this text, as I noted earlier, is the *time* of the "uncanny talk" Lepselter captures: the 1990s, leading up to the millennium. She marks the millennium as explanatory because her interlocutors do: "that's the way it used to be" (93), they say; "nothing is what it used to be" (127), and "people don't know what's coming" (137, 141). Periodization rather than locale forms the axis of difference for Lepselter's analysis, through which she identifies a distinctive way of theorizing power among her interlocutors and in the "public culture" they share (157), that encompasses but exceeds conspiracy theory.

As I argued in Part 1.3, conspiratology situated in the United States often determines context by periodizing, as Lepselter does, though often in a more pointed way: by marking out eras or epochs within which American culture can be read symptomatically in eruptions of conspiracy theory—or, as Bratich reframes them, conspiracy panics—which implicitly contrast with a normal time before and a (presumably) better time ahead. In such works, culture is understood as part of the context only by way of historical comparison, not by way of cross-cultural comparison.

Conspiratology in the Cypriot context of conspiracy attunement, on the other hand, operates much closer to the ground: at least as close as what Clifford Geertz, contrasting the "theoretical development" of "cultural interpretation" to the "imaginative abstraction" of other sciences, had in mind with his notion of "thick description" (Geertz 1973, 24). In this, Yiannis Ioannou is an exemplary and avowedly symptomatic reader of conspiracy theory, in a context he marks as distinctively Cypriot by amassing detailed accounts of the "self-destructive" [αυτοκαταστροφικό] "irrationality" [παραλογισμό] (Ioannou 2009, 18, 11) at the heart of political culture in Cyprus. In his analysis, the Cypriot "culture of 'conspiracy'" (14) is Greek-Cypriot culture, defined by its separation from and antagonism toward the Turkish-Cypriot community; there is no question here of a unified and coherent pan-Cypriot culture. His approach is densely particularist, bound to a locale that serves as explanatory context.

The fact that locale does not (or not necessarily) serve as context in this way for conspiratologists in and of the United States is to be expected, perhaps, given the geopolitical position of Cyprus—a specific, peripheral somewhere—vis-à-vis the United States, a general, imperial anywhere and everywhere. The frequent invocation by Cypriot conspiracy theorists of Cyprus's victimization by the Great Powers, to which Ioannou alludes in the passage quoted in the Introduction, speaks to this geopolitical-theoretical asymmetry—a condition of anthropological theory from the beginning, as Talal Asad makes clear in his introduction to *Anthropology and the Colonial Encounter* ([1973] 1975). Here, Asad shows how the theory of functionalism in British social anthropology was fashioned on colonized African ground, requiring, in order to become as dominant as it was in the first half of the twentieth century, both the proximity to colonized people that anthropologists enjoyed, facilitated by colonial-military governments in sub-Saharan Africa, and the impossible distance separating those people from western centers of theory production.

This colonial structure of anthropological knowledge-making created a profound and durable legacy that, itself, has become a focus of anthropological theorizing. In a brief essay published in 1986, Appadurai explores the special relationship between theoretical foci in anthropology and the particular places, taken as empirical sites, where early ethnographic research was conducted by theorists whose work became foundational to "the field." He observes that the "prestige zones of anthropological theory," such as Australia, Melanesia, and sub-Saharan Africa, were historically occupied by "certain forms of sociality (such as kinship), certain forms of exchange (such as gift), certain forms of polity (such as the segmentary state)" by virtue of anthropologists' attraction to "the small, the simple, the elementary, the face-to-face" in their research (Appadurai 1986, 357). By contrast, outside these "prestige zones" were located "complex traditional civilizations" such as those that anthropologists found in India and China, which they approached via "gatekeeping concepts" like "hierarchy" and "filial piety" (as well as "honor-and-shame" in the Mediterranean, a regionalizing concept to which Michael Herzfeld and other anthropologists of Greece have turned their critical attention[51]). Compiling a long list of additional factors that have shaped—largely imperceptibly to practitioners—the relation between place and theory in anthropology, Appadurai warns,

> The discussion of theoretical issues tends (surreptitiously) to take on a restrictive local cast, while on the other hand, the study of other issues in the place in question is retarded, and thus the over-all nature of the anthropological interpretation of the particular society runs the risk of serious distortion. (358)

In a decisive and intricately argued paper that serves in some respects as a rejoinder to Appadurai's essay, Rena Lederman tunes into this "distortion" as an interesting and productive site of disciplinary self-reflection and self-provocation in anthropology. Connecting conceptualizations of "culture area" that framed ethnographic research around national traditions in the early twentieth century to the postwar consolidation of the "area studies" framework and its later dismantling by "globalization" studies,[52] Lederman notes, "Culture areas were at least equally about culture theories as about areas. They operated as heuristics, organizing grounded particulars for theoretical and comparative ends" (2008, 312). Indeed, throughout the paper, Lederman insists (as Appadurai does) on the comparative and general—or general *because* comparative—nature of anthropological theory that has referred to and refracted the particularities of place through all of its logistico-theoretical arrangements.

Reading Appadurai against the grain in several ways, however, Lederman makes the crucial point that it is not only topics, concepts, and theoretical foci that have developed in this special relationship with place in anthropological theory, but also "research *methods*" (317, emphasis original). Methods have to do with the extent and the quality of interaction that anthropologists have sought and been able to achieve with their interlocutors—conditions of research (among other things) that, she shows, determine to a large degree the questions anthropologists pursue and how they do so. Melanesianist anthropology serves as a complex paradigm for Lederman here: an example of and a model for a regional anthropology at the same time as it stands (and has always stood, she argues) as a "heterodox" and "destabilizing" provocation to comparative theory (311, 323, 325). On her account of it, all the questions about cultural and local particularity that are asked at the level of general theory—that is, at the level of cross-cultural comparison—are also posed by Melanesianist anthropologists to their own regional (that is, particularist) tradition of knowledge, which they have made through dialogue and debate with Indigenous Melanesian knowledges as well as other regional anthropological knowledges. Melanesianist anthropology, and perhaps any regional anthropology, has thus achieved a paradoxical or indeterminate yet quite generative state of general-particularity and particular-generality in its synthesis of theory and ethnography.

Perhaps that indeterminate state is what it means for theory to be "from" a place. It is a different notion, at least in certain ways, from "the very simple" idea proposed by Jean and John L. Comaroff in their forceful book, *Theory from the South; or, How Euro-America Is Evolving toward Africa* (2012, 1)—which is not, as they are quick to acknowledge, simple at all. "Theory from the south," they explain, is a "counter-evolutionary" framing, pitched against the "Western enlightenment" narrative of modernity as "Euromodernity" (5). They make two key arguments here (and many others besides): first, that African modernity—a complex category that might encompass the entire global south or instead refer with great specificity to a particular regional context—exists in its own terms, and with its own history, rather than subsisting as a minor and subordinate derivative of Euro-American modernity; and second, that if anthropologists wish to study "capitalism-and-modernity in the here and now" (12), they would do well to look to Africa instead of Euro-America, since it is there that new kinds and organizations of capitalism and social relations are being invented and tested.

Theory from the South is a densely and self-consciously polemically argued text whose ambitions far exceed my own and do not, in many ways, meet them directly. What most pertains here to my line of thinking about locale and context is the Comaroffs' concern with the places of theory: where it is made and where it refers, which is also a way of saying, who makes it for whom and about whom. Among the exclusions from the "Western enlightenment" narrative of modernity that they contest most strenuously is the exclusion of "local intellectuals" from "writing the planetary history of the present" (4); the specific referents of "local" here are African, Indian, perhaps anyone "foreclosed" from the enjoyment of the universal subjectivity presumed by western political and social theory (3). Indeed, they begin the book by observing how western theorists have treated the global south as "a place of parochial wisdom, of antiquarian traditions, of exotic ways and means. Above all, of unprocessed data . . . reservoirs of raw fact . . . from which Euromodernity might fashion its testable theories and transcendent truths" (1)—or, as Srinivas Aravamudan puts it in his response to the book, "the theft of experience from the South rendered as intellectual property in the North" (Aravamudan 2012).[53]

Yet Aravamudan queries the Comaroffs on their use of "from" to describe the theory they have in mind as something whose provenance would reverse the direction of that extraction:

> The "from" is a representation where the theory is not any more from the South than it is from the North, as it is the product of the relational interaction between anthropologists such as the Comaroffs, who are just as comfortable in South Africa as in the United States. This might sound churlish, but there is something a bit over-earnest about needing to claim that the theory is from the South, as there is a certain alibi-producing aspect to that claim. (Aravamudan 2012)

Whether the claim is over-earnest depends on what the Comaroffs mean by "the South"; and as Aravamudan notes, they seem to have in mind a great number of things: a heuristic, a "developmental category," an originality, a relation, a paradigm. The Comaroffs describe it this way:

> The south cannot be defined, *a priori*, in substantive terms. The label bespeaks a *relation*, not a thing in or for itself. . . . Whatever it may connote at any given moment, it always points to an "ex-centric" location, an outside to Euro-America. . . . As such, whatever else it may be presumed to be, "the south" is a window on the world at large . . . a world that, ultimately, transcends the very dualism of north and south. (47, emphasis original)

The vantages (there are many) opened by the Comaroffs' labile elocution of "the south" are extraordinarily compelling. But it bears mention that the transcendent "world at large" they envision here through the window of "the south" might, if we are not exceedingly careful, turn out to be none other than that very "north" whose presumptive universality and at-largeness they take as a legacy of Eurocentric social theory that has been constituted through its variegated exclusions of "the south." The concept of "the south," as an ex-centric locale for theory, by definition risks this impasse.

The Comaroffs' imagination of "the south" as "a window on the world at large" expresses, I think, what Fadi Bardawil calls the "metropolitan unconscious" (1, 7, passim) of critical theory. In his remarkable book, *Revolution and Disenchantment: Arab Marxism and the Binds of Emancipation* (2020), Bardawil complicates "the south" as a locale for theory by training his laser-sharp focus on dialogues and debates among Arab thinkers situated in western or northern metropolitan academic settings and those located "at home" in the Middle East (xvii), whom he takes to be "theorists at the crossroads of transnational streams of discourse" (7). He closely examines a "minority Marxist tradition" (xi)—the Lebanese New Left of the 1960s—by way of texts and their travels through a range of "'ex-centric' vantage points" (5), as well as the trajectories of several key theorists themselves, Bardawil's primary interlocutors. It matters a great deal in his inquiry that the kind of theory he examines is Marxism, whose universalism, premised in "class as the universal grammar of inequality" (15), proposes revolutionary movements wherever it is read, translated, interpreted, applied to local circumstances, and passed along to others. These are the "generative labors," Bardawil writes, "that produce its universality in practice" (xii): a "political universality" in the form of "internationalist solidarity" (14), which always opens a question around theory's relation to political practice.

This question of practice, for Bardawil, becomes a question, too, of what "the field" in ethnographic research can bring to anthropological theory (10). Framing his own research as "fieldwork in theory" (8, passim), he considers not only what theory means in the context of particular theorists' lifeworlds but also what it does in those worlds, not taking for granted—as do many working in the traditions of Marxist and critical theory he reads here—that theory is politically effective:

> Granting critical theory both too much and too little are the result of adhering to a metaphysical image of theory that assumes that the practical effects it will produce in the world are contained a priori in its epistemology. Theory, then, is cast in either the heroic role of saving the world or the bad one of destroying it. (188)

Bardawil does not discount the efficacy of theory in this political sense—its efficacy is precisely what interests him—but neither does he assume it. Instead, he works to discern the specific effects Marxist theory yielded in the thinking and writing of particular Arab intellectuals situated in particular contexts, considering "how [theory] seduces intellectuals, contributes to the cultivation of their ethos and sensibilities, and authorizes political practices for militants" (8). It is these effects that Bardawil tracks as he follows "traveling theory" to and from its many locales.

In the process, Bardawil works across multiple axes of epistemological differentiation and political articulation at once, showing the incongruities and dynamic synergies among these axes as well as the inadequacy of any one alone as a basis of critique. They include, among others, the west vis-à-vis the Arab world; Arab thinkers "at home" vis-à-vis in the diaspora; the political critique offered by Marxist theory vis-à-vis the epistemological critique offered by the "unmasking of Eurocentric knowledges parading as universals" (which, Bardawil argues, "risks naturalizing the conceptual universal/particular distinction on a geographical East/West one," 21); the universalism of Marxist theory vis-à-vis the particularity of Arab society; the universalism of Marxist theory vis-à-vis universalisms understood by critics as "vectors of imperial violence cloaked in ideologies of liberation" (e.g., human rights, feminism, liberal democracy, xiii); and the homogeneity of Arab society as constructed in Orientalist works *and* anti-imperialist critiques vis-à-vis the "multiplicity of regional, familial, sectarian, and religious loyalties" (171) within Arab society—which multiplicity, when interpreted through a Marxist lens as a fragmentation of the people, could not be unified by concepts of class or hegemony in the work of his interlocutors (185).

Especially pertinent in Bardawil's train of thought to my analysis of conspiracy theory is his insistence on multiple paths—he specifies three—for theory to "attain universality" (15), a status that is not entirely consistent with what I have been calling *general theory*. While the "universal concepts" associated with empire ("say, rights, reason, and freedom") achieve universality by way of their assertion as "a priori" and "context-less" (15)—I would frame universality in this sense as a universalizing moment in the dialectical play of general theory—the universality of Marxism results rather from the way theory and theorists travel, inciting consciousness, militancy, and solidarity in a "common world" that is "fashion[ed]" precisely through this process (15). (The third path to universality derives from institutional authorization in metropolitan centers of theory production and is thus closely, though differently, related to the other two, if I follow Bardawil.) "What I am after," he writes,

> is an examination of the different analytical and political effects produced by traveling theories hopping from Paris to New York to eventually land in Beirut.... Traveling theories disable certain critical paths and open up new ones, stifling political projects while potentially boosting others. (179, 181)

In naming two western metropoles and one Middle Eastern city (his own) as locales for theory, what Bardawil resists here is not the importance of locale to theory but rather the framing of locale as either an origin or a destination of theory, as well as the *stability* of theory's reference to locale or its grounding in locale as it travels. If theory produces local change along the way and is also changed by its local articulations, then a determination as to which locales are central in this process and which peripheral, which are originary and which derivative, no longer makes sense.

In their response to Aravamudan, the Comaroffs insist in a less nuanced way than Bardawil that their concept of "theory from the south" does not refer simply to locale. Neither do they mean "theories of people who may be wholly or partially of the south, least of all ourselves. Nor is it ... simply theory 'about' the South. It is ... about the effect of the south *itself* on theory" (30). In registering thus the ways in which an already theoretical conception of place, carrying an implicit political organization of space, has influenced the way people talk about place as well as the way the people to whom they talk understand their talk—recaptured, respectively, in ethnographic research and anthropological theory—they join a genealogy of thought that I first encountered in Stacey Pigg's work on Nepali "belief" in shamans conducted in the 1980s, which I discussed in Part 1.1. Pigg's understanding of "locality" as "translocal (or transnational)," I recall, led her to examine "junctures" of "cross-talk" created by the "displacements" of modernity, and thence to theorizing modernity itself as transitive and conjunctural (Pigg 1996, 164–65)—and certainly not *local* or *global*, if we understand those terms as substantive categories isomorphous with cultures or nation-states.

Lederman shows us that the comparative nature of cultural theory does not depend on the scale—local, regional, global—at which it is carried out. Or, to translate this thought into Strathern's terms in *Partial Connections*, we can look at *place* in anthropology as a species of complexity, which does not increase or decrease with scale. I note here that this text by Strathern, while pitched as a work of comparative theory, is also as Melanesianist an ethnography as we might imagine, and thus makes Lederman's point perfectly.

In approaching conspiracy attunement in Cyprus, I follow the leads these ethnographer-theorists have offered in their complicated scrutiny of the terms by which we identify and complicate locality, and especially those terms by which we contrast local with global, particular with general, and vice versa. Only by reframing context itself can we dismantle the unwarranted and ethnocentric distinctions between reasonable and unreasonable paranoia, as between social theory and conspiracy theory, to which I have been objecting throughout Part 1 of this book.

By reframing context in this way, I am also raising the question as to what kind of place Cyprus is as a setting for the case study I present in Part 2.[54] Conspiracy theories are among the partial connections, in Strathern's term, that both tie Cyprus to other locales and demand its comparison with them. I see my task in this book as writing the story of those connections and their implications—the recursive and intertwined histories of Cyprus and the United States, for example—rather than particularizing Cyprus to a point beyond comparison. In order to reckon with conspiracy theory, it is crucial to examine context itself, critically reassessing the terms of the distinctions we implement to generate difference for heuristic purposes—especially cultural difference and historical difference. My central aim in this reassessment is to dismantle the ethnocentrism that stabilizes a diagnostic position for *us*, who know the truth, in relation to *them*, who believe in conspiracy theory. This aim is not a liberal or relativist proposal to make sense of and accommodate radical difference; it is rather motivated by the sense that conspiracy theorists are not so different, and in fact that "we" might appear to be the conspiracy theorists if the boundaries around "us"—the contextual parameters—were drawn differently. This redrawing of boundaries might also help to disrupt the desire for a general theory of conspiracy theory that so many conspiratologists seem to be after. Cyprus, as seen through a western ethnocentric lens—small, exotic, peripheral, insular in all senses, stuck in the past, remote from world centers of knowledge production, and so on—is as good a place as any, and perhaps better than most, to conduct that disruption.

INTERLUDE: *THE BODY ITSELF*

"They Desecrated Cyprus: An Unprecedented Crime of Sacrilege against the Entire People"

Thus ran the front-page headline of *Philelevtheros*—an independent mainstream newspaper with the highest circulation in the Republic—on December 12, 2009, the day after the theft of the body of Tassos Papadopoulos was discovered (*Philelevtheros* 2009). A week later, his daughter, Anastasia Papadopoulou, published an essay, also in *Philelevtheros*, entitled "The Rape of Our Dignity" (Papadopoulou 2009). In a blow-by-blow account, she described what it had been like to receive the news of the theft and behold her father's empty grave, the horror and pain her family had felt and were still feeling, the outpouring of love and support they had received from some but not all of the political class (she pointedly remarked on the absence of President Demetris Christofias from her father's one-year memorial service, held a day after the crime was discovered), and the ongoing aftermath:

> And after the memorial, too, all those thoughts remained. The attempt to understand why. To feel something other than the rage that flooded through me. The scenarios were making us crazy. Was it for ransom? They didn't leave us alone even at the memorial. Was it extremists? For what reason? What did they hope to achieve? What were they doing to him? Where did they have him? Other obscene scenarios were added to the ones we imagined ourselves. [That] we took him, [that] he planned it himself.... I laugh so that I don't cry.... Have I lost something more than what I lost last year [when he died]? Dignity [αξιοπρέπεια]. My

dignity as a daughter who didn't protect the body of her father. As a Greek [Ελληνίδα]. As a Christian. As a citizen of a Democracy that. . . . is unable to protect the symbols of its very being and of the institutions that make it a state. (Papadopoulou 2009)

Papadopoulou gave searing voice in this essay to the pain, alarm, and fury she experienced after the theft. Building from the attachment of a daughter to her father—an attachment so strong and intimate in her case that she felt as if to her own person the injury done to his remains—she rendered her father's body here as a replete symbol of the nation-state: specifically, the Republic of Cyprus. (The regime in the north and the people living there were not even mentioned.) By a swift concatenation of kinship, ethnonationality, religion, citizenship, democracy, and state institutions, she established a continuity and a family resemblance between the entailments of belonging in monarchical sovereignty and those operative in modern democratic states. In the movement of this concatenation, she summoned as the transcendent attribute of membership in the body politic a moral notion of *dignity* that was stolen from her and the Cypriot nation-state when the remains of her father were stolen. Religion and ethnonationality—that is, Christianity and Greekness (not Cypriotness, notably)—are presented here as the self-evident coordinates of this dignity, which Papadopoulou felt she had lost by failing to protect her father's body from violence. In not naming the perpetrators of this violence, despite the intensity of the feelings she expressed and the clarity of her Greek ethnonationalism, she was more measured here than some of her compatriots would turn out to be, who soon condemned the crime as an attempt to "humiliate the Cypriot state"[1] on the part of Turks or Turkish Cypriots.

In the Introduction, I observed that the story of the president's body has stuck with me over the years due in part to its reception, in and outside Cyprus, as a classic case of Cypriot conspiracy theory. Papadopoulou published her essay just as the theorizing was beginning. She railed against the relentless "scenarios" to which she and her family had been subjected in the days following the theft, which for the most part framed the crime as politically motivated. (Perhaps despite her avowed intentions, Papadopoulou implicitly reproduced this framing by characterizing as symbolic the nature of the harm done by the theft.) However, Papadopoulou also conveyed another factor in this story's stickiness: namely, in the words of a family friend, the "shock, disgust, and horror" many Cypriots expressed at the transgressive nature of the violence done to these special, presidential remains (Tzioni 2009).[2] Papadopoulou observed,

> The world's reaction has been very moving. Constant phone calls. Messages. On Facebook, the relevant group has already acquired 17,000 members. The reactions are practically unanimous. The same words are repeated over and over like an echo: "Rage," "condemnation," "disgust." (Papadopoulou 2009)

Here, Papadopoulou registered the "echo" of this burgeoning affective discourse as if from a distance: one more feature of the agonizing situation she found herself confronting as a person touched more directly than most by the crime.[3] The affective intensity of this public talk, and the specific affectivity of disgust and horror in that talk, were implicated in the theorizing it provoked; the key to the connection between the affect and the theory is in the "abhorrence" (Hadjiapostolou 2009)[4] for an act that was widely understood not only as "macabre" (L. Charalambous 2009) but also, crucially, as "unholy" (Tzioni 2009). (I come back to its unholiness shortly.)

In *The Cultural Politics of Emotion*, Sara Ahmed writes that disgust uniquely "sticks" to its object; unlike other affects that we might feel or understand "in the abstract," or that we might attribute to the object itself, disgust "is clearly dependent on contact" between one object and another (Ahmed 2015, 85). It is that contact—a "form of relationality," as Ahmed puts it—that potentiates and accounts for the stickiness of both (91). She is interested here in "sticky signs": words that convey rather than signify affect and that, through repetition, come to have a "'binding' effect" on the affect those words carry and provoke (92). Bodies can be sticky "surfaces" for such signs, she argues, and I hope to show in what follows that the president's body was especially sticky in its associations with other sticky signs. Ahmed notes that "some objects become stickier than others given past histories of contact" (92), and though she has in mind histories of contact between "European bodies" and "native" ones under colonial rule (82), we might also consider the history of contact—I would call it a history of violence—that prepared the body of Tassos Papadopoulos so comprehensively for the attachment of public affect in Cyprus.

Even while he was alive, the figure of this president was a knot of story threads tying the political history of Cyprus to the history of violence among

Greek Cypriots and between Turkish Cypriots and Greek Cypriots. But when his dead body was stolen from his grave, it was transformed into a different kind of discursive site. By *discursive site,* I mean a place where discourse takes place; among several kinds of discourse in question here is the one surrounding conspiracy theories about the theft of Papadopoulos's remains published in the Cypriot press in the months afterward, which I analyze in Part 2. In this Interlude, I aim to show why this discourse about conspiracy theories of the theft cannot be analyzed without recourse to the body itself. What *the body itself* might be is the enigma that I think contributors to that discourse were trying to work out.

A Cypriot friend of mine, who is also an incisive cultural critic, told me once that she thought the theft had been a publicity stunt, an attempt to "deify" Tassos (she used the word in English): *He wanted to be the next Makarios!* This was a reference to Archbishop Makarios, the first president of Cyprus, who served from 1960 to 1977, surviving the coup in 1974 and four assassination attempts before succumbing to a heart attack. As archbishop, he wore his clerical vestments in the conduct of all his presidential duties, standing as the very embodiment of intimacy between the Orthodox Church and the political regime in the new independent Republic. When I first encountered images of Makarios, all I could see were those vestments: thick, heavy black folds of fabric, forming an image of his body while shrouding the body itself. Even his head was largely concealed in the patriarchal headdress (κουκούλιον) that he donned in place of the ceremonial miter (μίτρα) when circulating among the people, which permitted only his face to show through. This costume seemed to me then (and still seems) a stark announcement of the church's presence at the center of power in the Republic—*the republic of priests led by Makarios,* as another Cypriot friend once described it to me—which was imagined into existence starting in the 1950s with the Greek-Cypriot armed nationalist movement against the British colonial state. How could the Republic of Cyprus be understood as a secular democratic state under Archbishop Makarios? How could Turkish Cypriots, as (mostly, at least nominally) Muslims, ever have felt represented in such a figure? Were those vestments even visible to those whose leader he was?

Tassos Papadopoulos did not wear clerical vestments. He was not a religious personage, even if, as my friend suggested, his supporters may have desired his deification. But as I show in Part 2, he worked in intimate association with Makarios throughout the latter's three terms in office; the assumption of the presidency by Papadopoulos in 2003 was understood by many Cypriots as a perpetuation of Makarios's policies and a tending of his legacy. During his own presidency, Papadopoulos partook of the sacredness immanent in the office, in the sense Katherine Verdery is after, I think, when she asserts, "authority always has a 'sacred' component" (Verdery 1999, 37)—even ostensibly secular authority, as in the transitional postsocialist states in eastern Europe that Verdery examines. For all that, however, Papadopoulos's body—unlike the body of Makarios, whose hands were kissed in reverence by citizens bowing or kneeling before him—was not overtly represented as sacred until his remains were stolen: a crime that, in the words of his daughter, Anastasia, "offends and provokes our religion and culture" (Papadopoulou 2009).

At that moment, I submit, the president's body was put "in a state of desecration," as Michael Taussig frames a variety of material symbols of nation when they are "defaced" (Taussig 1999, 1). For Taussig, the state of desecration is not equivalent to sacredness, but it is "the closest many of us are going to get to the sacred in this modern world" (1). On his telling, desecration wreaks "the wound of sacrilege," from which "emanates" a "strange" "something" with "mysterious force" (1). This force cannot, Taussig observes, be "confront[ed] head-on," because we register it only in reaction to the act of desecration—a reaction that may, if we are paying attention, shock us into awareness that we have been complicit all along with what he calls the "violence of daily life" (2). By this I think he means the everyday violence of sovereignty: what it costs *the people*, and some people especially, to invest the authority of the sacred in the state and thus to authorize, as sacred, the most routine and the most extreme operations of state power.

Following Taussig for the moment (I qualify this approach later), I want to try to work out the intuition nurtured in me by his text that the theft of Tassos's remains—this desecration of the president's body—instigated an eruption of discourse about state power in Cyprus that revealed something important about state power in Cyprus without making that something known in the terms of that discourse. Taussig says that defacement

> works on objects the way jokes work on language, bringing out their inherent magic nowhere more so than when those objects have become routinized and social, like money or the nation's flag in secular societies

where God has long been put in his place. Defacement of such social things, however, brings a very angry God out of hiding. (5)

Taussig is careful to seed doubt as to whether that angry God was really there all along, hiding beneath the apparent surfaces of the social (8). In the discourse on the president's body that I study in Part 2, it was the position taken by those who denounced the crime as a sacrilege perpetrated against the entire Cypriot nation that God really had been there all along, in (or as) the state; those who denounced the denouncers took the position that God had been made to *seem* to be there as a pretext for those in power to legitimate their power. Perhaps it is needless to say that this argument is not resolvable. It is the play between the two positions—the continuous play of essence and appearance—that Taussig theorizes under the rubric of public secrecy: the very fabric of social relations and state-religious authority, shot through with relentless suspicions among the people about a secret center of power, beyond or above them, the "active not-knowing" of which makes knowledge of it a modality of power (7). Taussig suggests in the opening pages of *Defacement* that putting an end to this play—a mysterious proposition that he does not venture to elaborate—would open up a nothingness, an "empty space" devoid of distinctions (1, 8), that we can only sense and insinuate from within modern discourses of knowledge.

When the remains of Tassos Papadopoulos were stolen from his grave, I said earlier, his body was put in a state of desecration. I have wondered, though, while reading all those theories and countertheories and metatheories of the event in Cypriot newspapers, what state the remains were in at the time they were missing: how much of a body, and what kind of body, did they "presence"?[5] Were they dry bones, still-decomposing flesh, or something else? In Greek Orthodox practice, to my knowledge, bodies are usually buried in a cloth shroud inside a plain pine coffin; assuming Papadopoulos's burial shroud had not lost its integrity at the time of the theft, it is possible the perpetrators did not touch directly or even see his remains. This question was material to the criminal investigation—specifically, to ascertaining whether any forensic evidence could be found at the scene that could support a theory as to how the perpetrators were able to transport and hide the remains. But nowhere in the press coverage of the investigation into their whereabouts, and their eventual discovery and redeposition, could I find any description of the remains themselves or even speculation about what they looked, felt, or smelled like. Surely some people knew, and others wanted to know; that desire is part of the horror.[6] Yet the material state of these remains, a year and more after the president's death, was apparently *unspeakable* in Cypriot public discourse. Instead, I suggest, it was expressed in reactions to the event in affective terms: shock, disgust, horror.

If defacement was enacted through the theft and disappearance of Papadopoulos's body, then it was his body *in its defacement*, as a missing body, that became a discursive site—not the material remains themselves, wherever they were located at the time (unknown), and whatever material shape they were in (also unknown). The remains themselves were, I have suggested, unspeakable: the very antithesis of a discursive site. Affective expressions of shock, disgust, and horror recorded in the pages of Cypriot newspapers, and "echoed" in the account given by Anastasia Papadopoulou, surely indicated the remains, but did not symbolize them as desecrated. Contestation over the symbolic meaning of the missing body was what took place in the discourse on conspiracy theory that arose at the same time. It is crucial to the argument I am making in this Interlude to observe the distinction and the intricate entanglement between that discourse on conspiracy theory through which the president's missing body acquired symbolic meaning—which I examine closely in Part 2—and the affective discourse on the unspeakable remains I am exploring here, indicated but not symbolized by expressions of shock, disgust, and horror. This discursive entanglement worked to redouble the already double status of the president's body as something symbolic and material, collective and singular, sacred and profane. Later in this Interlude, I dwell at length on this redoubling, as Papadopoulos's body was by no means the first or most prominent body of a political leader to experience such redoubling after death, and his case therefore carries rich potential for comparative, cross-contextual thinking of the kind I am pursuing in this book.

The unspeakability of Papadopoulos's remains helps explain the affective intensity of public reaction to the theft, while the unknowability of his missing body helps to account for why conspiracy theory surfaced as a metadiscourse at the same time. Conspiracy theories about the theft of Papadopoulos's body circulated in public talk as long as the remains were missing. Once they were found, however, on March 11, 2011, a re-sacralization took place. A funeral procession and reburial of the remains in Papadopoulos's tomb was attended by family members, politicians, supporters, and media representatives, who recorded the event for public viewing; priests gave the funeral liturgy and led the gathered crowd in singing hymns at Papadopoulos's gravesite. This event was a re-sacralization in the sense that the material remains were ritually placed at the discursive site of the missing body, uniting the doubles. "Our dear father can finally find peace," his son, Nikolas, told reporters[7]—even if this ritual was not, as I show later, entirely effective: even if doubts lingered and conspiracy theories continued to haunt Papadopoulos's legacy; even if some remembered the whole story in retrospect as absurd rather than horrific.

Part of my analytic strategy in this Interlude is to extricate (partially and temporarily) the affective discourse on the president's remains from the symbolic discourse on his missing body. My aspiration here is to pick out a path around conspiracy theories about that body in order to focus on *the body itself* as a predicate of sovereignty, insofar as it summoned a collective into shared affect that anticipated and helped to fix symbolic meaning, at least for some. Ahmed is, again, helpful here. On her account, the "fetish quality" of a disgusting event or object—such as the theft of the president's body, or the remains themselves—depends on the performativity of disgust as a speech act: an expression that produces what it names (Ahmed 2015, 94, 96; 92). She shows how an object of disgust, borne of such an expression, becomes "sticky" and makes other objects and signs sticky through a "transference of affect" when it comes into contact or association with them (94, 91). In thus framing the expression of disgust as a speech act, Ahmed highlights its social nature and implications. The "demand for a witness" carried by such an expression, she argues,

> generates a community of those who are bound together through the shared condemnation of a disgusting object or event. . . . The sharing of the physical process of both casting out and pulling away means that disgust works to align the individual with the collective, at the very moment both are generated. (94, 95)

Examining the online circulation of images and videos of the collapse of the Twin Towers on 9/11, Ahmed observes the performativity of disgust in a media space that did not require the physical co-presence of viewers for their "shared witnessing" to take place. One of its effects, she concludes, was "shared rage or anger *about the ingestion of the disgusting* (about the ways in which it saturates one's life, minute by minute)" (96, emphasis original). Sticky disgust in this case stuck to the "bodies of others" that were already sticky, already understood in the US context as fearsome and unwanted: the bodies of the perpetrators were, thus, "Middle Eastern," objects of shared disgust that soon became "the cause of our disgust" needing to be expelled (97, 98). This is what Ahmed means, I gather, by the "historicity" of sticky signs (93); this is a way of understanding their iterativity not through the conventionality of their signification—that is, their symbolic meaning—but rather through their accumulation of affective attachments over time, a process of *adherence* in which affects ramify and affect other objects, signs, and bodies, sometimes binding them in hard knots of association with mortal stakes.

It might even be the case that the performativity of disgust in the "shared witnessing" of 9/11 was part of the historical process of adherence that prepared Cypriot publics to register shock, disgust, and horror when the theft of Papadopoulos's body was revealed. That "witnessing" was surely "shared" well beyond US publics; who shares in witnessing—who is "aligned with the collective" in the historical process of affective adherence—is one of the questions Ahmed is opening around sticky signs. In Part 2.2, I discuss an op-ed published a few days after the theft by a conservative writer in the south, Michalis Papadopoulos (no relation to Tassos, as far as I am aware), who compared the theft of the president's body to the events of September 11 in terms of how they riveted and paralyzed Cypriots in front of their televisions, overcome by shock and unable to believe what they were seeing. Michalis Papadopoulos warned his readers,

> In the midst of anxious confusion anchored in violent feelings, it is necessary that thought remain sober, that it not hasten to be written down on paper, that it not get swept away in fiery speeches, that it be kept at a distance, until we can take the necessary step back from the mist surrounding the events and recall the freedom of calm. So that suspicions become clues, so that the game of fantasies can be grounded in tangible things. For now, all that exists is an empty grave. (Papadopoulos 2009, 2)

The distinction between affective and symbolic registers of public discourse could not be clearer. The author observed a distinction between the "violent feelings" provoked by the crime and whatever might too hastily be "written down on paper" about it or expressed in "fiery speeches"; affect was a "confusion" here, while thought was a choice that must be made soberly. He reminded readers that, in actuality, they were confronted only with an absence, an "empty grave," implying they should not rush to theorize the meaning of the missing body. The president's remains—the object of his readers' "violent feelings"—were absent not only from his tomb but also from the author's commentary.

Ahmed indicates that the historical process of adherence may be arrested or peter out rather than yielding *coherence* in the form of a durable consensus on the meaning of the event, object, or body in question (Ahmed 2015, 98). It is possible, I think, to discern just such a failure of coherence in the dynamics of theorizing and countertheorizing in Cypriot newspapers during the months following the theft of the president's body. This discourse on the meaning of that missing body emerged from and addressed not one community but several, in a Cypriot society fundamentally riven by partisan and ethnonational division; the status of the president's body as desecrated thus emerged as a matter of contestation among multiple reading publics. The affective speech acts of shock, disgust, and horror that animated and propelled this contestation in public media turned on the symbolic meaning of the theft as a desecration for some but not others. What they all shared in common, as I show in Part 2, was their attunement to conspiracy.

The question of desecration—more specifically, for whom the theft marked a desecration—was thematized explicitly in a charged op-ed published on December 20, 2009, a bit over a week after the theft, by the left-leaning Greek-language paper *Politis*. Adopting what I read as a tone of high sarcasm, the author, Loukas Charalambous, denounced the many right-wing politicians who had jumped at the chance to use the scandal to their advantage:

> The macabre act of stealing the remains of former President Papadopoulos from his grave has given our politicians the opportunity to show their weakness once again. . . . All the representatives of the rejectionist front[8] went ahead and decided that the crime was perpetrated by those who supposedly wish to impose an unacceptable solution to the Cyprus Problem. Worst of all was Lillikas,[9] who divined that the actors "wanted to send a message: they disappeared the symbol who embodied the resistance of Cypriot Hellenism to catastrophic plans." *Sigma* television

decided to lay blame for the act on "MIT agents." Most of Papadopoulos's political friends directed their moronic assessments toward Turkish Cypriots, declaring that "this practice could not have come from Greek Cypriots." They thought it was a good opportunity to stir up hatred against the Turkish-Cypriot community so that a solution would be even more difficult. To some extent they have been successful. . . . My question is how these people didn't think to say that the unfortunate Papadopoulos was not stolen from his tomb but was resurrected from the dead, like Jesus. Such an event would irresistibly lift our spirits to the sky and elevate our "Greek dignity," so that we can vote again for partition. (L. Charalambous 2009)

The author of this op-ed plainly mocked the notion he attributed to his adversaries that Papadopoulos was the symbolic embodiment of Cypriot Hellenism. The motif of the president's death and resurrection on the paradigm of Christ that Charalambous wielded sarcastically in this piece ran through the Greek-language press coverage of the theft, expressing a political theology combining elements of Hellenism and Orthodox Christianity and proposing the continuity, immortality, and transcendence of the Greek ethno-nation in Cyprus. Similarly, in reading the Greek-language press, I noted the prevalence of religious terminology to describe the crime, as in the headline from *Philelevtheros* reprinted at the opening of this Interlude. Terms such as desecration (βεβήλωση), sacrilege (ιεροσυλία), and despoilment (σύληση)—as in grave-robbing or the looting of holy relics—featured much more frequently than vandalism (βανδαλισμός), for example, a term used in the press coverage of damage done to other graves in Cyprus around the same time.[10] The president's body itself was most often referred to as relics or remains (λείψανα: specifically, the remains of saints), or as a corpse (σορός, which can also refer to a coffin or urn—that is, the vessel of a dead or cremated body—and even the body of an elderly person who is still alive), less often as remnants (απομεινάρια).[11] A lawyer connected to the case explained to me that the criminal charge of "insulting religion" brought against the three suspects was based in the legal conception of the burial ground as holy, since Papadopoulos's tomb was located in the graveyard of the Church of Agios Nikolaos in Deftera and thus on church property. According to Cypriot law, the body itself was not sacred, but like all dead human bodies according to international law, it had dignity that could be violated.[12]

It is the framing of that dignity as "Greek" in public discourse, venturing an equation between the president's body and the body of the ethnonation, that indicates the political theology at play in this case. In this case, the *Greekness* (as against the Cypriotness) of the sovereign's body and its dignity supported the ethnonationalist claim to sovereignty on the part of right-wing Greek Cypriots—a claim that required the concealment, forgetting, or erasure of Turkish Cypriots, along with other Cypriots who had no Greek ancestry or affiliation. In this case, then, it is not difficult to understand why the sacredness of Papadopoulos's body was at stake for many Greek Cypriots in the theft of his remains. Indeed, the theft of his body as *sacrilege* recalled the sanctity of the body of Archbishop Makarios, Cyprus's first president—Papadopoulos's predecessor and patron, who was known as the ethnarch (Εθνάρχης) of Cyprus at a time when Cyprus was experienced by ethnonationalist Greek Cypriots as a dismembered part of Greece that might yet be reincorporated. What happened to Makarios's body after his death thus offers some context for what happened to Papadopoulos's body after *his* death, by way of preparing Cypriots to register a deep connection between the two presidents in the same historical process of adherence, in Ahmed's term. This connection was expressed not only in widespread images of Papadopoulos reverently kissing Makarios's hand in life and in death, but also in shared affects of shock, disgust, and horror on the part of many Cypriots at what happened to both presidents' bodies, as well as their shared attunement to conspiracy in theorizing why it happened.

On April 3, 1977, Makarios was treated by his personal physician after suffering a heart attack. Exactly four months later, on August 3, he had three more heart attacks in quick succession and died. According to an account given by Panos Stavrinos, pathologist at the General Hospital of Nicosia at the time, Stavrinos performed an autopsy, but not at the hospital, as some people in Makarios's inner circle did not want his body taken to the morgue. The autopsy was performed instead where Makarios lay in his bed in the archdiocese. Stavrinos removed the heart, studied and weighed it, finding signs of hypertrophy consistent with heart disease; due to the irregularity of the procedure, he explained later, no official autopsy report was produced. Miltiades Christodoulou, then the government spokesman, instructed Stavrinos to transport Makarios's heart personally to London, where a pathologist confirmed Stavrinos's findings. Stavrinos embalmed the heart, took it back to Cyprus, and "handed it over for safekeeping to the Archdiocese" (Polydorou 2017).[13]

In the months following his death, a photograph of Makarios's embalmed heart preserved in a glass jar was published under the headline "The Ravaged Heart of Makarios" in a Cypriot newspaper and in a pamphlet that circulated in schools. Rumors that Makarios had been assassinated by poison floated in the press for months afterward, buoyed by talk of an unreleased medical report from London finding elevated levels of arsenic and lead in Makarios's heart tissue (*Reporter* 2019),[14] by the absence of an official autopsy report issued by the archbishop's physician, and by the fact that Makarios had already survived four assassination attempts by the time he died.

Makarios—dubbed the Great Martyr (Ο Μεγαλομάρτυρας) in press coverage following his death (*Reporter* 2019, quoting *Apoyevmatini* 1977)—was succeeded by Archbishop Chrysostomos I, who kept the jar containing Makarios's heart in his private chambers. At some point after Chrysostomos I died in 2006, his successor, Archbishop Chrysostomos II, apparently discovered the jar in those chambers, and in 2010 he ordered that it be buried along with Makarios's other remains in his tomb at the Throne of the Virgin Mary near Kykkos Monastery, thereby restoring the integrity of Great Martyr's body—a condition of resurrection on the last day, the second coming of Christ. The story of Makarios's "unburied heart" has been published in one Cypriot newspaper or another on August 3, the anniversary of his death, every year since it was finally buried in 2010.

The symbolic equation between the ethno-nation and the body of the sovereign is not particular to Cyprus, of course, even if that equation required special political-theological work to be done in a roundabout itinerary between Greece and Cyprus on the part of an ethnarch who was also a saint and a martyr. Katherine Verdery famously has written about the legitimation of political authority and national sovereignty in post-Soviet republics through the exhumation and reburial of political and religious leaders, along with those she calls "the nameless dead": combatants in long-ago wars, some preceding the Soviet period (Verdery 1999, 20, 97, passim). One of the common rules of "proper burial," as she puts it, "not just in Eastern Europe but elsewhere as well," is that *"our 'sons' must be buried in 'our' soil*, lest we be plagued by misfortune arising from the soul's continued distress" (47). Conversely, reburying the national war dead in "our soil" is a way of sacralizing and laying a definitive national claim to the land. In these burial practices, Verdery discerns a symbolic association of soil with blood in postsocialist nationalism; thus, the named *and* the nameless dead, being reburied in newly national terrain, were employed in rewriting history, scripting a new story of national triumph, sovereignty, and repletion out of the ruins of empire.

More recently, Francisco Ferrándiz has studied the controversial exhumation of Francisco Franco from a crypt in the Valley of the Fallen outside Madrid, in 2019. In this case, he shows, resurrection theology was central to Franco's decades-long nationalist project of memorializing the Spanish Civil War as a "sacred crusade" (Ferrándiz 2022, 210, 211, 213). Starting in 1959, this project entailed the exhumation of loyalist "martyrs" (210) from mass graves across the country and their reburial in the Valley of the Fallen—a massive pantheon with a basilica, constructed in close proximity to the sixteenth-century Monastery El Escorial. Here, too, was reburied the twice-exhumed body of José Antonio Primo de Rivera, the founder of the Fascist Party in Spain, along with Franco himself after his death in 1975. Ferrándiz worked on the expert commission convened in 2011 to determine the fate of Franco's body and tomb (215), which ultimately proposed the removal of the bodies of Primo and Franco from their tombs in the Valley of the Fallen and their reburial in private cemeteries. People on the extreme right—Franco's family and groups such as the Francisco Franco National Foundation and the Association for the Defense of the Valley—"denounced" the proposal as an attempt to "desecrate the corpse of a head of state" (231). But for the commission, the socialist government, and many on the left, Ferrándiz writes, the proposal was a crucial first step toward the comprehensive resymbolization of the Civil War and the bodies of all the war dead, which had been identified until then in factionist terms—Republican or Nationalist—that preserved the divisions of the war throughout the entire period of Franco's dictatorship.

The body of Tassos Papadopoulos, too, was symbolically entangled with the bodies of the war dead. I have in mind those nearly two thousand Cypriots who went missing during the violence of the 1960s and 1970s, culminating in the war and the division of Cyprus during the summer of 1974. In 2011–2012, I worked with the Committee on Missing Persons in Cyprus, a bi-communal Greek-Cypriot/Turkish-Cypriot agency established under UN auspices, whose forensic teams at the time of this writing are still locating and identifying the bodies of the missing. I followed and participated in the process by which their remains were located and identified, publicized, recognized and sometimes misrecognized, and ritually sanctified through reburial (Davis 2017a; 2017b; 2023). These investigations prepared me to see what was at stake in the desecration of the body of Tassos Papadopoulos, and to understand how this crime could appear to some Greek Cypriots—reflexively and falsely—as violence perpetrated by Turkish Cypriots or Turkish nationals.

In Part 2.3, I show how the fate of both kinds of bodies in Cyprus has been storied in conspiracy theories, and how the stories themselves are recursively intertwined and mutually implicated.[15] I take these stories as evidence of a Cypriot context of conspiracy attunement, which can help establish grounds of comparison between this context and others. Here, in this Interlude, I thematize comparison itself in my analysis of the president's dead body: its political-theological status and its discursive efficacy in both affective and symbolic terms. In what follows, then, I explore other cases in which the dead bodies of political leaders have been exhumed, handled, moved, studied, represented, debated—in other words, transformed into discursive sites—through a process of doubling.

Nearly every piece of scholarly writing I have read on the dead bodies of political leaders takes as a point of departure the celebrated work of historian Ernst Kantorowicz, *The King's Two Bodies: A Study in Medieval Political Theology*, first published in 1957 but composed mostly during the 1930s, when Kantorowicz, a Jew, was living out his last years in Nazi Germany before fleeing to the United States.[16] In this immense volume, Kantorowicz explores the innovations in legal thought, theology, political theory, burial practices, and works of theatre and literature—especially in Tudor England, but also before and beyond—through which the notion was invented and popularized that a sovereign installed by divine right had two bodies: a mortal body that would come to a natural end, and a mystical body, the body politic, that was immaterial, immortal, and eternal. In the language of Edmund Plowden's *Reports* (c. 1571), composed during the reign of Elizabeth I, where Kantorowicz begins, this twinning of the king's body made it possible for the body politic to be understood by jurists and policymakers as continuous over time and present everywhere that sovereign authority obtained; it was, Plowden wrote, "a Body that cannot be seen or handled, consisting of Policy and Government" (Kantorowicz [1957] 2016, 7). Kantorowicz likens this notion of the king's mystical body to other medieval theological and legal concepts such as the king's *character angelicus*, which was considered "Immutable within Time," like the angels; as well as the *persona mixta*, used by one fifteenth-century Italian legal scholar to characterize the dominance of one sex over another within the body of a "hermaphrodite," just as the king's body politic would predominate over his natural body in a "unit indivisible" (8, 10, 9). The king's mystical body also spoke to Kantorowicz of "the blending of spiritual and secular powers" in the dual status of medieval bishops, a conception developed earlier in the Christological "'twinned' being," the *gemina persona* of "Christ-centered kingship" (43, 49ff). According to the judgment rendered in an English court case dated 1561, the unity of the king's two bodies would be divided upon the death (more precisely, the "Demise") of the sovereign, and the body politic would be "transferred and conveyed" to another body natural—hence the slogan, "The King is dead! Long live the King!" Kantorowicz is quick to observe that this understanding of the body politic as the king's mystical body is clearly founded in the medieval theology of the soul and its "migration," though not equivalent, given that (among other features) the mystical body rendered the sovereign as such immortal (13). Through hundreds of pages, he traces the many proliferating figures of this mystical body—the Name,[17] the Dignitas,[18] the Crown, the Phoenix, and more—which were all, in one way or another, designed to resolve symbolically the fundamental paradox of sovereignty as public and corporate in nature, a representation of the people, while also being private and singular in its embodiment in the king.

Most relevant to the questions I am pursuing here, Kantorowicz offers remarkable and detailed commentary on the material symbolism of the king's two bodies in the context of death rites first documented at the funeral of Edward II in 1327, but practiced well into the eighteenth century in England and France.[19] He describes a number of funerals and tombs, from the fourteenth century onward, in which an effigy of the dead sovereign would be displayed, crafted from wood or leather and covered with wax or plaster, dressed in royal regalia and wearing or holding the symbolic instruments of sovereignty: the insignia, the crown, the scepter, the orb. In some cases, the effigy was displayed on top of the coffin that held the sovereign's corpse, but later rituals separated the effigy from the corpse altogether and displayed them in different places or at different times. Kantorowicz suggests that this separation addressed a contradiction created by the attendance of a funeral by the dead sovereign's successor, since the new sovereign, a mortal but living human already embodying the immortal body politic, could not be co-present with the effigy, which also embodied the immortality of the king's mystical body. "There was no other solution," Kantorowicz concludes, "except staying away" from the effigy while attending the corpse during funeral rites (428–29).

Kantorowicz reads the use of effigies—made not only of sovereigns but also of other *persona mixta*, such as bishops—as a materialization of the dichotomy between the king's two bodies; the corpse and the effigy both took material form. This practice effected, he suggests, a complex reversal of the symbolization of the two bodies during the sovereign's life: the normally invisible mystical body was made visible in the effigy, while the normally visible natural body was secreted inside a sealed coffin. In this way, the effigy became a *persona ficta* symbolically representing another *persona ficta*, the Dignitas (421). People who attended the funeral of a sovereign mourned the corpse but celebrated the Dignitas, sometimes parading the effigy triumphantly during the funeral procession. Some tombs, likewise, were constructed in two parts, with a sculptural representation of the "naked" and "pitiful corpse" below, or the burial of the corpse underground, with a sculptural representation of the living person above, dressed in full regalia, reclining as if resting with his eyes open (434). Thus, Kantorowicz observes,

> the decrepit and decaying body natural in the tomb, now separated from the awe-inspiring body politic above it, appears like an illustration of the doctrine expounded over and over again by medieval jurists: *Tenens dignitatem est corruptibilis,* DIGNITAS *tamen semper est, non moritur*—"The incumbent of a Dignity may decay, the Dignity itself is nonetheless forever; it does not die." (435–36)

These "imaginative fictions," worked out by medieval jurists to ensure the continuity of sovereignty after the death of the sovereign, were also, Kantorowicz suggests, means of contending with "feelings" about death that were culturally pervasive in fifteenth-century Europe, following the Black Death, the Great Famine, and continual bloody wars of conquest. The form given to these feelings that is best known to modern audiences is the danse macabre: an allegorical representation of the ephemerality and vanity of human life on earth featuring jolly corpses and skeletons dancing with death (436). Yet legitimating the governance of humans on earth—not elevating and glorifying the afterlife, as these allegorical images did—remained the primary task of these jurists, who had thus to make the most of the very mortal humans who successively occupied the throne. Kantorowicz concludes,

> Since life becomes transparent only against the background of death, and death against the background of life, the bone-rattling vitality of the late Middle Ages appears not devoid of some deeper wisdom. What one did was to build up a philosophy according to which a fictitious immortality became transparent through a real mortal man as its temporary incarnation, while mortal man became transparent through that new fictitious immortality which, being man-made as any immortality always is, was neither that of life eternal in another world nor that of the godhead, but that of a very terrestrial political institution. (437)

Kantorowicz thus frames the immanence of sovereignty in the body of the king as a "man-made" fiction of immortality that facilitated the dynastic succession of monarchs, and thereby the corporate integrity and continuity of medieval polities whose institution of kingship was increasingly independent from the church and the papacy. He traces an only apparently paradoxical double movement in political theology in the late Middle Ages, when the "new territorial and quasi-national state" was growing more "ecclesiastical" in its theories of legitimation, at the same time as the church was growing more "sociological" and "juristic," incorporating Christian society as such into its "mystical corporation" (207, 196, 201). The story Kantorowicz tells, then, across several centuries, is not of a straightforward shift in symbolic authority from the church to the state. What he shows instead is porosity and "borrowings" between these "orbits" of power in their conceptions of corporate authority, a "mutual influence" and dependence that continued into the early modern period (193).

Throughout his wide-ranging commentary, Kantorowicz emphasizes the "fiction" represented by the king's two bodies, pointing out (often with apparent delight) its many contradictions, its "follies" and outright absurdities, and the "havoc" it wreaked in medieval and early modern governance in Europe (18, 23; 3). But Eric Santner, in *The Royal Remains: The People's Two Bodies and the Endgames of Sovereignty* (2011), takes the king's two bodies deadly seriously, framing this political theory as a collective fantasy that worked to secure sovereign power in European kingdoms and showing what became of that fantasy when monarchical sovereignty in Europe ended, violently, in democratic revolution. In unraveling the political theology tying Kantorowicz's postulate of the king's two bodies to the persistence of sovereign violence in modern democratic states, Santner dwells insistently on the problem of legitimacy in the body politic. By *legitimacy*, he has more in mind than the consent of the governed; it is rather an existential matter of what Claude Lefort calls "the symbolic dimension of the political," which is to say,

> the dimension or element in which politics touches on the intelligibility of the social world more generally, on one's sense of the coherence, continuity, and vibrancy of a form of life into which one is inscribed and from which one derives one's most basic sense of orientation in the world.... What is at issue here is the authoritative grip of "how things are done" as well as one's own sense of *existential legitimacy*: that one has a place in the world that entitles one to enjoy a modicum of recognition of one's words and actions. (Santner 2011, 3 [emphasis original], citing Lefort 1988, 215)

In Santner's theory of political theology, this "existential legitimacy" sought by subjects is secured by the legitimacy of sovereign power, whether sovereignty is invested in a king or the people themselves. The very possibility of living and belonging in a social world is thus implied in the symbolic means by which people are governed as members of a political collective. Their existential legitimacy is anchored in corporeality—not (or not only) the bodies of the people animated by biological life, but something more: what Santner calls *the flesh*, "the locus" of a "surplus of immanence" (xxi, 61). This surplus of immanence does not rest easy in this flesh, however; it agitates and disturbs, driving people to invest themselves (libidinally, he explains at length) in the political collective—or, in his phrase, emphasizing its corporeality, the "political collective *as a body politic*" (Santner 2011, 37 [emphasis added]). In royal sovereignty, it was the king's body that materialized this "sublime substance," but with the emergence of popular sovereignty and the transfer of "symbolic authority" from the king to the people, the flesh—the "sacral soma" of the king, who embodied a "'vertical link' to a locus of transcendence—divine authorization"—was "dispersed 'horizontally' among the 'people,'" the "new bearers of the principle of sovereignty" (ix, xii, xxi; 61). For Santner, what remains of royal sovereignty in modern democratic states is this flesh, the immanent "soul-substance" where life and law are joined in the bodies of citizens, rendering them subject to biopower but as more than "bare life in the sense of animal existence" (27, 61).

What more? Here, Santner follows Foucault in delineating the relationship between the body of the sovereign and the bodies of the people during the complex, indeterminate historical transition from sovereign power to biopower in modernity. Foucault extrapolates from Kantorowicz's account of the king's two bodies a "symmetrical, inverted figure of the king" (Foucault [1975] 1977, 29): namely, the body of a person condemned by the king to death, a public and baroquely violent death like that of Robert-François Damiens, "the regicide," to whose description Foucault devotes the famous first pages of *Discipline and Punish*. In shifting from this scene of sovereign power to the terrain of the modern prison, Foucault tracks the movement of that "surplus power possessed by the king" that "g[ave] rise to the duplication of his body," now channeled into "another duplication": the doubling of the subject's body by the soul, that "prison of the body" created through penal techniques of "punishment, supervision, and constraint" (29, 30, 29).

Santner nominates *the flesh* as the site where that same "surplus" is rechanneled and reconfigured in modernity.[20] In royal sovereignty, he explains, the principle of the king's two bodies elevated the king's mystical body above his mortal body to contain the surplus; in modern democratic states, on the other hand, this surplus became a supplement to the bodies of citizens, who therefore exist as themselves and more than themselves at the same time. Reading Esposito, Arendt, and Agamben, Santner identifies this "surplus immanence" of the flesh with race in Nazi ideology (28ff.), exposed as genocidal by the Holocaust; and with national identity, exposed as an exclusionary and arbitrary privilege by the fate of "stateless people" after World War II (51ff.). In both forms, Santner reads the flesh as the "charismatic dimension of extralegality" that functions as the "'matter' of general equivalence" among the people (52): in other words, the symbolic substance shared by the people, and thus a criterion of collective belonging and recognition, logically prior to the legitimation of state power and unjustifiable by state law.[21] People who "enjoy the entitlements of citizenship," Santner argues, are at the same time "radically and intimately exposed to . . . lawless arbitrariness" (54), since the universality of law—the universal rights of man that first gave a legal form to popular sovereignty—is contradicted by its particularization in state law.

In his best-known writings, Giorgio Agamben ([1995] 1998) via Hannah Arendt elaborated *the state of exception* as the topos of this contradiction: the sovereign decision to suspend the protections of law for someone or many, on grounds that can only be arbitrary in the light of universal rights. The surplus immanence by which Santner identifies citizens as more than themselves—the flesh that connects them, and equates them as members of a body politic—cannot be accommodated by the symbolic order, as Santner frames law in Lacanian terms. The partiality and arbitrariness of nation cannot be represented in a national constitution or bill of rights; nation is instead represented as universal and legitimate, given by divine or natural law. That which disrupts this symbolic order—the Lacanian real, for Santner, which I read as difference and singularity in this context—takes determinate social form in the paradox of national borders, which, due to their extralegality, have to be legitimated politically and protected continually in order that, as Santner puts it, the "flesh of the social bond" may find "representational corporeality" in the "national community" (50). For him, what is at stake in this continual legitimation and protection is the "continuity" of the polity, its "endurance and flourishing" over time as a body politic (41, 34)—and, by implication, the existential legitimacy enjoyed by citizens of a nation-state.

What Foucault narrates as historically contingent and ever-shifting arrangements of power in and through the body—discipline in the context of secular democracy during the long nineteenth century in western Europe and the United States, for example—Santner develops as a general theory of sovereignty that matches, at the level of the collective, universal symbolic processes at the level of the individual psyche. In other words, Santner shows how individuals are suited to the body politic in which they find what Lefort calls "existential legitimacy": nationalism works! Modernity for Santner is not, then, a set of historically contingent arrangements, but rather a historical threshold marking the radical rupture of an old symbolic order and the emergence of a new one. With this conception of modernity as rupture, Santner's theory of sovereignty offers no resources for considering how mis-fit at the level of the collective might occur within modern nation-states—how nationalism might stop working—even if anomalous cases of individual mis-fit, such as Schreber's, lay bare the paradoxes of state power that fantasies of nation constantly work to cover up. And, though he writes about democratic nation-states in the twentieth century, Santner has little god, whether it was a political or rather a ritual institution, and—most directly in line with Graeber's interest—how divine kings came to stand outside society, transcending its laws and norms and thus defining *the people* as such through the enactment of "arbitrary violence," as only gods can do (4–5, 7; 10; 8).

Graeber argues that it was largely through the reinterpretation of Seligman's case study by Evans-Pritchard that the Shilluk institution of divine kingship came to be understood in terms of Kantorowicz's postulate of the king's two bodies. Especially striking as a point of comparison between the Shilluk institution and the medieval to early modern English one examined by Kantorowicz was the Shilluks' use of a wooden effigy to impersonate a king who had died, as in the funeral of Edward II in 1327, on Kantorowicz's account ([1957] 2016, 419–37).[23] The Shilluk effigy, Graeber explains, would serve as an interregnum until an aspirant to the throne defeated it in mock combat and was ritually installed as king through a transformation of his own body into a fetish. The capacity of the king's body to represent the Shilluk people was thus not given; it was *made* by the violence enacted by each new king to initiate the process of his installation. In line with Kantorowicz, Graeber observes, Shilluk effigies have been taken by anthropologists to represent "the eternity of the royal office, as opposed to the ephemeral nature of any particular human embodiment" (Graeber 2011, 23). The key to this interpretation is the role played in Shilluk cosmology by the founder of Shilluk society: Nyikang, the originary king, who "did not and could not ever die" and "remains immanent in his effigies and [in] the [liv]ed person of the king" (24; see also 3). Thus, each wooden effigy and [n]ew king together represent a division first enacted within the body of [Nyikan]g, who was both "eternal, universal 'kingship'" and "the particular, [liv]ing" (39).

[It is te]mpting, with all this ethnographic evidence, to elevate the postu[late of the ki]ng's two bodies to a general theory of sovereignty! Graeber em[braces this te]mptation and works rigorously to legitimate it. He carefully [sifts Shill]uk legends and practices, construing both a genealogy of [this hi]gh-stakes debate from discussions among anthropologists [... an]d meanings of the institutions of divine and sacred king[ship ... a] work of what he calls "comparative cosmologies" (13); he [offers "pro]positions" about divine kingship, sacred kingship, and [...] and concludes with "cross-cultural generalizations" that hold in all the societies he has addressed (48–49). By holding in all these societies, these generalizations authorize the comparisons Graeber has already made, which come to work, in the process of his argumentation, as examples or tokens of a widespread (not to say universal) political institution. It is a deft hermeneutic circle that Graeber draws with some ambiguity. In the last section of the article, he explains,

> I have framed my argument in cosmological terms because I believe one cannot understand political institutions without understanding the people that create them, what they believe the world to be like, how they imagine the human situation within it, and what they believe it is possible or legitimate to want from it. While every cosmology is in a sense unique, anyone coming at this material from a background in Judaism, Christianity, or Islam is unlikely to feel on entirely unfamiliar ground here ... though to some degree ... [these cosmologies] deal with issues that are universal. It would have to be so, or it would not be possible to make cross-cultural generalizations about "divine kingship," "scared kingship," or "scapegoats" to begin with. (48)

I have elided in this quotation from Graeber's text an intriguing but exhausting series of qualifications that he offers to gloss a history of debates over whether and with what implications (racism? universalism?) the similarities that anthropologists have observed between Nilotic and Semitic institutions of kingship should be explained by actual historical connections between these societies. As evident in the passage above, Graeber lands in equivocation; he observes that, even if such historical connections between Nilotic and Semitic societies can be successfully demonstrated, the cosmological thinking he associates with divine kingship in these societies deals "to some degree" with issues whose universality can also help to explain similarities in their ritual-political practices of kingship.

Graeber's reading of the ethnographic archive on divine kingship, explicitly starting from Frazer, evinces what Marilyn Strathern frames as a *historicist* mode of comparison. As I recounted in the Introduction, Strathern returns (critically) to the critique of historicist comparison on the grounds of its ethnocentrism that was made by generations of anthropologists after Frazer—a critique largely targeting the general theory of cultural evolution wielded by Frazer to motivate and make sense of his comparisons, which established a value scale of cultures with European civilization at the apex.

Graeber's approach thus appears a bit of a throwback (deliberate, no doubt) to those earlier anthropologists working in the historicist tradition, who sought to develop a general theory of divine kingship from the cross-contextual comparison of cultural features—even if his historicism is tempered by a relativist understanding of cultural context that Strathern associates with anti-Frazerian, modernist ethnography in the style of Malinowski. On her account, I recall here, Malinowski's comparative framework has *also* been understood as ethnocentric by later generations of anthropologists, due to the radical separation of self and other entailed by exploratory fieldwork forays into cultural contexts conceived by anthropologists as culturally whole and (thus) wholly different from their own—this difference being organized on an implicit value scale that, in retrospect, was found to resemble Frazer's evolutionary one to a great extent. Strathern compares these historicist and relativist modes of comparison by way of developing a more self-reflexive view of ethnocentrism as a positional venture on the part of anthropologists whose apprehension of the world is irreducibly plural—that is, composed of multiple cultural wholes, of which their own is implicitly one. Whether it is the *best* one on some universal scale of value is, in this line of thinking, a moral judgment additional to comparison rather than an essential attribute of comparison.

Graeber does not make such a judgment in his analysis of the Shilluk, and my reservations about his general theory of sovereignty have more to do with the incoherence of his comparative exercise than with his ethnocentrism in that moral sense. Determining whether and to what extent one society is like another through cross-cultural comparison, as Strathern shows, entails proposing the likeness of a cultural feature in both societies (e.g., divine kingship, for Graeber) that must be decontextualized in each case in order for their likeness to be construed. Construing their likeness permits an elaboration of the feature itself—this is what is meant by *general theory*—and a determination as to whether each society in question in fact "has" that feature. Yet the context that has thus been stripped away for the purposes of cross-cultural comparison recurs in the new questions borne of the comparison—Strathern calls them "remainders"—which are not contained in questions about cross-cultural likeness, but must be answered if culture is to be taken as explanatory *within* the contexts implicated in the comparison. I follow Strathern in proposing that legitimate grounds of cross-contextual comparison are found, instead, in the process of establishing contexts by generating and responding to remainders. Cross-contextual analysis undertaken this way can only be partial and will never yield an understanding of cultural wholes; conversely, comparing decontextualized cultural features (as Graeber does) can suggest connections between cultures, but cannot explain the features themselves.

My strategy in the rest of this Interlude is to develop, through juxtaposition, a series of comparisons that generate remainders: further questions whose answers help me to establish the contextual boundaries within which, and across which, I can examine the political-ritual status and discursive activity of Papadopoulos's dead body in Part 2 of this book. The key boundaries here are those that mark the "inside" and "outside" of conspiracy attunement, which I do not assume are national (Cypriot) or ethnonational (Greek/Greek-Cypriot or Turkish/Turkish-Cypriot), even if such boundaries inflect or intersect with them in some ways. It therefore matters a great deal that my earlier discussion of the theft of the president's remains as a defacement that creates sacredness—using the terms of Taussig's general theory, which I am now in a position to qualify—does not account for all the theorizing and countertheorizing published in Cypriot newspapers in the months afterward, as I noted earlier. Many pieces in the Greek-language press assumed a political motive for the crime; shared by the authors of these pieces was a perception of the crime as a desecration, that is, an act intentionally perpetrated as a transgression of the sacredness of the president's body, and thereby, the body politic. Other writers, especially in the Turkish-language press but also in the leftist Greek-language press, promoted a number of more worldly theories, such as ransom or mental illness, that placed financial motives, other personal interests, or personal idiosyncrasies at the heart of the crime—perhaps because, for these writers, the theft of Papadopoulos's remains was not already indelibly symbolized as a desecration of his body and the ethno-nation it represented. This discrepancy, as noted earlier, helps to account for why some readers found the theft shocking, disgusting, and horrifying, and others did not. As I hope to show in Part 2, the different reading publics addressed by these writers nevertheless *did* share, along with the writers, a context of conspiracy attunement, whose distinctive features can, I think, be discerned by way of its comparison with others.

What follows, then, in this last section of the Interlude is my reading of several cases in which the dead body of a political leader—somewhere, sometime—has become a discursive site. A general theory of political theology would suggest that, in each of these cases, the immutability of sovereignty was symbolically represented by the immortality of the sovereign; the treatment of the sovereign's corpse after his death would therefore serve as evidence of the efficacy and durability of that symbolic representation. Several authors of these case studies indeed follow that line of analysis. My interest, however, is not in general theorizing; it is rather in contextualizing the case of Tassos Papadopoulos's remains, and in the process, rendering explicit possible grounds of cross-contextual comparison.

I therefore track the generalizing and contextualizing moves made by the authors of these case studies, who overtly or implicitly toggle between the particular locale and epoch in which they consider the fate of a specific dead leader's body, on one hand, and a transhistorical, cross-contextual scenario in which dead leaders' bodies have and produce meaning, on the other. My aim is not to make an argument about the political theology of these dead bodies, but rather to pose context explicitly as a problem inherent in the play between general and particular in political theology—as in any general theory. If there is theorizing in my own method, it lies in suggesting what can be compared across contexts by teasing out points of noncomparison, points that establish the distinctiveness of a context. There is no attainment to the general in this procedure; thinking across cases does not entail movement between logical orders or levels of abstraction—as in Santner's theory of sovereignty and Taussig's more labile theory of the sacred—but rather juxtaposing a series of cases for comparison and following the remainders as they emerge along the way.

One of the most famous political corpses in modern world history is that of Vladimir Lenin, visited in his mausoleum in Red Square by 2.5 million people each year. The ongoing maintenance and public display of Lenin's body since his death in 1924 has inspired several remarkable studies. In one of these, based on ethnographic research at what he calls the "Mausoleum Lab" in Moscow, Alexei Yurchak closely examines the "top secret" procedures invented and implemented by teams of scientists over the years to preserve Lenin's "dynamic form" (Yurchak 2015, 116): techniques of re-embalming, bathing, and suffusing the body with fluids, replacing the original biological material with synthetic material, and "resculpting" any surfaces that were losing their original shape (127), thus maintaining the integrity of every inch of Lenin's body, the limberness of its joints, and its overall lifelike appearance. Yurchak notes that this preservation of Lenin's body "for posterity" (124) was not intended or planned by anyone in Lenin's inner circles after his death, but rather arose contingently, with much principled debate, and evolved along with a political theory of Soviet sovereignty that came to justify it. However, Yurchak shows that the decision was, in a sense, primed by the incidental (and unexpected) preservation of Lenin's body without embalming for almost two months after his death, facilitated by the extremely cold temperatures in Red Square where his body was displayed for mourners (125). Even more important, he suggests, were prior practices of "doubling" Lenin during the last year of his life, when he suffered several debilitating strokes and was secreted away by Party insiders who thus separated his body from his "public image" (121). During that time, Yurchak explains, the Politburo began "canonizing" a highly selective, decontextualized, and distorting assemblage of Lenin's writings to craft the new "doctrine Leninism," thereby "twinning" Lenin the person with Lenin the doctrine (121, 122):

> This secret approach allowed the truth of "'Leninism'" to appear to be the source rather than the product of the party's actions and policies. It also made it possible to present every new version of "'Leninism'" as the same, unchanging, consistent teaching of a genius, and to represent the party, to itself and others, as its unwavering implementer—not its arbitrary creator. (147)

The construction of Leninism and the science of preservation both "function[ed] as mechanisms of sovereign perpetuity," Yurchak argues, placing Lenin's body at the center of the Soviet state's practices of self-legitimation (136). He finds here a process of doubling or "twinning" in the Communist Party itself into "mortal and immortal parts" (135): the succession of mortal leaders and members who constituted the party over time, on one hand, and the immortal doctrine of Leninism itself, on the other (134).

All this doubling and twinning in Yurchak's analysis is evidently inspired by Kantorowicz's treatise on the king's two bodies and the work done by its interpreters, primarily Santner and Lefort, to associate this concept with the political theology of sovereignty *in general* (I return to this generality shortly). Yurchak is especially intrigued by uncanny similarities between the doubling of Lenin's body in the Soviet context and the doubling of the

The Body Itself 137

king's body in medieval Europe, especially the funeral effigies that Kantorowicz described. In the case of Lenin's body, what was preserved, he suggests, was not the "authentic biological substance" of Lenin's corpse, as with a mummy or relic, but rather his "anatomical image" (127, 128). This image reminds Yurchak of medieval funeral effigies so much that he dubs it Lenin's "body-effigy"—the double of Lenin's "body-corpse," his mortal body (146). What makes this doubling more complex than medieval effigies, on Yurchak's account, is that the body-effigy of Lenin was never seen by the public; to be more precise, visitors to Lenin's mausoleum did not *know* that it was a body-effigy they were seeing, as the techniques of preservation the lab scientists implemented to shape this "living sculpture" were kept entirely secret during the Soviet period (136), known only to the scientists and a few political insiders (146). What was visible to the public, then, were the hands and head (only) of Lenin's "body-corpse," which they perceived as his natural body despite its artificiality.

Like Graeber, whom he cites here, Yurchak indicates the possibility that the construction of such material doubles of dead sovereigns may be found in a variety of unrelated cultural contexts (he names several) because this practice resolves problems shared across these contexts: "It appears that a general divergence between the impermanence of the mortal sovereign's body and the permanent perpetuity of the sovereign office has led to the development of comparable cosmologies and rituals. The case explored by Kantorowicz was just one significant instance among comparable cultural models" (131). Yet Yurchak does not take the possibility of independent development in general as a sufficient explanation for the resemblance between Lenin's body-effigy and medieval European funeral effigies. He ascribes the resemblance largely to the inspiration the Bolsheviks drew from the "general revolutionary ethos of modern European states that focused on the sovereign body as the central site of their democratic transformation" (132)—a focus that was itself traceable to medieval European political theology. Rather than seeking precedents for Lenin's body-effigy in prerevolutionary Russian monarchical traditions or Russian Orthodox rituals, then, or speculating about the independent development of "the same" political-ritual practice in unrelated contexts, Yurchak finds a plausible historical connection between the Soviet "political cosmology" that supported the preservation of Lenin's body and the medieval European political theology that yielded the king's two bodies (131):

> As in these other cases, the underlying political meaning of the work directed at Lenin's body was to ensure that the party-sovereign remained perpetually embodied and anchored in foundational truth despite all internal crises of the party organization, purges of its members, denunciation of its leaders, and turns in its policy. In that process, preservation of the original biological remains of Lenin's body (as opposed to the perpetual re-sculpting of its form) was not only unimportant but also problematic. This approach to Lenin's body meant that it could not be reduced to a mortal individual biology. Instead, it literally transcended every individual body of party members, leaders, and even Lenin himself; it was, in fact, the immortal body of the sovereign. (145)

Katherine Verdery's earlier study of Lenin's body—which she (as against Yurchak) describes as a "mummy"—adds some interesting detail to this account, suggesting a religious significance to the body that may, depending on one's other objectives, place it within a longer history of precommunist Russian traditions. She points out that Lenin's body is both on display—visible inside a coffin with glass walls—and also buried, as the tomb containing the coffin is located "two meters below the ground level, as is proper in a burial" from an Orthodox perspective (Verdery 1999, 13). His being embalmed and not buried in the soil offends Russian Orthodox doctrine, she notes, as *"every* dead person should be interred" (45); and yet the preservation of Lenin's corpse provides ambiguous grounds for quasireligious worship by visitors. Where Yurchak insists that Lenin's natural body has been incrementally and inventively replaced rather than preserved, and thus cannot be compared to a mummy or religious relic, Verdery suggests that the perception among visitors that Lenin's "mummy" is biologically continuous with his natural body (a perception that Yurchak observes as well) facilitates a more "Orthodox" interpretation:

> A dead person is revealed to be a saint not only through miracles but also because the corpse does not putrefy. . . . Even though the incorruptibility of Lenin's corpse is a *human* achievement, he is still touched by these associations: dead people whose bodies have not decayed are holy. (45)

The sense that Lenin's body is holy or saintly, and that his preservation is continuous with precommunist Orthodox practice in some respects, has been nurtured by Vladimir Putin, as Yurchak points out (2015, 145)—part of Putin's long-standing and wide-ranging venture to rewrite Soviet history as ethnonational Russian history.

For Verdery, the case of Lenin's body is one of many that support an implicitly general theory regarding the symbolic efficacy of dead bodies. In asking after the political significance of corpses and remains, she pinpoints a number of features: their "protean" qualities (they are ambiguous and accommodate many meanings), their availability for personal identification (everyone has a body), and their affective charge: "The link of dead bodies to the sacred and the cosmic—to the feelings of awe aroused by contact with death—seems clearly part of their symbolic efficacy" (Verdery 1999, 32). Perhaps most important for Verdery, however, is their "localizing" power; she suggests that the "materiality" and "concreteness" of corpses and remains lend them a "thereness" that "localizes part of the symbolic capital they contain" (28, 27, 49). This localization implicates not only place but also time, she argues; burying or reburying dead bodies associated with past historical moments effects a "time compression" between the present and the past in a particular locale (98, 115), even across many centuries: "The politics and revisions of history occurring around dead bodies participate in an epochal kind of time shift, from which may ensue new paradigms for thinking about time and the future . . . 'reconfiguring time'" (124).

It is this last feature that facilitates Verdery's framing of postsocialism as a time and place where dead bodies have special political relevance and symbolic efficacy (52). Postsocialism is, in other words, the context of her theorization; if the cases she examines indicate somewhat different processes of meaning-making, and different entanglements of dead-body politics with religion, history, and nationalism, they are all drawn from the "epochal kind of time shift" occasioned by the collapse of the Soviet system and the consequent demand on surviving post-Soviet republics for new processes of political legitimation (124). Even so, Verdery insists, her accounts of dead bodies in the postsocialist context have potential "consequences" beyond that context because "the transformation of socialism is not an isolated occurrence but part of a wider process of global change" (126).

Verdery's contextualization thus takes a different turn from Yurchak's; where Yurchak finds a historical connection between western European political theology of the sovereign's body and the revolutionary ideology of the Bolsheviks, Verdery finds a historical connection between western European political theology of the sovereign's body and (Russian) Orthodox theology of saints' bodies, and then frames the transition from socialism as a rupture in revolutionary ideology that permitted that historical connection to resurface. Where Yurchak opens a question around the implications of such a historical connection for a general theory of sovereignty, Verdery ventures the outlines of a general theory of body symbology pertaining to the postsocialist retheorization of sovereignty.

In his article on the "return" of Francisco Franco, discussed earlier in this Interlude, Francisco Ferrándiz closely examines the political appropriation of theology to which Verdery and Yurchak both gesture (though to different ends). His paper offers an ethnographic exposition of political theology *as such* in the case of Franco's body, showing how, in fascism, Catholic theology of the body merged with the political theory of sovereignty in twentieth-century Spain to legitimate both his dictatorship and the treatment of his body—by some—as saintly. Ferrándiz explores the complex historical process of Franco's shifting "moral exemplarity," tracing this process from the time of the Civil War, when Franco constructed himself as the leader of a "sacred war" and the head of a righteous state in an "alliance with the Roman Catholic Church" (Ferrándiz 2022, 210, 211, 209), to his exhumation from the Valley of the Fallen in 2019, forty-four years after his death, under the newly elected socialist government. Over this span of nearly a century, Ferrándiz explains, "Franco's grave, and more specifically his remains, increasingly became the ultimate bastion of his regime's protracted but decaying sovereignty" (228, citing Yurchak).

In his analysis of the successive phases of Franco's moral exemplarity, then, Ferrándiz tracks the changing location and symbolism of his dead body. During the period after his death in 1975 and the transition to democracy in Spain, when he was buried across the main altar from José Antonio Primo de Rivera in the basilica of the Valley of the Fallen, what Ferrándiz calls a "tacit pact of oblivion" (215) about his legacy slowly gave way to the "negative exemplarity" of Franco's image as "a clownish and mediocre man who was able to win the war and cling to power only through pervasive, iron-fisted repression" (218). This repression brought the murder of tens of thousands of Republicans both during the war and afterward, "seeding the country with irregular mass graves," Ferrándiz writes, and helping to "consolidate Franco's dictatorial rule and extend its sovereignty" (214). During this same phase of negative exemplarity, those mass graves were starting to be identified and the buried remains exhumed ("unburied" is Ferrándiz's term), at the initiative largely of the grandchildren of the dead, in collaboration with humanitarian forensic practitioners from around the world. Franco's new phase of "neo-exemplarity" marked his "reemergence" as a fascist leader in the twenty-first century, aided, Ferrándiz argues, by much "historical revisionism" in the celebration of his legacy for Spain today (212). The final phase of Franco's "necro-exemplarity" followed the rise of the neofascist-populist party, Vox, in the 2010s, Ferrándiz explains. At this time, "the whereabouts of his corpse and the treatment it deserves" became the focus of "tense debates about his historical legacy," pitting the growing neofascist Christian movement against leftist public memory initiatives (219).

For these reasons, the "providential, semi-sacred role" in which Franco promoted himself as head of state (218), combining sovereign power with religious authority, cannot be relegated to the past, as Ferrándiz makes clear. This role is a recursive element of Franco's exemplarity and thus a facet of his unfolding legacy. Ferrándiz writes at length of this "semi-sacred role" played by Franco: from his investiture ceremony, which "incorporated elements of a Christian royal coronation" (209), to his overtly Catholic brand of fascism, which Ferrándiz characterizes as a "political religion" and "clerical fascism," and which Franco himself "connected to the medieval birth of the Christian nation" (208). Animating this political religion was his rhetoric promoting the Civil War as a "Second Reconquest" and a "sacred crusade"; as well as his "cult to the dead" surrounding the fallen (*caídos*) (209; 210, 211, 213; 210)—the "martyrs" of the civil war, soldiers and Franco supporters, whose bodies were exhumed from mass burials across the country, reburied in small pantheons constructed for their honor in local cemeteries, and later exhumed again and reburied at the Valley of the Fallen, served by a basilica tended by monks of the Benedictine order as a "permanent religious cult to commemorate their martyrdom and sacrifice" (210; 227, 232).[25]

Ferrándiz notes that the Spanish Law of Historical Memory passed in 2007 permits religious worship at the Valley of the Fallen while forbidding political displays. But this law might seem a secularist cry into the void of neofascism, as Franco legitimated his sovereignty—and his political descendants legitimate their neofascist movement—through an almost parodically medieval political theology in which symbolic authority is shared between the religious and political domains to such an extent that they cannot be separated. The transportation of Franco's body from the basilica at the Valley of the Fallen was broadcast live on Spanish television but, as Ferrándiz (who was enlisted as a radio commentator at the event) observes, "the television spectacle left the Spanish public with conflicting senses of relief, indifference, or outrage, depending on people's political leanings and whether they considered Franco a villain, a relic from the past, or a moral hero whose tomb had been shamefully desecrated" (233).

In a remarkably resonant paper, Igor Cherstich examines the itinerary of Muammar Gaddafi's body during the forty-two years of his rule in Libya, focusing less on political theology, however, than on political aesthetics.[26] He traces the insinuation of Gaddafi's body into visual public culture during his nearly half-century reign, observing a remarkable change in its status after the revolution in 2011, when Gaddafi was captured, tortured, and killed, and his body hidden away by the perpetrators so it could not be seen and mourned by supporters. During his time as sovereign, Cherstich observes, Gaddafi "depicted himself in posters and pictures as having a divine status 'not attainable by others'" (Cherstich 2014, 94, citing Khatib 2013, 188). He put his own body at stake visually, enacting a "'colonisation' of the visual space of Libya itself," Cherstich argues, which was "saturated" with his "symbolic and visual presence" even as he remained almost completely absent from public space (100, 102). This absence was crucial in the "colonisation," as it meant that the people's only visual relation to Gaddafi was through authorized pictures and posters provided by him. And he provided so many! Cherstich works through the different "looks" Gaddafi adopted at distinct phases over the years—starting from the fresh-faced, clean-cut, modern young general in the days of the coup (1969), to the elaborately military costume of the 1970s, to the "ethnic" Bedouin look of the 1980s, to the dashikis and other sub-Saharan African garments he wore in solidarity during the 1990s. From there unfolded his final phase, through the 2000s, when he grew a beard, underwent plastic surgery, and wore wigs, as if to disguise his aging body.

Cherstich shows how these visual personae mystified the status of Gaddafi's body while rendering it a rich site for political symbolism; the uprising in early 2011, he argues, made use of this preparation. Thus, he documents a new kind of visual culture that emerged in the late 2000s; iconic images

The Body Itself 143

of revolutionary leaders outside Libya (e.g., Che Guevara, Bob Marley) started to appear in public spaces in counterpoint to images of Gaddafi, soon followed by overt anti-Gaddafi graffiti and mocking caricatures. Images of him authorized by the regime were defaced, and he was rendered in drawings as Satan, or with ridiculous exaggerations of his physical traits. Cherstich reads these contributions to visual culture on the part of rebels as a "desire to give flesh" to Gaddafi, "whose body had been only a mere potentiality before the revolution" (106). The pervasion of public space by these images in a sense primed Gadaffi's body to be captured and murdered in reality: "After the revolution," Cherstich writes, "he *gained* a body: one that could be represented, touched and eventually destroyed" (94).

In this shift from visual representation to embodiment in the flesh, Gaddafi was "transubstantiated," Cherstich argues: "He was turned from *potentially man, maybe a ghost* into *just a man* (or *just a subject*, one might say)" (94). The argument turns on the spectral quality of Gaddafi's body for all those years before the revolution. Whether he had an actual human body, Cherstich shows, was a matter of speculation during this time, as people often said he might be superhuman, like a god or a ghost; one interlocutor wondered if Gaddafi would actually ever die (104). Cherstich is quick to insist on this ambiguity ("blurriness," as he puts it, 101) in the status of Gaddafi's body's during his rule, given the instability, ambivalence, and ultimate unknowability of people's "beliefs" about it. He thus reads the torture and killing of Gaddafi during the revolution as "the verification of a hypothesis" that Gaddafi was actually really human and mortal, with a physical body that could be ridiculed, hurt, and killed (114).

Cherstich takes as further evidence of this reality check the pervasive visualization of the "martyrs"—revolutionary combatants killed during the uprising—along with caricatures of Gaddafi during the revolution. Their bodies, too, were absent from public space and "given flesh" by way of visualization, Cherstich observes: "Putting up the posters of the dead, whose bodies were often missing, was a way to preserve or reconstruct the tangibility and corporality of the deceased" (107). As I read Cherstich, this public imagery, which reaffirmed the corporality of the martyrs that was already known and incontrovertible—it was, after all, the relatives, friends, and neighbors of living people devastated by their deaths who put up the posters—established a kind of symbolic equivalence into which Gaddafi's body could be placed. In this train of symbolic thought, people came to understand that the sovereign did not have a superbody, after all—that he was no more and no less than human. The sovereignty he embodied had ended with his death.

The question of sovereignty as immortal and transcendent was likewise at stake in the exhumation of Simón Bolívar's long-dead body from his grave in Venezuela on July 15, 2010. As Godofredo Pereira (2011) tells the story, the exhumation was ordered by then-president Hugo Chavez, who sought to determine the cause of Bolívar's death—long a matter of speculation, Pereira explains, but reopened for questioning by a US medical expert who suggested Bolívar might have died from arsenic poisoning instead of tuberculosis. On Pereira's account, Chavez's interest in this theory was bolstered by his own theory that Bolívar had been killed by Colombian assassins—a refraction, Pereira suggests, of Chavez's own sense of persecution by "Colombian agents," through which he sought to establish an identification between himself and Bolívar and thereby to legitimate (among other things) participation in the "continuous battles" between Venezuelan security forces and Colombian paramilitary forces in contested border areas (Pereira 2011, 91, 90). For Pereira, this is the explanatory value of the exhumation of Bolívar as a public event; the forensic examination of his dead body, he writes, "turned into an investigation of the very own 'body of the state'" in Venezuela (91).

This framing of Bolívar's body as a replete symbolic representation of the Venezuelan state counts on a general theory of political theology, which Pereira situates in a global forensic context where other exhumations—Ché Guevara in 1997, Nicolae Ceaușescu in 2010, Salvador Allende in 2011—have similarly been undertaken to establish the identity or cause of death of a political leader.[27] For Pereira, this "recent rediscovery of the dead" globally is not only facilitated but also in a sense motivated by new forensic technology (90): "It is clear that forensic analysis is today the most effective *ritual* procedure to allow 'things to speak for themselves'" (93). Pereira goes to some trouble to document the performance of this ritual procedure in Venezuela, which was "conducted in maximum secrecy," he writes, and filmed but not broadcast live (91). The convocation of experts and representatives of state authority, the choreographed movement of hazmat-suited forensic specialists around the holy sarcophagus of Bolívar, surrounded by Venezuelan flags while the national anthem played, was fully recorded but only partially shown to the Venezuelan public after the fact. Pereira attributes publicity around this event to Bolívar's status as "close to that of a saint," which helps account for objections to the exhumation as "a profanation of the dead" expressed by opponents of Chavez (91). Yet Chavez himself rhetorically verified Bolívar's sainthood, using the most reverent language on Twitter to express the sacredness of this presidential body on the occasion of its exhumation: "My God, my God . . . my Christ, our Christ, while I was praying in silence watching these bones, I thought of you! . . . How much I wanted and would have liked for you to arrive and order, as you did to Lazarus: rise Simón, this is not the time to die!" (90).

Taking a quick turn through Michael Taussig's analysis of spirit possession in Venezuela, where the figure of Bolívar actively participates in the trance-dancing and healing of the living, Pereira underscores the sacredness of Bolívar's remains by way of their symbolic efficacy: "Like medieval relics of saints traded for their sacred value, the contemporary remains of Bolívar are extremely powerful fetishes" (91). Indeed, the status of Bolívar as living or dead hovers as an unresolved question in Pereira's train of thought. According to one minister, he reports, even the suggestion that Bolívar was dead was an offense to the Liberator. For this minister, "as for most of those who support the revolution," Pereira explains, "Simón Bolívar is in fact alive and who he was or what he represents is not open to questioning" (91); if his bones were "witnesses" to a truth, then, it was because Bolívar could actively "speak" through them (93). The exhumation of his remains, Pereira observes, which involved a "crossing of the barrier, the circulation between living and non-living," sustained the feeling among the people that Bolívar was still alive in the immortality of the revolution—and, for Chavez and his supporters, embodied in Chavez himself (94). From this perspective, Chavez's exhortation to Bolívar that he rise from the dead like Lazarus and *live* was supported by the forensic ritual of exhumation, which affirmed the immortality of the sovereign and sustained his "constantly felt" presence in the eternal revolution (94).

In all these cases—Lenin, Franco, Gaddafi, Bolívar—authors frame the dead bodies of political leaders as discursive sites in which the sacredness of those bodies was debated. In some cases, it was a conspiracy theory discourse that took the body as its site. For example, while the whereabouts of the bodies of Franco and Lenin are well known, and their mausoleums have become sites of tourism and pilgrimage, the body of Gaddafi was not secured for public knowledge and remains a matter of speculation. Gaddafi was captured and killed by revolutionary militias; his dead body was displayed for several days on a bloody mattress in a refrigerated container in Misrata, where hundreds of Libyans visited and took photos of his rotting corpse while debates raged over whether he had been killed in the initial conflict or after his capture. Journalists reported that his burial site was deliberately kept secret by members of his tribe for security reasons, to prevent it from becoming a shrine or a target of vandalism (*Al Jazeera* 2011; see also Chulov and Black 2011).[28] In the case of Bolívar, Hugo Chavez's own death in 2013 was considered suspicious by some—including his successor, Nicolas Maduro, who accused the CIA of infecting Chávez with cancer, potentially by the hand of a close aide—thus playing out the resurrection of Bolívar in Chávez to its end in an assassination plot.

At the risk of belaboring these comparisons—which could be multiplied—I will point out, in conclusion, a few remainders they have generated, which will guide my inquiry into the theft of the body of Tassos Papadopoulos in Part 2.

First is the question as to whether comparison across these cases might be grounded in historical connections or, alternatively, whether only a general theory of sovereignty can sustain such comparison. The ontological status of Lenin's body, Franco's body, and Bolívar's body, like Papadopoulos's, might be understood in terms of a Christian theology of the body, whether Orthodox or Catholic. In this theology, the flesh of saints does not decompose but remains supple, capacitating a life-in-death that gives such remains a fetish quality, and opening the possibility that the dead might be resurrected in the body of the living—Bolívar in Chavez, for example, like Tassos Papadopoulos in his son, Nikolas, as I discuss in Part 2. Even the odd one out of the European imperial genealogy—Gaddafi—might be understood to have this ontological status; though Cherstich does not emphasize this, what he calls the "apotheosis" of Gaddafi subtends his idea that Gaddafi's self-depiction granted him "a divine status 'not attainable by others.'" But these bodies can only be understood this way—theologically—insofar as these men were already understood to transcend their humanity in their embodiment of sovereignty. Does the connection among these cases in religious or political history require a general theory of sovereignty to explain how these dead bodies met the fates and drew the attention—even worship—that they did?

Next is the question as to the nature and coherence of the publics—the subjects of sovereignty and of symbolic efficacy—framed in these works as audiences whose witness conveyed sacredness or immortality to those dead bodies. While Verdery and Pereira depict at least relatively successful ritual performances of sanctification, Cherstich observes persistent irresolution among Libyans about the status of Gaddafi's body as living or dead, ghostly or real; Yurchak examines ideological conflict among the Politburo insiders who initiated the manifold twinning of Lenin for an unwitting public, as well as the incompatibility between revolutionary ideology and Russian ethnonationalism in framing the immortality of Lenin's body; and Ferrándiz renders a complex picture of ambivalence about the exhumation of Franco's dead body—some outraged by a desecration, others convinced that a deep historical wrong was being righted—that reflected profound and enduring divisions within Spanish society. Like reactions among Cypriots to the theft of Papadopoulos's body, these cases show limits to the symbolic efficacy of the sovereign's body and the performances of sovereignty enacted through the management of that body after death.

I observed in the opening of this Interlude that the discourse on conspiracy theory provoked by the theft of the president's body in Cyprus cannot be analyzed without recourse to the body itself. I have argued in these pages that the body itself was actually two: the missing body of the president, whose symbolic meaning was a matter of debate in the terms of a shared attunement to conspiracy; and the remains of the president, whose material status was unspeakable in symbolic terms and instead was expressed in the affective terms of shock, disgust, and horror. The unspeakability of those material remains was contingent on the unknowability of the missing body (where it was located, who took it and why, whether it would be returned); when the body was restored, re-sacralized, and reburied, the material status of the remains was no longer a matter of shock, disgust, and horror. Conspiracy theories of the crime and meta-discourse about conspiracy theory flourished in the absence of the body *and* silence about the remains.

Earlier, reading Sara Ahmed on disgust, I considered the entanglement of the symbolic meaning of the body with affect as an index of the remains. Ahmed writes, "Disgust works to align the individual with the collective, at the very moment both are generated" (2015, 95), thus proposing that the historical process of adherence by which disgust comes to be a shared affect also determines the contours and membership of the collective that shares it. In the case of Papadopoulos's body, that adherence did not settle into coherence. The accretion of sticky signs such as disgust and horror turned on the religious significance of the president's body for only some of those who participated in the debate over the body's symbolic meaning. In Part 2, I offer a close reading of public discourse that evinces lines of division between those some and those others—lines that divided right-wing from leftist Greek Cypriots as well as Greek Cypriots from Turkish Cypriots generally. At stake in those divisions, I think, was a disjuncture between political theology and sovereignty. All contributors to the discourse had experienced Tassos Papadopoulos as a political leader, even if his leadership for Turkish Cypriots was radically attenuated by what Bryant and Hatay (2020) have called the "suspended" sovereignty of the Turkish Republic of Northern Cyprus; but only some experienced the theft of his body as a desecration that provoked "violent feelings," as journalist Michalis Papadopoulos put it. In other readers, it provoked fear, raised eyebrows, even prompted jokes. The limits of political theology as a theory of sovereignty can be found not only in places where consensus over symbolic meaning falters but also where affect is not shared or sustained. In light of these failures of coherence, focusing only on the symbolic meaning of the body of a dead political leader might yield a distorted picture of the collective so often glossed as *the body politic*. What other kinds of collectives might be implicated or activated by the fate of a dead leader's body?

These are among the questions that drive my examination of the Cypriot context of conspiracy attunement in Part 2. I hope this case study offers some answers, while raising more questions along the way.

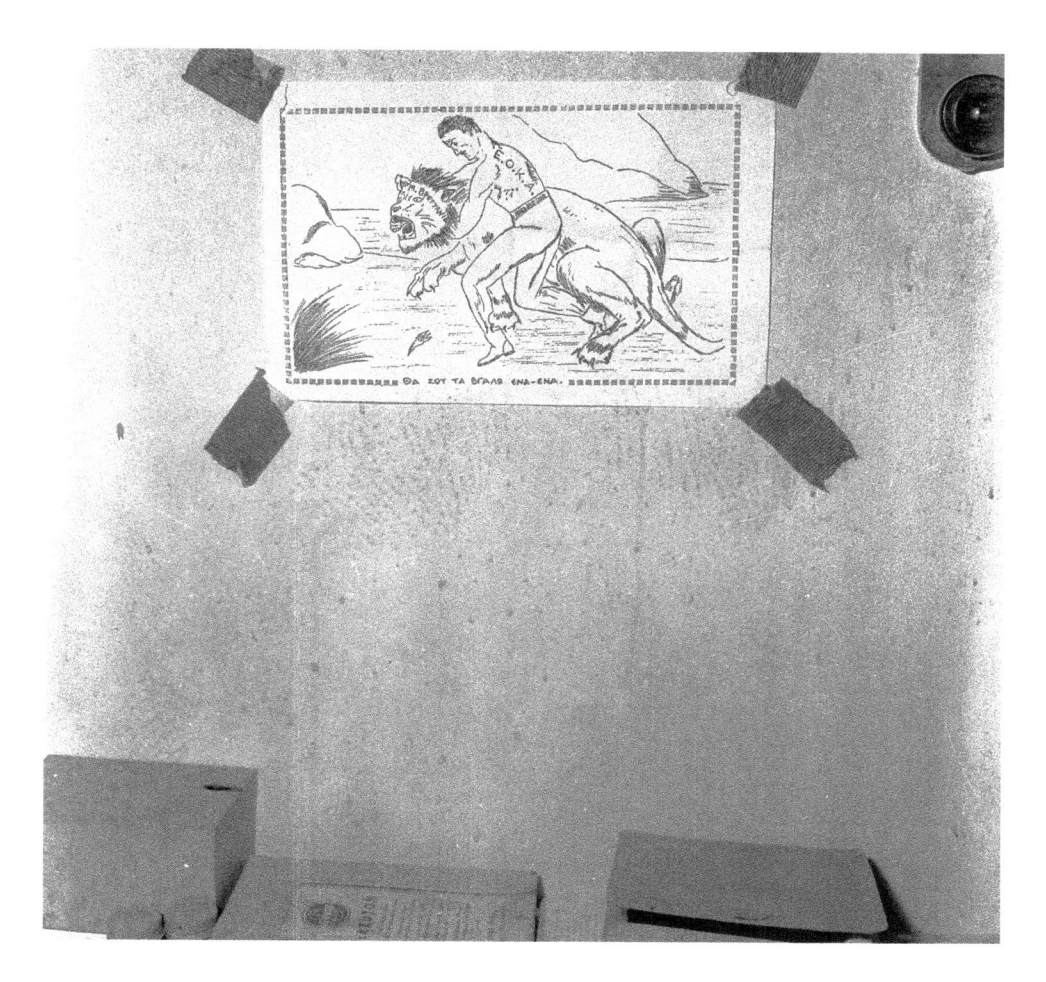

EOKA strangles Great Britain: "I'll take you out one by one" (θα σου τα βγάλω ένα-ένα). Lions are a long-standing symbol of British sovereignty in Cyprus; the British Cyprus flag depicted two red lions along with the Union Jack, and the unofficial flags of Akrotiri and Dhekelia—the two British military bases in the Republic of Cyprus that today, controversially, remain sovereign British territory—bear two golden lions. Archival note from the Press and Information Office (PIO) in the Republic of Cyprus: "Takis Ioannides collection, EOKA 1955–59. Military unit on the central road of Nicosia." Image supplied by the PIO photographic archives (24-191-18). Reproduced with permission.

Archival note from the Press and Information Office (PIO) in the Republic of Cyprus: "Episcopal Miter, 12/11/1973." This note may misidentify the miter shown here, which is the type worn by Orthodox bishops when performing ceremonial duties; the Episcopal miter is usually taller, shaped like a fan or cone, and crafted from embroidered cloth. Image supplied by the PIO photographic archives (A1-0979-0003). Reproduced with permission.

Tassos Papadopoulos kisses the hand of Makarios, a conventional gesture of respect and reverence for the office of archbishop, as well as the corporeal act that secures his blessing. Archival note from the Press and Information Office (PIO) in the Republic of Cyprus: "The President of the Republic, Archbishop Makarios III, receives the President and the Members of the House of Representatives, 20/07/1970." Image supplied by the PIO photographic archives (A1-0411-0009). Reproduced with permission.

Makarios addresses the crowd at a student demonstration for Cypriot sovereignty and against the Greek junta, held in Nicosia on February 16, 1972. Seen from the back, the figure of Makarios is a black shape, like a shadow or an empty set of vestments; his body is almost indiscernible, save for his waving hand, which conveys greeting as well as blessing. Some of the signs read: "Makarios, the only national leader of Cyprus" (Μακάριος, ο μόνος εθνικός ηγέτης της Κύπρου), "Makarios, the savior of our struggle" (Μακάριος, ο σωτήρας του αγώνος μας), "Makarios—guarantee" (Μακάριος—εγγύηση). Archival note from the Press and Information Office (PIO) in the Republic of Cyprus: "Demonstrations at the Presidential Palace organized by pupils, 16/02/1972." Image supplied by the PIO photographic archives (A1-0761-0003). Reproduced with permission.

Makarios addresses the crowd at a demonstration in front of the Archbishop's Palace in the center of the walled city of Nicosia on March 3, 1972. Makarios appears here at a great distance, addressing the assembled supporters from the second-story arched portico of the palace. He is a minute figure on the scale of the masses in attendance, but his waving hand is still visible. Archival note from the Press and Information Office (PIO) in the Republic of Cyprus: "Gathering at the Archbishopric, 03/03/1972." Image supplied by the PIO photographic archives (A1-0763-0001). Reproduced with permission.

At the same demonstration in front of the Archbishop's Palace in March 1972, Makarios appears on a poster held by supporters on the wall tracing the outer limits of the palace grounds: "My shield, the people" (ασπίς μου ο λαός). The same poster can be seen in Figure 6, on the far right of the image, facing Makarios; here, it faces the masses behind, in close proximity to the Greek flag, doubling the body of the archbishop, who stands some yards away. On the poster, the figure of Makarios, holding his staff and crosier and smiling toothily, stands on a map of Cyprus behind a line of people half his size, who are holding shields as if to protect him from the cartoonish villain who aims both a gun and a grenade at him. Makarios had already survived an assassination attempt by the time this photograph was taken and was widely believed to be a target of the Greek junta as well as the CIA. Is he rendered vulnerable here, in need of protection by the people of Cyprus, or is he a giant using the people as human shields? Archival note from the Press and Information Office (PIO) in the Republic of Cyprus: "Gathering at the Archbishopric, 03/03/1972." Image supplied by the PIO photographic archives (A1-0763-0057). Reproduced with permission.

Makarios among the people, accompanied by a bishop and two (visible) police officers as he visits a refugee camp in the south in December 1974. Some of the people gathered here are pushing to get close to the archbishop, presumably to touch him or talk to him. This photograph would have been taken four or five months after they had fled their homes in the war zones of the north. Archival note from the Press and Information Office (PIO) in the Republic of Cyprus: "The President of the Republic, Archbishop Makarios III, visits refugee camps, 09/12/1974." Image supplied by the PIO photographic archives (A1-1127-0004). Reproduced with permission.

"Makarios is alive." Photograph published in the book by Panos Ioannides, *Cyprus, Days of Rage in 555 Photographs* (Nicosia: Morphotiki, 1975), p. 285(a). The English caption from the book reads, "Immediately following the coup, Greeks and Cypriots living in the USA organize demonstrations in support of President Makarios." The coup began on July 15, 1974, at the Presidential Palace in Nicosia, which was burned to rubble; Makarios escaped to Paphos and was transported first to Malta and then London by the British Royal Air Force. His death was announced, falsely, on a CyBC broadcast the morning of the attempted coup, and he was widely believed to be dead until he made a broadcast of his own from Paphos the following day, before his evacuation from Cyprus. Image supplied by the photographic archives of the Press and Information Office in the Republic of Cyprus (285-A). Reproduced with permission.

"His Nobel Price." Photograph taken by Charalambos (Bambis) Avdellopoulos and published in the book by Panos Ioannides, *Cyprus, Days of Rage in 555 Photographs* (Nicosia: Morphotiki, 1975),p. 259(a). The English caption from the book reads, "Henry Kissinger's symbolic funeral along a Nicosia main street. Already messages are pouring in from Washington to the effect that Cyprus will sound the knell of Kissinger's policies. The people can see clearly who their executioners are." The Greek caption places a heavier accent on the burial being performed by the demonstrators: «το Κυπριακό θ'αποτελέση τον τάφο της πολιτικής Κίσσινγκερ» (The Cyprus Problem will be the grave of Kissinger's policies). Image supplied by the photographic archives of the Press and Information Office in the Republic of Cyprus (259-A). Reproduced with permission.

Tassos Papadopoulos at the funeral of Makarios, kissing the archbishop's dead hand this time, while mourners watch and wait their turn. Archival note from the Press and Information Office (PIO) in the Republic of Cyprus: "Snapshots from the funeral of His Beatitude and meeting of the leaders of the political parties, 04/08/1977." Image supplied by the PIO photographic archives (A1-1558-0007A). Reproduced with permission.

Η ΡΑΓΙΣΜΕΝΗ ΚΑΡΔΙΑ ΤΟΥ ΕΘΝΑΡΧΗ

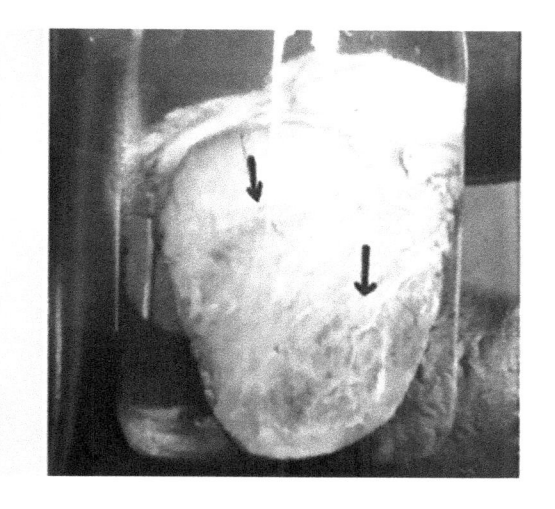

"The broken heart of the Ethnarch." This image of Archbishop Makarios's embalmed heart, indicating two areas of tissue damage, circulated in newspapers and grade-school pamphlets in the months following his death. The heart itself was secreted in the private chambers of the succeeding archbishop for thirty-three years and ultimately buried with the rest of Makarios's body in his tomb at the Throne of the Virgin Mary near Kykkos Monastery. The story of Makarios's "unburied heart" has been published in Cypriot newspapers around August 3, the anniversary of his death, every year since it was finally buried in 2010. The original photograph could not be sourced; this image, likely scanned from a newspaper dating to 1977, was published on To Thema Online, August 7, 2018, https://www.tothemaonline.com/Article/138142/h-ragismenh-kardia-toy-makarioy.

Spyros Kyprianou gives a press conference upon his appointment as acting president of the Republic, almost a month after Makarios's death on August 3, 1977. A photograph of the archbishop presides over the occasion while the assembled government officials mourn, one in a black armband. Archival note from the Press and Information Office (PIO) in the Republic of Cyprus: "Proclamation of Mr. Spyros Kyprianou as President of the Republic of Cyprus, 31/08/1977." Image supplied by the PIO photographic archives (A1-1568-0011). Reproduced with permission.

The front cover of Andreas Constandinos's book, *America, Britain and the Cyprus Crisis of 1974: Calculated Conspiracy or Foreign Policy Failure?* (2009), expressing the author's acute conspiracy attunement. The design is a heavy-handed metacommentary on conspiracy theories about the division of Cyprus, figuring Henry Kissinger, Archbishop Makarios, and James Callaghan as caricatures (or "caricatures") and amassing sham symbols of state secrecy—top-secret stamps, insignias of intelligence agencies, classified file numbers, and so on—to an absurd degree.

The front page of the Turkish-language newspaper *Halkın Sesi* (Voice of the people), on December 12, 2009. The headline reads, "Shock in the South: They Dug Up Papadopoulos's Grave, Removed the Coffin and Escaped with the Body." The uncredited photograph shows investigators in gloves and booties standing in and around the open grave of Papadopoulos; a placid olive tree stands nearby (which still grows in that spot at the time of this writing). The splashes of white on the tombstone were caused by the rain mingling with gypsum in the soil when it was dug up. Gypsum was soon identified as a key piece of evidence in conspiracy theories about the northern origins of the culprits.

The funeral of Tassos Papadopoulos held at the Cathedral of Saint Sophia in Strovolos, south Nicosia, on December 15, 2008. Cypriot National Guardsmen line both sides of the coffin, which is draped in the Greek flag and, on top of it, the Cypriot flag—the ethnonational symbol overlaid, but only partially, by the national symbol. A large portrait of Papadopoulos stands at the foot of the coffin, while the glass panel at the head reveals his corpse face: a modern effigy accompanying the body itself. Archbishop Chrysostomos I conducted the funeral service in the company of these bishops gathered in the cathedral's sanctuary. Archival note from the Press and Information Office (PIO) in the Republic of Cyprus: "Funeral of Tassos Papadopoulos." Image supplied by the PIO photographic archives (4v7o5142). Reproduced with permission.

ABOVE: The family receiving line at the funeral of Tassos Papadopoulos. First row facing front, left to right: Fotini (Michaelidi) Papadopoulou, his wife; Constantinos Georkadjis, his adopted son; Maria Georkadji, his adopted daughter; Nikolas Papadopoulos, his son with Fotini; and Anastasia Papadopoulou (embracing an attendee), his daughter with Fotini. Archival note from the Press and Information Office (PIO) in the Republic of Cyprus: "Funeral of Tassos Papadopoulos." Image supplied by the PIO photographic archives (PIO 06kid). Reproduced with permission.

FACING PAGE: A banner carried outside the cathedral where the funeral of Tassos Papadopoulos was held, bearing the concluding lines of his "No" speech broadcast on April 7, 2004, which also appear on his tombstone: "Greek Cypriot people, I call on you to defend justice, your dignity and your history." A sign held in the background, addressed in the familiar second person, reads, "Tassos, (we) thank you and bless you." Archival note from the Press and Information Office (PIO) in the Republic of Cyprus: "Funeral of Tassos Papadopoulos." Image supplied by the PIO photographic archives (4v7o5177). Reproduced with permission.

"Ελληνικέ Κυπριακέ Λαέ,
Σε καλώ να υπερασπιστείς το δίκαιο,
την αξιοπρέπεια και την ιστορία σου"

ΤΑΣΣΟ
Σ' ΕΥΧΑΡΙΣΤΟΥΜΕ
ΚΑΙ
Σ' ΕΥΓΝΩΜΟΝΟΥΜΕ

Achilleas Kyprianou, seated between his mother, Mimi, and his father, Spyros, then acting president of the Republic after Makarios's death. This photograph was taken at the public reunion of Achilleas with his parents on December 18, 1977, after he was kidnapped from the National Guard camp where he had been training and held for several days. The kidnapping has been the subject of much conspiracy theorizing. Archival note from the Press and Information Office (PIO) in the Republic of Cyprus: "Achilleas, the son of the President of the Republic, is set free by the kidnappers, 18/12/1977." Image supplied by the PIO photographic archives (A1-1601-0002). Reproduced with permission.

Tassos Papadopoulos shakes Spyros Kyprianou's hand at the latter's presidential investiture following his election in January 1978. Although Kyprianou, some six months after this photograph was taken, would fire Papadopoulos as head negotiator in the settlement talks with Turkish-Cypriot authorities and implicate Papadopoulos in a conspiracy against himself and his administration, they had apparently been friends for many years, and had even been housemates when they were law students at King's College London in the 1950s, when they cofounded a Cypriot student association (Smith 2009). Archival note from the Press and Information Office (PIO) in the Republic of Cyprus: "Mr. Spyros Kyprianou's investiture ceremony as President of the Republic, 28/02/1978." Image supplied by the PIO photographic archives (A1-1632-0002A). Reproduced with permission.

ΣΧΕΔΙΟ ΤΟΥ ΓΕΝΙΚΟΥ ΓΡΑΜΜΑΤΕΑ ΤΩΝ ΗΝΩΜΕΝΩΝ ΕΘΝΩΝ
ΓΙΑ ΤΗ ΣΥΝΟΛΙΚΗ ΛΥΣΗ ΤΟΥ ΚΥΠΡΙΑΚΟΥ ΠΡΟΒΛΗΜΑΤΟΣ

Το ερώτημα προς τους Ελληνοκυπρίους, όπως τίθεται στο Παράρτημα IX της Θεμελιώδους Συμφωνίας είναι το ακόλουθο:

«Εγκρίνετε τη Θεμελιώδη Συμφωνία με όλα της τα Παραρτήματα, καθώς και το Σύνταγμα της Ελληνοκυπριακής Συνιστώσης Πολιτείας και τις διατάξεις ως προς τους νόμους που θα ισχύουν, για να δημιουργηθεί μία νέα τάξη πραγμάτων με την οποία η Κύπρος θα προσχωρεί στην Ευρωπαϊκή Ένωση ενωμένη;»

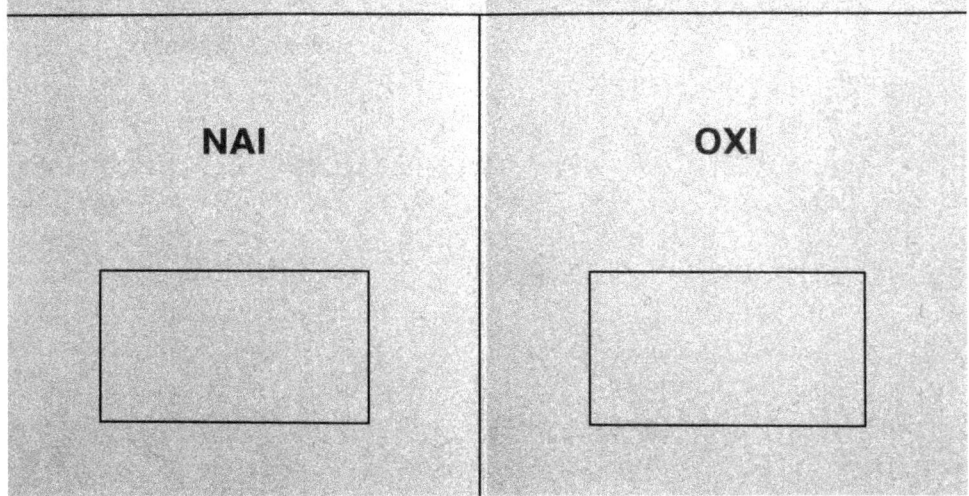

NAI	OXI

Ballot for the referendum on the Annan Plan as it appeared to voters in the Republic of Cyprus on April 24, 2004. The ballot reads, "The United Nations Secretary-General's Plan for the Comprehensive Solution to the Cyprus Problem. The question presented to the Greek Cypriots, as set out in Article IX of the Foundation Agreement, is the following: 'Do you approve the Foundation Agreement with all its Annexes as well as the Constitution of the Greek Cypriot Composite State and the provisions as to the laws to be in force, to bring into being a new state of affairs whereby Cyprus will join the European Union united?' Yes/No." Archival note from the Press and Information Office (PIO) in the Republic of Cyprus: "19/4/2004." Image supplied by the PIO photographic archives (img_1936). Reproduced with permission.

Tassos Papadopoulos casts his ballot—presumably "No"—in the referendum on the Annan Plan. Archival note from the Press and Information Office (PIO) in the Republic of Cyprus: "24/4/2004." Image supplied by the PIO photographic archives (01pap). Reproduced with permission.

The Tziaos Five, held at gunpoint by Turkish soldiers. This is one of the best-known photographs of the war in Cyprus, taken by Turkish photojournalist Ergin Konuksever, who was embedded with the Turkish army at the time. It circulated as a key piece of contested evidence in conspiracy theories about the missing from 1974 until 2009, when the remains of the five men were conclusively identified by the Committee on Missing Persons. The heads of four figures are circled here; the fifth, almost completely obscured, kneels behind the figure labeled "1." Archival note from the Press and Information Office (PIO) in the Republic of Cyprus: "Exhibition on the Black Bible of the missing (copy)." Image supplied by the PIO photographic archives (E4-053-013). Reproduced with permission.

Polykarpos Georkadjis kisses the hand of Archbishop Makarios as Tassos Papadopoulos stands to the left. No date is recorded for this photograph, but it was likely taken sometime during the middle of Georkadjis's tenure as minister of the interior, 1960–1968, while Papadopoulos, his close friend by all reports, was minister of labor (and/or finance, health, and agriculture). Georkadjis was implicated in the assassination attempt on Makarios in March 1970 and shot to death by "unknown" gunmen one week later—events that have figured prominently in conspiracy theories about the division of Cyprus. Image supplied by the photographic archives of the Press and Information Office in the Republic of Cyprus (A1-094-003). Reproduced with permission.

Tassos Papadopoulos, Polykarpos Georkadjis, and Archbishop Makarios III—along with a couple of National Guard officers and possibly Glafkos Clerides—on the tarmac at Nicosia International Airport in August 1964. Archival note from the Press and Information Office (PIO) in the Republic of Cyprus: "The President of the Republic, Archbishop Makarios III, accompanied by the Minister of the Interior and Defense Mr. Polykarpos Georghadjis, flew to Athens following invitation from the Greek government for talks on the Cyprus Problem, 25/8/1964." The Greek government in 1964 was pursuing Cyprus's union with Greece and attempting to avert an invasion of the island by Turkey. This meeting about "the Cyprus Problem" almost certainly had to do with the civil, police, and paramilitary violence largely perpetrated against Turkish Cypriots by Greek Cypriots from December 1963, following Makarios's proposal of fundamental revisions to the Cypriot Constitution, through February 1964, when the United Nations Peacekeeping Force in Cyprus (UNFICYP)—which still occupies Cyprus at the time of this writing—was formed and deployed. Papadopoulos is not mentioned in the archival note but he was serving as minister of labor (and/or finance, health, and agriculture) and a key adviser to Makarios at the time. Image supplied by the PIO photographic archives (16A-0739-0006). Reproduced with permission.

Tassos Papadopoulos tenderly greets children at a refugee camp on Easter 1975. Archival note from the Press and Information Office (PIO) in the Republic of Cyprus: "The Acting President of the Republic, Mr. Tassos Papadopoulos, visits refugee camps on the occasion of Easter, 04/05/1975." Papadopoulos was an independent member of the House of Representatives on the date recorded for this photograph; I am not aware of any service he performed as acting president of the Republic, at any time. Glafkos Clerides served in that capacity for a period of about five months in 1974 following the weeklong pretense presidency of Nikos Sampson, who was installed by EOKA-B and the Greek junta after the attempted coup on July 15; after Sampson resigned, following upon the first Turkish invasion of Cyprus on July 20, Clerides—by virtue of his office as president of the House of Representatives—was appointed acting president until Makarios returned to Cyprus from exile and resumed the presidency in December. Spyros Kyprianou also served as acting president when Makarios died, in August 1977, until he was duly elected president in January 1978. By May 1975, when this photograph was apparently taken, Makarios had already resumed his presidency six months earlier, and peace talks were taking place in Vienna, led on the Greek-Cypriot side by Glafkos Clerides. Image supplied by the PIO photographic archives (A1-1178-0011). Reproduced with permission.

Tassos and Fotini at church, nestled in the high-backed seats (στασίδια) of the nave, attended by the lieutenant general of the Cypriot National Guard. Archival note from the Press and Information Office (PIO) in the Republic of Cyprus: "Epiphany (Θεοφάνεια)"— an Orthodox holiday commemorating the baptism of Jesus Christ. No date is recorded for this photograph, but it was almost certainly taken during Papadopoulos's term as president (2003–2008). Image supplied by the PIO photographic archives (01ekklisia). Reproduced with permission.

Screenshot of a Facebook post by Nikolas Papadopoulos, Tassos's son and head of the DIKO party, on July 15, 2017, the forty-third anniversary of the attempted coup. Showing a great flair for conspiracy attunement, Nikolas implies here the involvement of the (then) current president of the Republic, Nicos Anastasiades, in the attempted coup. The post reads, "No mention of EOKA-B by N. Anastasiadis in his remarks today (about the anniversary). Only of the Athens Junta. Nor did he show up in Parliament." Superimposed over the image, along with a red arrow pointing toward the head of a man standing in the background, are these lines: "In the photograph, members of the treacherous organization EOKA-B, who had been arrested in Limassol in 1973 and were being transferred to Nicosia for trial. You can also make out the lawyer of Nikos Anastasiadis."

Coverage of the three suspects charged with the theft of the president's body in *Philelevtheros*, March 13, 2010, page 37. The headline reads, "Kitas is playing them for fools: Sudden transfer of the lifer from prison to the Paphos Gate." ("Paphos Gate" refers to a police station located along the western fortress walls of central Nicosia.) The caption beneath the large photograph of Antonis Kitas—aka the Cypriot Al Capone—reads, "yesterday for the third day in a row, the lifer was questioned for many hours, again saying various things to investigators, but he refused to put anything in writing." The small photograph on the right, above, is captioned, "Mamas Kitas"—the brother of Antonis. The small photograph on the right, below, is captioned, "The Indian who first confessed to the theft of the corpse." Friends who were in Cyprus at the time have told me they could not remember Sarbjit Singh's ever being named in the press; he was identified only as "the Indian."

PART 2
On Conspiracy Attunement: A Case Study

Readers who are not on intimate terms with the modern history of Cyprus might have difficulty assimilating the explicit and implicit contexts entailed and created by the talk about conspiracy theory I examine in Part 2. This difficulty is not incidental; the close-to-the-ground quality of talk about conspiracy theory in and about Cyprus is an artifact of the way locale operates, both geopolitically and theoretically. The density of "the local" in this meta-discourse about conspiracy theory is rather like that which characterizes anthropological debates about divine kingship, modeled by David Graeber in his review of ethnographic research on the Shilluk, which I discussed in the Interlude. It also characterizes contributions to the Melanesianist literature that Rena Lederman frames as regional yet cross-cultural in its comparative scope, which I discussed in Part 1.6. How dense "the local" appears to readers of such ethnographic texts may depend on the way they draw boundaries around what they consider (or assume) to be their own context—a point that I, following Strathern, began to argue in the Introduction.

In Part 2, I demonstrate this point in a case study of the president's body. Locale and epoch are my central concerns in this study, which is not about Cyprus as much as it is about relations: specifically, cross-contextual connections ("partial connections," in Strathern's term) between Cyprus and the United States in which I have found the president's body buried, so to speak. Conspiracy theory is one of those connections, and not only because conspiratology produced by theorists based in the United States often travels as general theory and is applied as such to the Cypriot context by scholars, journalists, tourists, and others. It is also because the United States is entangled with the Cyprus Problem itself in the form of conspiracy theories about the division.

Since the earliest inkling I had of this research project, then, I have conceived of the Cyprus Problem as, in part, an American problem. This conception is overtly expressed in the many conspiracy theories about the division that I address in Part 2.1—most of which position Henry Kissinger, US national security advisor and then secretary of state under President Richard Nixon, as the most powerful backstage actor in the disaster, agitated by anticommunist paranoia and wielding an unremitting sense of imperial entitlement to fit the world in what he styled as armor. Nixon resigned on August 9, 1974, under the threat of impeachment over Watergate, while a fragile ceasefire held in Cyprus and peace talks were underway in Geneva among representatives of the guarantor powers: Turkey, Greece, and the United Kingdom. The event known everywhere but in Turkey and northern Cyprus as the second Turkish invasion—the first having been launched on July 20, five days after the attempted coup—was the final military action that established the division of Cyprus as it stands today; it began on August 14, just a few days after Nixon's resignation.

Conspiracy theories about this history of conflict demand, I think, a historical approach other than periodization: an approach that credits the recursivity of the past in the present. While working on this project, I have spent a great deal of time learning and thinking about the early 1970s, and about the many and complex analogies and continuities between that time and the time of this writing. Does today really manifest the worst of all possible worlds, as I often hear friends and colleagues say, and as I sometimes fear? I find myself asking if it was not as bad in 1974, as the Vietnam War was only just starting to end, and the Pinochet dictatorship was just beginning in Chile, and the dictatorship of the Colonels blundered brutally on in Greece, and genocide was underway in East Timor and starting in Cambodia—to name just a few of the horrors facilitated if not instigated by the waging of the Cold War. The division of Cyprus is another of these horrors, smaller scale but no less damaging in its immediate and long-term consequences for those it touched, including all those whose stories never found a place in the public narratives that have settled into common sense since then. Among those public narratives is, of course, the Anglo-American conspiracy theory about the division of Cyprus, a theory of power that does not respect historical periodization, nor the boundaries of nation-states. (Where and when does Ottoman or British or American empire end?)

Thinking beyond these conventional ways of historicizing conspiracy theory brings me to conspiracy attunement. What Kathleen Stewart calls the "sensory labor" of attuning is not only a matter of registering a familiar feeling, of turning one's attention (again), of being drawn or thrown into a situation; it is also a matter of taking a stance toward the situation, in relation to others who are also taking a stance (Stewart 2011, 450). In the pages that follow, I trace this labor of attunement and pinpoint the stances taken by the many participants in the public discourse on conspiracy theory in the Cypriot context. In the first section, I examine the contentious discourse on conspiracy theories about the division of Cyprus, and what role archives can and should play in resolving that contention. In the second section, I consider a more contemporary archive of public discourse about the theft of Papadopoulos's remains, as represented in the Cypriot press in the months afterward; and I venture a view on what is public about that discourse. The third section explores the recursivity of conspiracy theories about the division in conspiracy theories about the theft—a recursivity that configures public discourse as a performative meta-discourse in the context of conspiracy attunement. As I try to capture something of this context in its dialogical dynamism, I am aware that any piece of evidence I encounter and any thread I follow leads to another and another, and therefore that what Part 2 shows is only the beginning of a process of becoming attuned to conspiracy.

1. DISCOURSE ON DIVISION

Conspiracy theories about the division in Cyprus form the foundational repertoire on which Cypriot conspiratology has been built, in much the same way that conspiracy theories about the assassination of JFK, UFOs, and 9/11 have figured in the crafting of the general conspiratology that has taken the United States as an unmarked locale. I call that conspiratology *general* because it has traveled so well and so widely; studies of conspiracy theory not only in the United States but also in India, Russia, Greece, and any number of other locales have drawn from the same repertoire of key texts—authored by Richard Hofstadter, George Marcus, Jodi Dean, and Frederic Jameson, among others—to frame and ground the analysis of what is, thereby, presented as a recognizable genre anywhere it is found. In other words, this conspiratology operates as general theory of conspiracy theory, rather than a local (American) theory or knowledge; and it operates this way despite the absence of cross-cultural comparison, conventionally the empirical basis for general theorizing in anthropology. In this section, I dwell on conspiracy theories about the division in Cyprus in order to unsettle the apparent consensus among conspiratologists on what the empirical grounds of a general theory of conspiracy theory are or should be. This is the first step in empirically motivating the shift away from conspiracy theory as an object of analysis and toward conspiracy attunement instead.

Yiannis Ioannou's book, which I discussed in Part 1, takes pride of place in a vast literature on conspiracy theories in Cyprus that seek to contextualize or account for the division. Since I began spending time in Cyprus in 2007, I have been collecting materials from this discourse on conspiracy published in Greek, Turkish, and English, the three official languages of Cyprus. I have been especially intrigued by a surge in journalistic and academic research, on the part of Cypriots as well as non-Cypriots, who aim either to corroborate these theories or to disprove them definitively, using newly available materials from British and American intelligence archives declassified in 2005. In this section I explore how different kinds of evidence are used by these differently positioned theorists to substantiate their claims: evidence such as hearsay and rumor, news stories without named authors or sources, interviews with state and para-state actors, and declassified intelligence documents, including diplomatic letters and reports. Disputes in this discourse over what counts as evidence, and over specific pieces of evidence, indicate to me the influence of an ideology of transparency that works to reproduce secrecy and doubt—even though many authors avowedly aspire, on the contrary, to establish historical facts according to knowledge-making procedures compatible with democratic norms of open dialogue and accountability.

It is with that contradiction in mind that I view debates and dialogues among those who explicitly position themselves as researchers with a stake in establishing the truth of the matter: journalists, historians, and political scientists, for the most part. Some are professional and others are "lay" researchers, but all engage in a self-styled *expert* and specifically *print* discourse; they have authored trade books, academic books, or self-published books, documenting empirical evidence and arguing from empirical evidence in ways that both presume and affirm the legitimacy of these practices as scholarship. The legitimacy of specific contributions to this literature is a matter of debate within the discourse, as I show here in my reading of key texts. Nevertheless, all contributors avowedly share a certain faith in archives as the source of truth about *what really happened* that led to the division of Cyprus in 1974.

The crux of debates in this literature is the purported collusion between the United States, in the figures of then–secretary of state Henry Kissinger and Undersecretary Joseph Sisco; the United Kingdom, in the figure of Foreign Secretary James Callaghan; the junta government then in power in Greece, in the figure of General Dimitrios Ioannidis; and Turkey, in the figure of Prime Minister Bülent Ecevit. These figures, and others associated with them, are widely thought to have colluded in the attempted coup against the president of the Republic of Cyprus, Archbishop Makarios, on July 15, 1974. There is not much dispute that the attempted coup was carried out by members of the Cypriot National Guard and the paramilitary group, EOKA-B; or that it was organized by the junta government in Greece and aided by Greek military officers, who installed Nikos Sampson as president after Makarios escaped. (Makarios was in fact reported dead the morning of the attempted coup, and many Cypriots did not know he had survived until days later.) On July 20, five days later, Turkish military forces invaded Cyprus with the goal—or the pretense, depending on one's perspective—of protecting Turkish Cypriots from the ethnonationalist Greek Cypriots then running the short-lived coupist government under Sampson. On July 23, a bit over a week after the attempted coup, an agreement for a provisional ceasefire was reached among Cypriot negotiators and Cyprus's guarantor powers—Greece, Turkey, and Great Britain—and Sampson was replaced as interim president by Glafkos Clerides, Speaker of the House at the time, while President Makarios stayed in Greece for his safety. Makarios ultimately returned and resumed his presidency five months later. The ceasefire did not hold, and Turkish armed forces invaded again on August 14. The ceasefire reinstated two days later—still in force as such today—demarcated the area of Turkish control in roughly the northern third of the island.

Conspiracy theories about the division, in broad brushstrokes, hold that officials and operatives in the United States and the United Kingdom had developed plans in the early 1960s to partition the island so as to weaken central authority and thereby, in the words of historian Andreas deal more to explain away than those who accept it. (Hitchens [1984] 1989, 164–65)[2]

Nearly every book on conspiracy theories about the division of Cyprus written after Hitchens's makes reference to it. Prominent among these is the self-styled definitive work by British journalists Brendan O'Malley and Ian Craig, *The Cyprus Conspiracy: America, Espionage, and the Turkish Invasion*. Published in 1999, the book is based, they explain, on their research "through top secret files, released in Britain and America, including Defense, Foreign Office and Colonial Office papers, Cabinet minutes, State Department and CIA papers, and interviews with a number of those closest to the crisis" (vii). O'Malley and Craig have no interest in distancing themselves from conspiracy theory, as Hitchens subtly does; they rather embrace it. In the opening pages of their book, they explicitly name a "conspiracy by America, as Britain stood by, to divide the island" (vii)—"an astonishing plot" (vii), a "deliberate Cold War plot" (x):

> Behind the plot is a secret world of intelligence and intrigue on Cyprus, an island bristling with radar and electronic intelligence hardware that made it a major military prize for the superpowers at a time when tracking advances in enemy nuclear missile technology, providing early warning of nuclear attack and monitoring military threats to the oil fields of the Middle East were critical to winning the nuclear arms race and the Cold War. (x)

O'Malley and Craig note that Greek Cypriots have held the United States responsible for the coup and invasion since the very outset,[3] whereas the accounts promoted publicly by the US State Department as well as British officials lay the blame on "intercommunal" conflict between Greek Cypriots and Turkish Cypriots that led, as if inevitably, to the division. O'Malley and Craig on the contrary frame these official American and British accounts as mystification, and emphasize the critical importance of their own work in dispelling the "myth that Cyprus is divided today purely because of ethnic hatred" (vii).

For books on conspiracy theory written after 2005, the declassification of British and American intelligence files on Cyprus is asserted by authors as the condition of their possibility as well as the proof of their legitimacy, in contrast with those texts that do not (and could not) refer to the files, such as Hitchens's. Many authors writing after 2005 present their works as the first to be based on extensive research with the declassified archival materials.[4] A good example is Jan Asmussen, a political historian who was teaching at Eastern Mediterranean University in Famagusta, in the TRNC, when he published his book, *Cyprus at War: Diplomacy and Conflict during the 1974 Crisis*, in 2008. Just a few pages into the introduction, Asmussen gives his assessment of the state of the field:

> Until now, the unbiased reader of the rich and varied literature on the topic of war and conspiracy in Cyprus will have found it extremely difficult to discriminate between a propagandistic or a scholarly work, since the facts presented seem to be conclusive in many respects. The art of propaganda *within the literature* has developed and supports divergent opinions, not by distorting but by selecting convenient facts in an intentional and manipulative manner. This has been exacerbated by research limited to secondary or non-auditable sources, i.e. memoirs, newspaper articles, and interviews. In 2005, this obstacle was cleared away. British and American archives opened most of their files pertaining to 1974. For the first time, previously unanswered questions can be addressed based on these newly released sources. . . . Through archival access it is possible now to move closer to the heart of the debate about whether Cyprus fell victim to a western conspiracy or if the local dimension was far more important then [sic] any outside factors. Conspiracy theories can also be checked in the light of primary sources that offer us a better idea of the actual intentions of British and American foreign policy making at the time of the crisis. That is the principal contribution of this book. (2–3, emphasis added)

Distancing himself from "the art of propaganda within the literature," Asmussen counterposes "hearsay"—a kind of evidence others have used—to the "records" of government activity (3) that inform his book:

> Thus a much better picture of the most recent history of the island emerges; misconceptions are corrected and disputed facts confirmed. Most importantly, the conspiracy theories about British-American involvement in the coup are conclusively discredited. . . . These open, and previously unanswered, questions are here addressed on the basis of recently released archival sources, thus establishing the "facts,"

rather than assembled rumours, speculations and politically manipulated "realities." (3)

Asmussen notes "an astonishing lack of academic literature describing the actual events surrounding the coup and the subsequent war of 1974." He goes on to qualify various contributions to this literature, using categories such as "reliable," "objective," "biased," and "scientific but nevertheless biased" (6–7). Throughout the chapter titled "Big and Little Lies," in which he considers narratives of Anglo-Greek and Anglo-Turkish collusion in the coup of 1974, he uses scare quotes around every instance of the terms "evidence" and "proved" or "proven," to emphasize their lack of legitimacy (243). He cites British diplomatic letters whose authors called the junta government in Greece a "lie factory" and blamed Greek leaders for fabricating these theories as the coup and invasion were unfolding. The letters, Asmussen argues, indicate that conspiracy theories were a matter of grave concern to the British government as soon as the coup happened, and thus support his own view that the coup could not have originated in British actions.

Largely in alignment with Asmussen in his endeavor to disprove conspiracy theories of the division is Andreas Constandinos, a diasporic Greek Cypriot born and educated in the United Kingdom. First trained as a barrister, he earned his PhD in modern European history with the research compiled in his book, *America, Britain and the Cyprus Crisis of 1974: Calculated Conspiracy or Foreign Policy Failure?* published in 2009, shortly after Asmussen's book, whose then-forthcoming publication he notes as the only instance of a work based on archival research (38n85). Like Asmussen, Constandinos concludes that there was no conspiracy behind the division of Cyprus. He offers a robust literature review in his introduction, where he notes that his book benefited from the "release and declassification of British and American government documents on the Cyprus crisis of 1974"—documents that allowed him "to test some of the claims of collusion [in] the coup against Makarios and the subsequent Turkish invasion, made against both Whitehall and more frequently, Washington" (37). "Up until now," he observes, "the lack of an account of these events based on archival research has been conspicuous only in its absence" (38). He specifies a "relatively transparent approach to the classification of government documents in the United States" (39), noting that CIA-backed coups against Allende in Chile and Papandreou in Greece, for instance, are well described in the documents now available. For Cyprus, on the contrary, he says, "Up until now, no such evidence has been found in relation to Makarios" (39). He concludes that such evidence must not exist, though he consistently qualifies his own claims in light of the "literature currently available" (46). He goes to some trouble, as Asmussen does, to evaluate the usefulness of this literature; for the most part, he dismisses works written before the declassification. He rejects the "journalistic" work of Brendan O'Malley and Christopher Hitchens, for example, whose "sources ... cannot be tested" (45). Asmussen, likewise, dismisses Hitchens's book as "a journalistic [work] basing its findings on literature and interviews; it does not provide actual proof for its main thesis" (5).

One note of special interest in Constandinos's introduction is his reference to the Greek-Cypriot researcher Athanasios Strigas as "a conspiracy writer and former NATO consultant." He briefly reviews Strigas's two books published in Greek: *Cyprus: Confidential File* (2000) and *International Conspirators: The Dark Side of the Moon* (1995). Strigas, he says, bases his argument on "a NATO and two State Department papers, revealing NATO and American complicity in the coup and invasion. However, at present these documents cannot be found in the U.S. National Archives. Until these documents can be found in the U.S. National Archives, their validity needs to be seriously questioned" (44). In this evaluation, Constandinos expresses a special trust in archives: a confidence not only that documents inside the archives can be trusted, but also, and more categorically, that what lies outside the archive is outside consideration—a matter of mere speculation.

The potential of archives to resolve urgent questions of truth definitively has also driven the work of Makarios Drousiotis, a Cypriot journalist and researcher, sometimes called a historian by readers,[5] though also an "autodidact historian" and a "conspiracy theorist" by those seeking to undermine his credibility, as I discuss in Part 2.2. For decades, Drousiotis has reported and written editorials for *Politis*, an independent, left-leaning Greek-language newspaper published in the south, along with other Greek-language papers in Cyprus, while also working as the Cyprus correspondent for the Greek newspaper *Elevtherotypia*. He is a well-known public figure in the south; during the period of my earliest fieldwork, he gave frequent newspaper and television interviews, often in connection with one of the many books he had written on the political history of Cyprus since the 1950s (Drousiotis 2002a; 2002b; 2003; 2005b; 2008; 2009a; 2009b; 2010a; 2014a;

2016; 2020; 2021; 2022; see also Drousiotis et al., 2004). More recently, he has been in the news for his trenchant critique of corruption in the Anastasiadis administration (2013–2023) and its "interested" failures to resolve the Cyprus Problem. He established his own press in Nicosia, Alfadi (Αλφάδι)—a "vanity press," a bookshop owner in Nicosia once told me—to publish these books, most running to many hundreds of pages, and some translated into English.

Drousiotis presents what I consider the very picture of conspiracy attunement. Throughout his career, he has argued vigorously against the conspiracy theories promoted by ethnonationalist politicians, media professionals, businesspeople, and lawyers in Cyprus, while also engaged in his own intricate documentation and theorization of their backstage deals and collusion in manipulating the public for power and profit. In a series of six books published between 2002 and 2010, Drousiotis marshaled extensive archival and interview evidence to establish, among other things, the agency of paramilitary and deep-state organizations in Greece, Turkey, and Cyprus in the attempted coup in July 1974, and especially close ties between the CIA and EOKA-B in the period leading up to the coup. Although he did not promote the Anglo-American conspiracy theory of the division in any of these works, his close attention to the CIA's activities in Cyprus and Greece throughout the 1960s and early 1970s, and to the impassivity at best of Kissinger before and after the Turkish invasions, was taken by some readers to be at least consistent with this conspiracy theory in its broad outlines.[6]

Drousiotis thus took much of his readership by surprise when he explicitly and laboriously denounced the Anglo-American conspiracy theory in a book published in Greek in June 2014 (Drousiotis 2014a); the English translation, *The Cyprus Crisis and the Cold War: USSR Duplicity versus US Realpolitik*, followed swiftly in 2016. This was the first of his books to be based on research with the declassified intelligence files. In a piece he wrote for the Anglophone newspaper *Cyprus Mail* in July 2014, he described what he discovered in the new evidence:

> When I was researching my recently published book . . . I found that the theory of a Western plot could not be documented and was, to a large extent, the product of Soviet propaganda at the time. In reality, the Soviet Union backed the Turkish invasion and consolidation of the status

On Conspiracy Attunement 163

quo to cause divisions within NATO and enhance its relations with Turkey. (Drousiotis 2014b)[7]

His main finding, in other words, was that there had been no Anglo-American conspiracy behind the division of Cyprus, whereas the Soviets had facilitated the division and perpetuated it; moreover, he argued, the Anglo-American conspiracy theory itself had Soviet conspirators behind it. In the book, Drousiotis addresses the durability of the Anglo-American conspiracy theory, arguing that Soviet operatives engaged in an extensive propaganda campaign to spread it among Cypriots:

> Despite the deeply embedded belief in Cypriot minds that the coup against Makarios and the Turkish invasion that followed was a UN and NATO plan as part of a broader conspiracy to transform the island into an "unsinkable aircraft," this theory remains completely unsubstantiated. Forty years after the events and with the release of US and British classified material, historical research debunks this conspiracy myth. (2016, 13)

In a footnote, Drousiotis locates the origin of the phrase "unsinkable aircraft" in the mouth of Khrushchev, who gave an interview to a Soviet paper in May 1964 that was quoted in the *New York Times* and circulated widely afterward. "Khrushchev's phrase," Drousiotis notes, insisting on the success of Soviet propaganda from the beginning of the conflict in Cyprus, "has become embedded in the Cyprus problem's terminology and is still used in contemporary Cypriot political dialogue" (2016, 370n32). He concludes,

> Entire generations of Cypriots have been nursed on the myth of a foreign conspiracy against Cyprus. What is documented is not the foreign conspiracy, but the abject failure of the country's leadership to manage its independence.... Projecting the coup—not the invasion—as a NATO operation was dreamed up by Soviet propaganda.... If one state benefitted from the Turkish invasion of Cyprus, without actually risking anything, it was the Soviet Union. Soviet intervention in the Cyprus crisis was one of the biggest successes of its propaganda machine during the Cold War. Moscow pushed for the Turkish invasion, intervening effectively in domestic Cyprus developments in order to maintain the status quo, without infringing upon Turkey, while embedding the perception among Greek Cypriots of all ideological hues that it was a persistent and

sincere ally of the Republic of Cyprus, as opposed to the West. This perception prevails to this day. (2016, 363)

Drousiotis's book saw a terrible reception in the south. He was attacked not only by the Russian ambassador to Cyprus but also by members of AKEL, the communist party in power until 2013, which he had criticized aggressively in the book for its susceptibility to Soviet influence in the years leading up to and following the failure of the Annan Plan in 2004. At that time, he argued, AKEL could have brought into being a solution and definitive end to the Cyprus Problem in the framework of a bizonal, bicommunal federation. In March 2013, after the elections in which AKEL lost power, Droustiotis was hired as a special assistant to Nicos Anastasiades, the newly elected (then reelected) president of the Republic and head of DISY, a conservative center-right party—not an obvious fit for Drousiotis, even if Anastasiades had been the sole party head to support the Annan Plan in 2004, thereby earning credit with progressives that he cashed in during the 2013 election. Drousiotis was thus already working in government when his book was published, and according to him, DISY was the only political party that did not denounce him when it came out, though it did not publicly support him either. Following the scandal, in November 2014, Drousiotis moved to Brussels to serve as personal assistant to Christos Stylianides, the European Union's commissioner for humanitarian aid and crisis management.

Drousiotis returned to Cyprus in the fall of 2019, having left government service and written a book in the meantime that became a best-seller soon after its publication in 2020; a second and third came out in 2021 and 2022, completing what he calls his "trilogy" on political corruption and incompetence behind the failure to solve the Cyprus Problem.[8] In talking with him, when we met in December 2021, I got the sense that he had distanced himself by then from debates over the Anglo-American conspiracy theory of the division as he grew more concerned with Soviet influence in Cyprus, and with corruption in contemporary Cypriot politics. He was even planning then to rewrite one of his early books dealing with the CIA in Cyprus, having revised his earlier views in light of his more recent archival research.

The faith in archives that Drousiotis evidently shares with Asmussen, Constandinos, and other conspiratologists of Cyprus represents what Jacques Derrida, in *Archive Fever*, frames as the positivist approach to archives. In his terms, the positivist approach names an aspiration to progress in historical knowledge, in relation to the relative incompleteness of the archive; it thus implies the possibility of completing historical knowledge through the discovery of new materials that "come out of secrecy or the private sphere" (Derrida 1995, 52). In other words, positivist researchers trust that the archives contain the knowledge they seek; the task of the researcher is to make discoveries, and in doing so, to add knowledge to the historical record in a cumulative, ever-progressive manner.

Derrida does not advance this positivist approach himself. He warns that the passage from "private" to "public" that archival materials make in the hands of researchers is not a passage from "secret" to "non-secret," as "there can be no archive [of the secret itself], by definition" (1995, 2–3, 101). The absence of the secret is a structural feature of the archive, for Derrida, that demands a psychoanalytic and political approach to the archive, one that acknowledges the destructive, "anarchival" or "archiviolithic" force that he likens to the death drive: a force of forgetting and erasure, of doubt and suspicion, of repression (in memory) and suppression (in social and political life) in the very recording and repetition of history (18–19). This force, he argues, determines the finitude of the archive: its limits and voids, its exteriority to memory, and the impossibility of knowing everything.

Saidiya Hartman (2008) seizes on this "anarchival" power as a rationale for the method of writing the past that she calls *critical fabulation*: a method of writing a "new story" that "exceed[s] the fictions of history—the rumors, scandals, lies, invented evidence, fabricated confessions, volatile facts, impossible metaphors, chance events, and fantasies that constitute the archive and determine what can be said about the past" (9). Ayşe Parla (2023) extends Hartman's reckoning with the instability and unreliability of archives in her conceptualization of *empirical fabulation*, which begins not from the violent silences, absences, and reductions of "the archive of slavery," as Hartman does (2008, 10), but rather from the fabulation of historical actors themselves—in this case, the court testimony given by Soghomon Tehlirian, who assassinated the "principal architect" of the Armenian genocide in 1921, and the memoir he wrote many years after he was acquitted of the crime (2023, 446). Both texts make veridically complex testament to the Armenian genocide that was (and is) concealed and denied by the Turkish state. Though working with radically different kinds of archives, Hartman and Parla both promote conscientious methods of speculation as a response to the "violence of the archive," in Hartman's term (1), which reproduces the violence of lived experience, facilitating the representation of power while erasing subjugation and dispossession from the book of history.

Quite on the contrary, one of the marks of the self-conscious scholarliness by which contributors to conspiratology in the Cypriot context have sought to legitimize their work is their tactic of discrediting other contributors by re-describing as *speculation* the discursive category to which their empirical evidence belongs, as Constandinos and Assmussen (among others) do. For these researchers, speculation approaches conspiracy theory itself as a low-status knowledge, or even a genre of nonknowledge. They do not consider how their aspiration to resolve definitively debates over "the true facts" might be foiled (or failed) by the archives in at least two distinct ways. The first is by dint of secrecy: that is, the deliberate omission or concealment of documentation that would otherwise provide a factual foundation for knowledge. Thus, in the case of the Anglo-American conspiracy theory of the division of Cyprus, diplomats and other political actors might have omitted to keep notes of meetings and to file reports, or have censored themselves in any number of ways, with a view to maintaining secrecy. By the same token, they might have fabricated documents, or passed impressions or half-truths off as facts in their filings, thus entrenching falsehoods or fallacies in the factual foundation that researchers seek to build from archival material. No matter how much new information one finds in the archives—and conversely, no matter how many times one fails to find new information—this research will not resolve the question of what really happened. What one most wants to know—what is most explanatory—does not exist in the archives.

The second way archives can foil the positivist approach is in changing historical narratives themselves—as Asmussen, Constandinos, and Drousiotis surely aspire to do (along with Hartman, Parla, and others who have long since taken their distance from positivism). From this aspirational vantage, new information discovered in archives carries the potential to change how people apprehend history, and thus the present as well; archival knowledge can instruct moral values and political action, triggering a change of consciousness and instigating social change. Here again, however, archival positivism is poorly founded, as the case of Drousiotis's book about the Soviet conspiracy attests. His demonstration that the Anglo-American conspiracy theory itself was in fact Soviet propaganda offered Cypriot readers

(Greek-Cypriot readers, especially) an opportunity to reverse their political positioning in relation to this conspiracy theory and thereby to the division itself: to denounce the Soviet conspiracy and ongoing Russian interference in Cypriot political and economic affairs today.[9] But it appears to have had no such effect. In terms of the political positioning of Cypriot publics toward the division, it seems to have had no effect at all. The Anglo-American conspiracy theory does not express "the political" in such terms, and by the same token, the facts established by archival evidence do not, alone, carry the power to realize themselves in political consciousness. What archival evidence can show is the context in which historical facts are debated and their role in political consciousness is determined. In the next two sections, I examine archival material in that way: that is, as evidence of the Cypriot context of conspiracy attunement.

2. THE PRESIDENT'S BODY

The body of Tassos Papadopoulos was stolen from his grave on December 11, 2009, one day before the first anniversary of his death and thus his one-year memorial—an important day of remembrance for any deceased person in Greek Orthodox tradition, but especially for one who had lived such an outsized public life. For the rest of that December and several months following, the identity of the thieves and the motive for their crime attracted intense speculation, figuring Papadopoulos as both the subject and object of conspiracy. The leading theories in many Greek-language newspapers attributed the theft to Turkish nationalists attempting to sow chaos in the south, or to Turkish-Cypriot or Greek-Cypriot progressives angered by the role Papadopoulos had played in defeating the Annan Plan in 2004.

My friend Nicos remembered this situation well, years later: *The big story after the theft was that it was Turkish Cypriots or Turks who'd done it*, he told me. The supposed proof for this theory was gypsum dust found around Papadopoulos's grave, which was tested and found to match samples from a mountain region in the north. The reporter in a public television broadcast on February 4, 2010, framed the facts this way, citing a report published in the *Philelevtheros* newspaper:

> It was determined that the gypsum scattered by the perpetrators when they desecrated the grave came from the occupied territories. . . . Stones

from the Pentadaktylos Mountains have the specific property that, when they are ground, they produce dust that is different from gypsum found anywhere in free Cyprus.[10]

Nicos laughed at the absurdity of this theory, which was premised on an absolute separation not only of people but also of stones between the north and the south, and which thus implied that it must have been Turkish Cypriots or Turkish settlers in the (occupied) north who had tracked the dust to the cemetery in the (free) south on their shoes. *Where do you think the soil and stone and building materials come from, for all those construction projects you see in the south?* Nicos exclaimed. *It all comes from the north, all of it, right across the border in trucks, legally—that's the border economy!* (RIK later reported that further testing proved the gypsum actually came from the Larnaca area, about thirty-five kilometers from the cemetery, in the south.[11]) Nicos also reminded me that Papadopoulos's son, Nikolas, who had been elected head of the DIKO party after his father's death, had supported the theory about Turkish or Turkish-Cypriot suspects publicly, in the press. *The other suspects were people like me—the "nainaikis,"* Nikos said. This term, he explained—"the yes-men," also meaning "traitors"[12]—referred to those (relatively few) Greek Cypriots who had voted to support the Annan Plan for reunification in 2004. *So, after the theft, my friends and I all went around whispering, "Where did you put them?"—meaning the bones. "Where are you hiding them?" It was hilarious.*

Though I stayed in Cyprus during the summer of 2010, when the trial of the conspirators began, and I moved there for a year starting in the fall of 2011, I was not in Cyprus when the theft of the president's body occurred in December 2009. I did not have the option of "being there," in the experiential sense valorized in ethnographic research since anthropology's early days—"an encounter and an exchange" with interlocutors, as John Borneman and Abdellah Hammoudi put it, a "co-presence" that "is also a source of knowledge that makes possible a transformation of what we know" (2009, 14).[13] I have tried to multiply the points of my experiential contact with the events: by visiting Papadopoulos's grave and the church where his funeral was held, as well as the village of the convicted conspirators, the Kitas brothers; by speaking with people close to the Papadopoulos family; and by interviewing journalists who reported on the theft and its aftermath, whose voluminous contributions to public discourse operated in a feedback loop from which "the modern concept of a public seems to have floated free" (10). Insisting on the importance of cross-contextual translation, Warner rejects the "nominalist skepticism" that, he observes, "too often passes as historicism in literary studies" (11)—a reticence, that is, to attribute universality to the category of "public" that has led scholars to conflate the analytic purchase of the concept of "public" with whatever publics are thought to be by the particular groups of people being associated with practices already understood by these scholars as public. Warner takes a less circular and more comparative tack, articulating the "metacultural dimension" of publics, which, he writes, "gives form to a tension between general and particular that makes it difficult to analyze from either perspective alone" (11).

Dwelling in this tension, while reading Habermas by turns with and against the grain, Warner entertains the notion of the public sphere as an "ideal," an "imaginary convergence point" of public discourse, an "implied but abstract point" that bears the "legitimacy" of "public opinion"; it is, he concludes, "an indefinite audience rather than a social constituency" (55). On his reading, publics are discursively mediated and mediating; they are not empirical groups circumscribed by locality, or "natural collections of people" (61), but rather virtual collectivities (Warner says "virtual entities," 88) that *become* social through their consumption and production of discourse—that is, by effectively being called into being through public address: receiving, enabling, sustaining, and transforming that address (67). Thus, Warner writes, "the notion of a public enables a reflexivity in the circulation of texts among strangers who become, by virtue of their reflexively circulating discourse, a social entity" (11–12). Indeed, he insists that public discourse cannot be addressed only to known persons: "A public is always in excess of its known social basis.... It must include strangers" (74). If everyone were "known personally" to one another, he argues, there would be no public (76); "strangerhood" is "constitutive" of publics, and in turn, publics make strangerhood "normative" (76). In order for speech to be public, then, it must be understood as addressed both personally (to us) and impersonally (to others). This dual address is part of the "social character" of public discourse for Warner, in that it shows the "social relevance" of what we might understand as our "private thought and life" through the "resonance" we sense between ourselves and others—strangers—whom we imagine are also addressed (77). We must be able to understand ourselves as strangers to others in order to imagine ourselves and strangers together as constituting a public. Thus, Warner concludes, "Strangers come into relationship [by means of a public], though the resulting social relationship might be peculiarly indirect and unspecifiable" (75).[14]

The significance of Warner's question as to whether and how a public is *social* has, I think, to do with scale. Undertaking the kind of comparative thinking about publics in which Warner is avowedly interested—a cross-contextual translation of the very concept of "publics"—I have devised a thought experiment. I imagine that the newspaper-reading publics in Cyprus in 2009–2010 are the kind that Warner cannot imagine: those made up of people known personally to the writers and directly addressed by them. Such publics might include some strangers, of course, but stranger-hood would not be as strongly normative in the constitution of these publics as Warner takes it to be for the publics implicitly in the background of his theorizing: big publics (where all people could not possibly know one another personally) occupying big spaces (where all people could not possibly cross paths). In the publics I am imagining here, by contrast—multiple overlapping publics, given the long-term division between Greek-Cypriot and Turkish-Cypriot communities and the different languages in play—writers and members of the publics they address are "in the know" together; they know one another, or at least know of one another, personally. This would account for the commonplace practice among Cypriot journalists of using epithets (e.g., "a certain autodidact historian") rather than proper names when lodging criticisms or accusations against colleagues or readers in their publications, and their common practice of omitting any kind of contextual background or framing of the events and ideas under discussion in their writing. Despite the intimacy of these publics—their low degree of strangerhood—writers might still invoke a public as an ideal, an abstract, an "imaginary convergence point," in Warner's terms, where they intend their discourse to land. But the social basis of such a public would be stronger and more substantive—traceable by ethnographic means—while the normative dimension of strangerhood would be weaker and more abstract.

By the same token, in these publics, the strong distinction Warner draws between gossip and public discourse would be untenable. For Warner, gossip "is never a relation among strangers" (78); it can only be face-to-face conversation with intimates—the sort of situated, dialogic speech that Stacey Leigh Pigg emphasized when arguing against the practice of attributing "belief" to others, as I discussed in Part 1.1. "Gossip in the usual sense," Warner writes, "by creating bonds of shared secrecy and calibrating highly particularized relations of trust, dissolves the strangerhood essential to public address" (79). When "gossip-based genres" of talk circulate widely, including among "professionals" (such as gossip columnists) to whom its objects are not personally known, it becomes "scandal," for him (79): a category whose distinctness from gossip can only be understood as an index or aspect of scale.

The scalar nature of distinctions between these low-status categories of discourse—gossip, scandal, rumor—has been missed entirely by some ethnographers who address gossip and rumor as a normative means of social control, which is to say, from a functionalist perspective. In their 2004 book, *Witchcraft, Sorcery, Rumors, and Gossip*, Pamela Stewart and Andrew Strathern trace this perspective to Max Gluckman's 1963 essay, "Gossip and Scandal," which they read critically, pointing to Gluckman's many implicit assumptions about the factual basis of gossip, the equal access of all group members to gossip, and its efficacy in bolstering solidarity despite and across social hierarchies.[15] They emphasize the tendency of anthropologists in Gluckman's line to focus on the "positive functions" of gossip (Stewart and Strathern 2004, 34), and they seek to counteract this tendency by exploring its potentially destructive impact, its fundamental ambiguity as to truth status, and the unknowability of its circulation, as well as by insisting on a performative understanding of "talk" in their extended comparison between gossip and witchcraft.

Despite this incisive critique, Stewart and Strathern nevertheless reproduce at least one of the implicit assumptions of the functionalist perspective on gossip they seek to move beyond: namely, the association between gossip as a category of discourse and the smallness of the societies in which anthropologists have, for the most part, studied it. It is the face-to-face conditions of sociality in small societies that facilitate the functionalist interpretation of gossip as a form of social control that Stewart and Strathern reject; yet the distinction they draw between gossip and other types of low-status knowledges has no other grounds than scale. Indeed, they turn without comment to "urban legend" in their discussion of Patricia Turner's (1993) work on beliefs about white supremacist conspiracy among African Americans in the United States (Stewart and Strathern 2004, 48–49). And they introduce a categorical distinction—albeit hesitant and provisional—

between gossip and rumor that is entirely scalar in nature.[16] "Gossip takes place," they write,

> mutually among people in networks or groups. Rumor is unsubstantiated information, true or untrue, that passes by word of mouth, often in wider networks than gossip. . . . Gossip may proceed into circuits of rumor, and rumor may get into gossip networks. . . . Gossip may be the term used more frequently for local forms of the types of discourses we discuss here, while rumor is perhaps used more frequently for the extension of this process into wider areas. (38–39)

The association that Stewart and Strathern acknowledge but do not question between gossip and small-scale societies, and the categorical distinction they draw between gossip and rumor that indexes that association, perhaps account for the organization of the ethnographic material in their book by something along the lines of culture areas. The body chapters are titled "Africa," "India," "New Guinea," and "European and American Witchcraft," as if to suggest that, across broad areas of cultural homogeneity, gossip could be studied as an identifiable (and thus comparable) social phenomenon in small, face-to-face societies. Although they comment at length on the importance of context in conditioning the social efficacy of gossip and rumor (30, passim), they do not explain what they mean by context, nor how context might be stabilized for the purposes of the cross-cultural comparison they pursue successively through the chapters of the book.

In thus associating gossip with small-scale societies, Stewart and Strathern let scale operate implicitly in their analysis, as Warner does in drawing a sharp distinction between gossip and public discourse. Scale must, indeed, be one of the contextualizing frames for any translation of "publics," but I wish to push it from the implicit background to the fore of my own analysis. If we let go of these implicit associations between scale and categories of discourse, we can see that scale does not have any bearing on the source of information in circulation, the nature of truth claims being made, the theories of agency and causality in play, or any other epistemological characteristics of the discourse in question. What scale bears on is the linguistic register of that discourse. Is it pragmatic speech situated in a performative context, or is it semantic speech styled as propositional claims about the world? I suggest that one of the ways the Cypriot context may be distinguished by a particular conspiracy attunement is that in it, for reasons of scale, public discourse on conspiracy theory transpires in the register of pragmatic speech, and relations among writers and readers are robust social relations rather than relations of "stranger sociality," in Elizabeth Povinelli's term, drawing on Warner (Povinelli 2011, 156ff.). In examining press coverage of the theft of the president's body in Cyprus, I aim to show how scale thus expresses a relationship between *social* and *public*, using each concept against the other in order to emphasize the contours that substantively define them and formally limit them in their distinction. Tracing these contours is another way of understanding context.

In this case study, the material is, as I noted earlier, narrowly textual, but I do not see this as a radically limiting or distorting constraint on my analysis of the event. I follow Warner's line in seeing publics as inherently "intertextual"—that is, as "frameworks for understanding texts against an organized background of the circulation of other texts, all interwoven not just by citational references but by the incorporation of a reflexive circulatory field in the mode of address and consumption. And that circulation, though made reflexive by means of textuality, is more than textual" (16). Texts, in other words, are a great place to start if one wants to discern and analyze publics. In their circulation, they are the material by which publics make themselves, doing a special kind of "metapragmatic work," as Warner puts it, to summon publics into being through their address (12); texts are also the means by which publics recognize themselves as such, as they reflexively receive and redirect that address. The knowingness about conspiracy theory that I have framed as conspiracy attunement in the press coverage of the president's body in the Cypriot context is thus "more than textual" (16), too, arising as it does from the circulation of texts; writers carry this attunement into a public discussion already underway, structured at least somewhat by previous instances of performative public speech, and recasting those instances as the grounds of further discussion and an impetus to continue talking.

These are among the reasons I chose to study print newspapers rather than online media. I had other reasons, too. In 2009–2010, with the exception of a few still-incipient social media platforms, web-based media had not yet achieved the generality, popularity, and ubiquity they have in everyday life at the time of this writing. Online news media, in particular, were for the most part sparer versions of the print newspapers that circulated in Cyprus; I did not find full coverage of the events in the online editions archived by the newspapers I consulted after the fact. More to the point, print newspapers gave me a focused vantage on *readership*. Newspapers in Cyprus had (and have) explicit political identities, and many have political party affiliations. These affiliations have helped me substantiate what Warner calls "the social basis" (74) or "social character" (90) of the reading publics addressed by newspapers; that their readerships were (and are) identitarian to some degree facilitates my observations about the intertextuality of the publics constituted by readership. My speculation regarding who was addressing whom in their pages, who was witnessing that address, and who was feeling addressed by it is thus grounded in an ethnographically informed understanding of the social field that structured the theories and arguments pursued by journalists and opinion writers in their public discourse.

To get a sense of this discourse, I looked at four Greek-language newspapers published in the Republic, held in the digitized and microfilm collections of the Press and Information Office in Nicosia; and I looked at six Turkish-language newspapers published in the TRNC, held in the hard-copy collections of the National Archives and Research Department in Kyrenia/Girne.[17] These papers spanned the political spectrum. I also selected several independent publications, not associated with political parties, in each regime.

In the Republic, I consulted *Politis* (Citizen), an independent, left-leaning, pro-peace paper; *Simerini* (Today), a far-right-wing paper owned by the DIAS company along with *Sigma* television, one of the most popular networks in the Republic; *Philelevtheros* (The Liberal), a mainstream independent paper with the widest circulation in the south; and *Haravgi* (Dawn), the newspaper of AKEL, the communist party headed by President of the Republic Demetris Christofias, who was in power when Papadopoulos's body was stolen. In the TRNC, I looked at *Kıbrıs* (Cyprus), an independent, pro-peace paper with the widest circulation in the north; *Star*, a pro-peace paper aligned with the progressive government then in power; *Afrika*, an independent opposition paper with a unique history and position in Cypriot public culture that I discuss below; *Halkın Sesi* (People's voice), a right-wing paper with the longest history of any in the TRNC; *Güneş* (Sun), a small right-wing paper; and *Yeni Düzen* (New Order), the newspaper of the pro-peace Republican Turkish Party (CTP) headed by the president of the TRNC, Mehmet Ali Talat, who was in office when Papadopoulos's body was stolen.[18] I also accessed articles and op-eds published in the *Cyprus Mail*, an independent English-language daily published in Nicosia that has open online archives.

Differences between the regimes of media publicity in the north and south of Cyprus are many and complex; for my purposes, it is most important to highlight differences in the way authorship is attributed and sources are cited. Many of the news pieces covering events in the south that appear in northern newspapers are published without authorship attribution; such pieces addressing the president's body were nearly identical across most of the northern newspapers. This is due at least in part to the reliance of northern papers on the TRNC's Press and Information Office, whose staff prepare and distribute daily summaries of stories published in southern newspapers for news about the south. (In this respect, the Press and Information Office in the TRNC plays a role akin to that of commercial news agencies in Turkey that conglomerate and redistribute news stories to various media outlets; such stories, too, appear in Turkish newspapers without authorship attribution.) While the Press and Information Office in the Republic likewise prepares summaries of news pieces published in northern newspapers for distribution to southern newspapers, my research rarely concerned such news, given that the crime and its investigation took place in the Republic. I should also note that, due to the extremely repetitive quality of the news summaries published in most of the northern newspapers I consulted, I focus more in my analysis of those papers on op-eds and editorials, where I found richer and more varied discussion of the president's body, as well as named authors. In my analysis of southern newspapers, however, I consider news stories as well as op-eds and editorials, as both genres were usually explicitly authored and full of opinion.

All four southern papers that I consulted followed the same basic arc of news reportage. They announced the theft of the president's body immediately upon its discovery and gathered comments from Cypriot and foreign politicians; they covered Papadopoulos's one-year memorial, held at his gravesite, then an active crime scene, the following day; and they detailed the progress of police investigations. These started with the examination of the crime scene and moved on to a search of the Papadopoulos family's compound at Strakka, outside Nicosia; the discovery of a potentially distinctive stone dust (gypsum) at the crime scene; the analysis of DNA evidence, cell phone data, and satellite imagery; and the enlistment of investigators from

Interpol, the FBI, and Israeli intelligence. Finally, the investigation took a turn to the "underworld" to explore the possibility of an organized ransom scheme. By the end of December 2009, the investigations had reached a dead end and press coverage had for the most part dwindled to an occasional paragraph reporting the absence of news.

On January 9, 2010, however, an incident transpired that revived media attention to the theft. The Greek flag that had stood beside the Cypriot flag at Papadopoulos's tomb was found stripped off its pole, torn and discarded some distance away in a streambed. Many southern papers reported that police were not ruling out a connection between this act of what they variously called "desecration" or "vandalism," on one hand, and the theft of Papadopoulos's body less than a month earlier, on the other (Dalitis 2010; Orphanidou 2010; Azas 2010). A few days later, on January 11, the media mogul Andy Hadjikostis, CEO of the DIAS company, which owned *Sigma* television as well as the *Simerini* newspaper in the south, was shot to death outside his home. The following day, *Simerini* ran a full front page on the murder, suggesting its connection to the theft of Papadopoulos's body, the removal of the Greek flag from his tomb, the slogans written on walls in south Nicosia, and the vandalism—discovered the same day Hadjikostis was killed—of dozens of graves in the Agiou Nikolaou cemetery in the southern port city of Limassol, including the tomb of former president Spyros Kyprianou, reported in the same edition of *Simerini* (Ioannou 2010a).[19] In an unattributed piece on its front page, titled "We Will Not Succumb to Terrorism," *Simerini* underscored the suspiciousness of this series of events culminating in the murder of Hadjikostis:

> Someone is not letting this place relax. Someone doesn't want citizens to live in conditions of security and peace. The cold-blooded murder of Andy Hadjikostis appears to be aimed at inflaming passion and hatred. Perhaps at creating conditions of abnormality and terrorism. We hope we are wrong. The DIAS company, and especially *Simerini*, assure the Greeks of Cyprus that we will not be stopped. We will not be afraid. We will not be terrorized. (*Simerini* 2010)

Although, according to the police spokesman, the police hesitated to draw connections between Hadjikostis's murder and the two incidents at Papadopoulos's grave, editorialists were more eager. Two days after the shooting, Makarios Drousiotis, whom I discussed in Part 2.1, posted a blog entry tracking the theories that were already circulating by then in the southern press. Foremost among these was the theory published in *Simerini* connecting the murder to the theft of Papadopoulos's remains, based in the understanding that Papadopoulos and Hadjikostis had shared a common enemy in the supporters of a new solution to the Cyprus issue that would be discussed a month hence, in January 2010, when UN secretary general Ban Ki-moon visited Cyprus to aid in the peace talks that had resumed after Christofias's election as president (and Papadopoulos's defeat). Hadjikostis, whom Drousiotis described as an "apolitical, zealous and powerful businessman," was indeed "such a businessman," he said,

> that he recently signed a fat contract with the UNDP to produce television programs promoting a reconciliation campaign, in light of the new plan for a solution! Yes, you read it right: the new plan for a solution. And it is alleged that he was so trenchantly against a solution that they killed him! The utter absurdity. (Drousiotis 2010b)

In addition to this "absurd" theory of the Hadjikostis murder, Drousiotis mocked other journalists who had written that he was killed by MIT (Turkish Intelligence) or that it was "a conspiracy of foreign powers" to destabilize Cyprus: "the only evidence being that the victim's home [where he was shot] was near the American Embassy!" He continued,

> A worthy young man, murdered in the most cowardly way, leaving behind a family tragedy. And these hawks with their sick minds, these ... defenders of "principles and virtues" that they have never respected in any way up to today, now try to increase the value of their political stock by trading on an unburied corpse. Exactly the same as in the case of the theft of Tassos Papadopoulos's corpse, when they gathered like vultures to feed on his remains. (Drousiotis 2010b, ellipsis original)

For Drousiotis, the same ethnonationalist political motivations not only explained the surge of conspiracy theories penned by these "defenders of 'principles and virtues'" in both cases, but more: they explained the very same theories, implicating the very same repertoire of possible enemies. The connection between the two cases, rendered legible by conspiracy theory, was enhanced by Antonis Kitas himself, known as the "Al Capone" of Cyprus: the man who was eventually charged and convicted of masterminding the plot to steal Papadopoulos's body while serving a life sentence in the

Central Prison—and a true gift to Cypriot journalists. According to reports in *Philelevtheros*, when Kitas was questioned (in prison) by police about the theft in March 2010, he named as co-conspirators two men, unrelated to him—Alexi Mavromichali and Yiannou Ioannou—who were already suspects in the attempted murder of two yet other men, known as the Grigoriou brothers, one of whom—Andreas—was also implicated in the murder of Hadjikostis by Kitas. "A Darker Landscape Emerges," went one *Philelevtheros* headline, framing this conspiracy within a conspiracy (*Philelevtheros* 2010b).[20]

Meanwhile, in the middle of March 2010, papers reported that a different inmate in the Central Prison, Andreas Aristodimou, known as "the Yurouki,"[21] was bringing a libel case against the former director of the Central Prison for telling police the previous December, after the theft of Papadopoulos's body was discovered, that a "lifer" (ισοβίτης) in his custody—namely, Aristodimou—had threatened in the past to steal the remains of former president Spyros Kyprianou for ransom, and was therefore the likely culprit in the Papadopoulos theft (*Philelevtheros* 2010a). Aristodimou's name had circulated in the press as the prime suspect in the Papadopoulos case from December onward, establishing a connection between the two former presidents as the intended victims of the same crime. Once Antonis Kitas was named as the prime suspect, in March 2010, Aristodimou brought the libel suit to protest his innocence publicly, his lawyers said. His claims also underscored the plausibility of an inmate's masterminding a plot of this kind from inside the Central Prison, whose security procedures had already been discredited by Kitas's escape from custody in 2008. The theorizing and countertheorizing that ensued from the theft of Papadopoulos's body thus acquired additional temporal coordinates as time passed, opening onto new horizons of suspicion at the same time as they retraced and substantiated earlier theories.

The right-wing paper *Simerini* offered perhaps the most extensive coverage of all the southern papers I consulted. The day after the theft, on December 12, 2009, *Simerini* ran five full pages of news and opinion; the following day, it offered three pages on Papadopoulos's memorial and ran an uncredited "position" piece alongside the news:

> Public opinion has not yet recovered from its shock, abhorrence, and rage at the unprecedented grave robbing of former President of the Cypriot

Democracy, Mr. Tassos Papadopoulos. The theft of his corpse by unholy persons, as yet unknown, has provoked indignation among all citizens at this unbelievable outrage, which is an attack on our civilization, our ethics and traditions, our values and our principles as Greeks [Ελλήνων] and as Christians. Cyprus, once again, presents itself internationally as a place where anything can happen. . . .

In whose interest would it be to provoke and disturb the state, to embroil us in unrest and to drive us to catastrophe? First, the Turks. After the destructive opening of checkpoints, the free areas [i.e., the Republic] became an open field. To the extent that our National Guard wondered what to protect us from, were they concerned about the Attilas [i.e., Turkish military] or MIT agents [i.e., Turkish intelligence] behind them? . . . What security measures are in place for the ministries, for government services and buildings, for roads, airports, electrical and telephone installations, community and other buildings, etc.? Hardly any or, in fact, none. Why? Because there exists this delusion that such an attack could never happen to us. . . . Our best teachers, our Israeli neighbors, know very well how to defend themselves against internal and external enemies. (Loizou 2009)

Michalis Papadopoulos penned an op-ed the following day in *Simerini*, sounding a note of empathetic understanding for Cypriots horrified and enraged by the theft but warning against the "darkest fantasies" it had aroused. Comparing the theft of Papadopoulos's corpse to the events of September 11, he evoked the contradiction Cypriots were living through: "It can't be possible . . . but it is."

And yet, in the midst of anxious confusion anchored in violent feelings, it is necessary that thought remain sober, that it not hasten to be written down on paper, that it not get swept away in fiery speeches, that it be kept at a distance, until we can take the necessary step back from the mist surrounding the events and recall the freedom of calm. So that suspicions become clues, so that the game of fantasies can be grounded in tangible things. For now, all that exists is an empty grave. This empty, pillaged grave carries the body of unfulfilled history. (Papadopoulos 2009)

The same day, December 13, as if anticipating the securitarian xenophobia that would be expressed in *Simerini*, the left-leaning *Politis* published an op-ed by Chrysostomos Perikleous, warning of dire consequences should citizens rush to judgment in this case. Rather than denouncing conspiracy theory, however, Perikleous offered a counter-theory of his own, tracing a connection between the recent events and the "corrosive work" of nationalist ideology among Greek Cypriots promoted by the paramilitary National Front in the 1960s.[22] "There is no longer any doubt," Perikleous wrote,

> People are seeking to make trouble domestically by conspiring in acts of provocation. What are the conspirators trying to accomplish? Obviously, to interrupt the path that the President of the Democracy is taking toward a solution [to the Cyprus Problem]. First, attacks on Turkish Cypriots who were circulating in the free areas [i.e., the south]. Next, slogans like *Kıbrıs Turktur* [in Turkish: "Cyprus is Turkish"], written in red on walls in Nicosia. Now, the desecration of the grave of Tassos Papadolpoulos, the "symbol-in-chief of resistance to false solutions." The goal is obviously to provoke righteous indignation among "true patriots" that will legitimate the escalation of trouble in the pliable minds of brainless false patriots. The ultimate goal can be nothing other than to undermine any position from which we might achieve a solution. One necessary reminder. On 21 May 1969, the founding declaration of the National Front circulated, declaring their objective was "defense against external enemies," the "Hellenization" of Cyprus, and the cleansing of "vicious regimes." And in which the National Front, with its leaflet of 10 August 1969, demanded the resignation of Clerides [then the chief negotiator for President Makarios] and the interruption of the negotiations that were then close to finding a solution. The trouble inaugurated by the National Front was left practically untouched by the state and allowed to continue its corrosive work until the attack on the police in Limassol on 22 May 1970. And when the National Front finally dissolved, the trouble it was making was carried forward even more violently by EOKA-B, again with the goal of achieving "national dreams," until we arrived at the tragedy of 1974. Today, faced with a similar phenomenon, the immediate responsibility of the state is the investigations that will reveal the identity of the thugs and, above all, who is behind them. But it is equally a responsibility of all thinking citizens to react by showing that they are not apathetic spectators of these events. The Hydra dangerously spreads her plots in murky waters. We must stop this before it is too late. (Perikleous 2009)

In this piece, as in many others published in the weeks after the theft, writers drew a close connection between the theft of the president's body and the island-wide referendum on the Annan Plan five years earlier. Their theories explicitly addressed a deep and long-standing rift within Greek-Cypriot society—between left and right, or between those who supported reunification and those who were holding out for a different solution to the Cyprus Problem—along with the division between Greek Cypriots and Turkish Cypriots. Along these lines of division, on December 12, the first day of press coverage following the theft, journalist Aristos Michaelidis wrote in *Philelevtheros*,

> This act has no logic that would allow us to give it a logical explanation. But we can be certain that the sacrilege of the grave of Tassos Papadopoulos was not committed by a lunatic, in the medical sense of the term. It is not medical sickness but political sickness that is behind this act.... It is the result of fanaticism and extremism that has been growing, with ever greater intensity and danger, over the last five years. If we find out that the actors were not motivated by economic reasons, then it must be civil war [εμφύλιος], even if that characterization seems extreme and heavy-handed.... Already we are hearing theories, starting yesterday, expressed with an extremity that has affected everyone. Some say ... it was allies of Tassos who wanted to rally support around his symbol in view of developments in the negotiations, some that it was enemies of Tassos who wanted to send a threatening message. The government has done so much to ensure a good climate with Turkish Cypriots and with Turkey, but nothing to ensure a good climate among Greek Cypriots. On the contrary, it has made every effort, with both declarations and policies, to mobilize fanaticism and to leave the people ever more divided between "yes" and "no," even five years later. We have to say that we do not believe the people have come to the point of an "internecine" state because that is not even a question anymore. And that is why this was most likely an act of provocation to create fear, stress, rupture and conflict among Greek Cypriots. (Michaelidis 2009a)

Less than a week after the theft, in an op-ed eulogizing the "unforgettable" Papadopoulos in *Simerini*, Dinos Agoustis quoted at length from the "No" speech Papadopoulos had delivered on April 7, 2004, a few weeks before the Cyprus-wide referendum on the Annan Plan, encouraging Greek

Cypriots to vote against it. To characterize Papadopoulos's courage and patriotism, Agoustis invoked no less an authority than General Dimitris Alevromageirou, described as a decorated soldier who had served on the front lines during the "black summer of 1974," supporting the "eastern front of Hellenism" on the Green Line running through Nicosia and on the northern beach of Kyrenia, where Turkish naval ships had first landed that summer. Reacting to the theft of Papadopoulos's body, Alevromageirou said, according to Agoustis,

> To be sure, [the actors] were not Greeks (in essence or metaphorically). Today's imperialist dwarves are always afraid of the great ones. And Tassos Papadopoulos was not only a rock of Hellenism. He was a global fighter for freedom and democracy, and in 2004, with his speech, he slapped the red face of global conspiracy. (Agoustis 2009)

This theory, associating the theft of Papadopoulos's body with a "global conspiracy" to push the Annan Plan through, appeared frequently in the pages of *Simerini*. A few days after Agoustis's op-ed, on December 20, the paper ran a two-page spread in which Nikitas Kypriakou interviewed three close associates of Papadopoulos and talked them through the scenarios they found most plausible. One of the associates, Giorgos Iliades, hesitated to answer Kypriakou's questions directly, given the paucity of evidence: "I might have some thoughts on this, but then I would second-guess them. The one thing I can say is that I can't believe it could be Greek Cypriots who did this. The theft of a corpse is not in our 'culture,' even the corpse of a president. I think it's most likely that this was done by some secret service" (Kypriakou 2009). Asked by Kypriakou—as were all the associates he interviewed—whether Papadopoulos, after his death, was "still considered a threat inside or outside Cyprus," Iliades replied, "Yes, he is still a threat, even dead. The foreigners wanted a president for solution. Any kind of solution. They were indifferent to the content. It seems they have found their man in Christofias. But Tassos was a fighter" (Kypriakou 2009). His pinpointing "foreigners" who wanted "any kind of solution" here suggests that the "secret service" he had in mind was neither Cypriot nor Turkish but rather one operating locally on behalf of the Great Powers—perhaps the CIA or MI6—which had long occupied a critical place in conspiracy theories of the division in 1974.

Conspiracy theories that pointed to Greek Cypriots rather than to Turkish Cypriots, Turks, or other foreigners were less prominent in the press coverage and often attacked by unsympathetic journalists when they did appear. On December 14, for example, in a *Philelevtheros* op-ed, Aristos Michaelidis took a number of Greek-Cypriot politicians to task for doing nothing and saying nothing about the theft of the president's body. He noted that several political parties, including President Christofias's AKEL, had sent no representatives to Papadopoulos's memorial, held the next day; AKEL's newspaper, *Haravgi*, had put news about EU policies on climate change on the front page that day instead. "Another journalist," he continued,

> wrote an article identifying this unprecedented sacrilege with the bombing of the statue of Markos Drakos [an EOKA fighter] in 1963, and there are witnesses, he said, that it was done by Greek-Cypriot provocateurs [though blamed on Turkish Cypriots at the time] so it is not responsible on our part to accuse Turks of being behind this abduction of the dead and thus ruin the climate [for peace talks]. We don't know to what to attribute all these reactions. It seems that paranoia is not particular to sacrilege. (Michaelidis 2009b)

Indeed, in comparison to the other southern newspapers I consulted, the Communist Party paper, *Haravgi*, had little to say about the theft and its aftermath. On the first day of its coverage, December 12, the paper ran a brief news piece on the front cover below the fold and carried a longer piece on the investigation on page 7 (*Haravgi* 2009a), as well as a statement from President Christofias and other AKEL figures, all expressing horror at the sacrilege and calling on Cypriots to react with "composure" (ψυχραιμία) and to wait for evidence to emerge before making accusations (*Haravgi* 2009b). On December 14, *Haravgi* ran a brief op-ed on page 4 by "Niki," who expressed collective condemnation of the act and sought to distance it from the field of politics by pathologizing the actors:

> Whatever the motives of the actors—thieves of the remains of former president of the Democracy T. Papadopoulos—their minds and thoughts were certainly sick and disturbed. . . . [Our entire society] knows that our country is, one way or another, going through difficult times, and that

patriotic resistance should be leveled against our one and only enemy: occupation [by Turkey]! The people went through the tragedy of 1974, the killings of EOKA-B, and the dark days of the coup; we know the meaning of resistance and unity. ("Niki" 2009)

Journalists writing for different papers engaged in heated parleys with one another about their theories of the theft. A good example is the varied coverage of the Papadopoulos family after their compound at Strakka, outside Nicosia, was searched by police on December 20. *Simerini* journalists gave especially sympathetic accounts of the family in their reporting, repeatedly quoting the statement by Police Chief Michalis Papageorgiou that the search had been undertaken with the family's permission and their blessing, and going to great lengths to correct the "misstatement" made earlier by police spokesman Michalis Katsounotos that the family had received a ransom demand (Azas 2009).[23]

The dots being connected in many other papers, including *Politis*, suggested that the trip to Zurich by Papadopoulos's widow, Fotini, a few days after the theft of his body had been made in order to pay such a ransom. On December 21, *Simerini* printed a statement by Papadopoulos's son, Nikolas, that he had read at a press conference earlier that day after the family met with the police chief for an official update. In the statement, *Simerini* reported, Nikolas explained that Fotini had gone to Zurich on a planned business trip for the Red Cross and the Levendis Foundation, her family's charitable organization: "I can't understand why this specific newspaper [*Politis*], all the while knowing the truth, would try to shed suspicion on my mother's trip" (Pallikaridis 2009). *Politis* struck back the next day, denying that the paper had ever reported that Fotini had made the trip under suspicious circumstances. "That rumor had been circulating for several days," an editorial note read, "and we simply reported that it had not been confirmed. Taking the baseless and unethical journalism of *Simerini* as a pretext, Nikolas Papadopoulos has attacked *Politis* yet again" (*Politis* 2009).

Such conversations across newspapers worked to consolidate certain conspiracy theories (among politically aligned papers) and undermine others (among contending papers). The frequency with which journalists alluded to the authors of these theories in other papers without naming them outright indicates their acute and collective attunement to the discourse on conspiracy theory that they were in the process of shaping and reinforcing.

They also assumed a readership "in the know" who would be able to decode these references.[24]

A different kind of intimacy with this discourse was reflected in northern newspapers, which focused on widespread allegations in the southern press of a Turkish or Turkish-Cypriot conspiracy. A number of editorialists reported statements by Greek-Cypriot politicians and community leaders that Turkish nationalist organizations such as the Grey Wolves were likely responsible for the theft. Northern papers spanning the political spectrum repeated the words of Archbishop Chrysostomos, head of the Greek Orthodox Church in Cyprus, in the days following the theft: "*Our* people [i.e., Greek Cypriots] didn't do this." Editorialist Elvan Levent expressed fear in the December 13 edition of *Afrika* that Turkish nationalists might in fact have done it, as this would surely have terrible consequences for Turkish Cypriots (E. Levent 2009).

In many northern papers, including *Kıbrıs* and *Star,* the mafia—Russian or Romanian—was named as the likely culprit, with ransom as the motive (for example, Özcanhan 2009). This same theory did not appear until much later in the southern papers, when investigations into political motives had borne no fruit. On December 15, just a few days after the theft, *Kıbrıs* ran an op-ed by Bilbay Eminoğlu:

> If we look at examples from other parts of the world, we see that incidents like this are acts of theft for ransom without any political motive. But the fact that this incident is taken as "the handiwork of Turks" by fanatic Greeks in their theories shows the extent to which they are driven by their hostility against the Turks. It is especially worrisome that neither Christofias, the President of the Greek administration, nor any other Greek public official, has spoken out against the Greek fanatics who are blaming Turks. (Eminoğlu 2009)

Several articles in the northern papers referred to Papadopoulos's notoriously dirty dealings with Serbian war criminals. In 2001, after Slobodan Milošević was ousted, Papadopoulos was named in a series of investigations and lawsuits brought by private citizens and officials in the new (short-lived) Yugoslav government against his law firm, which had set up off-shore accounts used by Serbian military leaders during the 1990s.[25] The lawsuits are a matter of public record and were covered extensively by the Cypriot and international press. R. Jeffrey Smith of the *Washington Post,* for example, reported that the Serbian deposits included proceeds of the sale of the "state-owned cell phone company PTT Serbia" to Greek and Italian phone companies, as well as gold from the Bor mines that was illegally diverted from the national treasury (Smith 2001).[26] Of particular interest in connection with Papadopoulos was the case of Predrag Đorđević, a Serbian businessman and naturalized citizen of Cyprus who had brought a civil suit against Papadopoulos as well as the Laïki Bank in Cyprus (now defunct) in 2000, claiming that large sums of his legitimate business revenues had been deposited erroneously into the Laïki Bank account of an offshore company, Antexol, that was used to launder money by Milošević during the UN embargo in the 1990s (Hassapi 2009). According to Anna Hassapi, writing in the *Cyprus Mail*, "Antexol was identified by the International War Crimes Tribunal as one of the eight offshore companies that comprised a money-laundering network, while all of them had opened accounts in Cyprus with the [Laïki] Bank and were registered in Cyprus by the Tassos Papadopoulos law firm" (Hassapi 2009). On December 22, *Politis* along with *Alithia*, another Greek-language paper, reported that Đorđević had been interrogated and his home in the Republic searched by Greek-Cypriot police the previous day as they pursued him as a suspect in the theft of Papadopoulos's body (Kalatzis 2009). George Psyllides, writing for the *Cyprus Mail*, interviewed Đorđević, who told him, "'I was fighting Papadopoulos when he was alive so now they are trying to intimidate me.'" According to Psyllides, "[Đorđević] said the officers were all right towards him but 'the people who sent them here are definitely sending me a message'" (Psyllides 2009a).

On December 23, the northern paper *Kıbrıs* reported on this reporting in the south, describing the suspicion cast on Papadopoulos by the investigations into his business dealings and highlighting the nonpolitical nature of Đorđević's suspected involvement in the theft of his remains (*Kıbrıs* 2009). Several articles in other northern papers speculated that, since Papadopoulos had been paid by Serbian war criminals, his family had massive secret funds the ostensible kidnappers were trying to access by ransoming the body.

More whimsical theories published in the pages of northern newspapers included the possibility, raised by Arif Hasan Tahsin in *Afrika*, that Papadopoulos's body had been stolen by medical students, consistent with a long-standing tradition of body-snatching for medical research in Turkish

> We have to understand that as long as the spirit of EOKA and TMT is alive in Cyprus, we can expect anything like this to happen. Opening graves to take dead bodies out and putting live people in those graves to die: in the history of Cyprus, we have experienced all of this. (Dalgıçoğlu 2009)

By "all of this," Dalgıçoğlu was referring to the violence perpetrated by Greek Cypriots, Turkish Cypriots, and Greek and Turkish military personnel during a series of episodes in 1963–1964, 1967, and 1974, leading up to the attempted coup and during the war that followed it. Forensic investigations into the cases of people who had gone missing in these episodes were ongoing when the editorial was published (and still are); they were a popular subject of press coverage in the north and south.[28] What is striking about this editorial is the connection Dalgıçoğlu drew between Papadopoulos and those missing persons—insinuating, perhaps, that Papadopoulos had been involved in the violence, and that the theft of his own remains served as some kind of retribution. Famously, too, in a September 2004 interview with a foreign media outlet, Papadopoulos had publicly denied that any Turkish Cypriots had been killed by Greek Cypriots between 1963 and 1974.[29]

A few days later, *Afrika* initiated its own investigation of the Papadopoulos family, based on a tip that the family had moved his body to Paris for reburial. Journalists took as primary evidence for this theory the fact that his widow, Fotini, had left Cyprus in a private plane when the theft was discovered and that she was not questioned by police about it, even though talking to the family is always the first thing the police should do. In a series of articles and op-eds published between December 19 and 23, reporters and editorialists at *Afrika* pursued the story through front-page headlines such as "He's Buried in Paris" (Paris'e gömülmüş) (*Afrika* 2009c), "Embargo: Blackout on Tassos" (Tasos'a ambargo karartma) (*Afrika* 2009d), and "Operation: Suspect Fotini" (Operasyon Şüpheli Fotini) (*Afrika* 2009b). Two theories emerged from these pages: first, that, in moving the body, Fotini was following Papadopoulos's wish not to be buried in Cyprus until the Turkish occupation ended; and second, that Fotini had staged the theft and moved the body in order to revive the spirit of EOKA and sow discord and suspicion between north and south. On the day after the first pieces of this story came out, an article on the front cover of *Afrika* claimed that the paper's coverage from the previous day had been embargoed in the south even though, if the story had concerned Turkish-Cypriot suspects, the media there would surely have covered it. Editor Şener Levent disparaged the southern press for its propaganda and its censorship of news coming from the north; the summaries of northern papers put together every day by the Republic's Press and Information Office, he wrote, only translated the news that made Greek-Cypriots look good (Ş. Levent 2009b). This complaint about what another of the paper's editors called "*Afrika*-phobia" (*Afrika* 2009a)[30] on the part of the southern and northern press persisted through half a dozen other stories and op-eds in the days that followed, even as the paper reported that the Greek-Cypriot police had finally started an investigation of Fotini and the rest of the Papadopoulos family—a development for which *Afrika* claimed credit. This storyline faded after December 23, when Greek-Cypriot police announced they had found no evidence of the family's involvement after exhaustive investigations of their multiple homes in Cyprus as well as their international contacts.

I read these stories in *Afrika* as pure and deliberate, possibly mischievous, meta-commentary on conspiracy theory in Cyprus. This is particularly obvious in the storyline about Fotini, which offers a model of conspiracy attunement in purporting to uncover the way news reporting was driving conspiracy theorizing, which in turn was driving news reporting styled as the denunciation of conspiracy theory. Zooming in on this one storyline shows the recursive narrative threads woven together into a web of conspiracies: the theft of Papadopoulos's body, the misbegotten wealth of his and his widow's families, the legacy of EOKA, the Turkish occupation of the north, the question of free expression and the free press in Cyprus, and the "lateral" and "racism-based relations" (per Demetriou, Constantinou, and Tselepou 2023, 4) between post-colonial Cyprus and the African continent, among other threads. Zooming out, the storyline about Fotini in the pages of *Afrika* appears as just one of many equally densely recursive narrative threads entwining the president's body in an ever-expansive web spanning many other times and locales. (As Strathern argues in *Partial Connections*, the level of complexity does not change with scale.) Those other times (episodes of violence in the 1950s and 1960s, the war in the summer of 1974, genocide in the former Yugoslavia in the 1990s, the referendum on the Annan Plan in 2004) and those other locales (Turkey, Greece, the United States, the United Kingdom, the United Nations, Serbia, Zurich, Paris, Romania, Russia, offshore) cropped up all over the press coverage of conspiracy theories in the immediate aftermath of the theft of the president's body. The multiplicity, contiguity or continuity, and mutual entailment of these times and places that journalists offered as contexts for theorizing the theft raise a basic yet pressing question as to how context itself can be defined. In conspiracy theories about the theft, we see the recursion and recontextualization of conspiracy theories about the division and its long and complex afterlife. This process of recursion and recontextualization is what creates and sustains a Cypriot context of conspiracy attunement. In the next section, I document and theorize that process directly.

3. RECURSION AND THE CURSE OF CYPRUS

On a predictably searing day in July 2017, I visited Papadopoulos's grave in Defterá, a dusty strip of cottages, shops, and gas stations on the southern outskirts of Nicosia. Referred to as a "village," like so many neighborhoods in this part of the city, Deftera had been a distinct municipality before it was absorbed by the sprawling periurban development of Nicosia that followed the division in the south in the 1970s–1980s. The cemetery where Papadopoulos is buried belongs to the small church of Ayios Nikolaos, parts of which date to 1880, as I learned from tourist information provided at the rear entrance. I was directed to the "old" cemetery, half a mile away, by a priest whose attention was divided by a large Russian tour group, but who grew immediately gracious when I mentioned the reason for my visit, and offered to take me over in his car. I declined his offer, but I followed his directions down a winding dirt road to a remarkably modest cemetery packed with tombs. Tucked into the corner closest to the parking lot was Papadopoulos's monumental gravesite, which I recognized from photo after photo of the crime scene published in Cypriot newspapers in the weeks after the theft of his remains in December 2009.

When I visited, eight years hence, the grave had long since been restored; I found it pristine, the massive marble slabs composing the gravestone and its several framing facets polished to a high shine. A thriving olive tree grew to the right of the monument and the flags of Greece and the Republic of Cyprus stood to the left, heading plots of well-tended, well-hydrated grass on either side of the vault covering the grave. The slab to the right of the grave held a bronze Orthodox cross, but the slab to the left is where I found the most explicit expression of Papadopoulos's political persona: a photo-engraved bronze plaque bearing his visage in middle age, and beneath it, a message signed as if by hand:

Σε καλώ να υπερασπιστείς το δίκαιο, την αξιοπρέπεια και την ιστορία σου. [I call on you to defend justice, your dignity and your history.]

These very words composed the concluding line of Papadopoulos's famous "No" speech, broadcast on Cypriot television on April 7, 2004, just a few weeks before the island-wide referendum on the Annan Plan for reunification on April 24.[31] With almost 90 percent of voters on both sides of the division turning out for the referendum, the Annan Plan was supported by 65 percent of Turkish Cypriots but rejected by 76 percent of Greek Cypriots, a much larger electorate. The plan's defeat is widely attributed to the strong stance Papadopoulos took against it. In his fifty-four-minute speech, now easily found on YouTube, he appealed to the historical consciousness of his "compatriots" (συμπατριώτισσες, συμπατριώτες)—the "sovereign Cypriot people" (Κυρίαρχο Κυπριακό Λαό) and, later in the speech, the "Greek-Cypriot people" (Ελληνικέ Κυπριακέ Λαέ)—to underline the significance of the decision at hand: "Now, the Cypriot people are called upon, individually and together, to write the history of the future of Cyprus" [Τώρα καλείται ο Κυπριακός λαός, καλούμαστε ο καθένας χωριστά, αλλά και όλοι συλλογικά, να γράψουμε την ιστορία του μέλλοντας της Κύπρου]. But he also imagined other audiences who did not share these stakes, representing other interests that had infected the negotiations and threatened, in his view, to distort any rational consideration of the Annan Plan by Cypriots:

I hope that our foreign friends will respect the people and the Cypriot Democracy. I hope they understand that interventions and pressure harm the dignity of the Cypriot people; they run counter to an express provision of the United Nations Charter and, ultimately, end up being counterproductive.

[Ελπίζω οι ξένοι φίλοι μας να σεβαστούν τον λαό και την Κυπριακή Δημοκρατία. Ελπίζω να κατανοήσουν ότι παρεμβάσεις και πιέσεις προσβάλλουν την αξιοπρέπεια του Κυπριακού λαού, είναι αντίθετες προς ρητή πρόνοια του Καταστατικού Χάρτη των Ηνωμένων Εθνών και, τελικά, καταλήγουν αντιπαραγωγικές.]

At great length, Papadopoulos outlined a series of deficiencies and ambiguities in the fifth version of the Annan Plan then up for voting that, in the years since, have occasioned considerable debate. He also railed against unjust problems of process in the negotiations that, he said, catastrophically disadvantaged "our side" (την πλευρά μας). As a result, he insisted, "Cypriots are not satisfied with the final Annan Plan; what is completely satisfied is Turkey's endeavor to control and preside over Cyprus" (Με το τελικό Σχέδιο Ανάν δεν ικανοποιήθηκαν οι Κύπριοι αλλά ικανοποιήθηκε απόλυτα η επιδίωξη της Τουρκίας να ελέγχει και να κηδεμονεύει την Κύπρο). With his concluding words, Papadopoulos returned to the historical theme with which he had opened the speech:

> I call on you to defend justice, your dignity and your history. [Σε καλώ να υπερασπιστείς το δίκαιο, την αξιοπρέπεια και την ιστορία σου.]

As Stefanos Evripidou reported in the *Cyprus Mail*, this last line of the "No" speech was printed on banners, T-shirts, and stickers donned by Papadopoulos supporters in and outside the church where his funeral took place in Strovolos, Nicosia, on December 15, 2008 (Evripidou 2008). "The message was clear," Evripidou wrote, noting the almost complete absence at the funeral of any reference by attendees to any part of Papadopoulos's long political career besides his denunciation of the Annan Plan.

The "No" campaign against the Annan Plan spearheaded by Papadopoulos was thus memorialized at his funeral as the apogee of his political career. This makes some sense, perhaps, given the proximity of his death to the referendum in historical time. But the heavy symbolization of the "No" campaign as the meaning of Papadopoulos's political life given at his death also positions the "No" campaign as the historical node of recursion for a long history of other campaigns—other conspiracies—surrounding Papadopoulos, as I show in this section. These conspiracies all date to the period between the anticolonial struggle of the 1950s and the division in 1974: the time of the cannibals.

From a biographical perspective, that time began for Papadopoulos when he completed his law degree in the United Kingdom and returned to Cyprus in 1955—the year EOKA formed. According to the research of Makarios Drousiotis, Papadopoulos joined EOKA at that time and worked in EOKA operations before becoming president of its political wing, PEKA.[32] Many sources attest to his lobbying, from his position in PEKA, against the power-sharing agreement between Greek Cypriots and Turkish Cypriots that became the governing framework of the Cypriot Constitution in 1960. Both before and after the division in 1974, he served in a number of advisory and ministerial roles in the administration of President Makarios, and as a Member of Parliament from the 1970s through the early 2000s. His tenure as president (2003–2008) began just before the historic opening of checkpoints between north and south leading up to the referendum on the Annan Plan in 2004. He died from lung cancer in 2008, shortly after his defeat in the next elections by Demetris Christofias, who had served in the preceding years (2001–2008) as president of the House of Representatives, and who had—though performing great regret—joined Papadopoulos's "No" campaign against the Annan Plan in 2004.

Long before the theft of his body buried his legacy in conspiracy theories, Papadopoulos was understood among many peace-minded Cypriots as the embodiment of political paranoia. Konstantina Zanou, a Cypriot intellectual historian, observed in a 2010 review of Yiannis Ioannou's book that the period of Papadopoulos's presidency was the "golden age" of conspiracy theory in Cyprus (Zanou 2010). In a bitterly comic piece published in *Politis* in February 2005, Makarios Drousiotis detailed some of the reasons why, reflecting at length on the pronounced "political paranoia" among Greek-Cypriot politicians during the lead-up to the referendum on the Annan Plan and following its defeat (Drousiotis 2005a). Excoriating President Papadopoulos and Demetris Christofias, President of the House at the time, he framed their "preoccupation with conspiracy theories" as a "curse" "bequeathed" by former president Spyros Kyprianou, whose own conspiracy theorizing was notorious but not, Drousiotis noted dryly, crippling to his political career. Regarding the accusations made by Papadopoulos and Christofias about a "foreign conspiracy" to undermine Papadopoulos's leadership by "remov[ing]" future reunification talks from the "UN framework" after the failed Annan process, Drousiotis contended, "This government is possessed by a persecution complex, and automatically blames everything that goes wrong for it on the foreigners" (Drousiotis 2005a).

In the conspiracy theories promoted by Papadopoulos around the referendum, Drousiotis heard uncanny resonances with those advanced by Spyros Kyprianou almost thirty years earlier, when he became acting president of the Republic following President Makarios's sudden death from a heart attack in August 1977. A few months later, in December of that year, Kyprianou's nineteen-year-old son, Achilleas, was kidnapped from the National Guard camp where he was training, held for a few days, then released unharmed. Suspicions fell on EOKA-B members who had been detained after the attempted coup in July 1974 and were seeking safe passage out of Cyprus. In his article, Drousiotis cautioned that "the real circumstances of Achilleas Kyprianou's abduction and release have never been documented to their full extent," and no charges were ever brought (Drousiotis 2005a). He suggested that the abduction of Achilleas did wonders for Spyros Kyprianou's political career; it was only after his son's safe return, and his subsequent policy of "purging" all people connected with EOKA-B from the administration and civil service, that he became a viable candidate for president. Kyprianou ran unopposed in the presidential elections of 1978 and was reelected five years later despite his florid "paranoia," manifested most clearly, on Drousiotis's account, in his accusations against a fascist movement he called the "Black Internationale," for conspiring to undermine his political power and possibly to kill him. In a tape recording that he made of himself and then released to the media, Kyprianou named members of this conspiracy, including a German diplomat in Cyprus, an Israeli soccer coach, and Tassos Papadopoulos himself, whom he suspected of acting on orders from Kikis Constantinou, a hotelier in the southern resort town of Ayia Napa, identified by Kyprianou as a former EOKA-B chief.[33,34]

Papadopoulos had been acting as chief negotiator on the Cyprus issue during Makarios's last term but was fired by Kyprianou in 1978, when peace talks were suspended; Papadopoulos ran as an independent for Parliament in the next elections. But there were no hard feelings, apparently; at the end of Kyprianou's last term, in 1988, Papadopoulos "praised" his leadership on the Cyprus issue, according to Drousiotis, and in 2000 became head of the party, DIKO, that Kyprianou had founded in 1976.

In this article, Drousiotis was liberal in his assignment of blame for this history of suspicion and dysfunction. In terms both of the leadership of DIKO and of "political paranoia," he traced a direct line of transmission from Kyprianou to Papadopoulos in the press, which Drousiotis—a journalist himself—presented as a public sphere where conspiracy theory in Cyprus lived most vibrantly. He was especially critical of the newspapers—spanning the political spectrum from the right-wing *Simerini* to the independent *Philelevtheros* to the Communist Party paper, *Haravgi*—that not only published but also actively advanced Kyprianou's conspiracy theories and, decades later, did the same with the "paranoid" theories about the "unseen hand" of foreign conspirators against Cyprus promoted by Papadopoulos and Christofias. Drousiotis supported the Annan Plan along with his newspaper, *Politis*, which a journalist friend of mine told me was the only one in the Republic to criticize Papadopoulos overtly during his presidency.

Some months after he had published this piece in *Politis*, Drousiotis developed his critique of Papadopoulos's own conspiracy mongering around the referendum in a report titled, "The Construction of Reality and the Mass Media in Cyprus" (Drousiotis 2005b).[35] Published in Greek and English on his personal website in October 2005, the report was also, he notes in the Foreword, sent to "all competent officials and bodies in Cyprus, as well as the European Union" (Drousiotis 2005b, 5). Drousiotis undertakes here to dismantle a series of claims made by Papadopoulos and his allies that certain individuals in Cyprus—journalists, pro-peace politicians, and leaders of bi-communal nongovernmental organizations (NGOs)—were "paid agents" of the United States and the United Nations during the lead-up to the referendum (Drousiotis 2005b, 7, 10). They were "paid," according to Papadopoulos and company, from development funds totaling approximately $60.5 million that had been donated by USAID (the United States Agency for International Development) and the UNDP (United Nations Development Programme) for projects promoting peace and reconciliation in Cyprus between 1998 and 2004. Papadopoulos was elected at the tail end of that period and, according to Drousiotis, he "changed the political landscape" (Drousiotis 2005b, 6), interrupting the momentum toward reunification that had been building since 1999, when Turkey—setting its sights on accession to the European Union—changed its stance toward the Cyprus issue and began actively supporting negotiations, and Greece suspended its objections to Turkey's EU accession. After the defeat of the Annan Plan in April 2004, Drousiotis says, Papadopoulos and his political allies, chief among them Demetris Christofias, undertook an "orchestrated misinformation campaign," maligning individual Cypriots for having allegedly accepted US and UN development funds in return for supporting and promoting the Annan Plan before the referendum. Drousiotis presents a blow-by-blow narrative of this campaign, beginning from a report commissioned by the United States in 2003 (before the referendum) and conducted by a private consulting firm to evaluate the efficacy of US development funds in promoting reconciliation in Cyprus. On his account, Papadopoulos (whose many misleading statements on the funding issue are compiled in Appendix 6 of the report) and his allies egregiously misrepresented this report as containing evidence of quid pro quo transactions between the development agencies and supporters of the Annan Plan.

Drousiotis is detailed in his reporting on the pervasive, intentional inaccuracies in statements on this matter made by politicians, their refusal to substantiate their claims, their unremitting slander of their political opponents as traitors, and especially Papadopoulos's curious decision not to order an investigation into the scandal that he himself had purportedly discovered. The Cypriot public addressed by the referendum appears in the report as credulous and overly submissive to the authority of the president, himself positioned in political discourse as the defender of Cypriot sovereignty against unlawful interventions by foreign powers. But Drousiotis ultimately emphasizes a larger point about political discourse in Cyprus here. The Cypriot public, on his account, lacks independent mass media and effective professional organizations for journalists; Cypriot journalism thus suffers from deficiencies in quality control and ethical oversight, and fails to furnish the public any space for political dissent. It is under these conditions that conspiracy theories hold such sway over what Drousiotis repeatedly calls "public opinion" (Drousiotis 2005b, 5, 7, 11, 21, passim).

For all his indignation, however, Drousiotis is rather uncharacteristically restrained in his report, which mostly sticks to reporting on what he conceives as the "true facts" regarding which monies went where and for what purpose (Drousiotis 2005b, 7). He does not theorize the cultural or psychological features of Cypriot society that enabled Papadopoulos's misinformation campaign to succeed beyond finding, in a quite summary manner, that Papadopoulos and his government were responsible for creating a "climate of intellectual terror" (Drousiotis 2005b, 26, cf. 37). For Drousiotis, the referendum was the definitive test for political paranoia; those who publicly opposed the Annan Plan were the ones who inherited the "curse" of Cyprus from Kyprianou.

As if proving this point, in a *Simerini* op-ed a week after the theft of the president's body in December 2009, Kostas Mavridis chided *Politis* for its coverage of the event:

> *Politis* is the victim of its own political passion against Papadopoulos for the big "NO" he said to the referendum, to the point that it has managed

to turn the event [the theft of his corpse] toward its own "interest." *Politis* ran a poll asking its readers who they thought had done it, and one of the choices was "Greek-Cypriot fanatic friends of Tassos Papadopoulos, in order to revive his 'No' to a solution." Personally, I don't rule anything out from among the plausible scenarios. But I reject this disgraceful attempt to create impressions. Although *Politis* framed this as a poll, it did not follow scientific methodology. . . . It will be interesting to see how many of those who choose the above-mentioned scenario have a financial tie to *Politis*. . . .

Regarding the sacrilege of the grave, it is likely that we will never know who did it, especially if behind the action is a mastermind who designed it as a provocation, as the President of the Republic said. However, he is mistaken if the government does find the perpetrators and it turns out that there is a Turkish hand behind it all (e.g., an extremist organization). Note that the Government Spokesman, just returned from abroad (he was with the President), immediately excluded such a scenario: "It's outside common sense"! Without a shred of evidence to exclude a Turkish hand, he did so. Why? In the meantime, *Politis* works to contaminate public opinion with its "polls." And perhaps, some months or years later, some auto-didact historian will discover new "circumstances" and new conspiracies because we did not accept his extreme views. We emphasize that this specific colleague at *Politis* refuses to answer the question in public that we have put to him many times: an explanation from his "source," who discovered the murder of 4 Turkish Cypriots 6 hours before the proven murders of 5 Greek Cypriots at Tziaos, as to how he knew the exact time when the Greek Cypriots were killed, which remained unknown to everyone at the time? When, of course, this "witness" declared that he was not present at the murders of the Greek Cypriots but in some strange way "knew" the exact moment of their murder. There is another interpretation of this still-unanswered question: sick political minds, whatever ideology presides over them, have the same sickness. (Mavridis 2009)

That Mavridis here connected the theft of Papadopoulos's body to the referendum on the Annan Plan is not at all unusual for accounts in the southern press. What distinguishes this piece from other commentaries is the connection Mavridis drew between the theft and yet another event that had generated a similarly intense debate in the southern press only six months earlier. In August 2009, the Committee on Missing Persons identified the remains of five Greek-Cypriot soldiers who had been on the official list of missing persons since August 1974—the central figures in a widespread conspiracy theory holding that some of the Greek-Cypriot missing were still alive and being held in detention camps in Turkey and northern Cyprus.[36] The "Tziaos five," as they came to be known, had been positioned in this role largely due to photographs taken of them by Ergin Konuksever, a Turkish photojournalist embedded with the Turkish army, after they had been captured by Turkish forces during the second invasion in August 1974. These five men had been part of a contingent of Greek-Cypriot irregulars and guardsmen who had been holding the Turkish-Cypriot village of Tziaos/Serdarlı after the attempted coup in July; they were therefore implicated in the murders of Turkish-Cypriot villagers committed by Greek Cypriots during the month between the first and second Turkish invasions that summer.

As Catia Galatariotou, a Greek-Cypriot social historian and psychoanalyst, writes in her case study of this controversy (2012), the Greek-Cypriot authorities had ample evidence of the soldiers' deaths from multiple sources as early as August 1974, including from the photographer Konuksever, whose film rolls were confiscated by Greek-Cypriot soldiers when he was captured shortly after the shootings—as well as from several Turkish army officers and Greek-Cypriot soldiers who had been stationed at Tziaos at the time. But, Galatariotou relates, the authorities appear to have concealed this information in order to sustain the theory that Greek-Cypriot missing persons were still alive and being held by Turkey as bargaining chips in ongoing negotiations toward a political settlement. Konuksever's photographs of the soldiers being detained were first published in September 1974 in *Μάχη* (Battle), an ultra-right-wing Greek-Cypriot paper, and they circulated widely for decades afterward.

In her case study, Galatariotou examines the coverage in two southern newspapers, *Philelevtheros* and *Politis*, following the identification in August 2009 of the remains of the five soldiers, found in a well near Tziaos along with the remains of over a dozen other people (Galatariotou 2012, 259). She observes that "confusion arose as soon as the facts . . . emerged" (258), citing as one among many examples the fiery debate over contradictory reports by two Greek-Cypriot witnesses at Tziaos—one of whom claimed to have seen Greek Cypriots shoot four Turkish-Cypriot combatants six hours before the five Greek-Cypriot soldiers were shot by Turkish Cypriots. It appears that this witness is the anonymous source whose account Mavridis impugns in his *Simerini* article (Mavridis 2009), though the more overt target of his attack is the "auto-didact historian" who had used that witness as a "source" in his own article in *Politis*. The latter was, I think, almost certainly Makarios Drousiotis, who had published an article on the controversy in *Politis* on August 15, and who was the target of many other attacks in *Simerini* at the time Mavridis was writing, after the theft of Papadopoulos's body.[37]

In his *Politis* article about the Tziaos five, published on August 15, 2009 (Drousiotis 2009c), Drousiotis undertook to "put events in their correct series," addressing himself to the "average citizen" who had gotten "lost in the accumulation of reports, witness testimony, and interviews with the protagonists" that had "bombarded" the public since the soldiers' remains were identified the previous week. Reviewing the movements of the relevant contingents of the Greek-Cypriot National Guard and the Turkish army between the first and second invasions, Drousiotis noted that, according to his source at the Committee on Missing Persons, the photographer (Ergin Konuksever) and a Turkish army commander (Hakkı Brotaş) had given information to the committee at the time that made it clear the five soldiers had been killed. Drousiotis related the rest of the story of Konuksever who, along with his photographer colleague, Adem Yiavuz, was captured and beaten by Greek-Cypriot National Guardsmen before being transferred to a hospital in Nicosia. Yiavuz died there, but Konuksever was saved by a Greek-Cypriot doctor, with whom he was reunited in 2008 while visiting Cyprus from Turkey. A Greek-Cypriot guardsman who had confiscated the cameras of the two photographers when they were captured told the Cypriot state news agency, RIK, that he had sent the cameras and film rolls with a colleague to the National Guard headquarters; along the way, Drousiotis wrote, "It appears that the equipment and film were delivered as plunder." When the photographs of the soldiers, still alive in captivity, were published in Μάχη, that paper claimed it had purchased the photographs from an "unknown person." In his article, Drousiotis emphasized how hopes that the soldiers might still be alive were ignited and sustained among their relatives by these photos, along with the government's repeated statements that it had no knowledge as to the fate of the soldiers. He quoted the sister of one of the soldiers, interviewed in *Philelevtheros* after the remains were identified in 2009, saying, "They left us in ignorance and they used us for propaganda purposes. It appears that they used us. That's the most tragic part."

In Drousiotis's account, the mainstream *Philelevtheros* and right-wing *Simerini* were taking the discovery of the remains of the soldiers in 2009 as a pretext to campaign for bringing Turkey to court for war crimes; certain journalists of what he calls "the patriotic front" criticized the Greek-Cypriot government and other politicians who took a more moderate line (Drousiotis 2009c). One such journalist from "the patriotic front" was Michalis Ignatiou, a Greek-Cypriot columnist for the Athens-based *Kathimerini* (Daily), who called the moderates "spineless karaghiozi [καραγκιόζη] politicians." The reference to karaghiozi (Turkish, karagöz), the Ottoman traditional art of shadow puppet theater celebrated by many Greeks as national folklore, implied that they were acting as the puppets of Turkey. Drousiotis himself took the part of these moderate politicians who, he explained, were keeping quiet in order to protect the integrity of the investigations carried out by the Committee on Missing Persons, which operated with a mandate not to make findings as to cause of death or responsibility for death. Any violation of this mandate, Drousiotis warned, would endanger the committee's investigations, which depended on information from confidential witnesses who would refuse to participate if they felt vulnerable to criminal prosecution. Any attempt by the Republic of Cyprus to bring charges against Turkey, he concluded, would trap the Cyprus Problem "in an endless legal process that would benefit the politician-lawyers and the mass media . . . but the price would be paid, once again, by the relatives of the missing" (Drousiotis 2009c).

Between these two articles by Mavridis and Drousiotis we can discern the interference among multiple conspiracy theories: first, concerning the alleged cover-up of the murders and the deliberate propagation of anti-Turkish propaganda by Greek-Cypriot authorities in 1974 and for decades afterward; second, concerning the alleged fabrication of an eyewitness account from an unnamed Greek Cypriot who had been present in Tziaos when the murders occurred; and third, concerning Greek-Cypriot journalists who, in their coverage of the controversy, promoted the veracity of the evidence of a new government cover-up, allegedly on behalf of Turkey, for political reasons. (It is worth repeating here that Tassos Papadopoulos publicly denied that any Turkish Cypriots had been killed by Greek Cypriots between 1963 and 1974 in 2004, only five years before the story of the Tziaos five broke in the press, and the same year the Committee on Missing Persons finally commenced its forensic investigations after thirty years of impasse.) Mavridis categorically dismissed Drousiotis's claims as "extreme views"; he mocked and pathologized Drousiotis's attraction to "conspiracies" as the "same sickness" shared by other "sick political minds"—though he did not specify whether the sickness in question was conspiracy theory, or rather a reconciliatory attitude toward Turkey, or alternatively "political passion against Papadopoulos." In any case, from Mavridis's perspective, the account of the second eyewitness at Tziaos in 1974 was of a piece with the government spokesman's rejection of a "Turkish hand" in the theft of Papadopoulos's body in 2009. A Turkish conspiracy to conquer Cyprus via the invasions foreclosed the possibility of a Greek-Cypriot conspiracy to Hellenize Cyprus via the coup, and vice versa. The intricate, recursive interweaving of the war in 1974 and the unfolding present in Cyprus in 2009–2010 reinforced this foreclosure. For Mavridis, the "political passion against Papadopoulos" that he found in *Politis*, embodied in the figure of Drousiotis, composed the connective tissue between these events and these moments in time. For Drousiotis, conspiracy theory itself—the "curse" of Cyprus, personified in this case by Mavridis—played that role.

Despite the evident fixation on the Annan Plan in Cypriot conspiracy theories about Papadopoulos, then, this is only part of his story—the final part of his long career as a trenchant hard-liner on the Cyprus Problem. When I started asking Cypriot friends and colleagues about him during the early days of my field research, I heard an astonishing range of suspicions and accusations going back to his earliest political activities. Many concentrated on his work behind the scenes, both in EOKA in the 1950s and in the early years of the Makarios administration in the 1960s, to accomplish what is widely known as the "Akritas Plan"[38]—a self-described "top secret" document composed in late 1963 but first published on April 21, 1966, in the Greek-language newspaper *Patris* (Fatherland).[39] The Akritas Plan outlined a set of "external" (international) and "internal" (domestic) tactics for the Greek-Cypriot authorities to "create the impression," as its author(s) put it, that the power-sharing framework of the 1960 Constitution was impossible to implement.[40] This impression would facilitate their achieving the right to amend the Constitution unilaterally and thereby to bring about the union of Cyprus with Greece by plebiscite, against the strong resistance of Turkey and the minority Turkish-Cypriot population. By some, the plan is also linked with apparent plots among Greek-Cypriot extremists in the Makarios administration to exterminate the Turkish-Cypriot population of the island. Turkish journalist Kıvanç Galip Över, for example, describes a series of memos published in the same newspaper, *Patris*, on January 22, January 27, and February 1, 1967, as the "General Operation Plan" of Akritas (Över 2007, 32ff.), which provided a sector-by-sector map of locations in Nicosia and instructions to "defence groups," "security groups," and "sabotage groups" in those locations to secure Greek-Cypriot families, homes, and businesses and to destroy Turkish-Cypriot ones. This "operation plan" was not contained in the original text of the Akritas Plan published in 1966, and its link to Akritas is speculative, but many Cypriots, especially in the north, find the link persuasive and associate the Akitras Plan with genocide.[41] Some cite the text of the original published plan to support this interpretation, including passages from the section titled "Internal Front" that describe possible tactics for creating a sense of "immediate danger" among Greek Cypriots that would warrant "intervention" and lead to constitutional amendment:

> Such a reason could be an immediate declaration of *enosis* [union with Greece] before stages (a)–(c) or serious intercommunal violence, which would be presented as massacres of the Turks. . . . Since we do not intend, without provocation, to attack or kill Turks, the possibility remains that Turkish Cypriots, as soon as we proceed to the unilateral amendment of any article of the constitution, will react instinctively, creating incidents and clashes, or stage under orders killings, atrocities or bomb attacks on Turks, in order to create the impression that the Greeks have indeed attacked the Turks, in which case intervention would be justified, for their protection.[42]

Catia Galatariotou considers this question of genocidal intention to be the crux of the debate over the credibility and meaning of the Akritas Plan, offering it as one example of "important historical events in Cyprus's intercommunal history" that "remain muddled and disputed, thus in a profound sense *unknown* to the collective mind":

> What is the truth about the Akritas Plan? Its authenticity is no longer disputed in Greek Cypriot sources (Soulioti 2006, 275–81), but its true meaning certainly is. When the Turkish Cypriot leadership insisted the

plan was a blueprint for genocide, did they really believe this? Were they cynically and opportunistically exploitative? And in either case, were they in fact correct in their public interpretation regarding the intentions of the plan's authors? (Galatariotou 2012, 249, emphasis original)

The Akritas Plan is one of the crucial pieces of evidence used by fans and critics of Papadopoulos alike to demonstrate continuity between the stance in favor of union with Greece that he took in the early years of the Republic and the stance against the reunification of north and south that he took as president in the last years of his life. It is a long-standing object of conspiracy theories about the division—the focus of debates over when and why it was written, and especially by whom. Key players in the Makarios administration have argued over whether he knew about the plan, or approved it, or might even have contributed to writing it. In his memoirs, former president Glafkos Clerides declines to give a definitive answer, noting, "A great deal of time is wasted in discussions of whether the Akritas Plan was known to and had been approved by Makarios"—though he states explicitly that he finds the plan consistent with Makarios's views and intentions at the time (Clerides 1989, 209).

John Reddaway, a career British diplomat who served in Cyprus for some twenty years before its independence in 1960, takes the Akritas Plan as "conclusive proof" of a conspiracy within the Greek-Cypriot leadership in the first years of the new Republic to "overthro[w]" the 1960 Constitution (Reddaway 1986, 83, 133) and to "eliminate the Turkish Cypriot community" (83). Not acknowledging even that it is a matter of debate, he states that the plan was "approved by Archbishop Makarios" and was "prepared" and meant to be "carried out" by his then–minister of the interior, Polykarpos Georkadjis (124, 83).[43] It was published in *Patris* in 1966, he says, presumably by members of Makarios's own administration who were secretly working against him, in order to "expose the mishandling of the national cause by the Archbishop"; by 1966, Makarios was supporting negotiations with Turkish-Cypriot authorities over a new power-sharing agreement for a unified, sovereign Cyprus, as against the union with Greece still sought by extremists:

> In a series of articles published afterwards in the same newspaper [*Patris*], it was disclosed that the Archbishop had assumed responsibility for the implementation of the plan and that he had appointed the former

leading member of EOKA, Polycarpos Georkadjis, who was then Minister of the Interior, to be the "Chief Akritas." The plan had been drawn up by him in 1963 on the Archbishop's orders and in collusion with Greek Army officers then serving in Cyprus.... The plan was in fact a conspiracy to dissolve the Republic of Cyprus. (Reddaway 1986, 133–34)[44]

On the other hand, Stella Soulioti, minister of justice under Makarios from 1960 to 1970, then law commissioner and attorney general of Cyprus, insists on Makarios's distance from the Akritas Plan. Makarios was not the author, she asserts, since "the author of the document is known to [her] and it was not Makarios"; he did not give it his "blessing," she says, and was "in all probability ignorant of it" (Soulioti 2006, 279, 281, 279). She emphasizes the "exploitation" of the plan by "the Turks," who, she argues, republished the document with strategic omissions in order to distort its meaning (280–91). From her perspective within the Makarios administration, the plan appears to have been written before "intercommunal violence" broke out on December 21, 1963, and it functioned as a way of "feeding" the "more reactionary members of the Organization ... with the notion" that their original objective—self-determination on the part of Greek Cypriots, leading to Cyprus's union with Greece—remained the objective of the Makarios government, while tamping down their potentially "precipitous" actions by limiting their interventions to constitutional revision (279). Citing as evidence her own "personal knowledge as a minister in the Makarios government between 1960 and 1970" (551n19), she asserts, "Only those involved in the Organization (Georkadjis and one other) were in the know from the beginning" (280).

Soulioti does not, in her text, identify this "one other" person besides Georkadjis who knew about the Akritas Plan from its inception. Authorship has been attributed by some to Tassos Papadopoulos,[45] including by Glafkos Clerides, president of the Republic from 1993 to 2003, who included a version of the plan in his memoirs (Clerides 1989, 212–19). Many others, however, including Reddaway (as noted earlier), name as its author Polykarpos Georkadjis,[46] the EOKA leader who became a key figure and strongman in the Makarios administration of the 1960s.[47] Georkadjis had been an adviser to Archbishop Makarios during and immediately after Cyprus's independence in 1960; he served as minister of the interior during the early years of the Republic, and in that capacity worked closely throughout the

On Conspiracy Attunement 207

1960s with Papadopoulos, his close friend and colleague in the Akritas organization,[48] who was minister of labor during those years.

Niyazi Kızılyürek, a professor of political history at the University of Cyprus, and the first Turkish Cypriot elected to the European Parliament (in 2019), published a book in 2006 based on a series of conversations he had with Glafkos Clerides after the failure of the Annan Plan. Clerides had supported the plan, in direct opposition to Papadopoulos, who had defeated him in the presidential election the previous year (2003). Clerides told Kızılyürek,

> To tell you the truth, I was abroad when this document [the Akritas Plan] was prepared and I saw it on my return to Cyprus.[49] I believe most of the work on the document was done by Tassos Papadopoulos rather than Georkadjis. He [Georkadjis] did not have the legal or educational background to draft such a document, however I never asked who prepared it. In my estimation the work was done by Tassos Papadopoulos, but I may be wrong. I do not have any evidence. Georkadjis often called on Papadopoulos to draft things for him because he did not have a legal background, that is why he named him his Deputy, and Nikos Koshis was his Chief-of-Staff. But neither Koshis nor Georkadjis had a legal background. The only one of the three who could have prepared it was Tassos Papadopoulos, possibly in cooperation with some members of the Greek military serving in Cyprus. (Kızılyürek [2006] 2008, 77)

Kızılyürek explains in his book that "the Secret Organization" referred to throughout the text of the Akritas Plan is "The National Organization of Cypriots," otherwise known as the Akritas Organization (Clerides 1989, 209, 219–20).[50] It was members of this organization, he explains, who authored the plan (Kızılyürek [2006] 2008, 90n53).[51] In his conversations with Clerides, the latter denied that he had been vice president of the organization, as rumor had it. Along with another future president of the Republic, Spyros Kyprianou, Clerides was, he said, put in charge of a section of the organization "under Koshis" when he returned to Cyprus in 1963. "Certainly Archbishop Makarios knew about it," he told Kızılyürek:

> Georkadjis was continually informing Archbishop Makarios that the Turks were arming. It was not a plan that was inspired by Archbishop

Makarios but one that he endorsed when he was told that the Turks were armed and that we needed to be ready. (Kızılyürek [2006] 2008, 78)

On the question of arming, Kızılyürek asked Clerides about an "American document" that had recently been published by Makarios Drousiotis, indicating that "Tassos Papadopoulos visited the US Embassy in 1964 and told them that in the event that Turkey should try to invade Cyprus and enter Cypriot waters... we will have one hour and 45 minutes 'to clean up the Turks in Cyprus'" (107). "Did this approach," Kızılyürek asked Clerides, "represent the Archbishop Makarios government or only himself [i.e., Papadopoulos]? Was he just fantasizing?" Clerides, describing Papadopoulos as more of a hard-liner even than Georkadjis, replied,

> Tassos Papadopoulos was thinking along these lines in case of a Turkish invasion and he was a Deputy of the "Organization." He was caught making preparatory phone calls in various directions giving instructions to kill Turkish Cypriots in the event of an invasion. Both Archbishop Makarios and Georkadjis warned him that he would lead us into a situation where we would be accused of having committed crimes and told him to stop. He was, however, thinking along these lines. (107–8)

In Clerides's telling, then, in the 1960s, the organization behind the Akritas Plan was internally divided between those, including Georkadjis, who saw the plan as entailing violence against Turkish Cypriots only as self-defense in the event of a Turkish invasion, and those, including Papadopoulos, who were indeed "thinking" along genocidal "lines." By the early 1970s, this division between Georkadjis and Papadopoulos had perhaps deepened, as Georkadjis grew increasingly intent on securing the union of Cyprus with Greece at any cost while Papadopoulos carefully tended his place inside the Makarios administration, which had by then adopted the accommodationist policy of unifying Greek-Cypriot and Turkish-Cypriot communities in a sovereign, independent Cyprus. According to many accounts, including contemporary US intelligence sources,[52] on March 8, 1970, Georkadjis led an unsuccessful attempt to assassinate President Makarios. Only a week later, Georkadjis himself was killed by two gunmen who have never been officially identified. Two years later, Papadopoulos, who had stood as best man at Georkadjis's wedding, married his widow, Fotini

Michaelides. It is worth noting that Fotini is the daughter of the late entrepreneur Anastasios Leventis, whose family is among the wealthiest and most powerful in the Republic. The Levendis Foundation holds some of the most important archives and art collections in Cyprus, and funds a great deal of research and exhibition work; almost all the researchers I have come to know in the south—artists, teachers, historians—had worked with the Levendis Foundation at one point or another. Some of those whose work was overtly "political"—that is, antinationalist—had been restricted in their access to holdings as well as to funding and collaborations with Turkish Cypriots. As for Fotini: As noted earlier, she was investigated by the police in the Republic after the theft of the president's body and became a central figure in conspiracy theories published in the northern press.

I first took note of this strand in Papadopoulos's story after the election of Constantinos Georkadjis as the new mayor of Nicosia in 2012, while I was living there. I was talking over coffee with a friend of a friend, a young economist who had just returned to Cyprus after studying in the United Kingdom for some years. When I expressed my curiosity about the new mayor's name, the economist confirmed that Constantinos was indeed the son of Polykarpos Georkadjis. *He was a big EOKA guy*, he told me. *This means it will be EOKA people who get city contracts now, who get to fill MP seats. It's a big deal.* He asked whether I had ever heard the rumors that Georkadjis (the father) had been killed by Tassos Papadoupoulos. *Everyone has heard it*, he told me, *and some people believe it. But it didn't make any difference in his career. He was still elected president. He was one of the few people from that time who held so much power for so long. He had his hands in everything.* After his marriage to Fotini, Papadopoulos had raised Constantinos and Maria, Fotini's children with Georkadjis, as his own.

Sometime later, when I asked a Cypriot historian about this rumor, she pointed me toward a book, *Two Attempts and a Murder: The Junta and Cyprus, 1967–70*, by Makarios Drousiotis (Drousiotis 2009a).[53] In this work, Drousiotis documents the multiple conspiracies in which Georkadjis was involved during the last three years of his life: his cooperation with the Greek poet and activist, Alekos Panagoulis, in his effort to assassinate then-dictator of Greece, Colonel Georgios Papadopoulos, on August 13, 1968; his collaboration with members of the Greek and Greek-Cypriot military and police in their plot to assassinate President Makarios on March 8, 1970; and his own murder a week later, when he was ambushed by two gunmen on a road outside the village of Mia Milia (now known as Haspolat, in Turkish) in the late night of March 15, 1970.[54]

According to Drousiotis, Georkadjis had driven to that spot to meet a key co-conspirator in the assassination attempt on Makarios—namely, the Greek army officer, Dimitrios Papapostolou, commander in the Mountain Commandos Special Forces (Λόχοι Ορεινών Καταδρομών) in Cyprus. Georkadjis was by then already under suspicion for the assassination plot and had been physically removed from a plane he was trying to board to Beirut on March 13; on Drousiotis's account, Georkadjis now expected help from Papapostolou in leaving Cyprus or otherwise securing his personal safety. More urgent, however, was Georkadjis's desire to stop the coup that he believed Papapostolou and officers of the National Guard were planning as early as the following day, according to documents he had read for the first time that evening.[55] These documents, detailing what is known as the "Hermes" plot to overthrow Makarios, form the pivot around which Drousiotis marshals his evidence of a cover-up in the investigations into Georkadjis's murder as well as the assassination attempt on Makarios. From the moment the documents were brought to Makarios's attention, Drousiotis argues, Makarios denied their authenticity and refused to countenance the possibility that Greek military officers might be conspiring against him (Drousiotis 2009a, 295, 305ff.). He was convinced, however, that Georkadjis had played a critical role in the assassination attempt against him.

These fragments have come to serve as pieces of the puzzle Drousiotis assembles of Makarios's responsibility in covering for Georkadjis's murderers. He draws from a number of primary sources, including the account given to journalist Petros Petridis by Georkadjis's trusted friend Kyriakos Patatakos, a police officer in the Central Intelligence Service (ΚΥΠ) in Cyprus,[56] who was with Georkadjis nearly constantly in the time leading up to his death, including at the shooting.[57] Drousiotis takes Patatakos's account as "the most authentic description of events," and uses it to craft a detailed, blow-by-blow narrative of Georkadjis's every conversation, location, and movement in the days between the failed assassination attempt on Makarios and his own murder (Drousiotis 2009a, 279). Among other sources for this narrative, Drousiotis draws on an interview he conducted with Georkadjis's friend Takis Skarparis, who was with him the day of his murder (287n15);[58] an interview he conducted with an anonymous Special Forces agent about the suspicious behavior of Papapostolou that he witnessed the night of the murder (297n24); and the interview given by the journalist Antonis Farmakidis to the newspaper *Alithia* (Truth) on the fifth anniversary of the murder, about the phone call made to him that night by a former employee who was working at the National Guard dispatch office and was responsible for passing along critical information about the crime and crime scene (291n19).[59] Drousiotis also cites the "top secret" Central Intelligence file on the murder of Georkadjis held in the private archive of Georgios Tombazos, head of intelligence under Makarios (286n13).[60] This file was the only source of information about that night given by Papapostolou's mistress, who admitted to intelligence officers that the alibi she had supplied for him was false.

It is apparently Drousiotis's use of this "top secret" file—regarding the testimony of Papapostolou's mistress and throughout the book—that attracted the critical attention of Efrosyni Parparinou, an archivist at the State Archives of Cyprus. According to a *Cyprus Mail* article by Charles Charalambous published on July 2, 2009, Parparinou had sent Drousiotis a letter in which she accused him of being "in possession of public documents that rightfully belonged to the state body" and of having "quoted them in his latest book, *Two Attempts and a Murder: The Junta and Cyprus, 1967–70*." The article emphasizes the swift and strong reaction on the part of the Cyprus Union of Journalists against the threats of a "jail sentence and heavy fine" made to Drousiotis by Parparino, who was acting, according to Drousiotis, on a complaint made to the *Philelevtheros* newspaper by the Georkadjis Foundation. The union denounced the threats, which they characterized as "anachronistic, illiberal gagging regulations" with no "constitutional basis." Drousiotis himself expressed disbelief at this turn of events. He told the *Cyprus Mail* that he had been granted access to the files in the private archive of Georgios Tombazos by his son, who inherited his father's papers after his death. On the other hand, he said, he had made many requests to the State Archives to see the transcript of the trial of Georkadjis's murder "but was told this wasn't allowed, despite the fact that the trial was open to the public" (C. Charalambous 2009).

From a stance of conspiracy attunement like Drousiotis's, the state archivist's attempt to "gag" his research into the murder of Georkadjis is entirely consistent with the tenor of the state's official investigation, which Drousiotis characterizes in his book as an utter sham. His most controversial claim is that President Makarios actively aided in covering up crucial evidence that Papapostolou and Makarios's own bodyguard, Athanasios Poulitsas, were the two gunmen, and moreover, that he vigorously directed investigations away from them:

> Whoever has written about the events of this period, including the author of this very book, has made the case that Makarios averted his eyes because he feared the negative impact on the Cyprus issue or the threat of a coup by the Junta. These judgments are completely subjective and they are not substantiated by witness testimony or other evidence. (Drousiotis 2009a, 306)

Drousiotis argues instead that Makarios "facilitated" the murder of Georkadjis—not arresting him but also not allowing him to leave Cyprus—while noting, "There is no evidence that would link Makarios directly to the murder" (308). He avowedly speculates as to Makarios's motives for covering up the crime:

> A mild interpretation is that he found it too disparaging to himself and his legacy to admit that his close colleagues were conspirators against him and they had their chief in the Presidential Palace. Another interpretation is that Papapostolou and Poulitsas had him trapped in a bad position, in the creation of the National Front as well as the circumstances of Georkadjis's murder, and they leveraged this for their immunity.... Whatever his true motivations, it is beyond doubt that Makarios made the decision from the outset to absolve Papapostolou and Poulitsas. (308)

The investigation into the conspiracy to assassinate Makarios, too, was superficial and toothless, according to Drousiotis; it "did not even touch" two of the men he identified as Georkadjis's murderers, Papapostolou and Poulitsas,[61] who were also, on his account, two of Georkadjis's co-conspirators in the Makarios assassination plot. Already deceased, Georkadjis was never officially implicated in the plot, but six co-conspirators were charged in May 1970, all Greek Cypriots and none Greek military personnel: Costas Ioannidis, Antonakis Solomontos, Adamos Charitonos, Georgios Taliadoros, Antonis Yenakritis, and Polykarpos Polykarpou. The charges against Polykarpou were soon dropped due to insufficient eyewitness evidence; the remaining five suspects were indicted for conspiracy to commit the murder of Makarios, though Costas Ioannidis was soon released—due, again, to lack of evidence. Of the four remaining men who were convicted, two

(Adamos Charitonos and Antonis Yenakritis) escaped from prison two years later and the other two (Antonakis Solomontos and Georgios Taliadoros) were pardoned by Makarios (319, 320).

And where was Tassos Papadopoulos in all this? Drousiotis does not include Papadopoulos among the various officials who attended a series of meetings with Makarios in the weeks after Georkadjis's murder to determine the direction of the investigations. He does note that Papadopoulos was the only member of the Makarios administration to attend Georkadjis's funeral, along with an immense crowd of supporters (302). In his book about Glafkos Clerides, Niyazi Kızılyürek asks Clerides about his "feelings at that time," remarking, "Tassos Papadopoulos said about Georkadjis, 'One of the few times in my life that I cried was when Georkadjis was murdered.'" Clerides replied,

> I believe it was because he was one of those who . . . they were friends. He [Georkadjis] had made him [Papadopoulos] a lieutenant of EOKA in the Nicosia district, but I know that on some occasions he went behind Georkadjis's back and denounced him to the Archbishop. He may say this now because it suits him to, but there were one or two occasions on which the Archbishop asked me, "Is Georkadjis doing such and such?" I asked him, "Who told you that?" And the Archbishop revealed a number of names to me. (Kızılyürek [2006] 2008, 146)

In the rumors I have heard about Papadopoulos's involvement in the murder of Georkadjis, his very swift marriage to Fotini, Georkadjis's widow, after his death has struck a few of my interlocutors as the strongest evidence of something suspicious lurking behind their apparent friendship. The conversation between Clerides and Kızılyürek briefly indicates another possible conflict—namely, opposition to Papadopoulos on the part of the National Front, a paramilitary organization of which, according to Clerides, Georkadjis was either a member or an affiliate (Kızılyürek [2006] 2008, 147).[62] In his book, Drousiotis makes no mention of Papadopoulos in connection with the killing of Georkadjis, and I have not been able to find any version of this theory in print, in any language. I am inclined to think it has not achieved widespread currency, though one Cypriot friend observed to me that, given the prominence of various members of the Papadopoulos family in positions of power in Cyprus today, it is precisely the kind of theory that I should not expect to find published. I heard more about the murder of Georkadjis from an investigator I knew at the Committee on Missing Persons, whom I sought out in 2014, a couple of years after I had conducted fieldwork with forensic archaeologists and anthropologists working for the Committee. The investigator was telling me how much information about the violence of the 1960s and 1970s was actually "out there," even though no one wanted to discuss it, which made the committee's investigations very difficult. *It's like the American ambassador and Georkadjis*, he said. *You've heard of them? Everyone knows who killed them, but no one will touch it. Their interest is in keeping Cyprus stable so that they can use it as a base of operations for the rest of the world, especially the parts that really matter. It's always been that way. Everybody is here: CIA, Mossad, Iran, the Chinese, everyone. It's a small island with a small population, they think it's OK if we kill each other as long as the overall structure remains the same. None of the Great Powers who were here back then would share the information they had from 1963–4 and 1974. The Americans, the British, the UN, they all did their own investigations and had files on the events, lots of information. But they would never share it with us.*

At the time of our conversation in the summer of 2014, Papadopoulos's son, Nikolas, was in the headlines for attacking Nicos Anastasiades, then the president of the Republic, who had resumed peace talks that February with Derviş Eroğlu, then the president of the TRNC. Nikolas accused President Anastasiades of conceding too much to "the Turkish side" from the outset and leaving the Republic in an impossibly weak position to negotiate. For his part, according to a *Cyprus Mail* article, Anastasiadis characterized Nikolas as "driven by unexplainable obsessions" rather than a sense of "duty" to resolve the Cyprus Problem (Evripidou 2014a). The previous year, in December 2013, five years after Papadopoulos's death and two years after the conviction and incarceration of the Kitas brothers and Sarbjit Singh for the theft of his remains, Nikolas had been elected leader of his father's political party, DIKO. Critics of DIKO in the Greek-Cypriot press noted that the theft of his father's remains in 2010 was the best thing that could have happened for Nikolas's political career. If, as Michalis Papadopoulos wrote in his *Simerini* op-ed after the theft, the "empty, pillaged grave" of Papadopoulos "carrie[d] the body of unfulfilled history" (Papadopoulos 2009), then Nikolas appeared on the political scene to fulfill that history by embodying the legacy of his father.

In that same summer of 2014, discussing party politics in the Republic with a Cypriot teacher I knew and his friend, a retired UN diplomat living in Nicosia, I asked them what they thought of Nikolas, less than a year into his leadership of DIKO. The diplomat looked at us with an expression of exaggerated surprise: *Did you hear that Jesus rose again in Cyprus?* My friend laughed: *I would never have thought someone could defeat the Annan Plan after death, but he's managed to do it! Tassos is still saying "No"!* The resurrection of Tassos in the body of his son, Nikolas, to spread the gospel of "No" to any solution to the Cyprus problem: this appeared to be the legacy of Tassos Papadopoulos.

And perhaps also the curse, in Drousiotis's term, as Nikolas also demonstrated a robust attunement to conspiracy. On July 15, 2017, the forty-third anniversary of the attempted coup, he posted a photograph on Facebook that he captioned thus: "No mention of EOKA-B by N. Anastasiadis in his remarks today [about the anniversary]. Only of the Athens Junta. Nor did he show up in Parliament." The photograph itself, a black-and-white street shot, depicts a dozen or so men milling about; in the Facebook posting, the following words were superimposed over the photograph, along with a red arrow pointing toward the head of a man standing in the background: "In the photograph, members of the treacherous organization EOKA-B, who had been arrested in Limassol in 1973 and were being transferred to Nicosia for trial. You can also make out the lawyer of Nikos Anastasiadis." These men were presumably being arrested for the bombings of police stations by EOKA-B that took place throughout the year 1973, leading up to the coup in July 1974. In his posting, Nikolas appeared to be indicating Anastasiadis's implication in the bombings, and by extension, in EOKA-B. Coming from the son of Tassos Papadopoulos, who was aligned with EOKA-B at least in its objectives, and stood to gain power after their coup if it were successful, this accusation of complicity might seem a bit rich. But just as conspiracy attunement does not imply *belief*, so does it not accommodate *hypocrisy*. It entails a vocabulary, a style of talking, and a range of performative affects—from cynical to rueful to playful—that indicate the speaker's knowingness about the prevalence of conspiracy theory in public discourse. The ends to which particular speakers wield that knowingness, and their efficacy in doing so, serve not to support or undermine their claims but rather to affirm the shared nature of the attunement itself.

INCONCLUSION (RECONTEXTUALIZATION)

You should be careful! F. told me, her eyes wide, laughing. A friend from the south, a scholar who had done her own research on the secret history of violence in Cyprus, F. always laughed when I reminded her that one of the topics of my research in Cyprus was the story of the president's body. The first time, a few years earlier—a few years after the conviction of the Kitas brothers and Sarbjit Singh—when I asked her if she knew anything about it, she laughed and told me she remembered the story, but not all of it; she recalled the involvement of the Kitas brothers, but not the outcome of the trial. *Mostly what I remember is that the story never made sense. Why would the Kitas brothers do this? They didn't need the money. The ransom just didn't seem like a good motive. And why would that poor Indian guy be involved?* She recalled how strange and funny it had been when the story finally came out that it had been the Kitas brothers and not Turkish nationalists who had stolen the body after all: *What an embarrassment for all those people who felt so sure of themselves!*

Now, years later, in the summer of 2017, I was organizing a day trip with Nicos, a mutual friend, to visit Athienou, the village where the Kitas brothers had lived. I asked F. if she wanted to come along but she declined, laughing again. *Do you think it'll be safe for you? They still have family living there.* She suggested I talk to the police about the case, but then warned, *No, on second thought—they have networks in the police, you shouldn't just show up asking questions, it'll get back to them. Even if Antonis is still in prison, it doesn't matter—they have people everywhere, they're running things from inside the prison.* She made an exaggerated gesture, raising her eyebrows and wiggling her fingers to suggest, I thought, either a puppet master or the sticky tendrils of a spider web. I asked her whether she thought they were really so powerful and dangerous; from the stories I had heard, it seemed possible they might just be foolish and incompetent. *Maybe they were making trouble, having fun, manipulating public opinion, muddying the waters,* she suggested, implicitly rejecting the possibility of their incompetence by underlining the success of the strategy she imputed to them.

The village of Athienou, when I saw it, was larger and more affluent than I had expected. Nicos and I followed the road there from Nicosia around the curving edges of barbed-wire fences marking the territory of the TRNC. These informal border lines, Nicos explained to me, which mostly kept to the contours of the hills spanning the plains between Nicosia and Larnaca, had been carved around Louroukina, a "mixed" village before the division that had ended up on the northern side of the buffer zone. We came upon a small blockade where the road turned east and saw a UN-branded farm outbuilding in the distance. In the hills beyond the road stood a series of watchtowers with the flags of Turkey and the TRNC flying high. The plains where we were driving, full of small cultivated fields, were Republic territory. There was not a person in sight.

Newly constructed villas on large lots, some with swimming pools, began to appear along the road as we drove into Athienou. We were soon picking our way down narrow village streets of brightly painted two-story homes and their well-kept gardens. Nicos knew where to go. He had documented dozens of coffeehouses in Cyprus for a photobook he had published some years earlier, and that morning we followed his research protocol: we located the church in the central plaza of the village, seated ourselves in a coffeehouse next door, greeted the patrons—all middle-aged or elderly men—and waited for them to engage us. A DIKO flag was flying above the front entrance, marking its alignment with the party of Papadopoulos, father and son. We sat for a time, chatting and drinking coffees to which we had been treated by one of the older patrons, but it was not until we moved to get up and leave that anyone came to talk with us.

Two elderly men—one more and one less—approached our table and introduced themselves. They addressed Nicos, asking where he was from, one's ancestral village being a commonplace for locating parentage, political orientation, and generation, indicating birth before or after the war in 1974. Nicos had spent the first year of his life in Varosha, a district of Famagusta, in the north—before the war—and this piece of information opened a conversation, itself a commonplace, about what life had been like in Cyprus back then. The younger of the two men, perhaps in his seventies, who was from the same region, recalled a village with many Turkish Cypriots who, he said, did not even speak Turkish. *They spoke Greek! They would get baptized!* They talked a bit, too, about the villages of Louroukina and Potamia, near Athienou, which had been "mixed" before the war and ended up on opposite sides of the buffer zone. The older man told us that Athienou had never been a "mixed" village. Panagia, the Virgin Mary, had always protected it, he said, and she saved it when the Turkish air force began bombing in the summer of 1974: *Panagia repelled the missiles from the church! Later on, a Turkish-Cypriot woman came here to rent a house, but she left the next day because Panagia appeared to her in the night and told her to leave.*

One of the younger patrons at the coffeehouse, sitting at the next table, slowly turned toward us, obviously listening to the conversation. Finally, he asked Nicos and me why we were visiting the village that day. Nicos took the opportunity to mention the name of Kitas. The man said he knew him. He laughed when Nicos explained that I was interested in the story of the president's body and how the Kitas brothers were involved. Between nudges from Nicos and me, he warmed up and started to offer observations of his own. He had grown up in Athienou, he told us, and he had known Antonis Kitas, who was a few years older; they had not been friends. Antonis had left the village when he was in his twenties and had been gone a long time, the man said. There were four children in the family, and only the youngest daughter was "good"; she still lived in the village and worked as a teacher. The other three siblings were "the bad ones," he said, though only Antonis was a murderer; the others, he thought, were mostly into drugs. Their mother was still alive but lived in a nursing home. And the patriarch of the family, Prokopis, whose name Antonis carried, had died just a few months before. Antonis had been released from prison so that he could attend the forty-day memorial service, accompanied by a large group of police officers who were paying special attention, since he had escaped from custody once before and they feared he would run. (His petition to the Parole Board for early release from prison due to ill health—made in 2021, at the age of sixty-one—was denied, and he is still in prison at the time of this writing [*Sigmalive* 2021].)

Prokopis died of marazi (μαράζι), the man said to us—a Cypriot word of Arabic origin that Nicos later translated for me as *sorrow*. Nicos understood the man to be saying that the father had died on account of the grief and shame brought to the family by his son's bad deeds and reputation. He asked the man if the village had any stigma due to Kitas, and the man very quickly dismissed the idea: *No, no!* He told us that he had actually seen one of Kitas's victims—*the one with a Russian name*—when he coincidentally passed by Kitas's car and saw her, dead in the back seat. Unsure whether I believed him, I asked him why he thought Kitas had murdered this woman. *Back then, Antonis had a relationship with Fanieros,* he explained. *Maybe it had something to do with him. They split later on, they're not close anymore, but back then they were. Fanieros was very powerful in this area.*

Fanieros: another notorious name in Cyprus, another connection with organized crime. I had already heard of Antonis Fanieros from a friend who was related by marriage to one of his distant cousins. I learned from my friend that the Fanieros family represented a power base in the Larnaca area; a different family, Aeroporos, controlled the Limassol area. I remembered a series of car bombings in Limassol when I was living there during the summer of 2010, which I thought had been connected to organized crime, and my friend confirmed the connection; it was the latest episode in a decades-long turf war between the two families, he explained. The Fanieros patriarch, Antonis, had been shot in the neck in the late 1990s but survived, and his businesses thrived after that. According to his legend, he had been captured and tortured by the Turkish military during an episode of mass violence in 1967, and later worked as a bodyguard for President Makarios, who had by then survived several assassination attempts as well as the attempted coup. By the 1990s, the Fanieros family owned hotels and nightclubs in the Larnaca area where they made money from prostitution and gambling. They ran a protection racket through a security firm in Larnaca and operated Larnaca airport. But Antonis Fanieros had also built a nursing home and contributed large sums of money to the poor. His extended family seemed to share his special synthesis of criminality and benevolence. My friend, who knew Fanieros's distant cousin, described the cousin as a "Robin Hood" figure: *He always came across as a very kind man who loved his family and helped people. Don Corleone. But that's how they work: they do you a kindness, then you have to do them a kindness. Favor for favor. Organized crime families are just like other families! I met him a few times at family gatherings—what a sweet man. Smiling, gracious, a sweetheart. You'd never know what he was involved in, stealing and having people killed.* I found it reported in several Cypriot papers that Antonis Fanieros had sought to get his criminal record expunged in 2016 so that he could run for Parliament as an independent. He died a year later from cancer.[1]

Nicos and I had talked a few days earlier about the Kitas family and he had warned me that villagers in Athienou might not be thrilled to talk with me about them. *People think of them as the worst criminals: brutal, filthy, shameful,* he said. *It's very different from how people felt about Fanieros. He had a kind of romance about him—more like the American Mafia.* Nicos had been a young adult when Antonis Kitas was tried for rape and murder; he remembered watching footage from the trial on the evening news.[2] *He was like a wild animal,* Nicos told me, *urinating in the courtroom, just the worst of the worst.*

Finishing our coffees, we got directions to the village cemetery from the old men at the table, explaining that we wanted to see the Kitas family tomb and visit Prokopis, who had died so recently. It was nearby, on the outskirts of the village, and quite large, especially in comparison to the cemetery where Papadopoulos is buried. We might have had trouble locating the Kitas grave, but we found the groundskeeper, who was watering plants that visitors had placed around a large family tomb, and he helped us. At first, when I asked him if he knew where the Kitas family tomb was, he seemed confused. *The only Kitas buried here is Prokopis, the father,* he said. *And his grave is fresh, they haven't even built the tomb yet.*

He pointed to the row of graves closest to the cemetery gate. All had gravestones adorned with photographs, wreaths, and flowers, but there were no granite vaults; the bodies were still above ground, buried in mounds of dirt. The groundskeeper asked me, *Are you family of Kitas?* I told him no, we were just interested in the story. *Well, there isn't a family tomb here,* he told us, *just the old man's grave.* Nicos remarked to me how modest the grave was, with so little adornment—only two small wreaths—in comparison to the one next to it. The photograph placed at the head of the grave showed old Prokopis to be a small, humble person, and poor, like a farmer, he said. There was no sign of family wealth or status here, no sign even of visitors. It was not the grand tomb I had been expecting for the patriarch of an organized crime family.

(Recontextualization)   221

A few days after our visit to Athienou, I went to see an acquaintance of mine, a middle-aged woman who identified herself as a Maronite—a Syriac Christian minority in Cyprus—and a refugee; her family had been forcibly displaced from their ancestral village in the north and fled to Nicosia during the war in 1974. When I told her about seeing the grave of Kitas's father, she told me she had always had suspicions about the crime. She did not recall much of the story—she could not, for example, remember who was tried and convicted—but the theft had left a strong impression. *From the very beginning, I always thought that it was the family of Papadopoulos who did it*, she told me. *Maybe I'm just mean, but I always had that feeling. He had lost the election, he was fading from importance, lots of people were angry with him by the time he died. I thought maybe his family wanted to create some attention and sympathy for him.* I told her that I had come across this theory published in newspapers; that the compound where his wife lived had been searched by the police in the days after the theft, that she had made a suspicious trip to Zurich, and so on. *Some people were really not convinced that it was the Kitas brothers*, I said to her, prompting. *I wasn't, either*, she replied, nodding.

Indeed, I have heard quite a number of alternative theories of the crime over the years. Another acquaintance, an academic, laughed when I told her I was working on a case study about the theft of Papadopoulos's body, and said immediately: *It was a scam!* She told me she had never believed the Kitas brothers were behind the plot: *It didn't make sense. Why would they go to all that trouble for some ransom money?* She thought it had been an attempt to get publicity for Tassos after his death. In 2008, she explained, when he lost the election to Christofias, he and his supporters grew angry and resentful; they felt betrayed by the left, who were supposed to support him in the elections and did not. Her theory was that the theft had been organized by yet another politician, a minister in Papadopoulos's administration and the architect of his "No" campaign to defeat the Annan Plan. The campaign was very successful in that purpose, she said, but it made Papadopoulos into an international pariah; no diplomats or heads of state would talk to him after that. He carried the shame of ostracization by the international community into the next elections, when he was defeated. The theft of his body only a year later, she suggested, was designed to redeem his political legacy.

By way of affirming the plausibility of this theory, she told me another story of another scam, some years earlier. This other scam had to do with the fabrication of a letter, purportedly penned by surviving members of EOKA-B, threatening to kill all traitors to the nation. The letter was received by a new media company just as it was beginning television broadcasts, and its TV station carried exclusive coverage of the letter—good for business, as the letter caused an uproar and drew many viewers to the new station. As it turned out, my acquaintance explained, the letter was a hoax, cooked up by the same politician she thought was behind the theft of Papadopoulos's body. *He is very experienced in public relations!*

I also read and heard ample criticism of the police investigation, which a number of my interlocutors considered a cover-up. As I noted in Part 2.2, Antonis Kitas implicated two men in the crime, one of whom he also implicated in the murder of Andy Hadjikostis. A person who had been involved in the investigation told me he knew for a fact that the two men fingered by Kitas for the theft of the president's body had indeed assisted in the theft, but they were given an immunity deal by the police in exchange for information that helped them solve the Hadjikostis murder. *The theft could never have been carried out only by two men,* he told me. *They had to have help.*

On March 21, 2010, nearly two weeks after the Kitas brothers and Sarbjit Singh were arrested for stealing the president's body, the *Philelevtheros* newspaper ran a full-page interview with Anastasia Papadopoulou, Tassos's daughter, regarding what by then had been established publicly as the police's theory of the crime (Kallinikos 2010). Papadopoulou responded to several questions about the speculation and rumors that had dominated the media during the previous months, including theories implicating her family. She had harsh criticism for all those who had politicized the theft and never apologized after the culprits were charged. She also blasted the police for their handling of the case; it was wrong, she insisted, in the days following the theft, to arrest and interrogate people due only to their political views, whatever those were. Her own first thought when the crime was discovered was that it was about ransom; she was afraid to think it might be connected to the "national question" (that is, conflict over a solution to the Cyprus Problem), though she acknowledged that "the motive doesn't have to be about 'the national question' to be characterized as 'political.'" The only issue that suggested to her a political motive in those early days was the date of the theft, one day before her father's one-year memorial service; this interpretation was strengthened a month later, when Spyros Kyprianou's grave was also disturbed.

Although Papadopoulou affirmed the likelihood of the Kitas brothers' guilt in the interview, she said she was not convinced that Antonis Kitas was the mastermind of the plot. "It appears that he certainly had some involvement," she said, "and likely he was the mastermind. I am not saying it wasn't him. But I'm not convinced that it was him. Besides, he denied it in the letter that 'Sigma' [a television network] discovered last week." It was hard for her to believe that two people alone—Mamas Kitas and Sarbjit Singh—could have removed and replaced the massive granite slab on her father's tomb by themselves. There were still some gaps in the story, she maintained, and the police made contradictory statements day after day. This alone sufficed to sow "doubt" [αμφιβολίες].

In this interview, Papadopoulou expertly navigated the "murky waters"[3] in which conspiracy theories mingled and melded with the forensic investigation of the criminal conspiracy. Without asserting *belief* in the police's theory of the crime, she spoke *as if* it were true, at least in broad brushstrokes, reasoning through the alternative theories and weighing the evidence in order to reach this conclusion. Her responses to the interviewer's questions, though clear and direct, were also quite knowing. What she knew was that her words could make things happen. She knew that the interview was taking place in a discursive context that was performative in register—attested by her striking analysis of the media coverage that had fostered an atmosphere of suspicion and doubt animated by the same political motivations being attributed to the crime itself. In other words, Papadopoulou showed herself to be both experienced and exquisitely skilled in conspiracy attunement.

The context of Papadopoulou's attunement was not novel, nor particular to the setting of the interview. In fact, her father had coined a phrase many years earlier that captures the context precisely. In his 2005 report on the mass media in Cyprus, Makarios Drousiotis recounts the invention of this phrase, six months after the defeat of the Annan Plan in April 2004. That October, he explains, rumors circulated that Demetris Christofias—head of the AKEL party and president of the House of Representatives—had accused the *Politis* newspaper of "selling out" to "the Americans," who supported the Annan Plan. (*Politis* had been critical of AKEL for backing Papadopoulos and his "No" campaign during the referendum earlier that year.) In a press conference on October 14, 2004, according to Drousiotis, Papadopoulos responded to a question about these rumors, wryly characterizing them as "phrases whispered by some" (φράσεις ότι έχουν λεχθεί ψιθυριστά από κάποιους) that could not be substantiated (Drousiotis 2005b, 10–11[4]), and mocking the hypocrisy of those who credited the rumors as fact while demanding substantiation from Christofias for his purported accusations against *Politis*. In the absence of "stamped receipts," Papadopoulos said, "many things can be deduced from behavior. Other things can be deduced from the ambient atmosphere [περιρρέουσα ατμόσφαιρα]" (Drousiotis 2005b, 10–11).[5] *Politis* ran a front-page story about Papadopoulos's comments the following day, expressing outrage that the president of the Republic—dubbed "the chief of dark whispers" (ο αρχηγός του σκοτεινού ψιθύρου)—could publicly impugn a person's (or a newspaper's) motivations based on the "ambient atmosphere" (*Politis*, October 15, 2010, 1). The phenomenological register of this phrase, to which Papadopoulos granted evidentiary status in the absence of documentation that did not and *could not* exist, indicates the dialogical context of performative discourse on conspiracy theory in which he and the assembled journalists—especially key figures like Drousiotis, who helped to elevate and popularize the phrase[6]—all implicitly counted on the public to register its meaning and implications.

The phrase stuck; it has cropped up time and again in media coverage of Cypriot politics in the years since the referendum, and I have heard it uttered by my own interlocutors in conversations about conspiracy theory in Cyprus. A perfectly recursive concept, ever available for repurposing, it was borne of conspiracy attunement—an "atmospheric attunement," as Papadopoulos helps me to reframe Stewart's concept (Stewart 2011)—and perpetually works to re-charge it. For Stewart, atmospheric attunement is "the activity of sensual world-making," "a labor that arrives already weighted with what it's living through" (446, 448). She addresses this concept to a gap or discontinuity between such sensual activity and its discursive representation. To bridge that gap in writing, Stewart favors "'weak theory'" that "tries to stick with something becoming atmospheric" (445[7]), as against the kind of theory—paranoia, perhaps, which Sedgwick (clearly invoked here) describes as a "strong theory" (Sedgwick 2003, 130, 133–36)—that changes the nature of experience by re-presenting it. The "sensory labor" of "being *in* whatever's happening" is what Stewart seeks to capture in writing about atmospheric attunement (Stewart 2011: 447, 450, 451).

These are the terms in which I have tried to capture the Cypriot context in regard to conspiracy theory: a context of conspiracy attunement whose

(Recontextualization)

boundaries are not cultural, historical, or ethnonational but rather affective, sensory, and dialogical. (Not all Cypriots are "in" it; some non-Cypriots are, myself included.) And, as Stewart suggests, its durability cannot be predicted or generalized: "Particular attunements can become habitual and rind up, or they can slough off as they are replaced by what comes next" (2011, 451). Whether something comes next that can instigate the sloughing off of conspiracy attunement is the key question posed by the recursivity of conspiracy theory in this context. The Akritas Plan, the Anglo-American conspiracy, the assassination plots against Makarios, the Hermes plot and the attempted coup itself, the fate of the Missing, the defeat of the Annan Plan, the laundering of war plunder—these conspiracies, which overlap one another in the figure of Tassos Papadopoulos, are only the most widely discussed of the events and experiences that charge and re-charge conspiracy attunement. In this context, people might take a positivist approach to the past, as a place to seek new information—new facts that might change the story. Or they might take a paranoid approach, learning again the story they already know, thereby reinforcing it as a kind of shield against the future. But embracing the recursivity of the past describes a different orientation to knowledge: not a revolutionary project of seeking change by design, but rather an openness to being struck by whatever arises from the past, and to reworking what one finds already there: reversing figure and ground, zooming in or panning out, scaling up or down, shifting angle or tack—in short, recontextualizing. Letting go of ethnocentric contextualization means letting time do this recursive work.

ACKNOWLEDGMENTS

This book began as part of another book, which grew beyond all reasonable proportion and necessitated much careful disaggregation in order that this text might emerge on its own terms. I am finding it next to impossible, then, to separate my deep gratitude to all the people who have contributed to the project as a whole—initiated some fifteen years ago, at the time of this writing—from that which is due uniquely for this book. I think I cannot go wrong by starting with thanks to friends who have contributed research, labor, advice, and their own thoughts and stories about conspiracy—though I hasten to assert that the book itself is my responsibility alone. David Hands, my collaborator on a documentary film touching on the president's body, has followed any number of "leads" with curiosity, humor, and cross-contextual fluidity that never stops educating me; his sensibility for the dark and absurd has been a wholesome influence over the years I have been working in Cyprus. Nicos Philippou, who knows the story of the president's body inside out, and whose variegated memories form a framing narrative in this text, kept discovering new threads and new sites to explore with me, which he did with a bearing of radical critique and a penchant for mind-bending recontextualization that decisively shaped my own disposition toward the material. Onur Günay accompanied me to the National Archives at Girne/Kyrenia during the summer of 2016, showing endless patience and healthful bemusement with Tassos Papadopoulos as he helped me read through and translate the Turkish-language press coverage discussed in Part 2.2 of this book. His care for my then-toddler, Ruby, not to mention his tolerance for the summer heat and the obscenity of Girne harbor, mean more than I could ever fairly ask. Rebecca Bryant, Olga Demetriou, Ellada

Evangelou, Mete Hatay, Despo Pasia, Theopisti Stylianou-Lambert, Constantinos Taliotis, and Konstantina Zanou shared with me their recollections, laughter, and critical impulses about conspiracy theories and presidents' bodies; whether they intended it or not, I owe to them much honing of my conspiracy attunement in the Cypriot context.

I could not have written this text as it is without the generous and incisive feedback of many people over the years. I send special thanks to the extraordinary graduate students at Princeton who read and discussed pieces of this manuscript in progress in an anthropology course, Conspiracy Theory and Social Theory, in Fall 2019; an interdisciplinary humanities course, The Problem of Context, in Spring 2020; and an IHUM reading group in Fall 2020. I am especially grateful to Luke Forrester, Hazal Hürman, Navjit Kaur, and Cate Morley, who offered rich close readings, provocative questions, and resonant research of their own that pushed me to think more carefully and more radically about conspiracy theory and context. Charles Stewart and Campbell Thomson read the entire manuscript and did me the great honor and favor of intensively discussing the material with me, broaching connections, metaphors, and comparative contexts to think with that I could not have imagined beforehand. Yelena Baraz, Zahid Chaudhary, Jessica Cooper, Karen Emmerich, Saygun Gökarıksel, Liz Harman, and Ayşe Parla read pieces of the manuscript with laser-sharp eyes and immense generosity. Neni Panourgiá, Theo Rakopoulos, and Mick Taussig inspired me with conversations and writings about sovereignty, conspiracy, and public secrecy. Jody McAuliffe and Vangelis Calotychos—separately—referred me to Tengiz Abuladze's 1984 film, *Repentance*, which reverberates in without resolving the story of the president's body that I tell in this text.

I thank Fadi Bardawil and Rena Lederman for riveting dialogue and the inspiration of their work. I am grateful to other colleagues at Princeton, too, for their ongoing support and interest: João Biehl, Julia Elyachar, and Serguei Oushakine, in particular, along with the members of the 2015–2017 cohort of Behrman Faculty Fellows and the 2019–2021 cohort of postdoctoral and faculty fellows in the Society of Fellows in the Liberal Arts, to whom I presented pieces of this manuscript in progress. It should not go without saying that I could not have produced this book (at long last) without the unflagging help and strategic advice of Carol Zanca, Mo Lin Yee, and Patty Lieb over the years I was working on the project, as well as Ryan Noll, Kelly Lake, and Joe Capizzi in the last stretch.

My research and writing on conspiracy theory have been enlivened and transformed by a series of collective ventures in spaces of shared obsession. Joe Masco and Lisa Wedeen invited me to join the incomparably fantastic C/T project and hosted me twice to present my work in progress. Moyukh Chatterjee, Saygun Gökarıksel, Giacomo Loperfido, Ayşe Parla, Theo Rakopoulos, and Steven Sampson organized conference panels that became exciting contexts for collective thinking. For their generative comments and questions, I thank the audiences who convened for presentations I gave at the Chicago Center for Contemporary Theory; the Culture, Power, Social Change seminar at UCLA; and the Princeton Athens Center, as well as departments of anthropology at Johns Hopkins University, Washington University, CUNY Graduate Center, the University of Oslo, and Panteion University, Athens. I am particularly grateful to colleagues and friends who took the interest, time, and care to organize those events: Joe Masco, Laurie Kain Hart, Dimitris Gondicas, Alessandro Angelini and Anand Pandian, Talia Dan-Cohen, Jeff Maskovsky and Leo Coleman, Theo Rakopoulos and Ingjerd Hoëm, Katerina Rozakou and Dimitra Kofti.

I feel beyond lucky to have worked on this project with Tom Lay, my editor at Fordham University Press, whose open-mindedness, judiciousness, and overall generosity and good humor made the process of publication a pleasure. I also want to thank the series editors of Thinking from Elsewhere—Clara Han, Bhrigupati Singh, and Andrew Brandel—for their support and encouragement, along with two anonymous reviewers who offered incisive and tremendously helpful feedback; their suggestions and provocations reinvigorated and reshaped this text at a critical stage.

I have been very fortunate to receive generous funding from Princeton University for my research and writing in this project, including a Stanley J. Seeger Hellenic Studies Sabbatical Research Grant, a Richard Stockton Bicentennial Preceptorship, a Behrman Faculty Fellowship in the Humanities, and several research grants from the University Committee on Research in the Humanities and Social Sciences. I have also enjoyed the immeasurable benefit of two sabbaticals at the Institute for Advanced Study in Princeton, in the School of Social Science and in the School of Historical Studies. My second year at the IAS was made possible by a Frederick Burkhardt Residential Fellowship for Recently Tenured Scholars awarded by the American Council of Learned Societies; I thank the administrators and reviewers at the ACLS sincerely.

A version of some material in this text was previously published as a chapter in a collective volume: "Conspiracy Attunement and Context: The Case of the President's Body," in *Conspiracy/Theory*, edited by Joseph Masco and Lisa Wedeen (Duke University Press, 2024, pp. 104–126). The publication of this book was made possible in part by a subvention grant from the University Committee on Research in the Humanities and Social Sciences at Princeton University. I am grateful for the committee's continuing generosity.

I give the very last and most loving word of thanks to my family: my husband, Rob, and my daughter, Ruby. Rob has stepped up countless times as a partner and caregiver to accommodate both the long-term slow burn and the episodic urgencies of my research and writing, while remaining curious about the project itself in a way that reassured me of its value. Ruby has witnessed me working and tolerated my occasional absences with a growing fascination for writing and books; if that is the main effect of this project in her life, I will count it worthwhile.

NOTES

INTRODUCTION: THE TIME OF THE CANNIBALS

1. These massacres took place in quick succession between what is known in the Republic as the first Turkish invasion (July 20, 1974) and the second (August 14–16, 1974).

2. For more detailed accounts of these events, see Bryant and Hatay (2020), Demetriou and Gürel (2008), Davis (2023, 1, 305–6n2), and PRIO Cyprus Centre (2012).

3. Angastiniotis's short documentary film, *Memory*, about a Turkish-Cypriot man and a Greek-Cypriot man who fought in Lekfa on opposite sides of the war in 1974, and who met again and became friends and peace activists thirty years later, was screened at Cine Studio (University of Nicosia) on October 11, 2011.

4. Angastiniotis's self-identification is complex. While he was working on the *Voice of Blood* films, he involved himself in raising awareness about the genocide of First Nation children in Canadian Indian Residential Schools as the Truth and Reconciliation Commission of Canada was conducting investigations. In recognition of this work, according to a bio page based on interviews Angastiniotis gave to the Cypriot newspaper *Afrika* in the mid-2000s, the Elders of the United Cherokee Nation appointed him Clan Chief in 2007, and a Cree elder, Morning Star, named him Night Eagle (https://en-academic.com/dic.nsf/enwiki/6580974). Angastiniotis has used Night Eagle as part of his name ever since. After the release of his films in 2004 and 2005, under pressure of threats, Angastiniotis moved from the Republic to the TRNC and took a position in the Faculty of Communication and Media Studies at Eastern Mediterranean University, though he does not have an active university webpage or any recent web presence at the time of this writing.

5. EOKA is the National Organization of Cypriot Fighters [Εθνική Οργάνωσις Κυπρίων Αγωνιστών]. TMT is the Turkish Resistance Organization [Türk Mukavemet Teşkilatı]. See my discussion of these organizations in Davis (2023).

6. See my discussion of this fraught terminology in Davis (2023, 2).

7. See Demetriou, Constantinou, and Tselepou (2023) on the manifold significance of Cyprus's nonaligned position.

8. Masco (2014) examines national security affect in the United States from the Cold War to the post-9/11 war on terror by means of both statecraft and security culture.

9. See Rakopoulos (2023) for a rich discussion of the growth of the offshore banking sector in the Republic of Cyprus after 1974, and the new economy in "golden passports"—citizenship purchased by investment—taking shape since the banking crisis in 2013, which Rakopoulos frames as "offshoring by other means" (79).

10. See Psyllides (2009b).

11. My usage of this term differs from that of Bratich (2008, 5), who thus describes researchers of conspiracies who are seeking scientific legitimacy for their representation of the facts, rather than (as I do here) theorists of conspiracy theories whose factual claims may be beside the point.

12. Examples include Comaroff and Comaroff 1999; 2003; Dean 1998; Harding and Stewart 2003; Marcus 1999; Stewart 1999; West and Sanders 2003.

13. Lepselter (2016, 54) cites Urban (2001) on "metaculture."

14. *Slow Burn*, Season 1, Episode 6, "Rabbit Holes," first released on January 9, 2018. Neyfakh continued to explore conspiracy and conspiracy theory in American political culture in Season 2 of *Slow Burn*, "The Clinton Impeachment" (especially Episode 6, "God Mode," released September 19, 2018). He acknowledged to an interviewer that the podcast's return to the Watergate scandal and the Clinton scandal(s) was motivated partly by his experience of American political culture during Trump's presidency. See Tu 2020.

15. For example, Taussig (1999), Aretxaga (2005), Nelson (2009), and Harsin (2008), respectively, address the Dirty War in Colombia, the Franco dictatorship in Spain, the genocide in Guatemala, and the Bush II years in the United States.

16. See my discussion of Occupy the Buffer Zone and ELAM, the National Popular Front in Cyprus (Davis 2023, 23–29, and 4ff.).

17. Cf. Olga Demetriou's writing on event temporality and political subjectivity in the Republic of Cyprus (Demetriou 2007).

18. See also Giannakos 2010, 32: "The most serious charges the three [suspects] face are: conspiracy, desecration [βεβήλωση] of the corpse [σορός] of Tassos Papadopoulos, illegal entry into the place of the grave, exhumation [εκταφή] of the corpse, insulting the memory [μνήμη] of Savvas Ptolou of Dikomo (in whose grave they put the corpse of Tassos Papadopoulos), and extortion of money. In addition, the first charged (Singh) faces charges of impersonation, circulating with forged documents, and illegal stay in the Democracy [i.e., the Republic of Cyprus]. Only Singh and Mamas [Kitas] are charged with the exhumation and

insulting the memory of Savvas, while Antonis [Kitas] is accused of encouraging them to exhume the corpse. Singh admitted to the charges but the Kitas brothers have not admitted to any of the charges. Hearing is set for 12 July."

PART 1: ON CONSPIRACY THEORY AND CONTEXT

1. Jean Comaroff and John L. Comaroff gloss this juncture slightly differently as the "Age of Futilitarianism . . . in which the rampant promises of late capitalism run up against a thoroughly postmodern pessimism" (Comaroff and Comaroff 1999, 292).

2. See also Stewart (1999), Harding and Stewart (2003), Melley (2000, 8, and chapter 4).

3. This phrase is cited (in a slightly different form) in Melley (2000, 9).

4. Fassin cites Turner (1980).

5. Fassin does briefly discuss a European example (2021, 131): the false accusation of an anti-Semitic assault made by a French woman against two Arab men, and the rush to judgment by the French media and government that, he suggests, expressed a collective disposition to believe her story. Since Fassin does not claim or show that the accusation was a conspiracy theory, however, nor examine the conditions of the credibility granted reflexively to the accuser (though see Fassin 2014), this example does not much elucidate the heuristic approach to conspiracy theory that he advocates in this article.

6. It bears mention that relabeling "conspiracy theory" as "theory of conspiracy," as Pelkmans and Machold do, does not solve the problem of incommensurability that I introduced at the beginning of Part 1.2. If conspiracy theory cannot be stabilized by inherent meanings or epistemological features across contexts or polarized perspectives, neither can conspiracy itself. One person's executive privilege or executive session in an otherwise transparent, democratic government, for example, is another person's nefarious conspiracy; there is no way to define conspiracy such that these two interpretations can be distinguished. "Theory of conspiracy" just restates "conspiracy theory" as the impossible object of the theory in question.

7. This phrase is quoted in Pelkmans and Machold (2011, 73) as well as Bratich (2008, 3), citing Christopher Hitchens (2004).

8. Mahon (1992, 60) writes that this phrase (*dans le vrai*), borrowed from Georges Canguilhem, was first used by Foucault in his inaugural lecture at the Collège de France on December 2, 1970.

9. See Fassin (2021), Greenwood (2022), and Parmigiani (2021), among many studies comparing these practices.

10. French anthropologist Lucien Lévy-Bruhl famously took the position that the "primitive mind" was fundamentally "irrational" in his 1910 (1985) work, *How*

Natives Think, later targeted by Evans-Pritchard for critique. See Heinz (1997); see also George Stocking's discussion of the rationality debate in his introduction to his edited volume (1989), and Hollis and Lukes (1982). See also Magliocco (2012), who complicates the received wisdom about Lévy-Bruhl's "ethnocentrism," citing his later work, which hypothesized "the co-existence of the two contrasting ways of thought—the rational-logical and the mystical—in all human societies" (11).

11. Good takes this phrase from a chapter of Dan Sperber's 1985 book, *On Anthropological Knowledge: Three Essays*. He suggests that Sperber evades the very epistemological problem he sets out to solve—namely, the problem of apparently irrational beliefs—by coming to the conclusion that people do not really believe what they seem to believe (irrationally).

12. In her acknowledgments, Pigg cites Favret-Saada ([1977] 1980) and Taussig (1987) as formative influences.

13. In emphasizing the performative efficacy of speech in witchcraft situations, Favret-Saada is aligned (at least in this respect) with Bronislaw Malinowski's approach in his two-volume ethnography, *Coral Gardens and Their Magic* ([1935] 1978). Favret-Saada does not discuss Malinowski's work, published just two years before Evans-Pritchard's much more widely read *Witchcraft, Oracles, and Magic among the Azande*, itself targeted critically by Favret-Saada as the very model of scientistic objectivity that would foreclose any real understanding of witchcraft. Unlike Evans-Pritchard, Malinowski studied in depth the "active pragmatic speech" of magic spells (214), theorizing the "specific magical influence" (213) of supposedly meaningless "nonsense" words uttered by Trobriand magicians during the planting and caring for gardens, to which Trobrianders attributed the health and growth of their crops. Malinowski asserted that the "coefficient of weirdness" (218ff.) in these spells—their "esoteric allusions" (230) and their odd grammar, vocabulary, phonology, and rhythm—marked them as a special kind of locution that only had meaning in the ritual context of their utterance. In this context, an "accredited magician" would utter magical words and phrases he had inherited from predecessors in a chain of transmission as long as the history of Trobriand society itself, invoking and directly addressing the plants, animals, and other creatures in the garden. On Malinowski's account, this ritual setting was required but not sufficient for a magic situation to take shape. Magic situations were, he argued, fundamentally "created by native belief" (215)—specifically, the belief that a magical spell was "coeval with that aspect of reality which it ha[d] to influence" (229). The efficacy of magical words was thus based in a principle of natural sympathy between words and things, and that principle is what Malinowski identified as the object of Trobrianders' belief. Magical words were untranslatable, he argued, though their meaning—which he understood as "the effect of the words within their ritual context" (223, cf. 214)—was nonetheless "explicable" (230). This distinction between the translatability and explicability of

magic speech gave Malinowski room for ethnographic knowledge of a particular sort. In Part VI of *Coral Gardens*, he recounted the difficulty of studying these mysterious spells, which ordinary Trobrianders did not know; he acknowledged that it was only through dissimulation that he was ultimately able to apprentice himself to a particular magician and learn the tools of the trade. This ethnographic procedure preserved Malinowski's positionality as an outsider to magical situations—which is to say his status as an unbeliever, which he did not question—and rendered his knowledge of spells ineffective insofar as they were written down in the pages of his book. This ethical-methodological crux of outsider unbelief is where Favret-Saada parts company with Malinowski.

14. Among the cultural analyses of "conspiracy theory" that Bratich considers symptomatological are Melley (2000), Fenster (2008), and most of the contributions in Marcus (1999), along with many others.

15. Cf. Marasco (2016, 237–38).

16. Melley (2000) likewise observes an "all-or-nothing conception of agency" in his examination of conspiracy narratives in American culture: that is, "a view in which agency is a property, parceled out *either* to individuals like oneself *or* to 'the system'—a vague structure often construed to be massive, powerful, and malevolent" (2000, 10).

17. Fenster pays special attention to Chomsky's widely read work *Rethinking Camelot: JFK, the Vietnam War, and US Political Culture*, originally published in 1993, shortly after the first Gulf War, and revised and updated in 2015. Here, Chomsky disparages "conspiracy theories" of the assassination of John F. Kennedy and furnishes evidence that Kennedy was in no way planning to end the Vietnam War, as hypothesized by many theorists. On Fenster's reading, Chomsky insists on the "structural causes" of foreign policy decisions as against the secret machinations of individuals (46).

18. See, for one example, Stuart Hall's discussion of subject positions (Hall [1997] 2013).

19. See also Birchall (2004; 2006, esp. chapter 3); Dean (2002, esp. chapter 2); Sedgwick (2003).

20. This phrase, originally in Hofstadter (1964), has been cited or reproduced often in conspiratology. See, for example, Marcus (1999, 1); Oushakine (2009, 106).

21. Philosopher Patrick Stokes (2018) observes precisely this: "There are conspiracies we all agree happened—Watergate, Iran Contra, etc.—and the search for a (non-question-begging) definition of 'conspiracy theory' that would exclude beliefs about these accepted conspiracies, but include those wacky theories we want to dismiss, appears doomed to failure" (25).

22. I use the term "particularist" in reference to the scope of the contextual parameters within which conspiratologists relativize the meaning of conspiracy theories. This is quite a different usage of "particularist" from the common

parlance in philosophical debates over the definition of conspiracy theory (for example, see Dentith, Ed., 2018). Patrick Stokes (2018), citing Dentith (2016), develops a critique of what they both understand as *generalism*—"the view that conspiracy theories as a class of explanation are intrinsically suspect"; but Stokes also argues against *particularism*, "whereby we only judge individual conspiracy theories on their merits, rather than judging them based on their membership of that class" (25). Arguing that "the very act of entertaining a conspiracy theory as a *worthwhile hypothesis for investigation* may come at a serious moral cost" (26, emphasis original), Stokes articulates a position for the "reluctant particularist," who "holds that we should be reticent to indulge conspiracy theories enough to investigate them" (35) as an "epistemic stance" that accounts for the ethical freight of conspiracy theories as social practices without entailing the "blanket refusal" of the generalist (36, 35).

23. On this point, see Rakopoulos (2018).

24. Personal communication with the author, November 9, 2021.

25. For a comprehensive literature review and meta-analysis of psychological research on conspiracy theories, see Douglas et al. 2019.

26. This overview of the Schreber case study is drawn from my prior writing on Freud and paranoia; see Davis (2012): 284n80. See Freud (1911) 1963.

27. Widespread critique of Freud as homophobic has centered on this theorization of paranoia. See Boyarin (1995) for an intricate, compelling reading of homophobia and anti-Semitism in Freud's writing on Schreber as well as his correspondence with Wilhelm Fliess.

28. Cf. Blanuša 2009, 115.

29. Marasco draws here on Melanie Klein's theorization of ego formation as the movement from a "paranoid-schizoid position" to a "depressive position"— which Sedgwick (2003) associates, respectively, with paranoid and reparative hermeneutic approaches.

30. Cf. "participatory knowledge" in Parmigiani (2021, 520, 523).

31. On this point, see Sedgwick (1996; 2003), on whom Marasco draws extensively in her piece.

32. See, for example, Luke Forrester Johnson's rich discussion of differential racial paranoias (2021).

33. Sedgwick, for her part, as Marasco notes (2016, 239), observes the "distinctly Oedipal regularity and repetitiveness" of the "generational narrative" at the heart of paranoid epistemology, which leaves no room for change; this is a key point in her critique of paranoid reading as "anti-queer." But Sedgwick levels this critique at critical theorists whom she respectfully (even affectionately) takes as her peers, rather than at anything like western or Euro-American culture or civilization. Marasco seeks to recuperate even this critique of paranoid epistemology in psychoanalysis via affect theory (à la Sedgwick) as an "autocritique of

psychoanalysis," finding within "the rich history of psychoanalytic thought" some "surprising resources for queer living" (239).

34. See Birchall's terse and illuminating discussion of Fiske and Fenster's response (Birchall 2006, 66–69).

35. My summary addresses the version of the essay published in 1974 in *Black Scholar*. See Eddie S. Glaude Jr.'s very interesting critique of the theory on epistemological grounds (Glaude 1991).

36. Blanuša and Hristov (2020) note that, in later work, Rogin "revisited the realist versus symbolist debate" and turned toward psychoanalysis to account for what both approaches failed to address: namely, "unconscious fantasies that motivated even the most exploitative forms of political thought" (68).

37. Despite this instability, Fenster lands on a definition of conspiracy theory as a "populist theory of power . . . an ideological misrecognition of power relations, calling believers and audiences together and into being as 'the people' opposed to a relatively secret, elite 'power bloc'" (89).

38. See also Birchall (2004; 2006).

39. See McIntosh (2022) on QAnon's "stylized language" (9).

40. Also relevant here is the distinction Henrik Sinding-Larsen (2008) draws between externalized ontologies (true by reference to external facts) and relational ontologies (true by means of relationships). In these terms, conspiracy attunement is a relational ontology.

41. I thank Zahid Chaudhary and Charles Stewart, respectively, for suggesting these auditory parallels in musical performance and dog whistling.

42. Cf. Fenster's analysis of "realist" vis-à-vis "symbolist" interpretations of conspiracy theory (Fenster 1999, 53–62, 74), which I discuss in Part 1.5. In these terms, in focusing on the intentions of conspiracy theorists, Rakopoulos is more aligned with the "realist" approach.

43. Along these lines, Parmigiani includes her notes to self about the time a pagan friend "crossed a line of gullibility" in asking for her opinion on a news item concerning a "pedo-satanic" attack on a New York City tunnel repelled by Trump in Operation "Q-force" (Parmigiani 2021, 513).

44. Parmigiani derives her sense of "micro" and "macro" context directly from Magliocco, who, she writes, understands belief as "a response to macro-contextual (i.e. historical, social, political, and cultural) and micro-contextual (i.e. unique to one specific performative context) forces" (Parmigiani 2021, 514, citing Magliocco 2012, 7).

45. In this, I am aligned with Rakopoulos, who writes of conspiracy theory experts in Thessaloniki, "While I do not refrain from using the term 'conspiracy theory' to describe what my interlocutors do, I distinguish this practice from assigning them the identity label 'conspiracy theorist,' and engage in how they use it to characterise each other" (2022, 48).

46. I thank Charles Stewart for an inspiring and clarifying conversation on this point.

47. Indeed, as Giovanna Parmigiani (2023) argues in her most recent article on conspiracy theory and conspirituality, "While oppositional in nature (conspiracy theories are, *de facto*, counter-narratives) . . . conspiritual beliefs are not necessarily divisive in practice" (9). She explores a "neo-animist" philosophy of "interconnectedness" and "participatory consciousness" espoused by her pagan interlocutors in southern Italy (10), who elaborate a distinction between "separating" as the "acknowledgment, and even the creation of, new entities" (9) and "dividing" as a "'seeing against,'" associated with discrimination and judgment (9). Parmigiani wrestles with the easy inclusivity entailed by their embrace of separation over division, which positioned them to accept without trouble her decision to be vaccinated against COVID despite the strong and "affectively charged" anti-vax stance they had taken online and with her (12). On Parmigiani's account, her interlocutors understand their approach to the extreme polarization taking shape in Italian society around online conspiracy discourse as more expansive, inclusive, and communitarian than the approach of debunkers, who only seek division. Although, as Parmigiani observes, this mindset offers them "an inclusive way to inhabit current 'digital wars'" (15), it does not have any bearing on the social fact of polarization ensuing from the attribution of conspiracy theorizing to them by others who seek to debunk their beliefs. The same could be said for the interlocutors of Theodoros Rakopoulos (2022, 53ff.), who have perhaps a similar mindset. Although some are accused—by others—of fascism, Rakopoulos finds their discourse oriented toward truth rather than division: "For them, conspiracy discourse is 'a matter of dreaming, not of hating'" (58).

48. This theory is also cited in Zanou (2010).

49. I was fascinated to discover mention of these events in Elana Freeland's book, *Chemtrails, HAARP, and the "Full Spectrum Dominance" of Planet Earth* (2014), in which she works to substantiate the chemtrail theory from a global perspective. Freeland quotes a *Simerini* item (Ioannou 2010b) covering a Green Party demonstration at the British Royal Air Force Base at Akrotiri (Freeland 2014, 110n73), and then a *Cyprus Mail* article discussing the demand made by then-head of the Green Party, Ioanna Panayiotou, for an investigation into chemtrails over Cyprus on April 6, 2011 (Freeland 2014, 110). She interprets chemtrail controversies in what she calls the "Case of Greece and Cyprus" in relation to financial crisis in the two countries, drawing a direct causal link between public outcries over chemtrails and the fiscal punishment of Greece and Cyprus by the Troika in, respectively, 2008 and 2012 (192–94).

50. See Part 2.3 for a longer discussion of this concept.

51. Herzfeld's masterwork on the locations of anthropological theory, *Anthropology through the Looking-Glass: Critical Ethnography in the Margins of*

Europe (1987), was published one year after Appadurai's essay on "Theory in Anthropology." See my discussion of Herzfeld's work in Davis (2012, 119–22).

52. This latter shift from area studies to globalization studies, and its implications for ethnographic research and anthropological theory, are subjects that Appadurai treats in depth in *Modernity at Large* (1996).

53. Cf. Bardawil (2020) on this point: "I seek in this work to hold the tension between the interconnectedness of our world and the structural imbalance of power that makes some intellectual theorists to be engaged and others autochthonous intellectuals to be studied, or native informants to be used. I seek to avoid both highlighting an interconnectedness, which does not take power into account, and an erasure of interconnectedness, which is itself a symptom of power" (Bardawil 2020, 7; see also xiv and 5).

54. I discuss the issue of locale in relation to representations of Cyprus at greater length in Davis (2023, 31–32).

INTERLUDE: THE BODY ITSELF

1. This phrase comes from the screed published in *Simerini* (2009).

2. Tzioni had been director of the Diplomatic Office under President Papadopoulos. President Christofias apparently expressed "horror" in his first press conference after the theft (*Haravgi* 2009a; 2009b). Mikaellas Loizou, writing for *Simerini*, characterized the reaction of "public opinion" in terms of "shock, abhorrence, and rage" (Loizou 2009).

3. Papadopoulou expresses her own reaction differently, in terms of "rape": "What is the feeling that overwhelms me? What has filled the void? What's left but a dent in the pillow? Just one word. Rape. How else do you describe such an invasion of your personal life, your own space? The revilement of a body, even if the soul is immaterial? . . . And who did the vandals finally rape? . . . They raped our dignity" (Papadopoulou 2009).

4. Hadjiapostolou is quoting a person here who is described as being "very close to the Papadopoulos family," and might be Giorgos Iliades, a friend of Papadopoulos (see Part 2.2).

5. This is Taussig's term (1999, 4, 32, 33, passim).

6. Ahmed contends that the physical or emotional act of recoiling, of "pulling away" from a disgusting object or event, imbues it with a "fetish quality" that fascinates those who recoil and "saturat[es] the subjective world," drawing them toward the event in "a perpetual recontamination," as if in traumatic repetition (2015, 95, 96, 94, 96).

7. RIK evening broadcast, March 11, 2011, "Ενταφιασμός" [Entombment]. Archival record: item code 4589763, DVC number 310/00760, timecode 47:26:24–50:02:02.

8. Charalambous is referring to politicians (the vast majority in the Republic) who rejected the Annan Plan for a solution to the Cyprus problem in 2004 and supported Papadopoulos's successful "No" campaign to defeat it. I discuss this campaign and its role in conspiracy theories of the theft of the president's body in Part 2.

9. Lillikas is a politician, originally of the communist party, AKEL (Ανορθωτικό Κόμμα Εργαζόμενου Λαού, Working People's Reform Party), and later independent, who served as minister of commerce and industry and then as foreign minister in the Papadopoulos administration.

10. See, for example, the article published in *Simerini* on January 12, 2010 (Ioannou 2010a), which addresses the "vandalism" of dozens of graves in a cemetery in Limassol, including the grave of former president Spyros Kyprianou, only a month after the theft of Papadopoulos's remains.

11. I do not believe I saw a single instance of κόκκαλα, the term for "bones" used in medical anatomy, or πτώμα, meaning corpse or carcass.

12. Adam Rosenblatt (2015) explores how "dignity" operates in human rights law and humanitarian forensic ethics as a universal principle of humanity imbued in human remains, and the complicated ties between this legal notion of dignity in human personhood and religious notions of the sacredness of dead bodies and graves. See my discussion of this issue in Davis (2023).

13. In this piece, Polydorou juxtaposes the story of Makarios's heart with that of the heart of General Giorgos Grivas Digenis, a Nazi collaborator during the Greek occupation and a mastermind of EOKA-B's campaign of terror in Cyprus in the early 1970s. Polydorou quotes at length from Anastasiadis (2016). An article in *Sigmalive* (2023) gives an almost identical account, also citing Anastasiadis's book.

14. This article quotes at length from the front-page article published by the newspaper, *Apoyevmatini* [Evening], on November 19, 1977: "Συγκλονιστικό. Ανάλυση και έκθεση Άγγλου ιατρού υπονοεί ότι δολοφονήθηκε ο Εθνάρχης. Μεγάλα ποσοστά μολύβδου βρέθηκαν στην καρδιά του. Τι κατέδειξαν οι αναλύσεις του αίματός που έκανε Άγγλος ειδικός. Υπάρχει επίσημο πόρισμα να δημοσιευτεί!" [Shocking: Analysis and report by English doctor suggests that the Ethnarch was assassinated. High levels of lead were found in his heart. What the analysis of the blood done by an English expert showed. There is an official conclusion to be published!].

15. See Drousiotis (2000) for an acutely critical examination of conspiracy theories about the missing. See also Δεκατρία Περιστέρια [Thirteen doves] (1997), by Greek journalist Petros Kasimatis, a master work in conspiracy theory about the Greek-Cypriot missing (and denial about the Turkish-Cypriot missing). The book is written as a journalistic account of rescue missions to save Greek-Cypriot prisoners of war being held in a Turkish prison camp, using four of Turkish

photojournalist Ergin Konuksever's photographs of the "Tziaos five" (Kasimatis 1997, 216–18; see Part 1.3)—who were in fact killed in the summer of 1974—intercalated with purportedly top-secret government and military documents.

16. The authors of the introduction and preface to the 2016 Princeton Classics edition of *The King's Two Bodies* make much of this timing, given the distance between Kantorowicz's early biography of Emperor Frederick II, which celebrated the emperor's legacy for the German nation and became "a Nazi favorite" (Jordan [1997] 2016, xxviii), and his later work, inaugurated during the first years of Nazi rule as a critical history of political theology, a concept closely associated with Carl Schmitt's writings, themselves widely understood as a legitimation of authoritarian rule (Leyser 2016, xii–xiii).

17. An English jurist cited by Plowden averred, "King is a Name of Continuance, which shall always endure as the Head and Governor of the People (as the Law presumes) as long as the People continue . . . ; and in this Name the King never dies" (Kantorowicz [1957] 2016, 23).

18. Kantorowicz ([1957] 2016) presents Dignitas as a concept that "referred chiefly to the singularity of the royal office, to the sovereignty vested in the king by the people, and resting individually in the king alone" (384); as a shade of the king's mystical body, "the dignity does not die" (386).

19. Kantorowicz ([1957] 2016) argues that effigy ritual was brought to France due to the coincidence in the year 1422 of the deaths of Henry V and Charles VI, and later elaborated during the Renaissance with borrowed elements of Roman practices "discovered" from antiquity (421, 427–28).

20. Santner's theorization of the flesh in *The Royal Remains* avowedly owes much to Foucault's work on biopolitics; he enlists Foucault to play "on the same team" with Freud in his own book, to examine how "the 'intensification' of the body" is connected with "disorders or shifts in the resources of representation available to subjects and in the capacities of subjects to use those resources to discharge the normative pressures they introduce into the life of subjects" (2011, xiii).

21. Here, Santner parts company with Rafael Sánchez, who takes the body of the leader as "a sort of general equivalent, publicly and visibly expressing what the heterogeneous majorities equally yet unknowingly share as members of a single, homogenous 'people'" (Sánchez 2016, 13).

22. Many others have written about this, of course; Rafael Sánchez's analysis of the figure of Simon Bolívar in Venezuelan populism comes to mind (Sánchez 2016).

23. See also Santner (2011, 42).

24. Graeber (2011) distinguishes divine kingship ("the human capacity to become a god through violence," 54) from sacred kingship, a ritual but not

necessarily a political office achieved through ritual "domestication" (1) and "tam[ing]" (1, 9). In Graeber's view, a divine king can be rendered "merely sacred" (i.e., transformed into a sacred king) by "turning [him] into a fetish or scapegoat" (9).

25. According to Ferrándiz, archival and forensic research has shown that, contrary to the official state policy of relocating the bodies only of "martyrs" to the Valley of the Fallen, the dead buried there included Republicans as well as Nationalists.

26. Indeed, although Cherstich (2014) describes Gaddafi's rise to power as an "apotheosis" (94), he argues in a footnote that most Libyans' talk about the ghostly status of Gaddafi's body in life was conducted in general supernatural terms that did not recur to the "'more Islamic' category of *Jinn* . . . as attested in the Qur'an" (116n3). He also offers an intriguing but brief note on the *Jamahiriya*, which he translates as "'state of the masses,' a unique political system based on a mixture of socialist and 'Islamic' elements introduced by Gaddafi" (117n5).

27. Pereira even signals to the then-future exhumation of Lech Kaczynski, former president of Poland, which eventually took place in 2016.

28. A similar case is that of Saddam Hussein, who was executed by hanging after his conviction in an Iraqi court for crimes against humanity. He was first buried in al-Awja, nearby his family shrine, in a tomb that became a pilgrimage site and was later destroyed in an air strike. The current whereabouts of his body are a matter of dispute. Years after Hussein's execution, rumors circulated that his body had been exhumed from his tomb and reburied in a secret location, or that he was actually still alive and it was his body double who had been executed and buried. *Alarabiya* (2018) quoted a Baghdad resident claiming, "Saddam's not dead. . . . It was one of his doubles who was hanged."

PART 2: ON CONSPIRACY ATTUNEMENT: A CASE STUDY

1. See Demetriou, Constantinou, and Tselepou (2023) for a rich discussion of Cyprus's complex position as a "white colony" (3) and "an island between three continents" (2) that shaped its relations with other decolonizing countries after its independence from Great Britain. They read Cyprus's "peripheral" position in colonial and imperial formations of power as a special mode of implication, and they develop the concept of "lateral colonialism" to capture the ways in which Cyprus's nonalignment during the Cold War facilitated various "lateral" and "racism-based relations" (4) with African countries that ranged from exploitation to anticolonial solidarity.

2. This passage is also quoted in Constandinos (2009, 45).

3. O'Malley and Craig present as evidence the assassination of Rodger Davies, US ambassador to Cyprus, during anti-American protests outside the embassy in

Nicosia on August 19, 1974; he had only just arrived in Cyprus to take up the post a month earlier (July 10). The protesters were demanding US action against Turkey in response to the second Turkish invasion of Cyprus only a few days before. EOKA-B gunmen were tried for the crime several years later.

4. See also Dimitrakis (2010). Dimitrakis is a Greek war historian, educated in Greece and the United Kingdom, based in Athens. His book focuses on British military intelligence and does not even use the word "conspiracy"; it contains no discussion of methodology.

5. See Nicolet (2009).

6. Indeed, Drousiotis is read as a supporter of the theory by Claude Nicolet, a French historian who cannot be counted as a political detractor. On an invitation from *The Cyprus Review*, Nicolet reviewed Drousiotis's 2006 book, *Cyprus 1974: Greek Coup and Turkish Invasion* (a condensation and English translation of two books he had previously published in Greek; it was republished in 2009 by Alfadi [2009b]). Here, he expresses acute disappointment that Drousiotis, whom he considers "well informed on the many common conspiracy theories or nationalist propaganda produced over the past decades from domestic authors," nevertheless failed to include a "scientific introduction" to the book in which he would "point out the specialties of his work that would make his conclusions all the more trustworthy as opposed to the mass of unserious authors from whom he can distance himself" (Nicolet 2009, 242). He praises the book for combining "US archival research with vast Greek material and Cypriot oral history," a unique feat in extant scholarship on the events of the summer of 1974 (242); but he accuses Drousiotis of having "fallen into the trap" of a preconceived conclusion about American involvement in the coup, and points to the absence of proper citations and "adequate source critique" that would indicate a scholarly assessment of evidence. He concludes that Drousiotis, "a well-known Cypriot journalist, has an obvious claim to have his publication considered as the work of a historian—but he is mastering the tools and methodologies of historians only partially" (241).

7. This event is explored (sympathetically) by Stefanos Evripidou in his interview with Drousiotis (Evripidou 2014b).

8. Drousiotis's trilogy includes his books published in 2020, 2021, and 2022.

9. See Rakopoulos (2023) on the question of Russian influence in the economy and government of the Republic since 2013.

10. The quoted passage is drawn from my transcript of the RIK evening news broadcast on February 4, 2010 (CyBC archives, file 4589380, 310/00759). RIK [Ραδιοφωνικό Ίδρυμα Κύπρου] is the term used in Greek for the Cyprus Broadcasting Corporation (CyBC). While the CyBC promotes itself as a pan-Cypriot service, its offices and archives are located in south Nicosia, and Greek is the language of almost all its employees and broadcasts (see Davis 2023, 331n13). At the CyBC archives in Nicosia, I viewed all available RIK broadcasts relating to the

theft of Papadopoulos's remains between December 11, 2009 (when the theft was discovered) and mid-March 2010 (when the remains were found and the suspects charged). I attempted to locate archives for television stations operated by private media companies in the south, but I was not able to confirm that any other stations actually kept archives. For example, representatives of Sigma Live, owned by the DIAS company (which also owns the far-right newspaper *Simerini*), told me that many broadcasts were streamable on the Sigma website, but only recent ones, as broadcast recordings were saved for about six months and then discarded.

11. RIK evening news segment, "Τέλος στο μακάβριο θρίλερ" [End of the macabre thriller], aired March 9, 2010 (CyBC archives, file 4585756, 310/00244).

12. The term "ναιναίκοι" (yes-men) uses the Greek word for "yes" (ναι) to make a homonymic play on the derogatory term, "νενέκοι," connoting "traitors"—a reference to Dimitris Nenekos, the chief of Patras in the Greek revolutionary war era (c. 1825), who "sold out" to Ibrahim Pasha, an Egyptian general, during clashes between Egyptian and Ottoman forces in parts of what are now Crete and mainland Greece.

13. In their introduction to their edited collection, *Being There: The Fieldwork Encounter and the Making of Truth* (2009), Borneman and Hammoudi offer a summary critique of textualism in anthropology after the so-called crisis of representation in the 1980s, which, as they read it, cast suspicion on ethnographic authority and thus on the ethnographer's experience as a source of knowledge—to the detriment of anthropology, at least in the United States, in their view.

14. Following Bourdieu, Warner (2005) notes that the modern technique of opinion polling contrives to "characterize a public as social fact independent of any discursive address or circulation" (71), even though polling is one of the forms of mediation that helps constitute the public—the very object it is supposed to measure as if it were occurring independently (71–72).

15. Cultural studies scholar Clare Birchall, drawing on the same genealogy of functionalist anthropology, also identifies Gluckman as a founding ancestor, but unfortunately stops there. Her interest, unlike Stewart's and Strathern's, lies in how such anthropologists have taken for granted the low status of gossip in relation to official knowledges, including the knowledge they themselves produce. She finds a strong similarity here between anthropologists and the cultural studies scholars who criticize them, insofar as the latter, while celebrating the impropriety of gossip as a means of subversion, have "left intact" the distinction between gossip and knowledge conventionalized in functionalist ethnographic accounts (Birchall 2006, 108). Birchall herself pursues a deconstructive approach to gossip, following Derrida's critique of writing in showing that much official knowledge, and especially academic knowledge, acquires legitimacy through derivational and citational practices of "borrowing and repetition" (123) that

render impossible its tracing to an original source or "ultimate authority" (127). In this, Birchall finds an essential resonance between gossip and "legitimate knowledge" in their shared speculativeness: their "uncertainty" and "undecidability" as to status (125). Gossip, then, she concludes, is not a category distinct from legitimate knowledge but rather is "constitutive" of it (108), as gossip is already "within the cognitive practices and knowledges associated with more legitimate endeavors" (120). The constitutive nature of gossip in relation to legitimate knowledge that Birchall thus illuminates is obvious in the discourse on conspiracy theories of the division of Cyprus that I explore in Part 2.1.

16. Stewart and Strathern distinguish both gossip and rumor from scandal, which they specify not by scale but rather by content and effect: "Scandal is news that is unambiguously deleterious to those it is directed against, whereas gossip and rumor need not be so (though they often are)" (2004, 39).

17. Translations from the Greek-language press in this chapter are mine. I am profoundly grateful to Onur Günay for his patient and expert assistance in reading and translating material from the Turkish-language press.

18. My sense of the political shadings of these papers as well as their circulation and impact among Cypriot readerships was informed in part by Ersoy's discussion of peace journalism in Cyprus (Ersoy 2010, 87).

19. See also Kostakopoulos (2010) and Drousiotis (2010b).

20. See also Chatzivassili (2010) and Chatzistylianou (2010).

21. This nickname (ο Γιουρούκκης) is a relatively common surname in the Macedonian region of Greece and the Greek diaspora from this region; it appears to have been an ethnonym for settlers in northern Greece who came from the Konya region of Turkey during the fourteenth and fifteenth centuries. The Yurouks (Turkish, Yörükler; Greek, Γιουρούκοι) were seminomadic and known as bandits during the early centuries of Ottoman rule; the ethnonym thus evokes a history of tribal criminalization comparable to that of "Gypsy." The name pejoratively implies not only Turkish origin but also criminal predation on subjugated Greeks.

22. The National Front was a sort of intermediary paramilitary group operating between the end of EOKA (which formed in 1955 and officially disbanded in 1959, on the eve of Cypriot independence) and the beginning of EOKA-B (which formed in 1971, with personnel and resources from the junta in Greece, and disbanded after the failed coup in 1974, when many members were jailed). According to former president Glafkos Clerides, Polykarpos Georkadjis was either a member of the National Front or "placed one of his people in the organization" (Kızılyürek [2006] 2008, 143 [Cf. 264]).

23. Indeed, the family, according to evidence that emerged during the 2010 trial, had been contacted by one of the conspirators, who asked for money and assistance in leaving the country.

24. I borrow the phrase "in the know" (in scare quotes) from Diane Nelson, who theorized this position in her many works on knowledge production around the genocide in Guatemala (see especially Nelson [2009, xxiii, passim]).

25. See forensic reports by Torkildsen (2002), for the ICTY, and Van Duyne and Donati (2006), for the UNICRI, concluding that Cypriot banks (particularly Laïki) had been extensively involved in laundering Serbian monies to finance the Yugoslav government, army, and police during the wars.

26. See also Howden's (2003) reportage on the scandal in *The Independent*.

27. A disturbing incident took place on January 22, 2018, when the paper's offices in north Nicosia were violently attacked by the Grey Wolves and other Turkish ultranationalists, after Turkish president Erdoğan encouraged his "brothers in north Cyprus" to give "the necessary response" to an editorial published by *Afrika* on January 21, 2018, likening the recent Turkish invasion of Afrin (northern Syria) to the Turkish occupation of Cyprus. See Calik (2018a; 2018b).

28. See Davis (2023), Introduction and Part 1.

29. See Charalambous (2004), citing Papadopoulos's interview with journalist Mohammed Galadari in the *Khaleej Times*.

30. Under the headline "*Afrika*'nın haberi giderek doğruluk kazanırken" [*Afrika*'s reporting grows increasingly accurate], the unnamed columnist wrote, "*Afrika* fobisenden muzdarip Kıbrıs Türk medyası ve iletişim kanalları, tıpkı Rum tarafı gibi, bu haberimize ambargo koymuş ve yayınlamamıştı" [The Turkish-Cypriot media and communication channels, suffering from *Afrika* phobia just like the Greek-Cypriot side, put an embargo on this news and did not publish it] (*Afrika* 2009d).

31. Cyprus SAT footage of Papadopoulos's "No" speech on YouTube, accessed February 19, 2018, https://www.youtube.com/watch?v=JMrlnhsSepc.

32. PEKA is the Pancypriot Committee of the Cypriot Struggle [Παγκύπρια Επιτροπή Κυπριακού Αγώνα]. See Drousiotis (2009b, 99).

33. On this conspiracy theory, see Psyllides (2011; 2016). Passing references to this conspiracy as well as the conspiracy to abduct Achilleas were included in *The Yellow Book of Spyros Kyprianou* [Το Κίτρινο Βιβλίο του Σπύρου Κυπριανού], a collection of press clippings and statements by Kyprianou published first in 1978 by Alekos Konstantinidis; a second edition was published in 1981 (see Konstantinidis ([1978] 1981, 14–17, 28.ii, 46–47). The title of the book, explained in its first pages, was a reference to *The Red Book of Chairman Mao* (6), as well as to *The Little Black Book of Makarios*, apparently devised during Makarios's life but never published, which would contain "the wisdom and a selection of quotations from the Great Leader" (7). "It is too late now for Makarios's *Little Black Book*," the author writes. "In its place, we decided to publish *The Little Yellow Book of Kyprianou* by today's Leader of Cyprus, continuing the work of the Great Leader" (7).

34. Kikis Constantinou, also the longtime chairman of the Anorthosis soccer club, died in October 2023, while I was visiting Nicosia. One of my friends there expressed surprise at the very public celebration of his life taking place in Cypriot news media and social media at that time, given his notoriety as a key figure in EOKA-B. She recalled that Kikis had been connected with Papadopoulos in the 1970s, though she could not remember the details. *It's no wonder there were so many conspiracies surrounding Tassos*, she said. *He was a threat to everyone!*

35. Citations to Drousiotis (2005b) are to the English version of the piece.

36. The names of these five men were Antonis Korellis (Αντώνης Κορέλλης), Panayiotis Nikolaou (Παναγιώτης Νικολάου), Christoforos Skordis (Χριστόφορος Σκορδής), Ioannis Panayiannis (Ιωάννης Παναγιάννης), and Ioannis Chatzikyriakos (Ιωάννης Χατζηκυριάκος). See Kasimatis (1997), Drousiotis (2000), and Drousiotis (2009c).

37. Drousiotis (2009c) relates that one eyewitness, Greek-Cypriot guardsman Yiannakis Christodoulos, the brother-in-law of one of the murdered soldiers, who escaped capture and watched the events from a distance, gave his account to the state news agency (RIK) at the time. Christodoulos acknowledged that the Greek-Cypriot National Guard had "done so many things" to Turkish-Cypriot villagers in Tziaos that he understood the murder of the five Greek-Cypriot soldiers as retribution. (See also Galatariotou, who offers the material published in Drousiotis's article as transparent fact [2012, 258].) Drousiotis also presents information from another eyewitness, a second lieutenant in the National Guard, who identified himself to *Politis* but wished to remain anonymous in its coverage; according to Drousiotis, he told *Politis* that four Turkish Cypriots had been killed six hours before the murder of the five Greek-Cypriot soldiers, in the same manner—that is, by firing squad. It is this second eyewitness whose account was questioned by Mavridis in his *Simerini* op-ed.

38. The plan took its name from its supposed author. It was signed, "The Leader AKRITAS," recalling the hero of a ninth-century Byzantine epic, Digenis Akritas, known as the "border warrior" for his dual Greek-Arab ancestry and his strength and valor defending the eastern borders of Byzantium from Arab invaders. One of the epic tales features his magical leap to Asia Minor from the Pentadactylos Mountains in northern Cyprus. "Akritas" has been identified by many sources as the code name of Polykarpos Georkadjis (Kızılyürek [2006] 2008, 253; Reddaway 1986, 134; Clerides 1989, 209–10), while the EOKA leader, Georgios Grivas, who took the same hero as his ancestor, was known as "Diyenis." Grivas, a Greek Cypriot who became a Greek citizen and general in the Greek army, and a well-known Nazi collaborator during the German occupation of Greece, returned to Cyprus in the 1950s to spearhead EOKA's armed activities and then to build Cyprus's National Guard and defenses in the mid-1960s. He was exiled to Greece in 1967, having been blamed for a massacre of Turkish-Cypriot

villagers, but returned secretly in 1971 to work with the Greek-Cypriot guerillas then organizing themselves as EOKA-B. Elderly and in poor health by then, Grivas died of a heart attack in January 1974, six months before the attempted coup staged by EOKA-B and Greek military personnel.

39. Constandinos (2009, 34) cites as a source Soulioti (2006, 275–78), who observes that the text was first published in April 1966 but was most likely written "just before" Makarios presented his thirteen points of constitutional amendment on November 30, 1963. The text of the plan has been reprinted in full, in English, in Kızılyürek ([2006] 2008, 265–71), Hakki (2007, 90–97), Över (2007, 24–38), and Reddaway (1986, 199–206), among other sources. It appears to me, from pervasive differences in phrasing, that the English translations of the plan reprinted in Över, Kızılyürek, and Hakki are distinct. In his review of Hakki's volume, Andrekos Varnava points out that the original source of the version reprinted therein is not noted (2008, 138); it could be a new English translation of the original text published in *Patris*, or the English translation published by Clerides in his own memoirs, to which it is nearly identical. See Clerides (1989, 212–19).

40. Akritas Plan (section A.b.), Hakki (2007, 91).

41. Turkish-Cypriot political historian Niyazi Kızılyürek, in his 2006 book of interviews with former president Glafkos Clerides, says to Clerides, "I have studied the Plan and let me tell you that I do not agree with Turkish historians that this was a plan to wipe out the Turkish Cypriots. To my mind the Akritas Plan was more a legal and political document which could be used by the Greek Cypriot side to push for *Enosis*, that is to say by showing the outside world that Cyprus could not function as a state and that the right to self-determination had never been granted to Cyprus. The aim was to reopen the chapter on self-determination and *Enosis*. Of course it had a military substrata" (Kızılyürek [2006] 2008, 77).

42. Text of the Akritas Plan as reprinted in Hakki (2007, 94).

43. The text, Reddaway notes, was "circulated to the UN General Assembly and the Security Council on 30 May 1978 (A/33/115; S/12722)." Reddaway cites Patrick (1976, 42) on the UN document.

44. Constandinos (2009, 34) largely agrees with Reddaway, whom he cites; the Akritas Plan was published, he says, "in an attempt to expose Makarios' inability to deal with the Turkish Cypriots" and "appears to have been put together by the influential Minister of the Interior, Polykarpos Georkadjis" (citing US intelligence document NARA: RG59, CFPF, 1964–66, Political & Defense, Military Operations, Cyprus, Appendix 9). He notes that there is substantial disagreement among researchers today as to whether Makarios contributed to the plan.

45. See, for example, Loukas Charalambous (2017), who asserts that Glafkos Clerides named Papadopoulos as the author.

46. For example, Constandinos (2009, 34–35), who notes debates over the extent to which President Makarios was involved in writing the plan.

47. This phrase appears in the telegram from US ambassador David Popper to the US State Department on March 28, 1970 (document #355, point 6, in Miller, Selvage, and Van Hook 2007, 876).

48. According to Drousiotis (2009b, 48–49), the third member of "Akritas" was Glafkos Clerides.

49. In his memoirs, by contrast, Clerides says that he did not see the Akritas Plan until "after it was published, some years later, in a Greek Cypriot newspaper," presumably *Patris* in 1966 (Clerides 1989, 209).

50. Clerides notes that Makarios supported the formation of two other paramilitary groups in addition to Georkadjis's "Akritas" organization, one led by Dr. Lyssarides and the other by Nikos Sampson, in order to "balance the growing power around Yiorgadjis [Georkadjis]" (219).

51. On the membership of the organization, Reddaway quotes the conclusion drawn by Richard Patrick (1976): "Archbishop Makarios, President of the Republic, entrusted Greek-Cypriot military preparations for the future conflict to a triumvirate composed of Glafkos Clerides, President of the House of Representatives, Tassos Papadopoulos, Minister of Labour, and Polycarpos Yeorgadjis [Georkadjis], the Minister of the Interior" (Reddaway 1986, 134; Patrick 1976, 36).

52. See Constandinos (2009, 79n207), Drousiotis (2009a), and Mallinson ([2005] 2009, 69). See also US Department of State memos and reports, including the Intelligence Information Cable of March 9, 1970 (document #351) and telegrams from US ambassador David Popper on March 17, 1970 (document #352) and March 28, 1970 (document #355), reporting on Makarios's reaction to the assassination attempt and his private vis-à-vis public framing of it (Miller, Selvage, and Van Hook 2007, 867–77).

53. This is one of Drousiotis's books that has not been translated into English.

54. O'Malley and Craig (1999, 134) give a brief account of Georkadjis's murder, based on Stanley Mayes's (1981) biography of Makarios, that matches Drousiotis's narrative in broad brushstrokes. They note in addition that the minister of the interior who succeeded Georkadjis (whom they erroneously identify as "T. K. Anastasiou") implied that "Georghadhis [*sic*] and the Americans were mixed up" in the coup plot that Georkadjis had tried to warn Makarios about. Hitchens ([1984] 1989, 70) likewise refers to connections among Georkadjis, Papapostolou, and the CIA in Athens in the plotting of a coup in 1970.

55. Glafkos Clerides, in conversation with Niyazi Kızılyürek, indirectly corroborated certain details of Drousiotis's account concerning Clerides's own involvement the night of Georkadjis's murder—including that Georkadjis's friend, Kyriakos Patatakos, who escaped the shooting, immediately went to Clerides to show him the "Hermes" documents (as Georkadjis had instructed him to do if anything should happen to him); he and Clerides then went to the archbishopric to show the documents to Makarios. Clerides also advanced the view here that

Georkadjis had been killed by his co-conspirators in the plot to assassinate Makarios (Kızılyürek [2006] 2008, 145).

56. The Central Intelligence Service (Κεντρική Υπηρεσία Πληροφοριών, ΚΥΠ) was officially established in 1970, the same year as the assassination attempt, and closely linked to the Greek Intelligence Service (ΕΥΠ) under the junta. In 2016, the service was renamed the Cypriot Intelligence Service (Κύπριακή Υπηρεσία Πληροφοριών) with the same acronym (ΚΥΠ). Drousiotis writes that an "unofficial intelligence service" (2009b, 42)—which elsewhere he calls a "para"-intelligence service ("παραΚΥΠ") (2002a, 353)—was formed by Georkadjis much earlier, in 1960, during the interim period after Cyprus's independence, "with the assistance and support of the later Greek dictator Colonel George Papadopoulos" (2009b, 42), in whose assassination attempt Georkadjis was later implicated.

57. Patatakos lived to tell the tale because, as he attested, Georkadjis had instructed him to get out of the car and wait while Georkadjis drove a few hundred meters down the road to meet the people who turned out to be his assassins.

58. Drousiotis first published this interview in "The 'Invasion' of the Junta in Cyprus" (207).

59. The original source is *Alithia* [Αλήθεια] (1975).

60. The "top secret" memo was titled, "The Assassination of Georkadjis" ("Η δολοφονία του Γιωρκάτζη").

61. Drousiotis identifies as a "likely" third gunman one Georgos Aslandis, the son of Constantinos Aslandis, a lieutenant colonel in the Greek junta who had been active in Cyprus. Drousiotis (2009a, 299; 2009b, 63).

62. In Kızılyürek ([2006] 2008), see note 77 on the National Front.

INCONCLUSION (RECONTEXTUALIZATION)

1. A bit of the Fanieros legend is captured by news items published upon his death; see Psyllides (2017) and *Philenews* (2017).

2. In 1994, Antonis Kitas was convicted of the murder of Oxana Lisna (from Ukraine) and the rape and murder of Christina Ahfeldt Constantinidou (from Sweden), both in 1993.

3. This was the phrase used by Chrysostomos Perikleous in his December 2009 op-ed to characterize the unfolding situation a few days after the theft of the president's remains (2009, cited in Part 2.2). In the piece, he cautioned readers against jumping to conclusions by reminding them—recursively—of the National Front's "corrosive work" that derailed peace negotiations in 1969 and ultimately instigated the formation of EOKA-B.

4. Drousiotis quotes Papadopoulos from a Cyprus News Agency report, October 15, 2004.

5. Many thanks to Theo Rakopoulos for suggesting to me the phenomenological relevance of this phrase.

6. Drousiotis used this phrase as the Greek title of his IKME report (2005b) as well as the Greek and English titles of his 2006 documentary ("Η περιρρέουσα ατμόσφαιρα" / "The Case of the Ambient Atmosphere"). The documentary is streamable on Drousiotis's website (http://www.makarios.eu/cgibin/hweb?-A=980&-V=specials) as well as on YouTube (https://www.youtube.com/watch?v=SL8RM7t5EMo).

7. Stewart cites Sedgwick here (1997, 452).

BIBLIOGRAPHY

Agamben, Giorgio. (1995) 1998. *Homo Sacer: Sovereign Power and Bare Life.* Translated by Daniel Heller-Roazen. Stanford, CA: Stanford University Press.
Ahmed, Sara. 2015. *The Cultural Politics of Emotion.* London: Routledge.
Anastasiadis, Lakis. 2016. *Κυπρίων ιατρών έργα ̈η ιατρική στην Κύπρο 1950–2015* [The work of Cypriot doctors: Medicine in Cyprus, 1950–2015]. Nikaia, Greece: Εκδόσεις Εντύποις [Entypois].
Angastiniotis, Tony. 2005. *Trapped in the Green Line: The Story behind the Documentary, "Voice of Blood."* Nicosia: Rüstem.
Appadurai, Arjun. 1986. "Theory in Anthropology: Center and Periphery." *Comparative Studies in Society and History* 28(2): 356–61.
Appadurai, Arjun. 1996. *Modernity at Large: Cultural Dimensions of Globalization.* Minneapolis: University of Minnesota Press.
Aravamudan, Srinivas. 2012. "Surpassing the North: Can the Antipodean Avantgarde Trump Postcolonial Belatedness?" Society for Cultural Anthropology Fieldsights forum, "Theorizing the Contemporary," edited by Juan Obarrio. February 25. https://culanth.org/fieldsights/surpassing-the-north-can-the-antipodean-avantgarde-trump-postcolonial-belatedness.
Aretxaga, Begoña. 2005. *States of Terror: Essays.* Reno: University of Nevada Press.
Asad, Talal. (1973) 1975. "Introduction." In *Anthropology and the Colonial Encounter*, edited by Talal Asad, 9–19. Amherst, NY: Humanity Books.
Asmussen, Jan. 2008. *Cyprus at War: Diplomacy and Conflict during the 1974 Crisis.* London: I. B. Tauris.
Bakalaki, Alexandra. 2016. "Chemtrails, Crisis, and Loss in an Interconnected World." *Visual Anthropology Review* 32(1): 12–23.
Bardawil, Fadi. 2020. *Revolution and Disenchantment: Arab Marxism and the Binds of Emancipation.* Durham, NC: Duke University Press.

Best, Stephen, and Sharon Marcus. 2009. "Surface Reading: An Introduction." *Representations* 108(1): 1–21.

Birchall, Clare. 2004. "Just Because You're Paranoid, Doesn't Mean They're Not Out to Get You: Cultural Studies on/as Conspiracy Theory." *Culture/Machine* 6. https://culturemachine.net/deconstruction-is-in-cultural-studies/just-because-youre-paranoid-doesnt-mean-theyre-not-out-to-get-you/.

Birchall, Clare. 2006. *Knowledge Goes Pop: From Conspiracy Theory to Gossip*. Oxford: Berg.

Blanuša, Nebojša. 2009. "The Structure of Conspiratorial Beliefs in Croatia," *Anali Hrvatskog politološkog društva* [Annals of the Croatian Society for Political Science] 6(1): 113–43.

Blanuša, Nebojša, and Todor Hristov. 2020. "Psychoanalysis, Critical Theory and Conspiracy Theory." In *Routledge Handbook of Conspiracy Theories*, edited by Michael Butler and Peter Knight, 67–80. New York: Routledge.

Boon, James A. 1982. *Other Tribes, Other Scribes: Symbolic Anthropology in the Comparative Study of Cultures, Histories, Religions, and Texts*. Cambridge: Cambridge University Press.

Borneman, John, and Abdellah Hammoudi. 2009. *Being There: The Fieldwork Encounter and the Making of Truth*. Berkeley: University of California Press.

Bourdieu, Pierre. [1980] 1990. *The Logic of Practice*. Trans. Richard Nice. Stanford, CA: Stanford University Press.

Boyarin, Daniel. 1995. "Freud's Baby, Fliess's Maybe: Homophobia, Anti-Semitism, and the Invention of Oedipus." *GLQ* 2(1–2): 115–47.

Bratich, Jack. 2008. *Conspiracy Panics: Political Rationality and Popular Culture*. Albany, NY: SUNY Press.

Bratich, Jack. 2017. "If Everyone Is a Conspiracy Theorist, Is Anyone? Trumpism, Mutually Assured Disqualification, and Communications Warfare." Lecture delivered at the Monroe Center for Social Inquiry, Pitzer College (Claremont, CA), November 14, 2017. https://www.pitzer.edu/mcsi/2017/12/14/jack-bratich-everyone-conspiracy-theorist-anyone/.

Briggs, Charles L. 2004. "Theorizing Modernity Conspiratorially: Science, Scale, and the Political Economy of Public Discourse in Explanations of a Cholera Epidemic." *American Ethnologist* 31(2): 164–87.

Bryant, Rebecca, and Mete Hatay. 2020. *Sovereignty Suspended: Building the So-Called State*. Philadelphia: University of Pennsylvania Press.

Chaudhary, Zahid R. 2022. "Paranoid Publics." *History of the Present* 12(1): 103–26.

Cherstich, Igor. 2014. "The Body of the Colonel: Caricature and Incarnation in the Libyan Revolution." In *The Political Aesthetics of Global Protest: The Arab Spring and Beyond*, edited by Pnina Werbner, Martin Webb, and Kathryn Spellman-Poots, 93–120. Edinburgh: University of Edinburgh Press.

Clerides, Glafkos. 1989. *Cyprus: My Deposition,* Volume 1. Nicosia: Alithia.

Chomsky, Noam. 1993. *Rethinking Camelot: JFK, the Vietnam War, and US Political Culture.* New York: Verso.

Comaroff, Jean, and John L. Comaroff. 1999. "Occult Economies and the Violence of Abstraction: Notes from the South African Postcolony." *American Ethnologist* 26(2): 279–303.

Comaroff, Jean, and John L. Comaroff. 2003. "Transparent Fictions; Or, The Conspiracies of a Liberal Imagination: An Afterword." In *Transparency and Conspiracy: Ethnographies of Suspicion in the New World Order*, edited by Harry G. West and Todd Sanders, 287–300. Durham, NC: Duke University Press.

Comaroff, Jean, and John L. Comaroff. 2012. *Theory from the South; or, How Euro-America Is Evolving toward Africa.* Boulder, CO: Paradigm.

Constandinos, Andreas. 2009. *America, Britain and the Cyprus Crisis of 1974: Calculated Conspiracy or Foreign Policy Failure?* Milton Keynes: AuthorHouse.

Csordas, Thomas. 1993. "Somatic Modes of Attention." *Cultural Anthropology* 8(2): 135–56.

Culler, Jonathan. 1983. *On Deconstruction: Theory and Criticism after Structuralism.* London: Routledge and Kegan Paul.

Davis, Elizabeth Anne. 2012. *Bad Souls: Madness and Responsibility in Modern Greece.* Durham, NC: Duke University Press.

Davis, Elizabeth Anne. 2017a. "Time Machines: The Matter of the Missing in Cyprus." In *Unfinished: The Anthropology of Becoming*, edited by João Biehl and Peter Locke, 217–42. Durham, NC: Duke University Press.

Davis, Elizabeth Anne. 2017b. "'The Information Is Out There': Transparency, Responsibility, and the Missing in Cyprus." In *Competing Responsibilities: The Ethics and Politics of Contemporary Life*, edited by Susanna Trnka and Catherine Trundle, 135–55. Durham, NC: Duke University Press..

Davis, Elizabeth Anne. 2023. *Artifactual: Forensic and Documentary Knowing.* Experimental Futures: Technological Lives, Scientific Arts, Anthropological Voices. Durham, NC: Duke University Press.

Davis, Elizabeth Anne. 2024. "Conspiracy Attunement and Context: The Case of the President's Body." In *Conspiracy/Theory*, edited by Joseph Masco and Lisa Wedeen, 104–26. Durham, NC: Duke University Press.

Dean, Jodi. 1998. *Aliens in America: Conspiracy Cultures from Outerspace to Cyberspace.* Ithaca, NY: Cornell University Press.

Dean, Jodi. 2002. *Publicity's Secret: How Technoculture Capitalizes on Democracy.* Ithaca, NY: Cornell University Press.

Dégh, Linda. 1996. "What Is a Belief Legend?" *Folklore* 107: 33–46.

Demetriou, Olga. 2007. "To Cross or Not to Cross? Subjectivization and the Absent State in Cyprus." *Journal of the Royal Anthropological Institute* 13: 987–1006.

Demetriou, Olga. 2018. *Refugeehood and the Postconflict Subject: Reconsidering Minor Losses*. Albany, NY: SUNY Press.

Demetriou, Olga, Costas M. Constantinou, and Maria Tselepou. 2023. "Lateral Colonialism: Exploring Modalities of Engagement in Decolonial Politics from the Periphery." *Third World Quarterly* 44(9): 2173–90.

Demetriou, Olga, and Ayla Gürel. 2008. "Human Rights, Civil Society and Conflict in Cyprus: Exploring the Relationships." Case Study Report WP3. *SHUR: Human Rights in Conflicts: The Role of Civil Society*. Rome: Programme of the European Commission.

Dentith, Matthew R. X. 2016. "When Inferring to a Conspiracy Might Be the Best Explanation." *Social Epistemology* 30(5–6): 572–91.

Dentith, Matthew R. X., Ed. 2018. *Taking Conspiracy Theories Seriously*. Lanham, MD: Rowman & Littlefield.

Derrida, Jacques. 1995. *Archive Fever: A Freudian Impression*. Translated by Eric Prenowitz. Chicago: University of Chicago Press.

Dilley, Roy. 1999. "Introduction: The Problem of Context." In *The Problem of Context: Perspectives from Social Anthropology and Elsewhere*, edited by Roy Dilley, 1–46. New York: Berghahn.

Dimitrakis, Panagiotis. 2010. *Military Intelligence in Cyprus: From the Great War to Middle East Crisis*. London: I. B. Tauris.

Douglas, Karen M., Joseph E. Uscinski, Robbie M. Sutton, et al. 2019. "Understanding Conspiracy Theories." *Advances in Political Psychology* 40(suppl. 1): 3–34.

Drousiotis, Makarios. 2000. *1619 Ενοχές· Τα λάθη, τα ψέματα και οι σκοπιμότητες* [1619 guilty: Mistakes, lies, and practicalities]. Nicosia: Diafaneia.

Drousiotis, Makarios. 2002a. *EOKA· Η Σκοτεινή Όψη* [EOKA: The dark side]. Nicosia: Alfadi.

Drousiotis, Makarios. 2002b. *1974· Το Άγνωστο παρασκήνιο της Τουρκικής εισβολής* [The unknown backstory of the Turkish invasion]. Nicosia: Alfadi.

Drousiotis, Makarios. 2003. *EOKA-β & CIA· Το ελληνοτουρκικό παρακράτος στην Κύπρο* [EOKA-B and the CIA: The Greek-Turkish parastate in Cyprus]. Nicosia: Alfadi.

Drousiotis, Makarios. 2005b. "Η περιρρέουσα ατμόσφαιρα." Translated into English by George Karaolides as "The Construction of 'Reality' and the Mass Media in Cyprus." October 2005. Nicosia: IKME (Institute of Socio-Political Studies). http://www.makarios.eu/upload/20051111/1131713084-12865.pdf.

Drousiotis, Makarios. 2008. *The First Partition: Cyprus 1963–64*. Nicosia: Alfadi. English translation of *Η Πρώτη διχοτόμηση: Κύπρος 1963–64* (Nicosia: Alfadi, 2005).

Drousiotis, Makarios. 2009a. *Δύο απόπειρες και μια δολοφονία· Η Χούντα και η Κύπρος* [Two attempts and a murder: The junta and Cyprus]. Nicosia: Alfadi.

Drousiotis, Makarios. 2009b. *Cyprus 1974: Greek Coup and Turkish Invasion*. Nicosia: Alfadi. English translation and condensation of Drousiotis (2002b) and Drousiotis (2003).

Drousiotis, Makarios. 2010a. *Η Μεγάλη ιδέα της μικρής χούντας" Η ΕΟΚΑ β και το πραξικόπημα της 15ης Ιουλίου 1974* [The big idea of the little junta: EOKA-B and its coup of July 15, 1974]. Nicosia: Alfadi.

Drousiotis, Makarios. 2014a. *Κύπρος 1974–1977: Η εισβολή και οι μεγάλες δυναμείς" Η realpolitik των ΗΠΑ και το διπλό παιχνίδι της ΕΣΣΔ*. Nicosia: Alfadi.

Drousiotis, Makarios. 2016. *The Cyprus Crisis and the Cold War: USSR Duplicity versus US Realpolitik*. English translation of Drousiotis (2014a). Nicosia: Alfadi.

Drousiotis, Makarios. 2020. *Η Συμμορία—Το Διεφθαρμένο σύστημα εξουσίας στην Κύπρο. Το Κούρεμα και η διαπλοκή πολιτικών και δικηγόρων. Από το ημερολόγιο ενός αυτόπτη μάρτυρα* [Gangs: The corrupt system of power in Cyprus. The haircut and the entanglement of politicians and lawyers. From the diary of an eyewitness]. Nicosia: Alfadi.

Drousiotis, Makarios. 2021. *Έγκλημα στο Κραν Μοντάνα—Πώς και γιατί η συμμορία ματαίωσε τη λύση του Κυπριακού. Διαφθορά, ανικανότητα και ξένες εξαρτήσεις* [Crime at Crans-Montana—How and why gangs killed a solution to the Cyprus Problem: Corruption, incompetence, and foreign dependency]. Nicosia: Alfadi.

Drousiotis, Makarios. 2022. *Κράτος Μάφια—Πως η συμμορία κατήργησε το κράτος δικαίου στην Κύπρο. Ολιγάρχες, Ξέπλυμα, Μίζες, Παρακολουθήσεις* [The mafia state: How gangs destroyed the rule of law in Cyprus. Oligarchs, laundering, kickbacks, surveillance]. Nicosia: Alfadi.

Drousiotis, Makarios, Ahmet An, Desmond Fernandez, and Iskender Ozden. 2004. *Το Βαθύ κράτος: Τουρκία, Ελλάδα, Κύπρος* [The deep state: Turkey, Greece, Cyprus]. Nicosia: Alfadi.

Ersoy, Metin. 2010. "Peace Journalism and News Coverage on the Cyprus Conflict." *The Muslim World* 100(1): 78–99.

Evans-Pritchard, E. E. 1937. *Witchcraft, Oracles, and Magic among the Azande*. Oxford: Clarendon Press.

Fassin, Dider. 2011. "The Politics of Conspiracy Theories: On AIDS in South Africa and a Few Other Global Plots." *The Brown Journal of World Affairs* 17(2): 39–50.

Fassin, Dider. 2021. "Of Plots and Men: The Heuristics of Conspiracy Theories." Eric Wolf Lecture delivered at the University of Vienna, October 24, 2019. *Current Anthropology* 62(2): 128–37.

Faubion, James. 2001. *The Shadows and Lights of Waco: Millennialism Today*. Princeton, NJ: Princeton University Press.

Favret-Saada, Jeanne. (1977) 1980. *Deadly Words: Witchcraft in the Bocage.* Translated by Catherine Cullen. Cambridge: Cambridge University Press.

Fenster, Mark. 1999. *Conspiracy Theories: Secrecy and Power in American Culture.* Minneapolis: University of Minnesota Press.

Fenster, Mark. 2008. *Conspiracy Theories: Secrecy and Power in American Culture.* Revised updated edition. Minneapolis: University of Minnesota Press.

Ferrándiz, Francisco. 2022. "Francisco Franco Is Back: The Contested Reemergence of a Fascist Moral Exemplar." *Comparative Studies in Society and History* 64(1): 208–37.

Fiske, John. (1993) 2016. *Power Plays, Power Works.* Second edition. London: Routledge.

Forrester Johnson, Luke. 2021. "Racial Reverb: 'Paranoia within Reason' and the Sounding of the Social." *symplokē* 29(1–2): 247–66.

Foucault, Michel. 1971. "The Discourse on Language." *Social Science Information* (April): 7–30 (Rupert Swyer, Trans.). Reprinted in Michel Foucault, *The Archeology of Knowledge and the Discourse on Language*, translated by A. M. Sheridan Smith, 215–38. New York: Pantheon, 1972.

Foucault, Michel. (1975) 1977. *Discipline and Punish.* Translated by Alan Sheridan. New York: Vintage.

Foucault, Michel. 1980. "Lecture One: 7 January 1976." In *Power/Knowledge: Selected Interviews and Other Writings, 1972–77*, edited and translated by Colin Gordon, 79–92. New York: Vintage.

Foucault, Michel. 1982. "Afterword: The Subject and Power." In *Michel Foucault: Beyond Structuralism and Hermeneutics*, edited by Hubert L. Dreyfus and Paul Rabinow, 208–26. Chicago: University of Chicago Press.

Frazer, James George. 1890–1915. *The Golden Bough: A Study in Comparative Religion / A Study in Magic and Religion.* London: Macmillan.

Freeland, Elana. 2014. *Chemtrails, HAARP, and the "Full Spectrum Dominance" of Planet Earth.* Port Townsend, WA: Feral House.

Freud, Sigmund. (1911) 1963. "Psychoanalytic Notes upon an Autobiographical Account of a Case of Paranoia (Dementia Paranoides)." *Three Case Histories*, edited by Philip Rieff, 83–160. New York: Collier Books.

Galatariotou, Catia. 2012. "Truth, Memory, and the Cypriot Journey towards a New Past." In *Cyprus and the Politics of Memory: History, Community, and Conflict*, edited by Rebecca Bryant and Yiannis Papadakis, 242–64. London: I. B. Tauris.

Geertz, Clifford. 1973. "Thick Description: Toward an Interpretive Theory of Culture." In *The Interpretation of Cultures: Selected Essays*, 3–30. New York: Basic Books.

Glaude, Eddie S., Jr. 1991. "An Analysis of the Cress Theory of Color Confrontation." *Journal of Black Studies* 22(2): 284–93.

Gluckman, Max. 1963. "Gossip and Scandal." *Current Anthropology* 4(3): 307–16.
Good, Byron J. 1994. *Medicine, Rationality, and Experience: An Anthropological Perspective.* Cambridge: Cambridge University Press.
Graeber, David. 2011. "The Divine Kingship of the Shilluk: On Violence, Utopia, and the Human Condition, or, Elements for an Archaeology of Sovereignty." *HAU: Journal of Ethnographic Theory* 1(1): 1–62.
Greenwood, Susan. 2022. "A Spectrum of Magical Consciousness: Conspiracy Theories and the Stories We Tell Ourselves." *Anthropology Today* 38(1): 3–7.
Hakki, Murat Metin, Ed. 2007. *The Cyprus Issue, a Documentary History, 1878–2007.* London: I. B. Tauris.
Hall, Stuart. (1997) 2013. "The Work of Representation." In *Representation: Cultural Representations and Signifying Practices*, edited by Stuart Hall, Jessica Evans, and Sean Nixon, 1–47. Second edition. London: Sage.
Harambam, Jaron, and Stef Aupers. 2017. "'I Am Not a Conspiracy Theorist': Relational Identifications in the Dutch Conspiracy Milieu." *Cultural Sociology* 11(1): 113–29.
Harding, Susan, and Kathleen Stewart. 2003. "Anxieties of Influence: Conspiracy Theory and Therapeutic Culture in Millennial America." In *Transparency and Conspiracy: Ethnographies of Suspicion in the New World Order*, edited by Harry G. West and Todd Sanders, 258–86. Durham, NC: Duke University Press.
Harsin, Jayson. 2008. "Rumor Bombs: American Mediated Politics as Pure War." In *Cultural Studies, an Anthology*, edited by Michael Ryan, 468–82. New York: Blackwell.
Hartman, Saidiya. 2008. "Venus in Two Acts." *small axe* 26: 1–14.
Heinz, Andreas. 1997. "Savage Thought and Thoughtful Savages: On the Context of the Evaluation of Logical Thought by Lévy-Bruhl and Evans-Pritchard." *Anthropos* 92: 165–73.
Herzfeld, Michael. 1987. *Anthropology through the Looking-Glass: Critical Ethnography in the Margins of Europe.* Cambridge: Cambridge University Press.
Herzfeld, Michael. (1997) 2005. *Cultural Intimacy: Social Poetics in the Nation-State.* Second edition. New York: Routledge.
Hitchens, Christopher. (1984) 1989. *Hostage to History: Cyprus from the Ottomans to Kissinger.* New York: Farrar, Straus and Giroux / Noonday Press.
Hofstadter, Richard. 1964. "The Paranoid Style in American Politics." *Harper's*, November 1964, 77–86.
Hollis, Martin, and Steven Lukes, Eds. 1982. *Rationality and Relativism.* Cambridge, MA: MIT Press.
Ioannou, Yiannis. 2009. Θεωρία της συνωμοσίας και κουλτούρα της διχοτόμησης˙ Δοκίμιο για τον πολιτικό πολιτισμό της Κύπρου [Conspiracy theory and the

culture of partition: Essay on the political culture of Cyprus]. Athens: Papazisi.

Jackson, John L. 2017. "What's Love Got to Do with It? Race, Conspiracy Theories, and Contemporary Hip-Hop Culture." Lecture delivered at the Monroe Center for Social Inquiry, Pitzer College (Claremont, CA), November 7, 2017. https://www.pitzer.edu/mcsi/2017/11/14/john-l-jackson-jr-whats-love-got/.

Jameson, Frederic. 1988. "Cognitive Mapping." In *Marxism and the Interpretation of Culture*, edited by Cary Nelson and Lawrence Grossberg, 347–60. Urbana: University of Illinois Press.

Jameson, Frederic. 1992. *Postmodernism, or, The Logic of Late Capitalism*. Durham, NC: Duke University Press.

Jarvie, I. C. 1964. *The Revolution in Anthropology*. London: Routledge and Kegan Paul.

Jordan, William Chester. (1997) 2016. "Preface (1997)." In Ernst Kantorowicz, *The King's Two Bodies: A Study in Medieval Political Theology*, xxv–xxxi. Princeton Classics Edition. Princeton, NJ: Princeton University Press.

Kantorowicz, Ernst. (1957) 2016. *The King's Two Bodies: A Study in Medieval Political Theology*. Princeton Classics Edition. Princeton, NJ: Princeton University Press.

Kasimatis, Petros. 1997. Δεκατρία Περιστέρια˙ Οι τελευταίοι επιζώντες αγνοούμενοι της Κύπρου. Οι μυστικές αποστολές σωτηρίας τους [Thirteen doves: The last surviving missing persons of Cyprus and their secret rescue missions]. Athens: Livani.

Keeley, Brian L. 1999. "Of Conspiracy Theories." *The Journal of Philosophy* 96(3): 109–26.

Khatib, Lina. 2013. *Image Politics in the Middle East: The Role of the Visual in Political Struggle*. London: I. B. Tauris.

Kızılyürek, Niyazi. (2006) 2008. *Glafkos Clerides: The Path of a Country*. Nicosia: Rimal.

Knight, Peter. 2000. *Conspiracy Culture: From Kennedy to the X-Files*. London: Routledge.

Konstantinidis, Alekos. (1978) 1981. *Το Κίτρινο Βιβλίο του Σπύρου Κυπριανού* [The yellow book of Spyros Kyprianou]. Second edition. Nicosia: Διαφωνία [Dissent].

Lederman, Rena. 2008. "Anthropological Regionalism." In *A New History of Anthropology*, edited by Henrika Kuklick, 310–25. Hoboken, NJ: Wiley.

Lefort, Claude. 1988. *Democracy and Political Theory*. Translated by David Macey. Minneapolis: University of Minnesota Press.

Lepselter, Susan. 2016. *The Resonance of Unseen Things: Poetics, Power, Captivity, and UFOs in the American Uncanny*. Ann Arbor: University of Michigan Press.

Lévy-Bruhl, Lucien. [1910] 1985. *Les fonctions mentales dans les sociétés inférieures* [How natives think]. Princeton, NJ: Princeton University Press.

Leyser, Conrad. 2016. "Introduction to the Princeton Classics Edition." In Ernst Kantorowicz, *The King's Two Bodies: A Study in Medieval Political Theology*, i–xix. Princeton Classics Edition. Princeton, NJ: Princeton University Press.

Magliocco, Sabina. 2012. "Beyond Belief: Context, Rationality, and Participatory Consciousness." *Western Folklore* 71(1): 5–24.

Mahon, Michael. 1992. *Foucault's Nietzschean Genealogy: Truth, Power, and the Subject*. Albany, NY: SUNY Press.

Malinowski, Bronislaw. (1935) 1978. "Part VI, An Ethnographic Theory of the Magical World." In *Coral Gardens and Their Magic: A Study of the Methods of Tilling the Soil and of Agricultural Rites in the Trobriand Islands* (Volumes I–II), 2:211–50. New York: Dover.

Mallinson, William. (2005) 2009. *Cyprus: A Modern History*. London: I. B. Tauris.

Marasco, Robyn. 2016. "Toward a Critique of Conspiratorial Reason." *Constellations* 23(2): 236–43.

Marcus, George E. 1999. "Preface: A Reintroduction to the Series" and "Introduction to the Volume: The Paranoid Style Now." In *Paranoia within Reason: A Casebook on Conspiracy as Explanation*, edited by George E. Marcus, ix–xiv, 1–12. Chicago: University of Chicago Press.

Masco, Joseph. 2014. *Theater of Operations: National Security Affect from the Cold War to the War on Terror*. Durham, NC: Duke University Press.

Maskovsky, Jeff, and Sophie Bjork-James. 2020. "Introduction." In *Beyond Populism: Angry Politics and the Twilight of Neoliberalism*, edited by Jeff Maskovsky and Sophie Bjork-James, 1–19. Morgantown: West Virginia University Press.

Maskovsky, Jeff, and Julian Aron Ross. 2022. "Laboring for Whiteness: The Rise of Trumpism and What That Tells Us about Racial and Gendered Capitalism in the United States." In *The Routledge Handbook of the Anthropology of Labor*, edited by Sharryn Kasmir and Lesley Gill, 166–79. New York: Routledge.

Mayes, Stanley. 1981. *Makarios: A Biography*. London: Palgrave Macmillan.

Mazzarella, William. 2019. "The Anthropology of Populism: Beyond the Liberal Settlement." *Annual Review of Anthropology* 48 (2019): 45–60.

McIntosh, Janet. 2022. "The Sinister Signs of QAnon: Interpretive Agency and Paranoid Truths in Alt-Right Oracles." *Anthropology Today* 38(1): 8–12.

Melley, Timothy. 2000. *Empire of Conspiracy: The Culture of Paranoia in Postwar America*. Ithaca, NY: Cornell University Press.

Miller, James E., Douglas E. Selvage, and Laurie Van Hook, eds. 2007. *Foreign Relations of the United States, 1969–1976, Volume XXIX, Eastern Europe; Eastern Mediterranean, 1969–1972*. Washington, D.C.: United States Government Printing Office.

Muirhead, Russell, and Nancy Rosenblum. 2019. *A Lot of People Are Saying: The New Conspiracism and the Assault on Democracy*. Princeton, NJ: Princeton University Press.

Nelson, Diane M. 2009. *Reckoning: The Ends of War in Guatemala*. Durham, NC: Duke University Press.

Nicolet, Claude. 2009. "*Cyprus 1974: Greek Coup and Turkish Invasion*, by Makarios Drousiotis." *The Cyprus Review* 21(1): 242–44.

Obeyesekere, Gananath. 1990. *The Work of Culture: Symbolic Transformation in Psychoanalysis and Anthropology*. Chicago: University of Chicago Press.

O'Malley, Brendan, and Ian Craig. 1999. *The Cyprus Conspiracy: America, Espionage, and the Turkish Invasion*. London: I. B. Tauris.

Oushakine, Serguei Alex. 2009. "'Stop the Invasion!': Money, Patriotism, and Conspiracy in Russia." *Social Research* 76(1): 71–116.

Över, Kıvanç Gaip. 2007. *Tassos Papadopoulos: Valley of the Greek Cypriots in Cyprus*. Istanbul: Kaknüs Yayınları.

Parla, Ayşe. 2023. "Hamlet after Genocide: The Haunting of Soghomon Tehlirian and Empirical Fabulation." *Comparative Studies in Society and History* 65(2): 446–70.

Parmigiani, Giovanna. 2021. "Magic and Politics: Conspirituality and COVID-19." *Journal of the American Academy of Religion* 89(2): 506–29.

Parmigiani, Giovanna. 2023. "'Separation, but Not Division': A Southern Italian Perspective on 'Lived Conspirituality.'" *Anthropologica* 65(1): 1–23.

Patrick, Richard Arthur. 1976. *Political Geography and the Cyprus Conflict, 1963–71*, edited by James H. Bater and Richard Preston. Department of Geography Publication Series 4. Waterloo (Ontario): University of Waterloo.

Pelkmans, Mathijs, and Rhys Machold. 2011. "Conspiracy Theories and Their Truth Trajectories." *Focaal: Journal of Global and Historical Anthropology* 59: 66–80.

Pereira, Godofredo. 2011. "Dead Commodities." *Cabinet* 43 ("Forensics"): 90–94.

Pigg, Stacy Leigh. 1996. "The Credible and the Credulous: The Question of 'Villagers' Beliefs' in Nepal." *Cultural Anthropology* 11(2): 160–201.

Pipes, Daniel. 1996. *The Hidden Hand: Middle East Fears of Conspiracy*. New York: St. Martin's Griffin.

Pipes, Daniel. 1997. *Conspiracy: How the Paranoid Style Flourishes and Where It Comes From*. New York: Free Press.

Popper, Karl R. (1963) 2002. "The Conspiracy Theory of Society" (from Chapter 4: "Towards a Rational Theory of Tradition"). In *Conjectures and Refutations: The Growth of Scientific Knowledge*, 165–68. Second edition. New York: Routledge.

Povinelli, Elizabeth A. 2011. "The Woman on the Other Side of the Wall: Archiving the Otherwise in Postcolonial Digital Archives." *differences* 22(1): 146–71.

PRIO Cyprus Centre. 2012. *Displacement in Cyprus: Consequences of Civil and Military Strife, Reports 1–7*. Contributions by Rebecca Bryant, Corina Demetriou, Olga Demetriou, Ayla Gürel, Mete Hatay, Fiona Mullen, Bozena Sojka, Nicos Trimikliniotis, and Christalla Yakinthou. Oslo: Peace Research Institute Oslo.

Rakopoulos, Theodoros. 2018. "Show Me the Money: Conspiracy Theories and Distant Wealth." *History and Anthropology* 29(3): 376–91.

Rakopoulos, Theodoros. 2022. "Of Fascists and Dreamers: Conspiracy Theory and Anthropology." *Social Anthropology* 30(1): 45–62.

Rakopoulos, Theodoros. 2023. *Passport Island: The Market for EU Citizenship in Cyprus*. Manchester: Manchester University Press.

Read, Jason. 2003. *The Micro-Politics of Capital*. Albany, NY: SUNY Press.

Reddaway, John. 1986. *Burdened with Cyprus: The British Connection*. Nicosia: K. Rüstem & Brother; London: Weidenfeld & Nicolson.

Riggan, Jennifer. 2020. "'Fed Up' in Ethiopia: Emotions, Civics Education, and Anti-Authoritarian Protest." In *Beyond Populism: Angry Politics and the Twilight of Neoliberalism*, edited by Jeff Maskovsky and Sophie Bjork-James, 237–58. Morgantown: West Virginia University Press.

Robins, Robert S., and Jerrold M. Post. 1997. *Political Paranoia: The Psychopolitics of Hatred*. New Haven, CT: Yale University Press.

Rosenblatt, Adam. 2015. *Digging for the Disappeared: Forensic Science after Atrocity*. Stanford, CA: Stanford University Press.

Sánchez, Rafael. 2016. *Dancing Jacobins: A Venezuelan Genealogy of Latin American Populism*. New York: Fordham University Press.

Santner, Eric L. 2011. *The Royal Remains: The People's Two Bodies and the Endgames of Sovereignty*. Chicago: University of Chicago Press.

Sedgwick, Eve Kosofsky. 1996. "Introduction: Queerer Than Fiction." *Studies in the Novel* 28(3): 277–280.

Sedgwick, Eve Kosofsky. 1997. *Novel Gazing*. Durham, NC: Duke University Press.

Sedgwick, Eve Kosofsky. 2003. "Paranoid Reading and Reparative Reading, Or, You're So Paranoid, You Probably Think This Essay Is about You." In *Touching Feeling: Affect, Pedagogy, Performativity*, 123–51. Durham, NC: Duke University Press.

Sinding-Larsen, Henrik. 2008. "Externality and Materiality as Themes in the History of the Human Sciences." *Fractal: Journal of Psychology* 20(1): 9–18.

Soulioti, Stella. 2006. *Fettered Independence: Cyprus, 1878–1964*. Volumes 1–2. Minnesota Mediterranean and East European Monographs 16. Minneapolis: University of Minnesota Press.

Sperber, Dan. 1985. *On Anthropological Knowledge: Three Essays*. Cambridge: Cambridge University Press.

Stewart, Charles. 2017. "Uncanny History: Temporal Topology in the Post-Ottoman World." *Social Analysis* 61(1): 129–42.

Stewart, Kathleen. 1991. "On the Politics of Cultural Theory: A Case for 'Contaminated' Cultural Critique." *Social Research* 58(2): 395–412.

Stewart, Kathleen. 1999. "Conspiracy Theory's Worlds." In *Paranoia within Reason: A Casebook on Conspiracy as Explanation*, edited by George E. Marcus, 13–20. Chicago: University of Chicago Press.

Stewart, Kathleen. 2011. "Atmospheric Attunements." *Environment and Planning D: Society and Space* (29): 445–52.

Stewart, Pamela J., and Andrew Strathern. 2004. *Witchcraft, Sorcery, Rumors, and Gossip*. Cambridge: Cambridge University Press.

Stocking, George. 1989. *Romantic Motives: Essays on Anthropological Sensibility*. Madison: University of Wisconsin Press.

Stokes, Patrick. 2018. "Conspiracy Theory and the Perils of Pure Particularism." In *Taking Conspiracy Theories Seriously*, edited by Matthew R. X. Dentith, 25–37. Lanham, MD: Rowman & Littlefield.

Strathern, Marilyn. 1987. "Out of Context: The Persuasive Fictions of Anthropology." Frazer Lecture delivered at the University of Liverpool, May 1, 1986. Edited text with commentaries and response: *Current Anthropology* 28(3): 251–81.

Strathern, Marilyn. (1991) 2004. *Partial Connections*. Updated edition. Walnut Creek, CA: Altamira.

Strigas, Athanasios K. 1995. Διεθνείς συνωμότες· Η σκοτεινή πλευρά του φεγγαριού [International conspirators: The dark side of the moon]. Athens: Νέα Θέσις [New thesis].

Strigas, Athanasios K. 2000. Κύπρος Απόρρητος Φάκελος [Cyprus: Confidential file]. Athens: Νέα Θέσις [New thesis].

Sutton, David. 2003. "Poked by the 'Foreign Finger' in Greece: Conspiracy Theory or the Hermeneutics of Suspicion?" In *The Usable Past: Greek Metahistories*, edited by K. S. Brown and Yannis Hamilakis, 191–210. Lanham, MD: Lexington Books.

Taussig, Michael. 1987. *Shamanism, Colonialism, and the Wild Man: A Study in Terror and Healing*. Chicago: University of Chicago Press.

Taussig, Michael. 1999. *Defacement: Public Secrecy and the Labor of the Negative*. Stanford, CA: Stanford University Press.

Theodossopoulos, Dimitrios. 2014. "On De-Pathologizing Resistance." *History and Anthropology* 25(4): 415–30.

Torkildsen, Morten. 2002. "Amended Expert Report of Morten Torkilsen, Office of the Prosecutor at the International Criminal Tribunal for the Former Yugoslavia (ICTY)." Case No. IT-02-54-T. June 7, 2002.

Tu, Chau. 2020. "*Slow Burn*'s Leon Neyfakh on Bringing His Watergate Series to Television—And What He Thinks about Donald Trump's Impeachment."

Slate, February 14, 2020. https://slate.com/culture/2020/02/slow-burn-watergate-epix-leon-neyfakh-interview.html.

Turner, Patricia A. 1993. *I Heard It through the Grapevine: Rumor in African-American Culture*. Berkeley: University of California Press.

Turner, Victor. 1980. "Social Dramas and Stories about Them." *Critical Inquiry* 7(1): 141–68.

Urban, Greg. 2001. *Metaculture: How Culture Moves through the World*. Minneapolis: University of Minnesota Press.

Van Duyne, Petrus C., and Stefano Donati. 2006. "In Search of Crime-Money Management in Serbia." UNICRI/OSCE Mission to Serbia Report. Turin: UN Interregional Crime and Justice Research Institute.

Varnava, Andrekos. 2008. "Review: *The Cyprus Issue, a Documentary History, 1878–2007*, edited by Murat Metin Hakki." *The Cyprus Review*, 20(1): 135–39.

Verdery, Katherine. 1999. *The Political Lives of Dead Bodies: Reburial and Postsocialist Change*. New York: Columbia University Press.

Warner, Michael. 2005. *Publics and Counterpublics*. New York: Zone.

Weber, Max. (1904) 1949. "'Objectivity' in Social Science and Social Policy" (1904). In *Max Weber, The Methodology of the Social Sciences*, translated by E. A. Hils and H. A. Finch, 49–112. New York: Free Press.

Welsing, Frances Cress. 1970. "The Cress Theory of Color-Confrontation and Racism (White Supremacy): A Psycho-Genetic Theory and World Outlook." *Black Scholar* 5(8): 32–40.

West, Harry G., and Todd Sanders. 2003. "Power Revealed and Power Concealed in the New World Order." In *Transparency and Conspiracy: Ethnographies of Suspicion in the New World Order*, edited by Harry G. West and Todd Sanders, 1–37. Durham, NC: Duke University Press.

Yurchak, Alexei. 2015. "Bodies of Lenin: The Hidden Science of Communist Sovereignty." *Representations* 129(1): 116–57.

Žižek, Slavoj. 1989. *The Sublime Object of Ideology*. London: Verso.

Žižek, Slavoj. 1992. "The Nation-Thing." In *Looking Awry: An Introduction to Jacques Lacan through Popular Culture*, 162–69. Cambridge, MA: MIT Press.

Žižek, Slavoj. 1997. *The Plague of Fantasies*. London: Verso.

Žižek, Slavoj. 2006. *Interrogating the Real*. London: Continuum.

NEWS MEDIA BIBLIOGRAPHY

Afrika. 2009a. "*Afrika*'nın haberi giderek doğruluk kazanırken." [*Afrika*'s reporting grows increasingly accurate]. December 22.

Afrika. 2009b. "Operasyon Şüpheli Fotini" [Operation: Suspect Fotini]. December 22.

Afrika. 2009c. "Paris'e gömülmüş" [He's buried in Paris]. December 19.

Afrika. 2009d. "Tasos'a ambargo karartma" [Embargo: Blackout on Tassos"]. December 20.

Agoustis, Dinos. 2009. "Βεβήλωσαν το Έθνος" [They desecrated the nation]. *Simerini*, December 17.

Al Jazeera. 2011. "Gaddafi's Body Removed for Burial." *Al Jazeera*, October 25, 2011. https://www.aljazeera.com/news/2011/10/25/gaddafis-body-removed-for-burial.

Alarabiya. 2018. "12 Years after His Death, Where Is the Body of Saddam Hussein?" Alarabiya News, April 16. https://english.alarabiya.net/features/2018/04/16/12-years-after-his-death-where-is-Saddam-Hussein-s-body-.

Alithia. 1975. "Επιχείρησις Γιωρκάτζη εξετελέσθη" [Operation Georkadjis complete]. March 3.

Apoyevmatini. 1977. "Συγκλονιστικό. Ανάλυση και έκθεση Άγγλου ιατρού υπονοεί ότι δολοφονήθηκε ο Εθνάρχης. Μεγάλα ποσοστά μολύβδου βρέθηκαν στην καρδιά του. Τι κατέδειξαν οι αναλύσεις του αίματός που έκανε Άγγλος ειδικός. Υπάρχει επίσημο πόρισμα να δημοσιευτεί!" [Shocking: Analysis and report by English doctor suggests that the ethnarch was assassinated. High levels of lead were found in his heart. What the analysis of the blood done by an English expert showed. There is an official conclusion to be published!]. November 19.

Azas, Andreas. 2009. "Αναλαμβάνουν ξένοι εμπειρογνώμονες· Η Αστυνομία 'όργωσε' τη Στράκκα, αλλά δεν βρήκε τίποτε" [Foreign experts take over; police "plowed through" Strakka, but found nothing]. *Simerini*, December 22.

Azas, Andreas. 2010. "Άλλο η σύληση του τάφου, άλλο η υφαρπαγή της σημαίας" [Despoiling the grave is one thing; hijacking the flag is another]. January 9.

"The Bug" [Ο Κοριός]. 2011. "Και τα Αντιβραβεία, 2010¨ Έτος πελλότοπου πελλόκοσμου" [And the anti-awards for 2010: The year in bizarro-world]. *Politis*, January 1.

Calik, Aydin. 2018a. "*Afrika* Suspected Attackers Detained for One Month Pending Trial." *Cyprus Mail*, January 30.

Calik, Aydin. 2018b. "Tense Day in North after *Afrika* Article Protest (Update 4)." *Cyprus Mail*, January 22.

Charalambous, Charles. 2009. "Union Throws Weight behind Writer Threatened by State Body." *Cyprus Mail*, July 2.

Charalambous, Loukas. 2004. "Does the President Have Memory Problems?" *Cyprus Mail*, September 12.

Charalambous, Loukas. 2009. "Το λείψανο της αξιοπρέπειας" [The relic of dignity]. *Politis*, December 20.

Charalambous, Loukas. 2017. "Political Stupidity Is Clearly Hereditary." *Cyprus Mail*, June 25.

Chatzistylianou, Michalis. 2010. "Ισοβίτης και παραμυθάς ο Αλ Καπόνε" [Al Capone, lifer and storyteller]. *Philelevtheros*, March 30.

Chatzivassilis, Michalis. 2010. "Νέες συλλήψεις για κλοπή σορού˙ Πολυσέλιδη κατάθεση Κίτα εμπλέκει δύο άτομα" [New arrests in the body theft; Kitas's multipage statement implicates two people]. *Philelevtheros*, March 23.
Chulov, Martin, and Ian Black. 2011. "Gaddafi Buried in Unmarked Grave in Libya Desert to Avoid Creating Shrine." *The Guardian*, October 25, 2011. https://www.theguardian.com/world/2011/oct/25/gaddafi-buried-in-unmarked-grave.
Dalgıçoğlu, Dolgun. 2009. "Papadopulos'un cesedinin düşündürdükleri" [What Papadopoulos's corpse suggests]. *Afrika*, December 14.
Dalitis, Frixos. 2010. "Ξανακτύπησαν οι βέβηλοι˙ Κατέβασαν την ελληνική σημαία από τον τάφο του Τάσσου" [The profaners struck again: They took the Greek flag down from the tomb of Tassos]. *Philelevtheros*, January 9.
Drousiotis, Makarios. 2005a. "Η Μεγάλη Συνωμοσία των εγκεφάλων" [The great conspiracy of brains]. *Politis*, February 27. English translation: http://www.makarios.eu/cgibin/hweb?-A=727&-V=English.
Drousiotis, Makarios. 2009c. "Η Αλήθεια για την κόλαση στο Τζιάος˙ Όλη η ιστορία των πέντε της φωτογραφίας" [The Truth about the hell at Tziaos: The whole story of the five in the photograph]. *Politis*, August 15.
Drousiotis, Makarios. 2010b. "Άντης Χατζηκωστής: Τον σκότωσε (κι αυτόν) η ΜΙΤ . . . Νωρίς το βράδυ της Δευτέρας έγινε στη Λευκωσία ένα άγριο φονικό." [Andy Hadjicostis: MIT killed him, too. . . . A brutal murder took place in Nicosia early Monday night.] Blog post (Protagon.gr), January 13. http://www.protagon.gr/apopseis/blogs/antis-xatzikwstis-ton-skotwse-ki-afton-i-mit-1053000000.
Drousiotis, Makarios. 2014b. "Soviet Duplicity in the Cyprus Crisis." *Cyprus Mail*, July 20.
Eminoğlu, Bilbay. 2009. "Papadopulos olayının faillerinden ses bekleniyor" [Perpetrators of the Papadopoulos case await word]. *Kıbrıs*. December 15.
Evripidou, Stefanos. 2008. "A Very Political Funeral." *Cyprus Mail*. December 16.
Evripidou, Stefanos. 2010. "Grave-Robbing Trial Opens." *Cyprus Mail*, July 16.
Evripidou, Stefanos. 2014a. "The 'Nicos vs. Nicolas' Spat over Deadlock in Cyprus Talks." *Cyprus Mail*, June 21. https://cyprus-mail.com/2014/06/21/the-nicos-vs-nicolas-spat-over-deadlock-in-cyprus-talks/.
Evripidou, Stefanos. 2014b. "Turning the Cyprus Problem Industry on Its Head." *Cyprus Mail*, July 20.
Fassin, Dider. 2014. "Les leçons de l'histoire" [The lessons of history]. *Le Monde*. July 20.
Giannakos, Christakis. 2010. "Αρνήθηκαν τις κατηγορίες για τη σορό" [They denied the charges for the body]. *Philelevtheros*, May 18.
Hadjiapostolou, Panayiotis. 2009. "Συγκλονισμός ανά το παγκύπριο για την κλοπή της σορού του Τάσσου Παπαδόπουλου˙ Κανένας δεν το πίστεψε από

την πρώτη" [Shock around the country at the theft of the body of Tassos Papadopoulos: No one could believe it at first]. *Politis*, December 12.

Haravgi. 2009a. "Καταζητούνται οι βέβηλοι" [The profaners are wanted]. December 12.

Haravgi. 2009b. "Αποτροπιασμός και αναστάτωση από την ειδεχθή πράξη" [Disgust and disturbance at the heinous act]. December 12.

Hassapi, Anna. 2009. "Serb Money Laundering Victim Sues Cyprus." *Cyprus Mail*, October 14.

Hazou, Elias. 2016. "Minister Pledges Probe into Chemtrails." *Cyprus Mail*, February 17.

Hitchens, Christopher. 2004. "Unfairenheit 9/11: The Lies of Michael Moore." *Slate*. June 21. https://slate.com/news-and-politics/2004/06/the-lies-of-michael-moore.html.

Howden, Daniel. 2003. "Cypriot Leader's Law Firm 'Broke Milosevic Sanctions.'" *The Independent*, April 16.

Ioannou, Yiannis. 2010a. "Νεκροταφεία υπό επιτήρηση" Η Αστυνομία σε κινητοποίηση για τη βεβήλωση του τάφου του Σπύρου Κυπριανού" [Cemeteries under surveillance: Police mobilized after the desecration of Spyros Kyprianou's grave]. *Simerini*, January 12.

Ioannou, Yiannis. 2010b. "Aerial Spraying: Mobilization around the Cyprus Bases." *Simerini*, June 25. Cited in Freeland (2014, 110n73).

Kalatzis, Manolis. 2009. "Κάλεσαν τον Πρέντραγκ Τζόρτζεβιτς" [They called Predrag Đorđević]. *Politis*, December 22.

Kallinikos, Giorgos. 2010. "Όσα βιώσαμε στο φρικτό τρίμηνο" Η Αναστασία Παπαδοπούλου εξομολογείται τα πάντα για τη φοβερή περιπέτεια" [What we lived through in that horrific three months: Anastasia Papadopoulou confesses everything about the terrible adventure]. *Philelevtheros*, March 21.

Kıbrıs. 2009. "Sırp şüphesi!" [Serbian suspicion!]. *Kıbrıs*, December 23.

Kostakopoulos, Yiannis. 2010. "Πήραν τις σημαίες" Βεβήλωση και στο μνήμα του πρώην προέδρου Σπ. Κυπριανού στη Λεμεσό" [They took the flags: Another desecration, at the tomb of former president Sp. Kyprianou in Limassol]. *Politis*, January 11.

Kypriakou, Nikitas. 2009. "Ποιο και γιατί σύλησαν τον τάφο του Τάσσου Παπαδόπουλου; Τρεις στενοί συνεργάτες του τέως Προέδρου καταθέτουν τις απόψεις για την αποτρόπαια αυτή πράξη" [Who robbed the grave of Tassos Papadopoulos and why? Three close associates of the former president give their views on this heinous act]. *Simerini,* December 20.

Levent, Elvan. 2009. "Uyanmak ve tesadüf . . ." [Awakening and coincidence . . .]. *Afrika*. December 13.

Levent, Şener. 2009a. "Çalınan ceset ve 'To be or not to be'" [The stolen body and 'To be or not to be'"]. *Afrika,* December 13.

Levent, Şener. 2009b. "Karartma" [Blackout]. *Afrika*, December 20.
Loizou, Mikaellas. 2009. "'Τη μνήμη του Τάσσου δεν μπορεί κανείς να τη σβήσει'" Ξεχείλισε η οργή και ν αγανάκτηση κατά το πρώτο ετήσιο μνημόσυνο του τέως Προέδρου" [The memory of Tassos cannot be erased: Overflowing anger and indignation during the first annual memorial service for the former president]. *Simerini*, December 13.
Mavridis, Kostas. 2009. "Ποιος νομίζετε ότι έκλεψε τη σορό του Τάσσου;" [Who do you think stole the body of Tassos?]. *Simerini*, December 20.
Michaelidis, Aristos. 2009a. "Ποιον εξυπηρετεί αυτή η εξαθλίωση" [Who is served by this misery?]. *Philelevtheros*, December 12.
Michaelidis, Aristos. 2009b. "Μπορεί να το χειριστεί το κράτος και η ηγεσία;" [Can the state and the leadership manage?]. *Philelevtheros*, December 14.
"Niki." 2009. "Αρρωστημένα μυαλά" [Sick minds]. *Haravgi*, December 14.
Orphanidou, Sophie. 2010. "Μακάβριο παιχνίδι νυκτοβατών" [The macabre game of the sleepwalkers]. *Politis*, January 9.
Özcanhan, Özcan. 2009. "Papadopulosu kim mezarından kaçırdı" [Who kidnapped Papadopoulos from his grave?]. *Star Kıbrıs*, December 19.
Pallikaridis, Adonis. 2009. "Ανεύθυνα δημοσιεύματα για Τάσσο¨ Δεν πήγε για λύτρα στη Ζυρίχη η Φωτεινή" [Unreliable reports about Tassos: Fotini did not go to Zurich for ransom]. *Simerini*, December 21.
Pantelides. 2011. "Body Snatchers Found Guilty." *Cyprus Mail*, April 5.
Papadopoulos, Michalis. 2009. "Ο ανοικτός τάφος" [The open grave]. *Simerini*, December 14.
Papadopoulou, Anastasia. 2009. "Ο βιασμός της αξιοπρέπειάς μας" [The rape of our dignity]. *Philelevtheros*, December 19.
Pehlivan, Alihan. 2009. "Papadapulos'un kemikleri" [The bones of Papadopoulos]. *Güneş*, December 19.
Perikleous, Chrysostomos. 2009. "Κόψτε τα πλοκάμια της ανωμαλίας" [Cut the tentacles of the monster]. *Politis*, December 13.
Philelevtheros. 2009. "Βεβήλωσαν την Κύπρο¨ Πρωτοφανές έγκλημα ιεροσυλίας εναντίον ολόκληρου του λαού" [They desecrated Cyprus: An unprecedented crime of sacrilege against the entire people]. *Philelevtheros*, December 12.
Philelevtheros. 2010a. "Ο Γιουρούκκης ενάγει τον τεώς διευθυντή των Φυλακών" [The Yurouki is suing the warden of the prison]. *Philelevtheros*, March 18.
Philelevtheros. 2010b. "Λαβύρινθος . . . στην κλοπή της σορού¨ Από τη σύλληψη και κράτηση ακόμα δύο προσώπων προκύπτει πιο ομιχλώδεις τοπίο" [Labyrinth . . . in the theft of the body. A darker landscape emerges from the arrest and detention of two more persons]. *Philelevtheros*, March 24.
Philenews. 2017. "Aradippou to Bury Fanieros on Wednesday." In-Cyprus.com. March 7.
Politis. 2009. "η 'Σημερινή' και ο Νικόλας" [*Simerini* and Nikolas]. December 22.

Politis. 2010. "Η Δημοκρατία στο γύψο˙ Ο αρχηγός του σκοτεινού ψιθύρου" [The democracy in dust: The chief of dark whispering]. October 15.

Polydorou, Michalis. 2017. "Άταφη για 33 χρόνια η καρδιά του Μακαρίου, άφαντη μέχρι σήμερα του Διγενή" [The heart of Makarios, unburied for 33 years; Digenis's heart never found]. *Reporter*, August 3. https://reporter.com.cy/article/2017/8/3/283835/ataphe-gia-33-khronia-e-kardia-tou-makariou-aphante-mekhri-semera-tou-digene/.

Psyllides, George. 2009a. "Police Visit Serbian Businessman's Home in Papadopoulos Investigation." *Cyprus Mail*, December 22.

Psyllides, George. 2009b. "When Conspiracy Stretches to the Food on the Table." *Cyprus Mail*, September 20.

Psyllides, George. 2011. "Germany's 'Great Conspiracy.'" *Cyprus Mail*, January 8.

Psyllides, George. 2016. "The Players: Spyros Kyprianou." *Cyprus Mail*, December 20.

Psyllides, George. 2017. "Colourful, Controversial Fanieros Dies Aged 73." *Cyprus Mail*, March 6.

Reporter. 2019. "Ο θάνατος του Μακαρίου, τα περί δηλητηρίασης και η άταφη καρδιά του" [The death of Makarios, concerning poison and his unburied heart]. August 4. https://reporter.com.cy/article/2019/8/4/180170/o-thanatos-tou-makariou-ta-peri-deleteriases-kai-e-ataphe-kardia-tou/.

Sigmalive. 2021. ""Όχι" στην αποφυλάκιση του Κίτα: Οι δολοφονίες και η κλοπή της σορού του Τάσσου" ["No" to the release of Kitas: The murders and the theft of the corpse of Tassos]. November 22. https://www.sigmalive.com/news/local/872555/oxi-stin-apofylakisi-tou-kitaoi-dolofonies-kai-i-klopi-tis-sorou-tou-tassou#:~:text=σορού%20του%20Τάσσου-,"Όχι"%20στην%20αποφυλάκιση%20του%20Κίτα%3ΑΟι%20δολοφονίες%20και%20η,κλοπή%20της%20σορού%20του%20Τάσσου&text=Το%20Συμβούλιο%20Αποφυλάκισης%20Επ%27%20Άδεια,αναφέρει%20την%20εφημερίδα%20"Αλήθεια"

Sigmalive. 2023. "Ο θάνατος του Μακαρίου μέσα από πρωτοσέλιδα και ντοκουμέντα" [The death of Makarios through headlines and documents]. August 3. https://www.sigmalive.com/news/local/1132532/o-thanatos-tou-makariou-mesa-apo-protoselida-kai-ntokoumenta.

Simerini. 2009. "Η σορός του Τάσσου, το ΚΕΑ και η Κυβέρνηση" [The body of Tassos, the KEA and the government]. December 22.

Simerini. 2010. "Δεν υποκύπτουμε στην τρομοκρατία" [We will not succumb to terrorism]. *Simerini*, January 12.

Smith, Helena. 2009. "Obituary: Tassos Papadopoulos; Former President of Cyprus who Scuppered Reunification with the Turkish North." *The Guardian*, January 7. https://www.theguardian.com/world/2009/jan/08/cyprus-obituary-tassos-papadopoulos.

Smith, R. Jeffrey. 2001. "The Hunt for Yugoslav Riches." *Washington Post*, March 11.
Tahsin, Arif Hasan. 2009. "Olaylar ve Gerçekler." *Afrika*, December 22.
Tzioni, Tasos. 2009. "Η αρπαγή της σορού και οι ευθύνες μας" [The abduction of the body and our responsibilities]. *Philelevtheros*, December 14.
Washington Post. 2001. "The Oklahoma City Bombing." https://www.washingtonpost.com/wp-srv/nation/sidebars/okctimeline.htm. Accessed December 10, 2021.
Zanou, Konstantina. 2010. "Η Κύπρος στο επίκεντρο παγκόσμιας συνωμοσίας!" [Cyprus at the epicenter of a global conspiracy!]. Ta Nea.com. March 13. https://www.tanea.gr/2010/03/13/lifearts/by-the-book/i-kypros-sto-epikentro-pagkosmias-synwmosias/.

ON THE FRONTISPIECE

"Eustathios, the steadfast." Yiannis Gigas's icon-painting frames Tassos Papadopoulos as a saint. His portrait is surrounded by inscriptions stylized to resemble the epithets and biblical quotations characteristic of Byzantine iconography—even if, on authentic Byzantine icons, inscriptions usually appear within scrolls or books rather than pervading the background of the entire image. This iconography is blended with classical motifs, as Papadopoulos holds the golden head of Hercules wrapped in the skin of the Nemean lion. The highlighted text to the left of Papadopoulos reads: ο ακλόνητος Ευστάθιος (Eustathios, the steadfast); here, Papadopoulos's proper first name, Eustathios (after Saint Eustache), which could translate as "steadfast," "sturdy," or "stable," is redoubled by his epithet, "the steadfast." The highlighted text on the right-hand side is his familiar name, Τάσσος Παπαδόπουλος (Tassos Papadopoulos). The artist, Yiannis Gigas, also known as Yiannis Gigas Thomas, is Greek—not Cypriot—and, among other works, he paints Greek Orthodox icons and religious murals, some commissioned by churches in Greece. The artist's statement for his installation at the 2018 Athens biennale, *The Temple of the Indomitables, 2004–2016*, describes the religious and political resonances of his practice thus: "A recent poll showed that a whopping 98% of Greeks [are] baptized Christian Orthodox and the Church has an active role in everyday life, politics, even in external affairs. Religious Iconmaking, *agiografia* (the depiction of the holy), is still taught in the largest school of fine arts in Greece. Yiannis Gigas is informed by an early Christian, proto anarchist, school of thought and Christian doctrine. In his daily life, he paints frescoes and murals in churches, yet in his artistic practice he confronts the orthodox canon with themes and icons of revolutionary heroes mixed with emblematic cultural and historical figures, from Frank Zappa to Ernesto Che Guevara. These are the saints, the martyrs, and the idols of the oppressed and the common folk alike. Iconography is the orthodox visual pop art, the equivalent of comics. Yiannis Gigas' icons stand as archetypes of heroes in a pantheon of patron saints and demigods" (https://anti.athensbiennale.org/en/artist/gigas.html).

I understand from my communication with the artist that the point of view of this painting—decidedly situated in Greece and therefore rather distant from the experience of recursive violence and the context of conspiracy attunement in Cyprus that I explore in this book—is to heroize and sanctify Papadopoulos. In this sense, the painting is an exemplary visualization of the symbolic meaning of the president's body instigated by the theft of his remains. Considered in comparative perspective, as a work in a series comprising Gigas's alternative pantheon of "indomitables," this painting places Papadopoulos in the company of revolutionary and folk heroes across time and place, expressing a global populism ambiguously melding right and left political associations.

This image was supplied to me by the artist and is reproduced here with his permission. I am most grateful to Gigas for his willingness to share his work with me in the context of this book.

INDEX

Photo insert images are indicated by *p1*, *p2*, *p3*, etc. Photo insert follows page 150.

Adorno, 70
African modernity, 103
Afrika, 176, 187–92, 231n4, 246n27,n30
Agamben, Giorgio, 129, 130
agency panic, 52
Agoustis, Dinos, 183–84
Ahmed, Sara, 112, 117–19, 121, 148, 239n6
AIDS, heterodox theory of, 34
Akritas, Digenis, 247n38
Akritas Organization, 208
Akritas Plan: authorship of, 207–8; Clerides on, 249n49; *Enosis* and, 248n41; genocidal intention and, 205–6; Greek-Cypriot leadership and, 206; sources of, 248n39; as top secret document, 204; Turkish Cypriots and, 248n44
Alarabiya, 242n28
Albert, Michael, 51
alien abductions, 8, 99–100
alienness, of conspiracy theories, 12–13, 16
Aliens in America (Dean), 7
Allende, Salvador, 145, 161
America, Britain and the Cyprus Crisis of 1974 (Constandinos), 161, *p10*
Anastasiades, Nicos, 165, 215–16, *p17*

ancestral land, of Greek-Cypriots, 5–6
Anderson, Benedict, 170
Angastiniotis, Tony, 98; death threats against, 23–24; genocide awareness by, 231n4; *Memory* film by, 231n3; time of cannibals from, 4, 23–24; *Trapped in the Green Line* by, 2; *Voice of Blood* films by, 1–2
Anglo-American conspiracy theories, 163–65, 167–68
angry politics, 81–82
Annan, Kofi, 5
Annan Plan, 5; Cyprus curse and, 199; Cyprus-wide referendum on, 183–84; Drousiotis supporting, 198; failure of, 208; global conspiracy pushing, 184; Greek-Cypriots rejecting, 194; Greek-Cypriots supporting, 169; Papadopoulos, T., body connection with, 200–201; Papadopoulos, T., outlining, 195; Papadopoulos, T., role in defeating, 189–90; referendum ballot for, *p13*–*p14*; Turkish Cypriots supporting, 194; U.S. support of, 224
Anons, 67–68, 75, 86

Anthropology and the Colonial Encounter (Asad), 101
anticolonial struggle in Cyprus, 4, *p1*
"Anxieties of Influence" (Harding and Stewart, K.), 33–34, 57
Appadurai, Arjun, 57, 88, 102–3
Aravamudan, Srinivas, 104
Archbishop's Palace, *p4–p5*
archival materials, declassified, 156, 158–63
Archive Fever (Derrida), 165
Arendt, Hannah, 130
Aristodimou, Andreas, 180
Asad, Talal, 101
Aslandis, Georgos, 250n61
Asmussen, Jan, 160–62, 165, 167
Athienou village, 217–19, 221–22
attachments withdrawal, 64–65
Aupers, Stef, 43, 90–91
authoritarianism, 9
Avdellopoulos, Charalambos, *p7*

Bakalaki, Alexandra, 97–98
Bardawil, Fadi, 105–7, 239n53
Being There (Borneman and Hammoudi), 244n13
"belief systems," 38–40
Best, Stephen, 30
Beyond Populism (Maskovsky and Bjork-James), 81
biomedicine, 40
Birchall, Clare, 49–50, 77, 79, 83, 237n34, 244n15
Bjork-James, Sophie, 81
Blanuša, Nebojša, 64–66, 70, 74, 237n36
bodies. *See also* dead bodies; Papadopoulos, T., body: fetish quality of theft of, 117; king's two, 127–29; relocation of, 242n25; sticky signs on others, 118; as sticky surfaces for signs, 112

body politic, 130, 149
body symbolism, 111, 116–20, 122–24, 126, 140–41, 143–46, 148–49
Bolívar, Simón, 145–46
Borneman, John, 169, 244n13
Bourdieu, Pierre, 51
Branch Davidians, 8
Bratich, Jack, 8, 42, 96; on conspiracy panics, 84; *Conspiracy Panics* by, 45–46, 83; on conspiracy theories, 28, 232n11; conspiracy theory discourse and, 48; on moral panics, 83–84
Briggs, Charles, 36
British colonialism, 4, 6, 242n1
British Royal Air Force, 95–98
Bryant, Rebecca, 149
burial rules, 122–23

Callaghan, James, 157–58, *p10*
Calvary Chapel, 33, 57
capitalism, 7, 31–32, 48, 70, 74, 79, 104, 170, 233n1
Casebook (Marcus), 32, 55
case studies: of conspiracy theories, 79–80; of Papadopoulos, T., body, 153–54; textual material in, 175
Ceaușescu, Nicolae, 145
cemetery, with Papadopoulos, T., body, 193
Central Intelligence Service (Cyprus), 211–12, 250n56
Charalambous, Charles, 212
Charalambous, Loukas, 119–20, 240n8, 248n45
Chatterjee, Partha, 170
Chaudhary, Zahid, 67–68, 75, 86
Chavez, Hugo, 145–47
Chemtrails, HAARP, and the "Full Spectrum Dominance" of Planet Earth (Freeland), 238n49
chemtrail theory, 97–98

Cherstich, Igor, 143–44, 147, 242n26
children, refugee camp, *p16*
Chomsky, Noam, 51, 235n17
Christodoulos, Yiannakis, 247n37
Christodoulou, Miltiades, 121
Christofias, Demetris, 176, 196, 224, 239n2; Papadopoulos, T., defeated by, 5; Papadopoulos, T., memorial absence of, 110–11
Chrysostomos, Archbishop, 122, 187, *p9*
CIA-backed coups, 161–62
citizenship, 85, 232n9
class, inequality of, 105–6
classic conspiracism, 53, 79
clerical vestments, 113–14
Clerides, Glafkos, 157, 206–7, 214, 248n41; on Akritas Plan, 249n49; Georkadjis, P., murder and, 249n55
Clinton Impeachment, 232n14
cloud spraying, over Cyprus, 95–98
Cold War: geopolitics, 6; horrors facilitated by, 154; paranoia legacy of, 31
collective traumatic events, 66
colonized knowledge production, 18–19
Comaroff, Jean and John, 32, 56, 103–5, 233n1
Committee on Missing Persons in Cyprus, 123
community of sense (Rancière), 91–92
concept of totality, 71, 72
conspiracism, new, 52–53
Conspiracy (Pipes), 58
conspiracy attunement, 225–26, 237n40; apparent beliefs in, 91; contextualization and, 20–21; Cypriot context of, 124; in Cyprus, 108–9; dialogical context of, 87; Drousiotis on, 163; Papadopoulos, T., body and, 19–20; as paranoia alternative, 89; recursive discourse in, 170; recursive narrative threads in, 192–93; self-awareness in, 88–89; whole of Cyprus with, 93
conspiracy-believing (Parmigiani), 91–92
Conspiracy Culture (Knight), 7
conspiracy panics, 8, 45, 83; culture in, 101; as historical conjunctures, 60; media discourse and, 46–47
Conspiracy Panics (Bratich), 8, 45–46, 83
conspiracy theories: analysis of, 20, 29–30; Anglo-American, 163–65, 167–68; antigovernment, 8; approaches to, 27–28; Bardawil's multiple paths on, 107; believing in, 91–92; books on, 158–59; boundaries in, 109; Bratich and discourse on, 48; Bratich on, 28, 232n11; case studies of, 79–80; cloud spraying, 95–98; collective traumatic events in, 66; context of, 62–63; in Croatia, 74–75; culture of, 92; Cyprus diagnosis of, 14; Cyprus division and no, 161–62; about Cyprus divisions, 7, 19–21, 94, 153–55, 156; Cyprus's golden age of, 196; dead body theft, 148; discourse in, 238n47; disqualification of, 30, 46, 84–85; disqualifying label of, 44; emancipatory ambitions of, 79; embodied anxiety in, 33; epistemological approach to, 47–54; as fantasies, 68–69; Fenster on, 237n37; of Greek-Cypriots, 6, 185; in historical time, 61; identifying, 94–95; ideological cross-purposes in, 79; immanent diagnosis in, 46; intentions of, 90; Kasimatis on, 240n15; legitimate theory distinction with, 53–54; lingering functionalism in, 59; mainstreaming of, 10; narratives of, 235n16; in the Netherlands, 43; networks of belongings from, 92; new conspiracism in, 52–53; in newspapers,

Index 277

conspiracy theories (*continued*)
186–87; outside of U.S. and Europe, 35; Papadopoulos, T., promotion of, 196–97; of Papadopoulos, T., body theft, 116–17; paranoid, 31–32; particularist approach to, 54–63; political approach to, 76–87; political desires in, 71; populism link with, 81; powerlessness symptoms in, 70; psychoanalytic readings of, 71–76; psychological approach to, 63–76; Rakopoulos on, 43–44, 237n45, 238n47; reasonable and unreasonable, 57; reasonable paranoia in, 44–45; recursivity of, 99; satanic, 5; satisfactions from, 69; scale problem in, 56–57; secret and nefarious intentions in, 49–50; as sense-making practice, 58; social function of, 64; Stokes on, 235n21; symptomatic approach to, 28–47; theory of conspiracy and, 233n6; timeliness and alienness of, 12–13, 16; translations of, 95; traumatic disruptions in symbolic order, 67; in U.S., 9–10, 77–78; warranted and unwarranted, 50; witchcraft and, 42–43
Conspiracy Theories (Fenster), 79–80
"Conspiracy Theories and Their Truth Trajectories" (Pelkmans and Machold), 37
Conspiracy Theory and the Culture of Partition (Ioannou), 4
conspiracy thinking, Western, 59
conspiratology, 16, 27–28, 51, 101
conspirituality, 238n47
Constandinos, Andreas, 157–58, 161, *p10*
Constantinou, Kikis, 197, 247n34
contaminated critique, 71, 100
context: of conspiracy theories, 62–63; local, 59; in meaning, 61–62; modes of thinking and feeling in, 58; problem of, 54–55
contextualism, 16, 20–21, 62, 237n44
Coral Gardens and Their Magic (Malinowski), 234n13
counter-knowledges, 78
coup, 1, 2, 5, 22, 113, *p6*, *p16*, *p17*, 154, 157–64, 186, 191, 197, 201, 204, 211, 213, 216, 220, 226, 243n6, 245n22, 248n38, 249n54; Anastasiades and attempted, *p17*; CIA-backed, 161–62; Georkadjis, P., desire to stop, 211; "Makarios is alive" after, *p6*; U.S. responsibility of, 159
Craig, Ian, 159, 242n3
Cress Theory, 77–78
"The Cress Theory of Color-Confrontation and Racism (White Supremacy)" (Welsing), 77
crisis of representation, 13, 32
critical fabulation, 166
critical theory, 51–52, 63, 69–71, 105–6, 236n33
Croatia, 74–75
cross-contextual connections, 153–54
cross-contextual translation, 171
cross-cultural comparison, 11–12, 134–35
Csordas, Thomas, 89
CTP. *See* Republican Turkish Party
Culler, Jonathan, 61
cult to the dead, 142
cultural evolution, 11–12, 133–34
The Cultural Politics of Emotion (Ahmed), 112
culture: areas, 102–3; bounded, 14; conspiracy, 92; of conspiracy, 101; in conspiracy panic, 101; context in, 87; contextualism of local, 62; homogeneity of, 174; intimacy, 93–94; Ioannou on differences of, 14–15; popular, 99; relativism, 11; whole of, 134

CyBC. *See* Cyprus Broadcasting Corporation
Cypriot Hellenism, 120, 182
Cypriot Intelligence Service, 250n56
Cypriot National Guard, 157, *p11*, *p17*
Cyprus: Annan Plan and curse of, 199; Annan Plan referendum in, 183–84; body theft paralyzing, 118; cloud spraying over, 95–98; colonized knowledge production about, 18–19; conspiracy attunement context in, 124; conspiracy attunement for whole of, 93; conspiracy attunement in, 108–9; conspiracy theories about the division in, 7, 19–21, 94, 153–55, 156; conspiracy theories diagnosis of, 14; conspiracy to dissolve, 207; conspirators trial begins in, 168–70, 232n18; cross-contextual connections with, 153–54; culture of conspiracy in, 101; deeper look into, 3–4; embarrassing events in, 2–3; golden age of conspiracies in, 196; group identity in, 8; independent sovereignty of, 4; intelligence and intrigue on, 159; Ioannou on frozen in time of, 14; journalism in, 199; Kitas, A., as Al Capone of, 3; lateral colonialism of, 242n1; newspapers in, 176–77; no conspiracies in division of, 161–62; Papadopoulos, T., problem of, 1–2; political dialogue with, 164–65; political history of, 112–13; Republic of, 203, *p1*; sacrilege against, 115; secret history of violence in, 217; Turkey charged by, 203; Turkish invasion of, 154; as unsinkable aircraft, 164; U.S. history with, 108–9; Western conspiracy in, 160
Cyprus (Strigas), 162
Cyprus, Days of Rage in 555 Photographs (Ioannides, P.), *p6*–*p7*
Cyprus 1974 (Drousiotis), 243n6
Cyprus at War (Asmussen), 160
Cyprus Broadcasting Corporation (CyBC), 243n10, *p6*; as RIK, 169, 202, 247n37
The Cyprus Conspiracy (Craig and O'Malley), 159
The Cyprus Crisis and the Cold War (Drousiotis), 163, 165
Cyprus Mail (newspaper), 163, 177, 188, 195, 212, 238

Dalgıçoğlu, Dolgun, 190–91
Damiens, Robert-François, 129
Davies, Rodger, 242n3
dead bodies, 120; of Bolívar, 145; conspiracy theories on theft of, 148; decrepit and decaying, 126; exhumation and reburial of, 123–24; flesh of saints, 147; of Gaddafi, 143–44; of Lenin, 137–38; mass graves of, 141–42; as mummy, 139; Papadopoulos, T., and, 21; pitiful corpse and, 126; of political leaders, 21, 131, 135–36; proper burial rules for, 122–23; sacredness of, 146–47; sovereign, 125–26; symbolic efficacy of, 140; symbolic meaning of, 148–49
Dean, Jodi, 7, 30, 48, 96–97, 155
death rites, 125
death threats, 23–24
defacement, 114–16, 135
Demetriou, Olga, 18
democracy, 53, 83, 130
Derrida, Jacques, 165
desecration, 21, 23, 111, 114–16, 119–20, 123–24, 135, 143, 148, 168, 178, 182, 232
desire, 65–66, 71
dialectical theorization of habitus, 51
dialogical context, 41, 42, 47, 87, 89, 93, 155, 225

Index 279

dialogical polarization, 95
Digenis, Giorgos Grivas, 240n13
Dignitas, 126, 241n18
dignity, 240n12
Dilley, Roy, 54, 61
Dimitrakis, Panagiotis, 243n4
Discipline and Punish (Foucault), 129
discourse, production of, 171, 173
discursive site, 93, 113, 116, 117, 124, 136, 146
disqualification: of conspiracy theories, 30, 46, 84–85; of knowledge, 29
divine kingship, 131–34, 241n24
"The Divine Kingship of the Shilluk" (Graeber), 131
doctrine Leninism, 137
Đorđević, Predrag, 188
Drakos, Markos, 185
Drousiotis, Makarios, 98, 162, 202; American document published by, 209; Anastasiades as assistant to, 165; Annan Plan supported by, 198; book criticized of, 165; on conspiracy attunement, 163; *Cyprus 1974* by, 243n6; *The Cyprus Crisis and the Cold War* by, 163, 165; ethnonationalist political motivations and, 178–79; Georkadjis, P., murder argument of, 213; Mavridis dismissing claims of, 204; Papadopoulos, T., joining EOKA from, 195–96; phrase used by, 251n6; *Two Attempts and a Murder* by, 210, 212

Ecevit, Bülent, 157
Edward II, 125, 132
effigies, 126, 132, 138
effigy ritual, 241n19
Eminoğlu, Bilbay, 187
empirical fabulation, 166
empiricism, simple, 82
empiricist paradigm, 38

empty grave, 119, 181
enemies, stealing our enjoyment, 67
Enosis, 205, 248n41
EOKA (armed resistance group), 4, 23, 182, 210; Great Britain strangled by, *p1*; National Front after, 245n22; Papadopoulos, T., joining, 195–96
EOKA-B, 157, 163, 216
epistemological approach to conspiracy theory, 47–54, 56, 236n33
Epsilon theory, 90
Erdoğan, Recep Tayyip, 246n27
Eroğlu, Derviş, 215
esoteric allusions, 234n13
ethnarch, 121–22, 240n13
ethnocentrism, 109; concept of, 11; cross-cultural comparison and, 11–12; Lévy-Bruhl from, 233n10; in media discourse, 35; multiple cultural wholes in, 134; sense of alienness in, 12–13, 16
ethnographic research, 136–37
ethnography, 15, 44–45
ethnonational identity, 15
ethnonationality, 111
European Court of Human Rights, 2, 22
European imperial genealogy, 147
Evans-Pritchard, E. E., 39, 234n13
existential legitimacy (Lefort), 128
extremism, in paranoia, 70

Falireas, Vassos, *p9*
Fanieros, Antonis, 220–21
fantasy, 65–66, 68–69
fascism, 70–71
Fassin, Didier, 34–35, 233n5
Faubion, James, 8
Favret-Saada, Jeanne, 41–42, 234n13
Fenster, Mark, 30, 51, 77–78; on conspiracy theories, 237n37; *Conspiracy Theories* by, 79–80; on Kennedy, J.,

235n17; realist vis-à-vis symbolist interpretations by, 237n42
Ferrándiz, Francisco, 123, 141–43
fetish quality, 117, 147, 239n6
fieldwork in theory (Bardawil), 106
Fiske, John, 77–78
flesh of saints, 147
flesh, of social bond (Santner), 128–30
Floyd, George, 68
Folklore in the Old Testament (Frazer), 11
forensic analysis, 145
Foucault, Michel, 28, 95
Franco, Francisco, 123, 141–43
Frazer, James, 11, 15, 131
Frazer Lecture, 10–11, 16
Freeland, Elana, 238n49
Freud, Sigmund, 64–65, 236n27
functionalism, 37, 59
funeral, 138; of Georkadjis, P., 214; of Makarios, *p7*; of Papadopoulos, T., *p7*, *p11*; symbolic, *p7*

Gaddafi, Muammar, 143–44, 147, 242n26
Galatariotou, Catia, 201, 205
gambling, 220
gamification of paranoia, 67
Geertz, Clifford, 101
genealogy, 28
generalism, 235n22
General Operation Plan, 205
genocide, 205–6, 231n4
Georkadjis, Constantinos, 210–11
Georkadjis, Polykarpos, 206–7, 247n38; on airport tarmac, *p15*; Clerides and murder of, 249n55; death of, 209; funeral of, 214; Makarios hand kissed by, *p15*; murder argument about, 213; murder of, 249n54; Papadopoulos, T., division with, 209–10; Papadopoulos, T., involvement in murder of, 214; Patatakos's instructions to, 250n57
global conspiracy, 184
global south, 104–5
Gluckman, Max, 173, 244n15
The Golden Bough (Frazer), 11, 131
Good, Byron, 38–40
gossip-based genres, 173–74, 244n15
Graeber, David, 131–34, 153, 241n24
graves: empty, 119, 181; gypsum dust at, 168–69, 177–78; mass, 141–42
Great Britain (metaphorical), *p1*
Great Powers, 7, 101
Greece, 59, 97–98, 161, 178
Greek-Cypriot National Guard, 202, 247n37
Greek Cypriots, 1–2, 22, 149; Akritas Plan and leadership of, 206; ancestral land displacement of, 5–6; Annan Plan rejected by, 194; Annan Plan supported by, 169; anti-Turkish propaganda by, 203; conspiracy theories of, 6, 185; Papadopoulos, T., friends and, 200; power-sharing with, 204; soldiers, 201; Turkish Cypriots conflict with, 159–60, 172, 183, 201–2; Turkish Cypriots power-sharing with, 196
Greek junta, 4
Greek-language press, 135
Green Line, 5
Grivas, Georgios, 247n38
Guevara, Ché, 145
Güneş (Sun), 176
gypsum dust, Papadopoulos, T., grave with, 168–69, 177–78
gypsy, 245n21

Hadjiapostolou, Panayiotis, 239n4
Hadjikostis, Andy, 178–79, 223
Halkın Sesi (People's voice), 176, *p10*

Index 281

Hammoudi, Abdellah, 169, 244n13
Harambam, Jaron, 43, 90–91
Haravgi (Dawn), 176, 185
Harding, Susan, 33, 57
Hartman, Saidiya, 166–67
Hassapi, Anna, 188
Hastürer, Hasan, 189
Hatay, Mete, 149
hearsay evidence, 160–61
heart, embalmed, *p8*
heart attack, 121
Heaven's Gate group, 33, 57
hermeneutics of suspicion, 59
Herzfeld, Michael, 39, 93–94, 102
"He's Buried in Paris" (headline), 191
heterodox theory of AIDS, 34
The Hidden Hand (Pipes), 58
historical conjunctures, 60–61
historicism, 60–61
historicist comparison, 133
Hitchens, Christopher, 158–59, 162, 249n54
Hofstadter, Richard, 30, 69, 80–81, 155
homogeneity, of culture, 174
homophobia, 236n27
Hoover, J. Edgar, 79
Horkheimer, 70
Hostage to History (Hitchens), 158
Hristov, Todor, 64–66, 70, 237n36
human rights, 240n12
Hussein, Saddam, 37, 242n28
hyperreal knowledge, 49

idealization of power, 69
identity formation, 73
ideology, theory of, 51
ideoscapes, 57–59
Ignatiou, Michalis, 203
Iliades, Giorgos, 184, 239n4
imaginary convergence point, 172
immanent diagnosis, 46

Indigenous Delta residents, 36
inductive reasoning, 29
inequality, of class, 105–6
initiation rites, 16–17
intercommunal conflict, 6, 159
International Conspirators (Strigas), 162
internationalist solidarity, 106
interpretations, 73–74
intimacy, 73–74, 93–94
Ioannides, P., *p6–p7*
Ioannidis, Costas, 213
Ioannidis, Dimitrios, 157
Ioannidis, Yiannou, 180
Ioannou, Yiannis, 5; Cold War haunting from, 6; *Conspiracy Theory and the Culture of Partition* by, 4; on cultural differences, 14–15; Cypriot culture of conspiracy from, 101; Cyprus as frozen in time from, 14; on Cyprus conspiracy theories, 156; their times questions from, 13
Italy, 238n47

Jameson, Fredric, 32–33, 155
January 6th, 2021 insurrection, 67, 75, 85
Jarvie, I. C., 11
journalism, in Cyprus, 199
junta government, in Greece, 161

Kantorowicz, Ernst, 124–25, 138; decrepit and decaying bodies from, 126; Dignitas from, 241n18; on effigy ritual, 241n19; *The Kings Two Bodies* by, 241n16; sovereign immanence from, 127
karaghiozi (shadow puppet theater), 203
Kasimatis, Petros, 240n15
Katsounotos, Michalis, 186
Keeley, Brian, 49–51, 53
Kellner, Douglass, 83
Kennedy, John F., 235n17

Khrushchev, Nikita, 164
Ki-moon, Ban, 179
king's two bodies, 127–29, 132
The Kings Two Bodies (Kantorowicz), 124, 241n16
Kissinger, Henry, 154, 157, 163, *p7*
Kitas, Antonis Prokopiou, 22–23, 219, 221; as Al Capone of Cyprus, 3; co-conspirators of, 180; murder conviction of, 179–81, 250n2; others implicated by, 223; Papadopoulos, T., body theft trial of, 168–70, 250n2, *p18*
Kitas, Mamas Prokopiou, 22
Kitas brothers, 168–70, 217
Kıbrıs (Cyprus), 176, 187–88
Kızılyürek, Niyazi, 208, 248n41, 249n55
Klein, Melanie, 236n29
Knight, Peter, 7, 96
knowledge: archival, 167; colonized production of, 18–19; counter, 78; disqualified, 29; epistemology on problem of, 47–48; Good on beliefs distinctions from, 39–40; hyperreal, 49; past events in, 17; practices of, 17–18; subjugated, 28–29
Konstantinidis, Alekos, 246n33
Konuksever, Ergin, 201–2, 240n15
Koshis, Nikos, 208
Kouyialis, Nicos, 96
Kypriakou, Nikitas, 184
Kyprianou, Achilleas, 197, 246n33, *p12*
Kyprianou, Mimi, *p12*
Kyprianou, Spyros, 178, 180, 196–97, 208; Falireas with, *p9*; movie premiere attended by, *p9*; Papadopoulos, T., shaking hand of, *p13*; press conference by, *p8*; public reunion with, *p12*

Lacan, Jacques, 65–66, 130
Laclau, Ernesto, 81

Larnaca area, 169, 218, 220
LARPing. *See* live action role-playing
lateral colonialism, 242n1
Lederman, Rena, 102, 108, 153
Lefort, Claude, 128
left-progressive political critique, 80
Lenin, Vladimir, 136–39
Lepselter, Susan, 8–9, 99–100
Levent, Elvan, 187
Levent, Sener, 189, 192
Leventis, Anastasios, 210
Lévy-Bruhl, Lucien, 233n10
liberalism, 82
Lillikas, 119, 240n9
linear chronology, 60
live action role-playing (LARPing), 67–68, 75
local context, 59–60
Loizou, Mikaellas, 239n2
A Lot of People Are Saying (Muirhead and Rosenblum), 52

Machold, Rhys, 37, 45, 50, 57, 233n6
Maduro, Nicolas, 147
magic spells, 234n13
Magliocco, Sabina, 39, 42, 68, 91
Makarios, Archbishop, 4, 157; on airport tarmac, *p15*; assassination conspiracy about, 213; crowd surrounding, *p6*; embalmed heart of, *p8*; figure of, *p3*, *p5*; Georkadjis, P., kisses hand of, *p15*; as Great Martyr, 122; heart attack and death of, 121–22; Papadopoulos, T., at funeral of, *p7*; Papadopoulos, T., kissing hand of, *p2*; student demonstration addressed by, *p3*–*p5*; Turkish Cypriots and, 248n44; unburied heart of, 122; vestment images of, 113
"Makarios is alive," *p6*
Malinowski, Bronislaw, 11, 54, 134, 234n13
Marasco, Robyn, 50, 67, 71–72, 75, 236n33

Marcus, George, 8, 30, 49, 55, 155
Marcus, Sharon, 30–31
Marxism, 105–7
Masco, Joseph, 6, 232n8
Maskovsky, Jeff, 81, 85–86
mass graves, 141–42
Mausoleum Lab, 136
Mavridis, Kostas, 199, 202, 204
Mavromichali, Alexi, 180
Mayes, Stanley, 249n54
Mazzarella, William, 82–83
Mbeki, Thabo, 34
McVeigh, Timothy, 78
meaning, context in, 61–62
media discourse, 35, 46–47
medieval European funeral effigies, 138
medieval theology, 125
Melanesianist anthropology, 103
Melley, Timothy, 52, 79, 235n16
Memory (film), 231n3
metacultural dimensions, 171
metapragmatic work, 175
Metsos, Christopher, 3
Michaelidis, Aristos, 183, 185
milieu, 90–91
Milošević, Slobodan, 187–88
misinformation campaign, 198–99
Miter, Episcopal, *p2*
modernity, capitalism and, 104
Modernity at Large (Appadurai), 88
modern mass society, 70
money-laundering, 3
moral exemplarity, 141
moral panics, 83–84
mortal body, of sovereign, 138
Muirhead, Russell, 52–53, 79, 83, 85
mummy, dead body as, 139
murder: of Georkadjis, P., 213–14, 249n54, 249n55; of Hadjikostis, 178–79; Kitas, A., conviction of, 179–81, 250n2
mystical body, 125–26, 129

National Archives, U.S., 162
National Front, 182, 213, 214, 245n22, 250n3
National Guard officer, *p15*
native belief systems, 40
necro-exemplarity, 142
Nelson, Diane, 246n24
Nenekos, Dimitris, 244n12
neoliberalism, 81
Nepali villagers, 41
nervous illness, 64
the Netherlands, 43
networks of belongings, 92
new conspiracism, 52–53
news media, 175–76
newspapers, 175, 197–98; articles published in, 206–7; conspiracy theories in, 186–87; in Cyprus, 176–77; northern, 177, 187; southern, 177, 201–2
Neyfakh, Leon, 10
NGOs. *See* nongovernmental organizations
nickname (*ο Γιουρούκκης*), 245n21
Nicolet, Claude, 243n6
Nilotic people, 131–33
9/11 terrorist attack, 117
Nixon, Richard, 154
Non-Aligned Movement, 158
nongovernmental organizations (NGOs), 198
northern newspapers, 177, 187
"No" speech, by Papadopoulos, T., 194, 200, 216, *p12*
Nyikang (king), 132

Obeyesekere, Gananath, 74
observer/observed dichotomy, 12–13, 15–16
Oedipus complex, 74
Oklahoma City bombing, 78
O'Malley, Brendan, 159, 162, 242n3

On Anthropological Knowledge (Sperber), 234n11
online conspiracy discourse, 238n47
"Operation: Suspect Fotini" (headline), 191
opinion polling, 244n14
organization membership, 249n51
Ottoman Empire, 60
Över, Kıvanç Galip, 205

Panagoulis, Alekos, 210
Panayiotou, Ioanna, 238n49
Papadopoulou, Anastasia, 224; interview with, 223; public talk intensity and, 112; on rape, 239n3; shock, disgust and horror expressed by, 111–12, 116–21, 148–49; symbolic meaning from, 116
Papadopoulou, Fotini, 191–92, 210, *p17*
Papadopoulos, Georgios, 210
Papadopoulos, Michalis, 118, 149, 181, 215
Papadopoulos, Nikolas, 117, 147, 169, 186, 215, *p17*
Papadopoulos, T., body, 98; Annan Plan's connection with, 200–201; arrests for theft of, 222–23; case studies of, 153–54; cemetery with, 193; conspiracy attunement and, 19–20; conspiracy theories about theft of, 116–17; corpse or remains violation and, 120; Cyprus conspirators trial and, 168–70, 232n18; Cyprus paralyzed by theft of, 118; Dalgıçoğlu's op-ed on, 190–91; desecration of, 114–16; discursive site of, 93, 116; empty grave and, 119, 181; flesh of saints and, 147; gypsum dust at grave of, 168–69, 177–78; Hadjikostis's murder and, 178–79; Kitas, A., conviction for, 179–81, 250n2; Kitas, A., theft trial and, 168–70, 250n2, *p18*;
Kitas brothers involvement in, 219; police's crime theory about, 224; politicians showing weaknesses and, 119–20; press coverage of, 170–71; public reaction to theft of, 116–17; shock disgust and horror from theft of, 111–12, 116–21, 148–49; sticky signs and, 149; theft as publicity stunt of, 113; theft as sacrilege to, 121; theft of, 110; trial for theft of, 2–3, 22–23, 168–70, 232n18, *p18*; war dead and, 123
Papadopoulos, Tassos: Agoustis eulogizing, 183–84; on airport tarmac, *p15*; Akritas Plan authorship and, 207–8; Annan Plan defeat role of, 189–90; Annan Plan outlined by, 195; ballot cast by, *p14*; Christofias absent from memorial for, 110–11; Christofias defeating, 5; at church, *p17*; clerical vestments not worn by, 113–14; conspiracy theories promoted by, 196–97; courage and patriotism of, 184; Cypriot Hellenism embodied by, 120, 182; Cyprus problem and, 1–2; dead bodies and, 21; Đorđević civil suit against, 188; EOKA activity of, 23; EOKA joined by, 195–96; funeral of, *p7*, *p11*; funeral receiving line for, *p11*; Georkadjis, P., division with, 209–10; Georkadjis, P., murder involvement of, 214; Greek-Cypriots friends of, 200; as hard-liner, 209; Kyprianou, S., shaking hand of, *p13*; at Makarios funeral, *p7*; Makarios hand kissed by, *p2*; misinformation campaign by, 198–99; "No" speech banner and, *p12*; "No" speech by, 194, 200, 216; refugee camp children greeted by, *p16*; Serbian war criminals dealings with, 187; violent history and, 112

Index 285

Papadopoulou, Anastasia, 110–11
Papageorgiou, Michalis, 186
Papapostolou, Dimitrios, 211
Paphos Gate, *p18*
Papua New Guinea, 16
paramilitary groups, 249n50
paranoia: agency panic and, 52; attachments withdrawal in, 64–65; Cold War legacy of, 31; collective psychological disturbance in, 69–70; conspiracy attunement alternative to, 89; conspiracy theories with, 31–32; epistemology of, 236n33; extremism characterized in, 70; Freud's theorization of, 64–65; gamification of, 67; general structure of desire in, 65; groups, 33; Hofstadter's deployment of, 80–81; political, 30, 71; psychoanalytic theory intimacy with, 72–73; within reason, 45, 55; reasonable, 38, 44–45, 62–63; relations formed through, 67; right-wing, 70
Paranoia within Reason (Marcus), 8
"The Paranoid Style in American Politics" (essay), 30
Parla, Ayşe, 166
Parmigiani, Giovanna, 91–92, 237nn43–44, 238n47
Parparinou, Efrosyni, 212
Partial Connections (Strathern, M.), 16, 56, 62
partiality, 56
participatory consciousness, 68
particularist approach to conspiracy theory, 54–63, 235n22
Pasha, Ibrahim, 244n12
Patatakos, Kyriakos, 211, 249n55, 250n57
peer-to-peer skepticism, 85
Pehlivan, Alihan, 189
Pelkmans, Mathijs, 37, 45, 50, 57, 233n6
Perdikis, Giorgos, 95–96

Pereira, Godofredo, 145–46
Perikleous, Chrysostomos, 182, 250n3
periodization, 10, 100, 154
Petridis, Petros, 211
Philelevtheros (The liberal), 110, 120, 176, 203, 223
Pigg, Stacy Leigh, 40–42, 88, 108, 172
Pipes, Daniel, 58
Plowden, Edmund, 124, 241n17
"Poked by the 'Foreign Finger' in Greece" (Sutton), 58
polarization, 95
political leaders, dead bodies of, 21, 131, 135–36
politicians, weaknesses of, 119–20
politics, 63–64, 133, 135, 178–79; angry, 81–82; body, 130; conspiracy theories approach of, 76–87; conspiracy theories with desires in, 71; Cyprus's history of, 112–13; Cyprus with dialogue in, 164–65; left-progressive critique of, 80; paranoia in, 30, 71; populism and movements in, 81–82; theology in, 128; transformation in, 57; U.S. paranoia in, 71
"The Politics of Conspiracy Theories" (Fassin), 34
Politis (Citizen), 176, 181–82, 186, 199–200, 202
Polydorou, Michalis, 240n13
popular culture, in U.S., 99
populism, 80–83
positivist approach, 166–67
Post, Jerrold, 30
postmodernism, 13, 66
postmodernist ethnography, 15
postplural epistemology, 56
Poulitsas, Athanasios, 213
Povinelli, Elizabeth, 175
power, idealization of big, 69
press conference, by Kyprianou, S., *p8*

press coverage, 170–71
prestige zones of theory, 102
primitive rationality, 39
Primo de Rivera, José Antonio, 123, 141
prostitution, 220
psyche, symbolic process of, 64
psychic life, 74
psychoanalytic approach, 63, 71–76
psychological approach, 63–76
psychological disturbance, 69–70
Psyllides, George, 188
public discourse, definition, 118–19
Publics and Counterpublics (Warner), 170
public talk intensity, 112
Putin, Vladimir, 140

Al Qaeda, 37
QAnon, 9–10, 67, 75, 85–86

race-thinking, theory of, 51
racism, 36, 190
Rakopoulos, Theodoros, 48, 79, 232n9; on conspiracy theories, 43–44, 237n45, 238n47; milieu used by, 90–91
ransom scheme, 178
rape, Papadopoulou, A., on, 239n3
"The Rape of Our Dignity" (essay), 110–11
"The Ravaged Heart of Makarios" (headline), 122
realist vis-à-vis symbolist interpretations, 237n42
reality, beliefs and, 39
reasonable paranoia, 38, 44–45, 62–63
reasoning, inductive, 29
reburial, 123–24
recursive narrative threads, 192–93
recursivity, 99, 170
Reddaway, John, 206–7, 249n51

referendum ballot, for Annan Plan, *p13–p14*
relativism, 45, 56
religion, 111
religious fundamentalists, 38
remainders, questions as, 17
Reports (Plowden), 124
Republican Party, 79
Republican Turkish Party (CTP), 176
Republic of Cyprus, 5
research methods, 103, 156–57
The Resonance of Unseen Things (Lepselter), 8
Rethinking Camelot (Chomsky), 235n17
Revolution and Disenchantment (Bardawil), 105
Riggan, Jennifer, 82
right-wing paranoia, 70
right-wing populism, 80
ritual performance of sanctification, 148
ritual-political practices, 133, 135
Robins, Robert, 30
Rogin, Michael, 237n36
Rosenblatt, Adam, 240n12
Rosenblum, Nancy, 52–53, 79, 83, 85
Ross, Julian Aron, 85–86
The Royal Remains (Santner), 127, 241n20
Russian Orthodox rituals, 138–39

sacral soma, 128
sacredness, of dead bodies, 146–47
sacrilege, 114–15
Sánchez, Rafael, 241n21
sanctification, ritual performance of, 148
Sanders, Todd, 32, 55, 57–58
Santner, Eric, 127–30, 241nn20–21
satanic conspiracies, 5
SBAs. *See* Sovereign Base Areas
scale problem, 56–57, 62
scandal, 245n16

Index 287

Schmitt, Carl, 241n16
Schreber, Daniel Paul, 64, 70, 130
secular democracy, 130
Sedgwick, Eve Kosovsky, 52, 236n33
self-awareness, 88–89
Seligman, Charles, 131
semi-sacred role, 142
sense of alienness, 12–13, 16
sensual world-making, 225
separations, 44–45
Serbian war criminals, 187
The Shadows and Lights of Waco (Faubion), 8
Shilluk institutions, 132, 134
shock disgust and horror, 111–12, 116–21, 148–49
"Shock in the South" (headline), *p10*
Simerini (Today), 176, 178–80, 183–86, 203
Sinding-Larsen, Henrik, 237n40
Singh, Sarbjit, 22, 217, 224
Skarparis, Takis, 211
slavery, archive of, 166
Slow Burn (podcast), 10, 232n14
small-scale society, 174
Smith, R. Jeffrey, 187
Smith, Wilfred Cantwell, 41
social media, 92, 175–76
social relationships, 172
social theory, 19, 31–33, 50–51
society, 57, 74, 127, 174
sociopolitical histories, 63–64
Soulioti, Stella, 207
southern newspapers, 177, 201–2
sovereign: dead bodies, 125–26; immortality of, 136; Kantorowicz on immanence of, 127; mortal body of, 138; mystical body of, 129; preservation of, 137
Sovereign Base Areas (SBAs), 158
sovereignty, 4, 130–33

Soviet Union, 164–65
Spanish Law of Historical Memory, 142
speeches, 174–75, 194, 200, 216, *p12*
Sperber, Dan, 234n11
state of exception, 130
Stavrinos, Panos, 121–22
Stewart, Charles, 60–61, 245n16
Stewart, Kathleen, 30, 33, 57, 71, 100, 155
Stewart, Pamela, 173–74
sticky signs, 112, 118, 149
Stokes, Patrick, 235nn21–22
stranger sociality, 175
Strathern, Andrew, 173–74, 245n16
Strathern, Marilyn, 10–11, 108; historicist comparison by, 133; observer/observed dichotomy from, 12–13; *Partial Connections* by, 16, 56, 62; postmodernist ethnography timeliness from, 15; question asking consequences from, 17–18; questions as remainders from, 17
Strigas, Athanasios, 162
structural agency, 51
structural inequalities, 36
student demonstration, Makarios addressing, *p3–p5*
subaltern strategies, 37
subjugated knowledge, 28–29
surplus of immanence (Santner), 128
suspended animation, 14
Sutton, David, 58–59
symbolic efficacy, 140, 148
symbolic meaning, 116, 148–49
symbolic order, traumatic disruptions, 67
symbolic representation, 145
symbolism, 80
symptomatic approach to conspiracy theory, 28–47
symptomatological approach, 45–46
systemic oppressions, 52

Taguieff, Pierre-André, 49
Tahsin, Arif Hasan, 188
Talat, Mehmet Ali, 176, 189
Taussig, Michael, 4, 114–15, 146
Tehlirian, Soghomon, 166
temporality topology, 60
terrorist attack, 9/11, 117
Theodossopoulos, Dimitrios, 76–77
theology, medieval, 125
theory from the south, 107–8
Theory from the South (Comaroff, John), 103–4
theory of ideology, 51
theory of race-thinking, 51
theory of social cohesion, 51
therapeutic culture, 34
time of the cannibals, 4, 23–24
TMT (armed irregulars), 4
Tombazos, Georgios, 212
totalitarian theories, 28
transparency, 156
Transparency and Conspiracy (West and Sanders), 32, 55
Trapped in the Green Line (Angastiniotis), 2
traveling theories (Bardawil), 107
trial: of Cyprus conspirators, 168–70, 232n18; Papadopoulos, T., body theft, 2–3, 22–23, 168–70, 232n18, *p18*
tribal affiliations, 79
TRNC. *See* Turkish Republic of Northern Cyprus
Trumptimes, 83–85
truth regimes, 38
Tshabalala-Msimang, Manto, 34
Turkey, 154, 203
Turkish-Cypriots, 149; Akritas Plan and, 248n44; Annan Plan supported by, 194; Greek-Cypriots conflict with, 159–60, 172, 183, 201–2; Greek-Cypriots power-sharing with, 196; villager massacres of, 1–2; villagers, 22, 120
Turkish-language press, 135
Turkish nationalism, 190
Turkish Republic of Northern Cyprus (TRNC), 5, 218
Turkish soldiers, *p14*
Turner, Patricia, 173
Turner, Victor, 35
The Turner Diaries, 78
Two Attempts and a Murder (Drousiotis), 210, 212
Tziaos five, 202, 240n15, 247n37, *p14*

UFOlogy, 8–9, 96, 100
unconscious fantasies, 237n36
United States (U.S.): Annan Plan support by, 224; conspiracy narratives in, 235n16; conspiracy theories in, 9–10, 77–78; conspiracy theories outside of, 35; conspiratology in, 101; coup and invasion responsibility of, 159; cross-contextual connections with, 153–54; Cyprus's history with, 108–9; heterodox theory of AIDS in, 34; National Archives, 162; political paranoia in, 71; popular culture in, 99; white supremacy in, 173–74
universalism, 45, 106–7
unsinkable aircraft, Cyprus as, 164

Valley of the Fallen, 123, 141–43, 242n25
Varnava, Andrekos, 248n39
Venezuela, 36
Verdery, Katherine, 122–23, 139–40
vestments, images of, 113
violence: Cyprus's secret history of, 217; Papadopoulos, T., and history of, 112; public discourse feelings toward, 118–19

Index 289

Voice of Blood (Angastiniotis), 1
Voice of Blood 2 (Angastiniotis), 1

war crimes, 203
war dead, 123
Warner, Michael, 170–72, 244n14
Watkins, Jim, 75
Welsing, Frances Cress, 77–78
West, Harry, 32, 55, 57–58
Western conspiracy, 59, 160
"We Will Not Succumb to Terrorism" (headline), 178
white supremacy, 77–78, 173–74
witchcraft, 39, 41–43, 68, 173–74, 234n13
Witchcraft, Oracles, and Magic among the Azande (Evans-Pritchard), 39, 234n13

Witchcraft, Sorcery, Rumors, and Gossip (Stewart and Strathern, A.), 173
The Work of Culture (Obeyesekere), 74

The Yellow Book of Spyros Kyprianou (Konstantinidis, A.), 246n33
yes-men (ναιναίκοι), 169, 244n12
Yiavuz, Adem, 202
Yurchak, Alexei, 136–38, 140–41

Zanou, Konstantina, 196
Žižek, Slavoj, 66, 70, 74–75

ναιναίκοι (yes-men), 244n12

ο Γιουρούκκης (nickname), 245n21

Elizabeth Anne Davis is Professor of Anthropology at Princeton University, where she is affiliated with the Seeger Center for Hellenic Studies. She is author of *Bad Souls: Madness and Responsibility in Modern Greece* (2012), which won the Gregory Bateson Prize, and *Artifactual: Forensic and Documentary Knowing* (2023).

THINKING FROM ELSEWHERE

Robert Desjarlais, *The Blind Man: A Phantasmography*

Sarah Pinto, *The Doctor and Mrs. A.: Ethics and Counter-Ethics in an Indian Dream Analysis*

Veena Das, *Textures of the Ordinary: Doing Anthropology after Wittgenstein*

Clara Han, *Seeing Like a Child: Inheriting the Korean War*

Vaibhav Saria, *Hijras, Lovers, Brothers: Surviving Sex and Poverty in Rural India*

Richard Rechtman, *Living in Death: Genocide and Its Functionaries.* Translated by Lindsay Turner, Foreword by Veena Das

Jérôme Tournadre, *The Politics of the Near: On the Edges of Protest in South Africa.* Translated by Andrew Brown

Cheryl Mattingly and Lone Grøn, *Imagistic Care: Growing Old in a Precarious World*

Heonik Kwon and Jun Hwan Park, *Spirit Power: Politics and Religion in Korea's American Century*

Mayur R. Suresh, *Terror Trials: Life and Law in Delhi's Courts*

Thomas Cousins, *The Work of Repair: Capacity after Colonialism in the Timber Plantations of South Africa*

Hélène Dumas, *Beyond Despair: The Rwanda Genocide against the Tutsi through the Eyes of Children.* Translated by Catherine Porter. Foreword by Louisa Lombard

Elizabeth Anne Davis, *The Time of the Cannibals: On Conspiracy Theory and Context*